INTERNATIONAL INSTITUTIONS
and
STATE POWER

Essays in
International Relations Theory

Robert O. Keohane
Harvard University

Westview Press
BOULDER, SAN FRANCISCO, & LONDON

Copyright © 1989 by Westview Press, Inc.

Published in 1989 in the United States of America by Westview Press, Inc., 5500 Central Avenue, Boulder, Colorado 80301, and in the United Kingdom by Westview Press, Inc., 13 Brunswick Centre, London WC1N 1AF, England

Library of Congress Cataloging-in-Publication Data
Keohane, Robert O. (Robert Owen), 1941–
    International institutions and state power.
    Bibliography: p.
    Includes index.
    1. World politics—1945–   . 2. International
relations. I. Title.
D843.K397 1989   327′.09′04   88-37827
ISBN 0-8133-0837-2
ISBN 0-8133-0838-0 (if published as a paperback)

Printed and bound in the United States of America

♾ The paper used in this publication meets the requirements of the American National Standard for Permanence of Paper for Printed Library Materials Z39.48-1984.

10   9   8   7   6   5   4   3   2

INTERNATIONAL INSTITUTIONS
and
STATE POWER

Contents

Preface

The essays in this book trace the development of my thinking about international institutions between 1980 and 1988. The introduction, written especially for this volume, summarizes and defends the "neoliberal institutionalism" that I advocate as a framework for understanding world politics. Chapter 2, "A Personal Intellectual History," provides a more personal and longer-term view of my intellectual journey as a student of international relations. Together, these essays indicate my present vantage point, from which I view the papers to follow.

Because states, though internally diverse, are constrained by their environments, students of world politics have sought to explain regularities in state behavior by understanding the structures and processes of international systems. In structural realist, or neorealist, theory, the structure of international systems is conceptualized as anarchic: in the absence of hierarchical authority, states must rely on their own capabilities. Although this theory provides a valuable starting point for analysis, it overlooks the fact that world politics at any given time is to some extent institutionalized. Formal international organizations and codified rules and norms ("international regimes") exist in particular issue areas; but at a more general level as well, much behavior is recognized by participants as reflecting established rules, norms, and conventions. To understand state behavior, we must not only take account of the relative physical power capabilities of states and recognize the absence of hierarchical authority, but we must also comprehend world political institutions—regardless of whether they are formally organized and explicitly codified.

As explained more fully in the Introduction, Part 1 includes what I regard as my most important theoretical and conceptual papers of the 1980s, arranged in increasing order of departure from the arguments of neorealism. Certain essays in the first half of this volume discuss the strengths and weaknesses of neorealist theory and the need for clearer specification of the role of institutions, broadly defined. Others are designed to account for the existence of international regimes and for their patterns of rise and decline; they also examine practices, such as that of reciprocity, which broadly characterize the conduct of international affairs. In short, the objective of Part 1 is to put forward ideas that will help us understand international institutions and to suggest directions for research on them.

Yet inasmuch as the international environment does not determine state action, no theory of the international system can be complete. Domestic sources of policy must also be explored. Furthermore, ahistorical theory is highly misleading: changes have occurred not merely in the characteristics of the international system but also in the way in which human beings think about their worlds. Accordingly, Part 2 of this volume discusses some of the specific policy choices faced by U.S. governments and firms, in an attempt to account for the sources and consequences of these choices for both the United States and the international political economy. Editorial changes have been made in Chapters 9 and 10 to take into account changes in the political economy of oil since the early 1980s.

This book was planned, and Chapters 2 and 7 were written, during 1987–1988 at the Center for Advanced Study in the Behavioral Sciences, Stanford, California, where I was a fellow. As those who know it can testify, the center is an incomparable place for reading, reflection, and collegial discussion, and its staff is devoted and highly competent. During my time there, my research was supported by National Science Foundation grant #BNS-8700864 to the center. Throughout that year, as well as the subsequent summer, during which Chapter 1 was written, I was supported by a senior fellowship from the Social Science Research Council Foreign Policy Program. For this assistance I am most grateful.

Susan McEachern of Westview Press reacted with alacrity to my proposal for this book of essays, and she provided prompt and wise editorial guidance throughout the process. For suggesting that I publish such a volume, I am indebted to Edward Elgar of Edward Elgar Publishing Limited, Great Britain— although the vagaries of the intercontinental mails ultimately prevented us from collaborating in this publishing venture. Finally, I am particularly grateful to Professor Stephan Haggard for his insightful comments on the collection of essays originally proposed for inclusion in this volume.

All of these essays benefited from both the intellectual counsel and the emotional support of my wife, Nannerl O. Keohane, teacher, scholar, and college president. This volume is dedicated to our children, Sarah, Jonathan, Stephan, and Nathaniel, who grew up while it was being written. Fortunately, I was not so immersed in my work not to notice.

Robert O. Keohane

Acknowledgments

All of the essays in this volume, with the exception of Chapter 1, have been previously published. They are reprinted here by permission of the publishers, for which I am grateful. The original sources are listed below.

Chapter 2: Joseph Kruzel and James N. Rosenau, eds., *Understanding World Politics* (Lexington, Mass.: Lexington Books, 1989), pp. 403–415. Reprinted with minor changes.

Chapter 3: Ada W. Finifter, ed., *Political Science: The State of the Discipline* (Washington, D.C.: American Political Science Association, 1983), p. 503–540.

Chapter 4: Ole R. Holsti, Randolph M. Siverson, and Alexander L. George, eds., *Change in the International System* (Boulder, Colo.: Westview Press, 1980), pp. 131–162.

Chapter 5: *International Organization*, vol. 36, no. 2 (Spring 1982), pp. 141–171. Reprinted by permission of The MIT Press.

Chapter 6: *International Organization*, vol. 40, no. 1 (Winter 1986), pp. 1–27. Reprinted, with minor changes, by permission of The MIT Press.

Chapter 7: *International Studies Quarterly*, vol. 32, no. 4 (December 1988), pp. 379–396.

Chapter 8: John Gerard Ruggie, ed., *The Antinomies of Interdependence* (New York: Columbia University Press, 1983), pp. 43–90. Reprinted with minor changes.

Chapter 9: *International Organization*, vol. 36, no. 1 (Winter 1982), pp. 165–183. Reprinted, with minor changes, by permission of The MIT Press.

Chapter 10: William Avery and David P. Rapkin, eds., *America in a Changing Global Economy* (New York: Longman, 1982), pp. 49–76. Reprinted with minor changes.

CHAPTER 1

Neoliberal Institutionalism: A Perspective on World Politics

E ven those observers of contemporary world politics who have emphasized the importance of transnational relations agree that "states have been and remain the most important actors in world affairs" (Keohane and Nye, 1972:xxiv). Furthermore, they recognize that international systems are decentralized: "Formally, each is the equal of all the others. None is entitled to command; none is required to obey" (Waltz, 1979:88). Although the term "anarchy" is loaded and potentially misleading because of its associations with chaos and disorder, it characterizes world politics in the sense that world politics lacks a common government (Axelrod and Keohane, 1985:226). "In the absence of agents with system-wide authority, formal relations of super- and subordination fail to develop" (Waltz, 1979:88).

Yet it is also generally agreed that anarchy implies neither an absence of pattern nor perpetual warfare: "world government, although not reliably peaceful, falls short of unrelieved chaos" (Waltz, 1979:114). It would not be true to say of Europe in 1988 what Hobbes declared in 1651: "Persons of sovereign authority, because of their independency, are in continual jealousies and in the state and posture of gladiators, having their weapons pointing and their eyes fixed on one another—that is, their forts, garrisons, and guns upon the frontiers of their kingdoms, and continual spies upon their neighbors—which is a posture of war" (Hobbes, 1651/1958:108, Part 1, Ch. 13). Kenneth Waltz acknowledges that "world politics, although not formally organized, is not entirely without institutions and orderly procedures" (Waltz, 1979:114).

To understand world politics, we must keep in mind both decentralization and institutionalization. It is not just that international politics is "flecked with particles of government," as Waltz (1979:114) acknowledges; more fundamentally, it is *institutionalized*. That is, much behavior is recognized by participants as reflecting established rules, norms, and conventions, and its meaning is interpreted in light of these understandings. Such matters as diplomatic recognition, extraterritoriality, and the construction of agendas for multilateral organizations are all governed by formal or informal understandings; correctly interpreting diplomatic notes, the expulsion of an ambassador, or the movement of military forces in a limited war all require an appreciation of the conventions that relate to these activities.

THINKING ABOUT
INTERNATIONAL INSTITUTIONS

The principal thesis of this book is that variations in the institutionalization of world politics exert significant impacts on the behavior of governments. In particular, patterns of cooperation and discord can be understood only in the context of the institutions that help define the meaning and importance of state action. This perspective on international relations, which I call "neoliberal institutionalism," does not assert that states are always highly constrained by international institutions. Nor does it claim that states ignore the effects of their actions on the wealth or power of other states.[1] What I do argue is that state actions depend to a considerable degree on prevailing institutional arrangements, which affect

- the flow of information and opportunities to negotiate;
- the ability of governments to monitor others' compliance and to implement their own commitments—hence their ability to make credible commitments in the first place; and
- prevailing expectations about the solidity of international agreements.

Neoliberal institutionalists do not assert that international agreements are easy to make or to keep: indeed, we assume the contrary. What we do claim is that the ability of states to communicate and cooperate depends on human-constructed institutions, which vary historically and across issues, in nature (with respect to the policies they incorporate) and in strength (in terms of the degree to which their rules are clearly specified and routinely obeyed) (Aggarwal, 1985:31). States are at the center of our interpretation of world politics, as they are for realists; but formal and informal rules play a much larger role in the neoliberal than in the realist account.

Neoliberal institutionalism is not a single logically connected deductive theory, any more than is liberalism or neorealism: each is a school of thought that provides a perspective on world politics. Each perspective incorporates a set of distinctive questions and assumptions about the basic units and forces in world politics. Neoliberal institutionalism asks questions about the impact of institutions on state action and about the causes of institutional change; it assumes that states are key actors and examines both the material forces of world politics and the subjective self-understandings of human beings.[2]

The neoliberal institutionalist perspective developed in Part 1 of this volume is relevant to an international system only if two key conditions pertain. First, the actors must have some mutual interests; that is, they must potentially gain from their cooperation. In the absence of mutual interests, the neoliberal perspective on international cooperation would be as irrelevant as a neoclassical theory of international trade in a world without potential gains from trade. The second condition for the relevance of an institutional approach is that variations in the degree of institutionalization exert sub-

FIGURE 1.1
Conditions for operation of neoliberal institutionalism

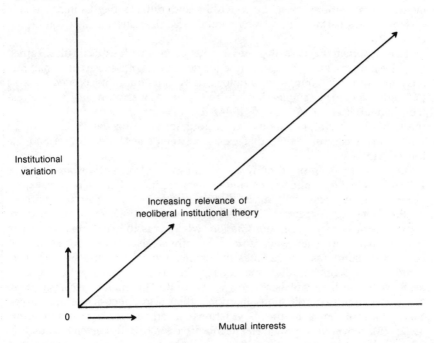

stantial effects on state behavior. If the institutions of world politics were fixed, once and for all, it would be pointless to emphasize institutional variations to account for variations in actor behavior. There is, however, ample evidence to conclude both that states have mutual interests and that institutionalization is a variable rather than a constant in world politics. Given these conditions, cooperation is possible but depends in part on institutional arrangements. A successful theory of cooperation must therefore take into account the effects of institutions.

The two conditions of mutual interest and institutional variation are graphically portrayed in Figure 1.1.

Organizations, Rules, and Conventions

Chapter 7 discusses in detail what I mean by "institutions" and how I think that international institutions should be studied. I define institutions as "persistent and connected sets of rules (formal and informal) that prescribe behavioral roles, constrain activity, and shape expectations." We can think of international institutions, thus defined, as assuming one of three forms:

1. *Formal intergovernmental or cross-national nongovernmental organizations.* Such organizations are purposive entities. They are capable of monitoring activity and of reacting to it, and are deliberately set up and designed by

states. They are bureaucratic organizations, with explicit rules and specific assignments of rules to individuals and groups.[3] Hundreds of intergovernmental organizations exist, both within and outside the United Nations system. Cross-national nongovernmental organizations are also quite numerous.[4]

2. *International regimes.* Regimes are institutions with explicit rules, agreed upon by governments, that pertain to particular sets of issues in international relations. In Oran Young's terminology, they constitute "negotiated orders" (Young, 1983:99). Examples include the international monetary regime established at Bretton Woods in 1944, the Law of the Sea regime set up through United Nations–sponsored negotiations during the 1970s, and the limited arms control regime that exists between the United States and the Soviet Union.[5]

3. *Conventions.* In philosophy and social theory, conventions are informal institutions, with implicit rules and understandings, that shape the expectations of actors. They enable actors to understand one another and, without explicit rules, to coordinate their behavior. Conventions are especially appropriate for situations of coordination, where it is to everyone's interest to behave in a particular way as long as others also do so. More specific contractual solutions—or regimes in the sense used earlier—are necessary to deal with prisoners' dilemma (PD) problems of major significance.[6] But as Russell Hardin emphasizes, conventions do not merely facilitate coordination in pure coordination situations; they also affect actors' incentives. Since nonconformity to the expectations of others entails costs (Hardin, 1982:175), conventions provide some incentive not to defect, even in situations when, without the convention, it would pay to do so. Conventions typically arise as "spontaneous orders," in Young's terminology. Traditional diplomatic immunity was a convention in this sense for centuries before being codified in two formal international agreements during the 1960s.[7] Reciprocity is also a convention: political leaders expect reciprocal treatment, both positive and negative, and are likely to anticipate that they will incur costs if they egregiously violate it—for example, by reacting disproportionately to barriers against their exports imposed by other states.

In thinking about international institutions, it is important to keep conventions in mind and to refrain from limiting one's frame of reference to formal organizations or regimes. Conventions are not only pervasive in world politics but also temporally and logically prior to regimes or formal international organizations. In the absence of conventions, it would be difficult for states to negotiate with one another or even to understand the meaning of each other's actions. Indeed, international regimes depend on the existence of conventions that make such negotiations possible.

Institutionalization in the sense used here can be measured along three dimensions:

- *Commonality.* The degree to which expectations about appropriate behavior and understandings about how to interpret action are shared by participants in the system;

- *Specificity.* The degree to which these expectations are clearly specified in the form of rules;
- *Autonomy.* The extent to which the institution can alter its own rules rather than relying entirely on outside agents to do so.[8]

An imaginary noninstitutionalized international system would lack shared expectations and understandings. Coordination would be impossible even when common interests existed. Policy in a true sense would be unknown, and state interaction would have a random quality. In practice, all international systems of which we have knowledge contain, or quickly acquire, conventions that permit coordination of action and alignment of interpretations of the meaning of action.

Conventions, however, do not necessarily specify rules with any precision. When international regimes are negotiated on the basis of previous conventions, they typically expand and clarify the rules governing the issues concerned. The process by which international regimes develop is therefore a process of increasing institutionalization.

But regimes cannot adapt or transform themselves. In the absence of international organizations, international regimes are entirely the expressions of the interests of constituent states. International organizations, however, evolve partly in response to their interests as organizations and partly in response to the ideas and interests of their leaders; and in this evolution they may also change the nature of the regimes in which they are embedded. Regimes with very clear rules could be more institutionalized than organizations with little autonomy and vague rules; but insofar as rules do not change, the emergence of international organizations indicates an increasing level of institutionalization.

The distinction among conventions, regimes, and organizations is not as clear in actuality as this stylization might seem to imply. Negotiated agreements often combine explicit rules with a penumbra of conventional understandings, which may be more or less ambiguous. Perhaps without exception, international organizations are embedded within international regimes: much of what they do is to monitor, manage, and modify the operation of regimes. Organization and regime may be distinguishable analytically, but in practive they may seem almost coterminous.

The Significance of Institutions

International institutions are important for states' actions in part because they affect the incentives facing states, even if those states' fundamental interests are defined autonomously. International institutions make it possible for states to take actions that would otherwise be inconceivable—for example, turning to the United Nations Secretary-General to mediate between Iran and Iraq, or appealing to nonproliferation rules in justifying a refusal to send nuclear reactor equipment to Pakistan. They also affect the costs associated with alternatives that might have existed independently: rules embodied in U.S.-Soviet arms control treaties increase the costs (especially for future agreements) of building antiballistic missile systems, and GATT rules on import barriers increase the costs of imposing formal discriminatory quotas on imports. Evasion is often possible, as the innovation of "voluntary export restraints" indicates; but institutions do affect behavior, even if they do not always attain the desired objective.

Yet it would be misleading to limit the significance of institutions to their effects on incentives. Institutions may also affect the understandings that leaders of states have of the roles they should play and their assumptions about others' motivations and perceived self-interests. That is, international institutions have constitutive as well as regulative aspects: they help define how interests are defined and how actions are interpreted.[9] Meanings are communicated by general conventions such those reflecting the principle of reciprocity and by more specific conventions, such as those that indicate what is meant in a diplomatic communiqué by a "full and frank exchange of views." Meanings are also embedded in the rules of international regimes, such as those of the General Agreement on Tariffs and Trade (GATT), which specify and implement the principle of reciprocity.[10]

The constitutive dimension of international institutions raises what Alexander Wendt (1987) has recently described as the "agent-structure problem." To what extent are the agents of international relations, principally states, "constituted" or "generated" by the international system? Wendt points out that it would be impossible to understand "capitalists" as agents without a concept of "capitalism," and he draws an analogy to international relations: "The causal powers of the state . . . are conferred upon it by the domestic and international social structures by virtue of which it is a state in the first place" (Wendt, 1987:360).

It is worthwhile to point out, as Wendt does, that the way in which leaders of states conceptualize their situations is strongly affected by the institutions of international relations: states not only form the international system; they are also shaped by its conventions, particularly by its practices. But this abstractly valid point should not be pushed too far. In modern international relations, the pressures from domestic interests, and those generated by the competitiveness of the state system, exert much stronger effects on state policy than do international institutions, even broadly defined. International "social structures" are manifestly weaker than those of small homogeneous communities or even of modern national societies. Thus, although I accept the "structurationist" advice to be alert to the reciprocal interaction between state and international institutions, I do not wish to be interpreted as accepting the view that the causal impact of international institutions on state policy is as strong as that of states on international institutions.

There is no strict relationship between the degree of institutionalization of an institution and its importance to world politics. In addition to asking questions about institutionalization, we need to inquire about effectiveness, which is not necessarily correlated with institutionalization. Highly institutionalized arrangements can become ossified, encapsulated, or irrelevant.

The International Court of Justice at the Hague, for example, is certainly highly institutionalized but is of relatively modest significance in world politics today. It sometimes serves to articulate and specify conventions or regimes (as it did in the case of the American hostages in Iran), but it is only rarely called upon, and states frequently fail to implement its decisions. Likewise, practices that are not highly institutionalized may be of supreme importance, insofar as they provide the basis for interpretation of action throughout world politics. Sovereign statehood was one such practice even before its rules had been codified. Whether increasing institutionalization leads to greater effectiveness should therefore not be assumed; the issue needs to be addressed with the usual combination of theory (under what conditions does institutionalization increase effectiveness?) and empirical research.

With this clarification of what I mean by international institutions in mind, we can now turn to a comparison between neoliberal institutionalist theory, as exemplified in this volume, and two established schools of thought: contemporary neorealist political theory and liberalism. Neoliberal institutionalism has affinities and disagreements with both.

NEOLIBERAL INSTITUTIONALISM, NEOREALISM, AND LIBERALISM

Labels play a large role in contemporary writing on international relations: Appellations such as "realist," "neorealist," "mercantilist," or "liberal" pervade the literature. These conceptual tags often help to focus issues and stimulate debate, but when they are obsolete or inappropriate, they obscure more than they clarify. My own work, as represented in this volume, has variously been described as "neorealist" and as "liberal," but in my view these labels are misleading descriptions both of my own writings and of works that I regard as intellectually congenial. In this section, accordingly, I will compare neoliberal institutionalism with both neorealism and liberalism, indicating what I see as the affinities and the differences of view between neoliberal institutionalism and these two competing tendencies.

Neoliberal Institutionalism and Neorealism

Contemporary neorealist international political theory, as elegantly outlined in Kenneth Waltz's work, has enhanced our understanding of world politics by clarifying the concept of structure, and by using this concept parsimoniously to account for certain prominent patterns of international political behavior, such as the formation of balances of power. Chapter 3 of this volume analyzes neorealism (there referred to as "Structural Realism") and provides an assessment of its strengths and weaknesses.

Neoliberal institutionalism, as reflected in the essays in this volume, shares some important intellectual commitments with neorealism. Like neorealists, neoliberal institutionalists seek to explain behavioral regularities by examining the nature of the decentralized international system. Neither neorealists nor neoliberal institutionalists are content with interpreting texts: both sets of theorists believe that there is an international political reality that can be partially understood, even if it will always remain to some extent veiled. Both also believe in trying to test theories, while recognizing that epistemology is also problematical: neither perspective is committed to the naive notion that reality can be objectively known.

Another reason for associating neoliberal institutionalism with neorealism is that both tendencies regard the international system as decentralized and take state power seriously. In the early part of my career I emphasized the significance of nonstate actors—then more often ignored than now. Subsequent research, especially that for *Power and Interdependence* (1977), persuaded me that these actors continue to be subordinate to states, although states may act in nontraditional ways due to changing systemic constraints. So I turned my attention back to states.

Finally, neoliberal institutionalists agree with neorealists that by understanding the structure of an international system, as defined by neorealists, we come to know "a small number of big and important things" (Waltz, 1986:329). As Waltz notes: "to the extent that dynamics of a system limit the freedom of its units, their behavior and the outcomes of their behavior become predictable" (1979:72). This is not to say that they become *perfectly* predictable: "Systems theories explain why different units behave similarly and, despite their variations, produce outcomes that fall within expected ranges. Conversely, theories at the unit level tell us why different units behave differently despite their similar placement in a system" (Waltz, 1979:72). Since no systems theory can be expected to account for the behavior of the units, we also have to look at policies and the exercise of state power—topics that require detailed empirical investigation and historical research.

Yet despite these affinities with neorealism, neoliberal institutionalism should be regarded as a distinct school of thought (Keohane, 1986:25–26, fn. 7). Although neoliberal institutionalists share the neorealists' objective of explaining state behavior insofar as possible through an understanding of the nature of the international system, we find the neorealist conception of structure too narrow and confining. Neorealism can account only for changes that result from shifts in relative state capabilities. Capabilities for Waltz refer principally to the economic resources and productivity of states, on the one hand, and to their military strength on the other (Waltz, 1979:98 and Chs. 7 and 8). Unless the positions of units change relative to one another, the neorealist cannot explain changes in their behavior. Yet, as indicated earlier, I believe that conventions in world politics are as fundamental as the distribution of capabilities among states: indeed, state action in the sense used by neorealists depends on the acceptance of practices such as sovereign statehood (see Chapter 7 of this volume). Thus I accept and generalize John Ruggie's argument that Waltz's conception of structure is unduly truncated, as well as static (Ruggie, 1983). Deeply embedded expectations are as fundamental to world politics as are the power resources of the units.

An implicit version of this appreciation of the role of expectations and conventions in world politics underlay the notion of "complex interdependence" that Nye and I developed in the 1970s, and that increasingly, it still seems to me, characterizes relationships among democratic industrialized countries, though not necessarily elsewhere in the world. The key characteristic of complex interdependence is the well-founded expectation of the inefficacy of the use or threat of force among states—an expectation that helps create support for conventions or regimes delegitimating threats of force. Western Europe, North America, and Japan form a zone of complex interdependence: power is an important element in relationships among these states (as well as between states and nonstate actors), but this power does not derive from the use or threat of force toward one another.[11]

Complex interdependence exemplifies the role of expectations and conventions in world politics—and therefore of institutionalization as defined above. My argument is that neorealism is underspecified because it fails to theorize about variations in the institutional characteristics of world politics. Because neorealists do not properly specify the nature of the international environment, their conclusions about self-help, about reliance on unit-level capabilities, and about sources of shift in patterns of interstate relationships are often wrong or at best misleading. Different international political systems have different degrees of institutionalization. In relatively non-institutionalized systems, the physical capabilities of states are most important: this is presumably what Waltz has in mind when he says of international relations that "authority quickly reduces to a particular expression of capability" (1979:88). But in relatively institutionalized international systems, states may be able to exert influence by drawing on widespread diplomatic norms, on legally institutionalized transnational financial networks, and on those international institutions known as alliances. During the Iran hostage crisis, for instance, the United States found these institutionalized arrangements more valuable in securing the honorable return of the hostages than military force—the archtypical realist capability (Christopher et al., 1985). An adequate understanding of state action in world politics depends on an appreciation of the strengths and weaknesses of institutionalization.

The essays in Part 1 of this volume, which were written between 1980 and 1988, all seek to contribute to our understanding of how and under what conditions world politics become more or less institutionalized. Chapters 3 through 5, written between 1980 and 1983, were part of my own intellectual struggle to come to terms with neorealism. Chapters 3 and 4 make quite a few concessions to neorealist arguments. In particular, Chapter 4, on the theory of hegemonic stability, displays a more positive evaluation of the explanatory power of neorealist theory than do my later writings.[12] Building on the earlier chapters, Chapters 6 and 7 explore the operation of reciprocity and examine the issue of institutional change via a comparison of rational-choice and reflective approaches to this issue.

Neoliberal Institutionalism and Liberalism

Liberalism is sometimes identified as a belief in the superiority of markets to state regulation of an economy. Thus defined, liberalism would be a highly inappropriate label for my work, which stresses the importance of international institutions, constructed by states, in facilitating mutually beneficial policy coordination among governments.[13] Another conception of liberalism associates it with a belief in the value of individual freedom. Although I subscribe to such a belief, this commitment of mine is not particularly relevant to my analysis of international relations. One could believe in the value of individual liberty and remain either a realist or neorealist in one's analysis of world politics.

But liberalism also serves as a set of guiding principles for contemporary social science. As a guide to social scientific thought, it stresses the role of human-created institutions in affecting how aggregations of individuals make collective decisions. It emphasizes the importance of changeable political processes rather than simply of immutable structures, and it rests on a belief in at least the possibility of cumulative progress in human affairs. In this sense, the work presented in this volume indeed reflects a liberal spirit. Institutions change as a result of human action, and the changes in expectations and processes that result can exert profound effects on state behavior.

Consider the way in which international cooperation is viewed by neorealists on the one hand and neoliberal institutionalists on the other. Neorealists and neoliberals agree that world politics lacks stable hierarchy and that, as Waltz (1959:186) puts it, "in anarchy there is no automatic hierarchy." But Waltz also admits that "there is no obvious logical relation" between this proposition and the statement that "among autonomous states *war* is inevitable" (1959:186, Waltz's italics). Neoliberals argue that establishing a necessary logical link between anarchy and war is impossible: any connection that may exist between lack of harmony and warfare will be conditional on the nature of prevailing expectations in the system and, hence, on institutions.

Neorealists declare that "in a condition of anarchy, relative gain is more important than absolute gain" (Waltz, 1959:198) and that "the fundamental goal of states in any relationship is to prevent others from achieving advances in their relative capabilities" (Grieco, 1988:498). These statements do describe, at least roughly, U.S.-Soviet relations since World War II, and they are applicable to many other relationships, such as those between India and Pakistan and between Iran and Iraq. They are also theoretically plausible whenever states expect all others to be hostile and deceptive, and when states' margins of survival are small.[14] But these statements do not accurately describe U.S. policy toward Europe or Japan for at least twenty years after World War II, or the relationships among members of the European Community (EC). And they are theoretically implausible when applied to situations in which substantial mutual gains can be realized through cooperation and in which governments do not expect others to threaten them with force.[15]

Such statements are not false in every case, but they are *conditional* on the nature of prevailing rules and expectations—that is, on international institutions as defined earlier. To understand world politics, we need to know about institutions, not merely about the existence of "anarchy" defined as lack of common government.

This is not to say that neoliberal institutionalism gives us the answer—only that it gets the question right. We need to understand which institutional patterns lead to more rather than less cooperative behavior among states; that is, we need testable conditional statements rather than dogmatic generalizations. Which conventions, regimes, and organizations promote cooperation? Since neoliberal institutionalists share with realists the assumption that leaders of states calculate the costs and benefits of contemplated courses of action, putting the issue in this way implies that we need to ask how institutions affect incentives facing states. Chapter 5, on the "demand" for international regimes, and Chapter 6, on reciprocity, explore issues of cooperation from this perspective.

These disagreements with neorealism may clarify my affinities with liberalism. In a fashion consistent with liberalism, I refuse to assume either unchanging definitions of interest in terms of relative gains or permanent patterns of conflict among states. For me, politics is open-ended and potentially progressive, rather than bleakly cyclical.

Yet my arguments diverge from those of much liberal international political theory. Liberalism in international relations is often thought of exclusively in terms of what I have elsewhere called *republican* and *commercial* liberalism (Keohane, 1989). Republican liberalism argues that republics are more peacefully inclined than despotisms. In its naive version, commercial liberalism argues that commerce leads necessarily to peace. The resulting caricature of liberalism posits the "harmony of interests" so tellingly criticized by E. H. Carr (1946). My own view is that republics are remarkably peaceful toward one another, but republics do not necessarily act peacefully toward nonrepublican states or toward societies not organized as states (Doyle, 1983). I believe that an open international economic environment, characterized by opportunities for mutually rewarding exchange under orderly sets of rules, provides incentives for peaceful behavior, but not that it necessitates or ensures such behavior. That is, cooperation must be distinguished from harmony. Cooperation is not automatic, but requires planning and negotiation. It is a highly political process inasmuch as patterns of behavior must be altered—a process that involves the exercise of influence. And influence is secured not only with the aid of persuasion and prestige but also through the use of resources—principally economic resources under conditions of complex interdependence, and military resources when conflicts of interest are very sharp and uses or threats of force are efficacious.[16] Neoliberal institutionalists accept a version of liberal principles that eschews determinism and that emphasizes the pervasive significance of international institutions without denigrating the role of state power.

SOME SUGGESTIONS FOR RESEARCH

I argued earlier that to understand international politics one must understand international institutions. At the end of its critique of neorealism, Chapter 3 makes a similar point in emphasizing that information, which reduces uncertainty, is both important and variable in world politics; and that one of the major functions of institutions is to retain and transmit information. Chapter 4 inquires into the extent to which patterns of change in postwar international economic regimes can be accounted for by shifts in power, as realists would predict. Chapter 5 uses rationalistic theory to examine the conditions—those of both "supply" and "demand"—underlying the emergence and maintenance of international regimes, and to elucidate some of the functions served by these regimes. Chapter 6 distinguishes between specific and diffuse reciprocity and explores how institutional innovations in international trade negotiations had the effect of combining aspects of both types of reciprocity in a way that facilitated multilateral trade agreements. Finally, Chapter 7 contrasts the rationalistic research program for understanding institutional change with "reflective" arguments stressing the role of human consciousness.

Chronologically, these essays reveal a progressively greater awareness of the importance and complexity of the institutional context of action in world politics. The earliest of them, Chapter 4, written in 1978–1979 and published in 1980, recognizes the importance of context but fails to specify its components or to theorize about institutions. Chapters 3 and 5, published in 1982–1983, are much clearer about the role of institutions in providing information, but the conception of institutions in these essays does not extend to conventions as defined above. The essay on reciprocity (Chapter 6) examines what I would now call the convention of reciprocity, and Chapter 7 argues that specific institutions are embedded in practices, which, as noted, constitute a type of convention. My personal intellectual history (Chapter 2), which was originally written for a collection of autobiographical essays, is designed to shed some light on these changes in emphasis by exploring how my family background, education, and professional roles have affected my perspectives on world politics.

The essays in Part 1 were written to clarify theory rather than to explore empirical or historical issues in depth. Yet theory and research should always be connected. It is misleading and pernicious to believe that the theorist does not have to be concerned with historical facts. Theory without empirical work is, in the long run, as empty as facts without theory. Thus the value of the essays in Part 1—particularly Chapters 3, 5 and 7, which make no empirical contributions—ultimately depends on the use that scholars make of my ideas in order to understand significant issues of world politics.

The essays in Part 2 at least gesture toward the need to use theory to explore history. Chapter 8 was written for a project, coordinated by John Gerard Ruggie, whose original impetus was provided by a question agitating students of the Third World in the late 1970s: could such countries benefit from dissociating their economics from the advanced countries of the West? Since my knowledge of the Third World was slight, I turned my attention to the antebellum United States experience. My previous work on international independence, rather than any sophisticated understanding of international institutions, provided my conceptual perspective for this essay; but despite its lack of close fit with the institutional emphasis of Part 1, "Associative American Development" at least indicates my interest in combining historical analysis with theoretical inquiry. Chapter 9, a detailed review essay on U.S. oil policy in the 1940s, indicates that despite my preoccupation with systemic theory of late, I have not forgotten the role of private power and corporate interests in foreign policy: policy depends not merely on systemic conditions but on domestic politics as well. Finally, Chapter 10 again emphasizes the impact of domestic politics by showing how U.S. policy during the 1950s permitted the demise of the strategy of hegemonic leadership by failing to ensure the maintenance of U.S. power resources that were essential to its continuation. It provides some background to the current belated debate about the decline of U.S. hegemony.

These essays take us to the threshold of an institutionalist research program. The theoretical chapters explain the need for a neoliberal institutionalist perspective, and the historical chapters illustrate the importance of domestic politics and the limited explanatory impact of system structure. But the link between theory and history is not forged; indeed, all of the historical essays were written before the major theoretical chapters. My 1984 volume, *After Hegemony: Cooperation and Discord in the World Political Economy*, does use institutionalist theory to explore the postwar international political economy in a relatively well-integrated fashion. But it deliberately eschews any attempt either to go more deeply into history or to use the institutionalist framework to analyze security affairs. Both deeper historical research and greater probing of security issues from an institutional standpoint should be on our research agenda.

What are the research implications of taking international institutions seriously? And where should we go next? Even to ask these questions seems to reveal a sort of *hubris:* Why should one scholar seek to define what other people should work on? Rather than sketching out a grandiose plan that no one would follow, therefore, I will simply indicate some general directions that seem to follow from the perspective outlined in this chapter. I will conclude by considering research that might help us to evaluate the comparative merits of neorealist and neoliberal institutionalist theory.

Neoliberal institutionalism calls for renewed attention to international organizations. During the last fifteen years, scholarship has followed policy in denigrating the significance of major international organizations such as the European Community and the United Nations. But despite what one might expect from the absence of literature on these organizations, there seems to be life in both of them. As I write these lines in September 1988, the EC is launching a major program to dismantle internal commercial barriers by 1992, under the Single European Act adopted by the member governments at the end of 1985. And the secretary-general of the United Nations has during the last few months arranged for the gradual withdrawal of Soviet troops from Afghanistan and for a cease-fire between Iran and Iraq. Both arrangements are to be policed by UN peacekeeping forces, which have just been awarded the Nobel Peace Prize for 1988. International organizations are not central to contemporary world politics, but they are more important than neorealist research has been willing to acknowledge.

Neoliberal institutionalism also insists on the significance of international regimes and the importance of the continued exploration of the conditions under which they emerge and persist. Judging from the literature in international relations journals, this battle has been won in the area of political economy: studies of particular international economic regimes have proliferated.[17] As generally recognized, it is important that domestic politics be taken into account in exploring how regimes operate, how they change, and what impact they have on governments, as Chapter 7 suggests. But we need to carry the investigation of international regimes further into the security area, as a number of authors have begun to do.[18]

The third type of international institution discussed at the beginning of this essay is the convention: an informal institution, with implicit rules and understandings, that shapes the expectations of actors. Conventions change over time, although the pace of change may be slow. To understand the changes in world politics over the course of centuries, we need to understand how conventions change. Otherwise, we are likely either to assume that the past must repeat itself (as realism so often assumes) or to be guilty of anachronism (that is, of reading the premises and values of the present back into the past). John Ruggie's exploration of sovereignty has shown the importance of exploring the premises and patterns of thought of previous generations (Ruggie, 1983), but his suggestive work has not yet been followed by detailed studies of conventions and how they change.[19]

As we understand more about the roles of institutions in world politics, the failure of neorealism to theorize about the causes or effects of institutions will become increasingly noticeable. With respect to issues on which states have substantial mutual interests, neoliberal theories have correctly anticipated that governments would create durable international regimes and organizations, and that the most extensive powers would be given to organizations with relatively few members, in which it would be feasible to monitor compliance with rules. The European Community, the Group of Five in international financial affairs, and the UN Security Council (as compared to the General Assembly) provide cases in point. On issues with substantial mutual interests (world trade is a prominent example), issue-linkages have often facilitated cooperation, as neoliberal theory would predict. It would be useful, as Joseph Grieco has proposed, to undertake systematic comparisons of neorealist and neoliberal theory as applied to the international political economy; there is much evidence to suggest that neoliberalism would be superior as a framework for analysis of these issues.[20]

It has often been assumed that neorealist theory is appropriate for the study of security issues; yet on some security issues, states have substantial mutual interests that can be realized only through institutionalized cooperation. Consider, for example, the phenomenon of international alliances. Currently, the theoretical literature on alliances views them from a neorealist perspective. According to this literature, alliances result from relations of major antagonism and are formed to supplement the capabilities of the parties (Liska, 1962:14–20; 26–27). They are viewed as fundamentally shaped by the structure of the system, defined in neorealist terms. For instance, Glenn Snyder (1984) argues that NATO's stability is assured by the structure of bipolarity; Robert S. Ross (1986) shows that changes in Sino-American relations have resulted from shifts in the Soviet threat and in the positions of the United States and China in the three-power triangle; and Stephen M. Walt (1987) examines the effects of shifts in capabilities and threats on alignment patterns in the contemporary Middle East. But none of these otherwise perceptive works takes advantage of the fact that alliances are *institutions*, and that both their durability and strength (the degree to which states are committed to alliances, even when costs are entailed) may depend in part on their institutional characteristics. None of them employs theories of institutions to examine the formal and informal rules and conventions on which alliances rely. Thus questions such as the following are not asked:

- Are formal alliances more durable or stronger than alignments based on informal agreements?
- How much difference do executive heads of alliance organizations, and their bureaucracies, make in terms of the durability or strength of alliances?
- To what extent do alliances provide information to their members that facilitates cooperation, therefore contributing to alliance durability or strength?
- Do alliances ever develop norms that are not subject to calculations of interest, and that are therefore genuine normative commitments for participants? If so, under what conditions (domestic as well as international) do such commitments emerge?
- Do open democratic governments find it easier to maintain alliance ties than closed authoritarian regimes?[21]

I believe that a comparison of neorealist interpretations of alliances with a sophisticated neoliberal alternative would show that neoliberal theory provides richer and more novel insights, without sacrificing the valuable arguments of neorealism. Similar conclusions may hold in other security issues, such as those concerning economic sanctions and unilateral versus multilateral arrangements for military procurement.[22] Indeed, the study of security and cooperation, using neoliberal theory, should be highly worthwhile during the next decade.

In comparing neoliberal institutionalism with neorealism, we must understand that neoliberal institutionalism is not simply an alternative to neorealism, but, in fact, claims to subsume it. Under specified conditions—

where mutual interests are low and relative gains are therefore particularly important to states—neoliberal theory expects neorealism to explain elements of state behavior. Thus a success for neorealism is not necessarily a failure for neoliberalism. Yet even under favorable circumstances, neorealism will fail to account for those aspects of behavior that have their source in institutional variation. For example, neorealism's account of alliances is valuable but thin. And under conditions in which concern for relative gain and threats of force are low, neoliberalism expects neorealism to yield false predictions.

During the last several years, debates between neorealists and neoliberal institutionalists have been both extensive and intensive (Keohane, 1986). Indeed, this controversy has now reached the point at which further theoretical controversy is likely to be fruitless: abstract argument must yield to empirical research and evaluation. I expect future research to show that where the predictions of neorealism and neoliberal institutionalism diverge, those of neoliberal institutionalism will be, on the whole, both richer and more accurate. Even in cases where neorealist predictions are essentially correct, attention to institutional variation will often provide additional insights. If these expectations are borne out, writing the essays in this volume will turn out to have been worthwhile.

ACKNOWLEDGMENTS

This essay was planned while the author was a fellow at the Center for Advanced Study in the Behavioral Sciences, 1987–1988. I am grateful for the financial support provided to the Social Science Research Council Foreign Policy Program and for National Science Foundation grant #BNS-8700864 to the center. Valuable comments on an earlier draft by Ernst B. Haas, Nannerl O. Keohane, and Andrew Moravcsik are also gratefully acknowledged.

NOTES

1. Joseph Nye (1988) refers to work such as mine as "neoliberal." Expanding Nye's phrase, Joseph Grieco employs the appropriate label of "neoliberal institutionalism" and provides a number of interesting critiques from the perspective of realist political thought. Unfortunately, however, he misinterprets my discussion of utility functions to imply lack of concern by states for the wealth and power of others. My assumption in *After Hegemony*, to which I continue to adhere, is that states' utility functions are independent of one another. This assumption, however, clearly does not imply that states ignore the effects of their actions on other states' power and welfare, insofar as these changes may affect the states' future actions toward themselves and, hence, their own utilities. Indeed, the focus on strategic interaction in my work clearly implies that actors must be careful to assess the *indirect* effects of their actions on their future payoffs (effects that operate through the power and incentives of their partners). Compare Grieco, 1988:496–497 with Keohane, 1984:Chs. 5–7 (especially p. 123).

2. Examples of neoliberal institutionalist thinking can be found in the following, among other works: Krasner, 1983; Oye, 1986; and Aggarwal, 1985.

3. This definition has been adapted from that given by Ernst Haas at a meeting on international cooperation and institutions. This meeting, supported by the Social Science Research Council, was held at the Center for Advanced Study in the Behavioral Sciences in Stanford, California, on January 29, 1988.

4. Transnational organizations, most notably multinational corporations, are a subject for another analysis. Often they are organizations with roots essentially in one country that operate transnationally—quite different from truly international governmental or nongovernmental organizations.

5. Extensive terminological discussion of regimes has convinced me that it is clearest to limit the term "regimes" to institutions with explicit rules, negotiated by states. As Haggard and Simmons point out, "focusing on 'implicit regimes' captures the convergence of actor expectations and may help us summarize a complex pattern of behavior, but it begs the question of the extent to which state behavior is, in fact, rule-governed" (Haggard and Simmons, 1987:494).

6. As Duncan Snidal argues, where a problem involves a relatively minor prisoners' dilemma element, convention may be adequate; but "successful resolution of major PD problems will require a higher level of institutionalization than in coordination problems" (Snidal, 1985:939).

7. Terminological confusion may be caused by the fact that in international law, such formal agreements are often known as "conventions." The agreements on diplomatic immunity are the 1961 Vienna Convention on Diplomatic Relations and the 1963 Vienna Convention on Consular Relations (Schacter, 1985). I use "convention," however, in the social theory sense rather than in the international law sense.

8. This criterion is suggested by Samuel P. Huntington, who includes *autonomy* as one of his criteria, meaning "the development of political organizations and procedures that are not simply expressions of the interests of particular social groups" (Huntington, 1968:20). Huntington's other three criteria—adaptability, coherence, and complexity—seem more relevant to the chief focus of his work—political organizations—than to institutionalization as used here.

9. On constitutive and regulative aspects of rules, see Giddens, 1984. My thinking on these issues has been helped by discussions with David Dessler and by a recent paper of his (Dessler, 1988).

10. Some conventions are deeply constitutive, in the sense that their rules cannot change without causing the fundamental nature of the activity to change. I refer to these conventions as *practices* in Chapter 7. In international politics, sovereign statehood is the best example of a practice: if the concept of sovereignty and the rules governing recognition of sovereign actors were to change, international relations as such would be fundamentally transformed. Insofar as they are intrinsically connected with sovereign statehood, diplomatic immunity and reciprocity can also be considered to have the status of practices. Practices originate as conventions, but they may become codified in the form of regimes. It should be emphasized, however, that not all conventions are practices. Many conventions are not sufficiently intrinsic to international relations to qualify as practices; indeed, they may reflect customary behavior that could change without fundamentally affecting the nature of world politics.

11. For a fuller discussion of the concept of complex interdependence, and of some difficulties in the way that Nye and I articulated it, see Keohane and Nye, 1987.

12. In "The Theory of Hegemonic Stability" (Chapter 4 of this volume) I conclude that "we should be cautious about putting the hegemonic stability theory forward

as a powerful explanation of events." However, I added that "to ignore its congruence with reality, and its considerable explanatory power, would be foolish." In *After Hegemony* (1984) I likewise argued that the theory of hegemonic stability provided a useful starting-point for analysis, which I saw as "suggestive but by no means definitive." But in that work I also characterized it as "somewhat simplistic," omitted any reference to its "explanatory power," and questioned its empirical basis as well as its logic. The two arguments are consistent, but my later language indicated more skepticism—as well as a desire to avoid the misinterpretations of my earlier paper as representing advocacy of the theory. In contemporary writing on international relations, avoiding misrepresentation requires attention not only to the substance of one's argument but also to tone and rhetoric.

13. It would also be mistaken to believe that I am particularly sympathetic to this neoclassical liberalism on normative grounds. I recognize the efficiency advantages of well-functioning markets and the liabilities of state control, but I regard unregulated markets as biased against people disadvantaged by lack of marketable skills, mobility, or sophistication. Some regulation is needed not merely to keep markets functioning efficiently but also to counteract the inequities that they generate.

14. Hardin (1982:213) points out that a reputation for trustworthiness cannot be acquired in a system in which there is a very low incidence of trustworthy behavior. "If almost no one is trusted, then I will not be trusted even if I am—alas, known only to me—utterly trustworthy. . . . This much we have in common with used cars: the incidence of enough lemons among us will wreck the reputations of us all."

15. If relative gain were unconditionally more important than absolute gain, as Waltz and Grieco claim, trade between great powers would be anomalous. One would expect export controls such as those applied by the United States against the Soviet Union to be the rule rather than the exception.

16. On cooperation and harmony, see Keohane, 1984:51–55. On the conditions of complex interdependence and realism, see Keohane and Nye, 1989:158–162 and Chs. 1 and 2.

17. For a partial listing, see Keohane and Nye, 1987:741, fn. 33.

18. Nye, 1987 (see especially pp. 374–378), cites the relevant works in his discussion of this issue.

19. Ernst Haas's forthcoming study of adaptation and learning in international organizations examines the related issue of how ideas guiding international organizations change. See Haas, 1988.

20. For the predictions of neoliberal theory about organizational size and durability, and about the effects of issue-linkages (which Grieco sees as *unlikely* to be substantiated), see Grieco, 1988:505–506. Grieco's statement of neoliberal theory is oversimplified however, inasmuch as he fails to emphasize that neoliberalism is a *conditional* theory. For situations with little mutual interest—in which international relations would approximate a series of zero-sum games—neoliberal theory's predictions considerably overlap with those of neorealism. Under these conditions, states will be reluctant to cooperate with each other and will choose less durable rather than more durable arrangements. Linkages, furthermore, may well impede cooperation. The divergence between the predictions of the two theories will become apparent only when opportunities for joint gains through cooperation are substantial. Under these conditions, according to neoliberal theory, states' obsessions with relative gains will diminish. They will join quite durable institutions, with explicit rules and organizations; and issue linkage will often, though not always, facilitate agreement.

21. A speculation to this effect appears in Keohane, 1984:95; but as far as I know, no one has sought to test this proposition.

22. Promising dissertations on these topics are being written at Harvard by Lisa Martin and Andrew Moravcsik, respectively.

REFERENCES

Aggarwal, Vinod K., 1985. *Liberal Protectionism: The International Politics of Organized Textile Trade* (Berkeley: University of California Press).

Axelrod, Robert, and Robert O. Keohane, 1985. Achieving cooperation under anarchy: Strategies and institutions. *World Politics*, vol. 38, no. 1 (October), pp. 226–254.

Carr, E. H., 1946. *The Twenty Years' Crisis, 1919–1939*, 2nd ed. (London: Macmillan).

Christopher, Warren, et al., 1985. *American Hostages in Iran: The Conduct of a Crisis* (New Haven, Conn.: Yale University Press for the Council on Foreign Relations).

Dessler, David, 1988. What's at stake in the agent-structure debate? (Williamsburg, Va.: Unpublished paper, Department of Government, College of William and Mary).

Doyle, Michael W., 1983. Kant, liberal legacies and foreign affairs. *Philosophy and Public Affairs*, vol. 12, nos. 3 and 4 (two-part article), pp. 205–231, 323–353.

Eckstein, Harry, 1975. Case studies and theory in political science. In Fred I. Greenstein and Nelson W. Polsby, eds., *Strategies of Inquiry*, vol. 7 of the *Handbook of Political Science* (Reading, Mass.: Addison-Wesley).

Giddens, Anthony, 1984. *The Constitution of Society* (Berkeley: University of California Press).

Grieco, Joseph, 1988. Anarchy and the limits of cooperation: A realist critique of the newest liberal institutionalism. *International Organization*, vol. 42, no. 3 (Summer), pp. 485–508.

Haas, Ernst B., 1988. *Adaptation and learning in international organizations* (Berkeley: Unpublished book manuscript).

Haggard, Stephan, and Beth A. Simmons, 1987. Theories of international regimes. *International Organization*, vol. 41, no. 3 (Summer), p. 491–517.

Hardin, Russell, 1982. *Collective Action* (Baltimore: Johns Hopkins University Press for Resources for the Future).

Hobbes, Thomas, 1651/1958. *Leviathan* (Indianapolis: Bobbs-Merrill).

Huntington, Samuel P., 1968. *Political Order in Changing Societies* (New Haven, Conn.: Yale University Press).

Kant, Immanuel, 1795/1949. Eternal peace. In Carl J. Friedrich, ed., *The Philosophy of Kant* (New York: Modern Library, 1949), pp. 430–476.

Keohane, Robert O., 1984. *After Hegemony: Cooperation and Discord in the World Political Economy* (Princeton, N.J.: Princeton University Press).

————, 1989. International Liberalism reconsidered. In John Dunn, ed., *Economic Limits to Modern Politics* (Cambridge: Cambridge University Press).

Keohane, Robert O., ed., 1986. *Neorealism and Its Critics* (New York: Columbia University Press).

Keohane, Robert O., and Joseph S. Nye, Jr., 1987. *Power and Interdependence* revisited. *International Organization*, vol. 41, no. 4 (Autumn), pp. 725–753. Reprinted in Keohane and Nye, 1989.

————, 1989. *Power and Interdependence: World Politics in Transition*, 2nd ed. (Boston: Little, Brown).

Keohane, Robert O., and Josesph S. Nye, Jr., eds., 1972. *Transnational Relations and World Politics* (Cambridge, Mass.: Harvard University Press).

Krasner, Stephen D., ed., 1983. *International Regimes*. Ithaca, N.Y.: Cornell University Press.

Liska, George, 1962. *Nations in Alliance: The Limits of Interdependence* (Baltimore: Johns Hopkins University Press).

Nye, Joseph S., Jr., 1987. Nuclear learning. *International Organization*, vol. 41, no. 3 (Summer), pp. 371–402.

————, 1988. Neorealism and neoliberalism. *World Politics*, vol. 40, no. 2 (January), pp. 235–251.

Oye, Kenneth A., ed., 1986. *Cooperation Under Anarchy*. Princeton, N.J.: Princeton University Press.

Ross, Robert S., 1986. International bargaining and domestic politics: U.S.-China relations since 1972. *World Politics*, vol. 38, no. 2 (January), pp. 255–287.

Ruggie, John Gerard, 1983. Continuity and transformation in the world polity: Toward a neorealist synthesis. *World Politics*, vol. 35, no. 2 (January), pp. 261–285.

Schacter, Oscar, 1985. International law in the hostage crisis: Implications for future cases. In Christopher et al., 1985, pp. 325–373.

Snidal, Duncan, 1985. Coordination versus prisoners' dilemma: Implications for international cooperation and regimes. *American Political Science Review*, vol. 79, no. 4 (December), pp. 923–943.

Snyder, Glenn, 1984. The security dilemma in alliance politics. *World Politics*, vol. 36, no. 4 (July), pp. 461–495.

Walt, Stephen M., 1987. *The Origins of Alliances* (Ithaca, N.Y.: Cornell University Press).

Waltz, Kenneth N., 1959. *Man, the State, and War* (New York: Columbia University Press).

————, 1979. *Theory of International Politics* (Reading, Mass.: Addison-Wesley).

————, 1986. A response to my critics. In Keohane, 1986, pp. 322–345.

Wendt, Alexander E., 1987. The agent-structure problem in international relations theory. *International Organization*, vol. 41, no. 3 (Summer), pp. 335–370.

Young, Oran R., 1983. Regime dynamics: The rise and fall of international regimes. In Stephen Krasner, ed., *International Regimes* (Ithaca, N.Y.: Cornell University Press), pp. 93–114.

CHAPTER 2

A Personal Intellectual History

Few people study world politics for purely intellectual reasons. Other disciplines, even in the social sciences, offer better prospects for intellectual rigor and cumulative progress in solving well-defined problems. In studying world politics, we examine the strategic interactions of small numbers of organizations—usually states. When actors' strategies are potentially "exploitable"—that is, when knowledge of one actor's strategies can allow its opponents to make gains at its expense—each party has an incentive to deceive and outguess the other.[1] Students of world politics therefore face *inherent* limitations to scientific prediction and to fully satisfactory explanation—limitations that we are unlikely ever to overcome. Economists who examine the strategic behavior of oligopolists face the same problem.[2] So do game theorists, who find that interesting games rarely have unique equilibria—points at which no players have incentives to change their strategies unless others do so.[3] The search for unique, deterministic outcomes of strategic interactions is a will-o'-the-wisp.

The realization that these limitations are inherent in our subject matter should make us humble. We do not have theories that can fully explain the past, and we certainly cannot predict the future. Prospectively, we seem to know too little to account for events; retrospectively, we know too much—since "everything seems relevant" and it is difficult to sort out causality. Past events seem "overdetermined"; the future is "underdetermined."[4]

The justification for spending one's professional life studying world politics cannot, therefore, be a purely scientific one. On the contrary, it is profoundly normative. We study world politics not because it is easily amenable to scientific investigation, but because human welfare, the fate of our species, and the future of the fragile global ecology itself depend on the ability of human beings to cope successfully with economic interdependence, nuclear weapons, and the world environment. We may be unable to understand world politics fully, but we know that our lives, and those of our descendants, depend on it. My own interest in international cooperation and discord—in particular, the conditions under which governments develop patterns of collaboration—reflects my personal aversion to conflict and violence, and my belief in the ability of human beings, through a combination of reason and empathy with others, to improve the world. I am a child of the Enlightenment—a chastened child, to be sure, but nevertheless a believer in the *possibility* of progress, though by no means in its inevitability.

FAMILY INFLUENCE AND FORMAL EDUCATION

My approach to world politics is rooted in my values, and my values were learned principally from my family. My father, Robert E. Keohane, taught in the College of the University of Chicago and later at Shimer College in Mount Carroll, Illinois, 130 miles west of Chicago. He was a social scientist who combined a deep love for history with a commitment to undergraduate education. He read deeply and widely in history and literature; he was a brilliant teacher who won a major teaching award at the University of Chicago; and he exemplified intellectual curiosity and integrity. Although he never became a major research scholar, his mind was much more interesting, and his conversation more enlightening, than those of many famous scholars whom I have subsequently known. His example has served as a warning to me against certain pitfalls of professionalism in our field, such as exclusive focus on a narrow range of problems, at the expense of extensive reading outside one's own specialty; disdain for teaching and for those who teach; and the temptations to pretend to more under-standing than one has attained and to publish when one has nothing to say. I fall short of his example on some of these dimensions, but an awareness of failings can itself be of value.

My mother influenced my values even more strongly than my father affected my intellectual development. Mary Pieters Keohane was born in Japan, the daughter of a Dutch Reformed missionary and the descendant of a long line of Calvinist ministers. Having rejected orthodox Calvinism early in her adult life, she directed her moral energy toward improving the human and natural world. In the 1930s she was a democratic socialist until converted by Franklin D. Roosevelt to the Democratic party; throughout her life she worked and spoke on behalf of social justice, civil rights, and peace; and during the last decade of her life, she was especially active as an environmentalist. In a career devoted to improving secondary school education in government and civics, she was the principal author (with my father and a collaborator) of two high school texts; she taught in the public schools of Los Angeles, Chicago, and Morrison, Illinois, for a total of about fifteen years; and for approximately five years she was engaged in the training of teachers.

I entered Shimer College, where my father taught, at age sixteen, after two years in the local rural high school. Shimer College in 1957 was a tiny offshoot of the College of the University of Chicago, itself established under the presidency of Robert Maynard Hutchins as an entity separate from the graduate departments; it had its own faculty and its own curriculum, centered on the "Great Books" of Western culture. Since Hutchins had a low opinion of American secondary education, bright students—"early entrants"—were admitted after only two years of high school, at age sixteen or younger. In terms of sheer I.Q., these early entrants (who constituted about one-third of the students) ranked higher than many graduate classes at first-rate universities today. The faculty included a large number of brilliant unknowns—experienced and dedicated explicators of the Great Books who, for a variety of personal reasons, had never become professional successes. Intellectually, I was most attracted by history and especially by the humanities: by Thucydides, Trotsky's account of the Russian Revolution, Aristotle's aesthetics, and James Joyce. But a life devoted to literary criticism or historical study was consistent with neither my personal commitment to social amelioration nor my activist streak. To combine my political and social concerns with my interests in study and reflection, it seemed natural—perhaps only too natural, given my background—that I attend graduate school in political science.

I did not really choose Harvard over other departments of political science: I went to Cambridge because of my ignorance of the alternatives and my unthinking acceptance of the Harvard mystique. To Yale, which probably had the world's most distinguished political science department at that time, I did not even apply. Berkeley, from which both my parents had received Master's degrees, offered me a three-year scholarship, far superior to what I had been offered anywhere else. But when I received a one-year national Woodrow Wilson Scholarship, and when Harvard accepted me, the die was cast. To my family, Chicago was "the university," and Berkeley was both respected and loved; but Harvard was the unattained pinnacle. Mythology is not absent even from the most rationalized lives.

I entered Harvard in the fall of 1961 knowing something about Western culture, quite a bit about contemporary U.S. politics, and very little about either modern social science or how to deal with Boston taxi drivers. Yet as one of my teachers, now a friend, said to me recently, I seemed, at twenty, to be in a terrible hurry. I *was* in a hurry, driven not so much by desire to begin my career but by fear of not finishing my Ph.D. My father, despite his brilliance and extensive research on the Second International, never completed his dissertation, and the specter of repeating his experience exerted an undue influence on my life at Harvard.

So, despite my relatively weak background in social science, I completed the work for my Ph.D. in little over four years, writing a dissertation on politics in the UN General Assembly. Proceeding so quickly seemed a good idea at the time, but in retrospect I regard it as a great mistake. At Harvard I became familiar with the rudiments of the international relations literature and with the history of classical political thought. Advised by Stanley Hoffmann, who was a very supportive dissertation supervisor, I spent a year in New York interviewing UN delegates about the sources of political influence in the UN General Assembly. My dissertation was well regarded by the department at the time, as it asked some interesting questions and exhibited a feel for the give and take of political bargaining. But it was neither theoretically nor methodologically ambitious. Since it did not require field work abroad or familiarity with a foreign language, I failed to develop the deep knowledge of another society that would have made me a more astute observer of international relations. And the speed with which I whisked through graduate school prevented me from developing the close personal and intellectual friendships that are often formed there; nor did I ever reach the point of talking with my professors as peers, rather than as student to faculty member. The average graduate student may take too long to get his or her Ph.D.; I did not take time enough. Like Henry Adams, I left Harvard without having yet attained an education.

MY PERSONAL TRAJECTORY, 1965–1988

Up to this point, my choices of college and graduate school had hardly been choices at all: I went to Shimer because it accepted early entrants and because my father taught there; I attended Harvard because of its aura in my household. That I benefited from both institutions was merely lucky. But in 1965 I actually made a correct decision largely for the right reasons.

The mid-1960s were boom times for colleges and for newly minted or about-to-be-minted Ph.D.s. Accordingly, I had offers of beginning positions from three first-rate institutions: Harvard, the University of Wisconsin, and Swarthmore College. Admittedly, in those days Harvard and Swarthmore still offered only instructorships to new faculty, even those with Ph.D.s; only Wisconsin was modern enough to dub its most junior faculty members with the lofty title of assistant professor. Despite this indignity, I chose Swarthmore. Although I liked Stanley Hoffmann, I had not particularly enjoyed my graduate years in what was then the quite formal and anomic environment of Harvard University: with respect to both the intellectual excitement of conversations among students and student-faculty interaction, Harvard compared unfavorably with the unknown college in the cornfields from which I had come. More to the point, I had sense enough to realize that it would be a mistake to begin my career where I had been a graduate student. Faculty members would still see me as a graduate student, rather than as a colleague; and I would inevitably always be looking over my shoulder to see whether Hoffmann and others approved of my work. Perhaps I recognized my own youth (I was twenty-four) and immaturity.

Wisconsin was too close to home and too cold in the winter. I was also intimidated by the prospect of lecturing to large audiences and teaching graduate students—those aspects of teaching that I now enjoy most. Swarthmore had a first-rate small department led by J. Roland Pennock, and it included among its members Kenneth N. Waltz, whose *Man, the State, and War* was already justly famous.[5] It seemed a good place to seek my own education.

It has become a cliché that one never knows a subject until one has taught it. At Swarthmore I learned about the field of international politics by teaching it, often in honors seminars with four to eight extremely bright students—seminars that typically begin at 1:30 and lasted until 5:30 or 6:00. No one who has been through that experience ever forgets the intensity of the discussions of students' papers, the thrill of recognizing new insights, or the comradeship that can develop not only among students but between students and faculty. I have always thought that my graduate education took place principally at Swarthmore College.

Swarthmore expected scholarly accomplishment from its faculty, but it did not make the enormous and often unreasonable demands made by universities for volume of scholarly output. I was therefore spared the extreme "publish or perish" syndrome that puts inordinate pressure on young people (especially those with family responsibilites) and can dampen rather than develop creativity. Ironically enough, I had come to Swarthmore partly because I saw myself more as a teacher, like my father, than as a research scholar. Just before my arrival at Swarthmore, several divisions of U.S. troops had been sent to Vietnam; and soon I was deeply involved in politics, spending almost the entire spring of 1968 and much of 1969–1970 directing political campaigns in our local congressional district, first for Eugene McCarthy and later for an antiwar candidate for the Senate. Had the candidates I supported been more successful, my career might conceivably have taken an entirely different direction at this point.

My first three or four years at Swarthmore were thus devoted principally to teaching, learning, and politics. Not having to publish a book or give up hope of tenure, I took a critical look at my dissertation and pronounced it mediocre. I restricted my publications from the dissertation to two articles that were based on it.

Ever since my years in graduate school, I had been critical of the then-dominant school of political realism, as represented most eloquently (if confusingly) by the works of Hans J. Morgenthau. My original reason for studying the UN General Assembly was to ascertain whether its institutional context significantly affected the outcomes of interstate relations taking place in the United Nations. Were power and interests the whole story, or did institutions also matter? Although I did not cast this issue in explicit terms, nor did I use social science theory to explore it, this puzzle was in my mind in 1964 and has remained a theme of my work ever since.

Teaching U.S. foreign policy at Swarthmore alerted me to what appeared to be another anomaly for realism in the 1960s: what I referred to in 1971 as "the big influence of small allies."[6] Why did Spain, Nationalist China, and Israel—and implicitly, Vietnam—seem to exert so much influence on the United States? My first year of leave came early, in 1968–1969, under Swarthmore's enlightened policy of providing a year's leave with half-pay every four years, and due also to the inauguration of the Council on Foreign Relations' International Affairs Fellowship program. I spent the year in Washington, doing research on the influence of small U.S. allies on American policy, and working for six weeks in the undersecretary's office in the State Department—my only experience then or since in government.

Meanwhile, as Joseph S. Nye has put it, "serendipity" struck when he and I, along with some other younger scholars, were asked to join the board of editors of *International Organization*. The established members of that board may well have been dismayed by the consequences of their decision, inasmuch as their new colleagues proceeded within five or six years to reconstitute the board totally. Even if the older board members paid a high price, becoming a member of the *I.O.* board was a turning point in my professional career. It marked the point of transition between orienting myself principally toward a particular intellectual and political community, on the one hand, and principally toward the "invisible college" of scholarship and study in international relations, on the other. Joe Nye was the most important person in this reorientation.

I want to say a word about our personal relationship, and its impact on me, not only because it is essential to this narrative but also because it says something about collaboration in social science. Joe Nye is almost five years older than I, and in 1969, when we began actively to collaborate, he was more than five years more mature. I had some interesting ideas, but they were not embedded in an overall framework; he had equally interesting ideas, but he also had a better sense of how they fit together, and how they related both to realist orthodoxy and to policy concerns. He arranged for me to come to the Center for International Affairs at Harvard during 1972 so that we could work closely together. Furthermore, he knew, as I did not, how to construct an *agenda* for scholarly work—that is, how to devise tasks in a progressive way that would lead from ideas to articles to a book. We were fully equal partners and we both benefited personally as well as intellectually from our collaboration; but in a professional sense, I am sure that I gained more from Joe than he did from me.

A collaboration this close is in many ways like a marriage. To be successful, it rests on deep mutual respect and trust. As we said in the preface to *Power and Interdependence:* "Friends have often asked us how we managed to collaborate so intensively over such a long period of time. The short answer is by swallowing our pride while we tore apart each other's chapters."[7]

Without mutual respect—and indeed affection—tough mutual criticism may become impossible. This failure to engage in mutual criticism leads to "least common denominator collaboration"—as painful for the reader as for the authors. Our collaboration was so close that it is not meaningful to ask "who wrote" each chapter, because each of them underwent four to eight drafts and many long sessions of argument and revision, usually at the Nyes' home on Lexington Green. Others can judge intellectual success or failure; we can judge our personal success.

By 1973 I was ready to leave Swarthmore. However exciting it was to teach bright undergraduates, I was ready for new challenges, and for the more diverse environment of a great university. So when Stanford asked me to direct a new undergraduate international relations program and offered a teaching position in political theory to my wife, Nan Keohane, we moved to California. During my first two and a half years at Stanford, an under-graduate international relations major (which continues to attract large numbers of students) was founded, I began graduate teaching with the aid and colleagueship of Alexander George and Robert North, and Joe Nye and I completed *Power and Interdependence.* In 1974 I began the first of my six years as editor of *International Organization,* a position from which I could observe the rapid growth of work on international political economy and exert some influence over it myself.

My interest in political economy actually dates back to my years at Swarthmore, where in 1970 I had taught a course on multinational corporations with Van Doorn Ooms, an international economist who eventually embarked on a distinguished career in government. Van Ooms did his best to teach me some economics, in which I had had almost no formal training; he certainly intrigued me with economic logic and the strategies of international business; and we wrote two articles together. My research for *Power and Interdependence* later led me to read extensively into the history of the international political economy during the twentieth century. So in 1976 I returned to this theme, reflecting on the political implications of economic advice; and in 1977–1978 I spent a year at the Center for Advanced Study in the Behavioral Sciences, at Stanford, working on the politics of U.S. foreign economic policy, the issue of international policy coordination, and the international politics of inflation.[8]

In retrospect, some of my work in this period seems to lack an incisive or original theme. Of course, any set of economic relationships has a political dimension—a dimension not only clear to Albert Hirschman, Karl Polanyi, and Jacob Viner in the 1940s but brilliantly analyzed by all of them.[9] Furthermore, in *Power and Interdependence* Nye and I had already sought "to integrate realism and liberalism by using a conception of interdependence which focused on bargaining."[10] Further work on the international political economy ran the risk of being only a set of extended footnotes to *Power and Interdependence*.

As I began to focus more explicitly on policy coordination, however, a new analytical puzzle began to emerge. Once again, I started out by expressing my dissatisfaction with the realist orthodoxy. If the realist emphasis on conflicts of interest and power were correct, how could so much cooperation persist in world politics during the 1980s? After all, the relative economic power resources of the United States had declined since the 1950s relative to Europe and were still declining relative to Japan. I did not assume that U.S. power was collapsing, or even that its decline was uniform—Chapter 9 of *After Hegemony* was entitled "the *incomplete* decline of hegemonic regimes" (italics added).[11] Nevertheless, in a realist world one should have expected sharply increasing discord, and even the formation of economic blocs—as prominent scholars had predicted during the disruptions of the early-to-mid 1970s. The fact that cooperation persisted—sometimes even increasing as in energy, sometimes under great stress as in trade—seemed puzzling.

I hadn't much of a clue to this puzzle until the very end of my year's leave. In the summer of 1978 I was present at a meeting in Minnesota with Charles Kindleberger, the famous international economist, who began to talk about the implications for international relations of theories of transactions costs, uncertainty, and risk. Upon my return to Stanford I began to think more explicitly about what I called, in a working paper of July 1978, "externalities and risks in international policy coordination." In 1979 Timothy McKeown was a graduate student at Stanford, working with James March as well as myself. McKeown accelerated my process of learning by introducing me to some of the contemporary microeconomic literature. Thus it is that students sometimes teach their professors more than their professors teach them! So I began to read works by such writers as George Akerlof, Ronald Coase, and Oliver Williamson, and to think about their implications for international relations.[12] James Rosse, a colleague of mine from economics and an associate dean (now provost) of Stanford, lent me an invaluable set of papers reproduced for his course on industrial organization. By the end of 1979 I had made some notes for a possible paper on "risk, information, and international regimes," which became "The Demand for International Regimes," which in turn formed the basis for the analytical heart (Chapters 5 and 6) of *After Hegemony.*[13]

To me, it was an exciting realization that international regimes could be accounted for in ways that are parallel to the modern theory of the firm— that political market failures result from transaction costs and uncertainty, and that these failures could be corrected, with benefits for all participants, through international institutions. I can still remember the "aha" feeling, in my fourth-floor office at Stanford in December 1979, when I glimpsed the relevance of theories of industrial organizations for understanding international regimes. Such a sudden realization has happened only once in my career, but December 1979 was a critical moment for me: before then, I was not sure what the key issues were; afterwards, I had an admittedly vague but nevertheless compelling image to guide me. And although others may judge differently, I regard the making of this connection as one of my most important contributions to the study of world politics.

I did not declare in my moment of revelation that "efficiency is all," nor that the rationality principle was perfectly enlightening—I had been too much instructed at Harvard in the significance of power politics and the vagaries of human history for that. Indeed, some friends have thought that during the 1980s I bent over backwards to express my respect for realism and neorealism. Some have even identified me as a "neorealist," despite my explicit self-identification as a critic of that point of view.[14]

By early 1980 I had formed a conception of a book on international cooperation that would deal with the puzzle of cooperation under declining hegemony, and that would use market failure theories to seek to resolve that puzzle. It took me almost four years to work out the argument, complete with chapters on the postwar international political economy, for which my research had been started during 1977–1978.

Meanwhile, Nan was unexpectedly appointed president of Wellesley College. A 3,000-mile commute did not appeal to either of us, particularly since we had three children living with us at the time. I was fortunate to be offered a position at Brandeis University, also west of Boston; and we were therefore able to move east together in 1981. At Brandeis the students were interesting and my colleagues, particularly Robert Art and Susan Okin, were stimulating and supportive. Mercifully relieved of my Stanford departmental chairmanship after only one year, I was able to concentrate on my manuscript. Brandeis offered a congenial environment for trying out my ideas as well as sufficient time to make progress with my writing. Although I had moved to Brandeis for personal rather than professional reasons, it turned out to be a productive shift of locale.

In 1985—twenty years after my departure for Swarthmore—I accepted a position in a much-changed Harvard Government Department, now both personally more congenial and intellectually more vibrant than I had found it as a graduate student. Despite my affection for Brandeis, the opportunity to return to Harvard—where both the quality of the students and the richness of the intellectual environment are unexcelled—was irresistible.

FUTURE PUZZLES AND POSSIBILITIES

No intellectual journey is smooth, since a necessary condition for discovery is confusion. I have spent much of my intellectual life being so confused that I couldn't even describe the questions I wanted to answer. Reportedly, Gertrude Stein asked on her death-bed, "What is the answer?" When her friends could not provide one, she said, "Well then, what is the question?" Understanding the right question on which to focus is often the most difficult part of a research project in international politics. It was probably 1973 before Joe Nye and I realized that our key issue could be posed in terms of the relationship between political power and economic interdependence; it was early in 1980 before I could pose my research question in clear terms: Why does institutionalized international cooperation persist as hegemony declines? In each case, three to four years of research and muddled thinking preceded the posing of the question, and a similar length of time was necessary to complete the study once the question had become clear. The essence of discovery is being deeply puzzled about questions on which one is supposedly an expert.

Since the completion of *After Hegemony*, I have been looking for a way to go beyond its rather rudimentary theory of international cooperation. To say that international regimes facilitate cooperation by reducing uncertainty, and that governments conform to regime injunctions largely out of concern for reputation, still makes sense to me. But this formulation is not very precise, and it does not take us very far. One possible approach to additional precision would be to use game theory rigorously rather than metaphorically; but game theory does not yield unique predictions even in the most interesting simple situations, and is of only heuristic value to those trying to understand complex multilateral situations. As a result of my involvement in a collective attempt to understand "cooperation under anarchy" through the use of simple precepts derived from game theory, I concluded that it was unlikely that greater formalization of game theory would provide a clear structure for precise and insightful investigation of world politics—and, in any case, that I was intellectually unequipped and temperamentally unsuited to making a contribution toward that enterprise.[15] The employment of game theory only highlighted the importance of the context within which games take place and the perceptions that affect decisionmaking in ambiguous situations.[16]

With the aid of a grant from the Ford Foundation, in 1985–1986 and 1986–1987, I co-directed a series of seminars at Harvard-MIT on international institutions and cooperation, and organized a conference on that subject with scholars from around the country. These meetings, and the urgings of my Harvard graduate students, reinforced my incipient view that the next major step forward in understanding international cooperation will have to incorporate domestic politics fully into the analysis—not on a merely ad hoc basis, but systematically. They also led more fundamentally to a new awareness of the limitations of static theory such as I employed in *After Hegemony*. World politics is path-dependent, as Paul David pointed out at the conference: Where we are depends not merely on the state of contemporaneous demographic, institutional, economic, and military factors but also on *how* we got there; and how we got there may itself have been strongly affected by random or conjunctural events.[17]

In these seminars Hayward Alker repeatedly urged a further claim: that sutdents of international relations must take *historicity* into account. As I understand it, historicity refers to the social process of reflection on historical experience that human societies undergo. This social process alters societies' understandings of themselves and, hence, the actions in which they engage. "Meaning matters." As a result, ahistorical economic accounts of human action, which attribute unchanging utility functions to their members, fail to capture the essentially historical and reflective nature of human collective life.

I am now trying to come to grips with domestic politics, path-dependence, and historicity in my reflections on how patterns of international cooperation change. Why are relationships between certain countries, or multilateral arrangements with respect to particular issues, characterized by general compliance with international agreements, whereas in other relationships the significance of past commitments is much less assured? If one believed in the realist worldview, compliance would be puzzling, since changing interests, and changing power relationships, should make agreements obsolete. "The strong do what they can and the weak suffer what they must," said the Athenian envoys to the inhabitants of Melos, according to Thucydides; and Bethmann-Hollweg in 1914 described the treaty guaranteeing the neutrality of Belgium as "a scrap of paper." In *After Hegemony* I relied in answering this question on reciprocity, with its implications of retaliation, and on governments' concern for their reputations. But reciprocity does not apply well between unequals in power, and not all valuable reputations involve being reliable partners: it may be useful sometimes to have a reputation as an egoist or a bully. I suspect that better answers to this question can be found if we look more closely at how domestic and international politics intersect, or at the relationship between domestic and international law.

At any rate, the central question that puzzles me now can be stated as follows: Why and under what conditions do governments ever take international agreements seriously in a world of anarchy? We must come to understand not only why governments take their commitments seriously but also what the sources of variation are in this deference to commitments. Why do some relationships develop, over time, such that each party takes agreements seriously, even when they do not always perfectly conform to their terms; and why do other relationships not develop in that way? Even the same country may behave differently in different contexts—consider the contrast between American behavior in the nineteenth century toward its agreements with Great Britain, on the one hand, and its behavior toward its treaties with the Indians or its immigration agreements with China, on the other. I am now working on U.S. foreign policy with this puzzle in mind. But if any published work comes out of this, the question may be different; it is not yet clear to me that this is the right question, or the right way of posing it.

If I turn out to be lucky enough to have a life-span of normal duration, I am now almost exactly at the midpoint of my professional career. Twenty-three years ago I was teaching in my first semester at Swarthmore; twenty-three years from now, if personal fate permits, world war is avoided, and the political and educational institutions on which our lives rest persist, I will be seventy years old and nearing retirement. So this is not an autobiography but, rather, a look backward and forward at the midpoint.

If it seems presumptuous to review my own past, it would be absurd to try to forecast my future. Fortunately, life's zest often lies in the unexpected. As one contemplates the future, hope and examples may be more useful than either experience or logic. Hope is necessary because it allows us to overcome the despair to which rational, probabilistic analysis can often lead. Examples are essential because they allow us to imagine our future in personal terms, giving us something specific to strive for. In addition to the examples of Hoffmann and Nye, a special role model for me is Ernst Haas of the University of California at Berkeley—whose student I would have been had the Harvard mystique not turned my head. Haas exemplifies the kind of scholarly life in which I believe: commitment to humanistic, cosmopolitan, and ecological values; persistence in pursuing consistent research themes (in his case, research into how people and organizations learn to cope with problems of international interdependence); support for his present and former students; and willingness to admit puzzlement and confusion in trying to come to grips with difficult theoretical problems that he cannot satisfactorily solve.

Reflection on Ernie Haas's career leads me back to my initial point about values. If we learn more about the processes by which international commitments are taken seriously, we may understand better the conditions under which cooperation not only occurs but becomes institutionalized and cumulative. Not all cooperation has worthy purposes—governments often cooperate to make war, to exploit others, and to conceal the effects of their depredations. But I believe that international cooperation, though not sufficient, is a necessary condition for life, liberty, and the pursuit of happiness in the twenty-first century. It remains, therefore, a worthy subject about which to be puzzled and confused.

NOTES

1. Robert Axelrod, *The Evolution of Cooperation* (New York: Basic Books, 1984), Ch. 2.

2. Herbert A. Simon, "From Substantive to Procedural Rationality," in Spiro J. Latsis, ed., *Method and Appraisal in Economics* (Cambridge: Cambridge University Press, 1976), pp. 129–148. Reprinted in Herbert A. Simon, *Models of Bounded Rationality* (Cambridge, Mass.: (MIT Press, 1982), pp. 424–443.

3. David M.Kreps, "Corporate Culture and Economic Theory" (Stanford, Calif.: (Unpublished paper, Graduate School of Business, Stanford University, August 1984), pp. 12–19.

4. James Kurth made this point in an unpublished paper about fifteen years ago.

5. Kenneth N. Waltz, *Man, the State, and War* (New York: Columbia University Press, 1959).

6. Keohane, "The Big Influence of Small Allies," *Foreign Policy*, no. 2 (Spring 1971).

7. Keohane and Joseph S. Nye, *Power and Interdependence: World Politics in Transition* (Boston: Little, Brown, 1977), p. ix.

8. Keohane, "Economics, Inflation and the Role of the State: Political Implications of the McCracken Report," *World Politics* 31 (1978), pp. 108–128.

9. Albert O. Hirschman, *National Power and the Structure of Foreign Trade* (Berkeley: University of California Press, 1945, 1980); Karl Polanyi, *The Great Transformation* (Boston: Beacon Press, 1944, 1957); Jacob Viner, "Power vs. Plenty as Objectives of Foreign Policy in the Seventeenth and Eighteenth Centuries," *World Politics*, vol. 1 (October 1948), pp. 1–29.

10. Keohane and Joseph S. Nye, "Power and Interdependence Revisited," *International Organization*, vol. 41 (Autumn 1987), p. 733.

11. Keohane, *After Hegemony: Cooperation and Discord in the World Political Economy* (Princeton, N.J.: Princeton University Press, 1984).

12. George Akerlof, "The Market for Lemons," *Quarterly Journal of Economics*, vol. 24 (April 1970), pp. 175–181; Ronald H. Coase, "The Nature of the Firm," *Economica*, vol. 4 (1937), pp. 386–405; Coase, "The Problem of Social Cost," *Journal of Law and Economics*, vol. 31 (1960), pp. 1–44; Oliver Williamson, "A Dynamic Theory of Interfirm Behavior," *Quarterly Journal of Economics*, vol. 79 (1965), pp. 579–607; Wiliamson, *Markets and Hierarchies: Analysis and Anti-Trust Implications* (New York: Free Press, 1975).

13. Keohane, "The Demand for International Regimes," *International Organization*, vol. 36 (1982), pp. 325–356 (also Chapter 5 of this volume).

14. Keohane, "Theory of World Politics: Structural Realism and Beyond," in Ada Finifter, ed., *Political Science: The State of the Discipline* (Washington, D.C.: American Political Science Association, 1983, 1986), pp. 503–540 (reprinted in Keohane, *Neorealism and Its Critics* (New York: Columbia University Press, 1986), pp. 158–203 (also Chapter 3 of this volume).

15. Kenneth A. Oye, ed., *Cooperation Under Anarchy* (Princeton, N.J.: Princeton University Press, 1986). This was the Fall 1985 special issue of *World Politics*.

16. Robert Axelrod and Keohane, "Achieving Cooperation Under Anarchy: Strategies and Institutions," in Kenneth A. Oye, ed., *Cooperation Under Anarchy* (Princeton, N.J.: Princeton University Press, 1986).

17. Paul A. David, "The Economics of QWERTY," *American Economic Review*, vol. 75 (1985), pp. 332–337.

PART ONE

International Institutions and Practices

CHAPTER 3

Theory of World Politics:
Structural Realism and Beyond

For over 2000 years, what Hans J. Morgenthau dubbed "Political Realism" has constituted the principal tradition for the analysis of international relations in Europe and its offshoots in the New World (Morgenthau 1966). Writers of the Italian Renaissance, balance of power theorists, and later adherents of the school of *Machtpolitik* all fit under a loose version of the Realist rubric. Periodic attacks on Realism have taken place; yet the very focus of these critiques seems only to reconfirm the centrality of Realist thinking in the international political thought of the West.[1]

Realism has been criticized frequently during the last few years, and demands for a "new paradigm" have been made. Joseph S. Nye and I called for a "world politics paradigm" a decade ago, and Richard Mansbach and John A. Vasquez have recently proposed a "new paradigm for global politics." In both these works, the new paradigm that was envisaged entailed adopting additional concepts—for instance, "transnational relations," or "issue phases" (Keohane and Nye 1972, esp. 379–386; Mansbach and Vasquez 1981, ch. 4). Yet for these concepts to be useful as part of a satisfactory general theory of world politics, a theory of state action—which is what Realism purports to provide—is necessary. Understanding the general principles of state action and the practices of governments is a necessary basis for attempts to refine theory or to extend the analysis to non-state actors. Approaches using new concepts may be able to supplement, enrich, or extend a basic theory of state action, but they cannot substitute for it.[2]

The fixation of critics and reformers on the Realist theory of state action reflects the importance of this research tradition. In my view, there is good reason for this. Realism is a necessary component in a coherent analysis of world politics because its focus on power, interests, and rationality is crucial to any understanding of the subject. Thus any approach to international relations has to incorporate, or at least come to grips with, key elements of Realist thinking. Even writers who are concerned principally with international institutions and rules, or analysts in the Marxist tradition, make use of some Realist premises. Since Realism builds on fundamental insights about world politics and state action, progress in the study of international relations requires that we seek to build on this core.

Yet as we shall see, Realism does not provide a satisfactory theory of world politics, if we require of an adequate theory that it provide a set of plausible and testable answers to questions about state behavior under specified conditions. Realism is particularly weak in accounting for change, especially where the sources of that change lie in the world political economy or in the domestic structures of states. Realism, viewed dogmatically as a set of answers, would be worse than useless. As a sophisticated framework of questions and initial hypotheses, however, it is extremely valuable.[3]

Since Realism constitutes the central tradition in the study of world politics, an analysis, like this one, of the current state of the field must evaluate the viability of Realism in the penultimate decade of the twentieth century. Doing this requires constructing a rather elaborate argument of my own, precluding a comprehensive review of the whole literature of international relations. I have therefore selected for discussion a relatively small number of works that fit my theme, ignoring entire areas of research, much of it innovative.[4] Within the sphere of work dealing with Realism and its limitations, I have focused attention on several especially interesting and valuable contributions. My intention is to point out promising lines of research rather than to engage in what Stanley Hoffmann once called a "wrecking operation" (Hoffmann 1960:171).

Since I have written on the subject of Realism in the past, I owe the reader an explanation of where I think my views have changed, and where I am only restating, in different ways, opinions that I have expressed before. This chapter deals more systematically and more sympathetically with Realism than does my previous work. Yet its fundamental argument is consistent with that of *Power and Interdependence*. In that book Nye and I relied on Realist theory as a basis for our structural models of international regime change (Keohane and Nye 1977:42–46). We viewed our structural models as attempts to improve the ability of Realist or neo-Realist analysis to account for international regime change: we saw ourselves as adapting Realism, and attempting to go beyond it, rather than rejecting it.

Admittedly, chapter 2 of *Power and Interdependence* characterized Realism as a descriptive ideal type rather than a research program in which explanatory theories could be embedded. Realist and Complex Interdependence ideal types were used to help specify the conditions under which overall structure explanations of change would or would not be valid; the term "Realist" was used to refer to conditions under which states are the dominant actors, hierarchies of issues exist, and force is usable as an instrument of policy (Keohane and Nye 1977:23–29). Taken as a full characterization of the Realist tradition this would have been unfair, and it seems to have led readers concerned with our view of Realism to focus excessively on chapter 2 and too little on the attempt, which draws on what I here call structural realism, to account for regime change (chapters 3–6).[5]

To provide criteria for the evaluation of theoretical work in international politics—Structural Realism, in particular—I employ the conception of a "scientific research programme" explicated in 1970 by the philosopher of science Imre Lakatos (1970). Lakatos developed this concept as a tool for the comparative evaluation of scientific theories, and in response to what he regarded as the absence of standards for evaluation in Thomas Kuhn's (1962) notion of a paradigm.[6] Theories are embedded in research programs. These programs contain inviolable assumptions (the "hard core") and initial conditions, defining their scope. For Lakatos, they also include two other very important elements: auxiliary, or observational, hypotheses, and a "positive heuristic," which tells the scientist what sorts of additional hypotheses to entertain and how to go about conducting research. In short, a research program is a set of methodological rules telling us what paths of research to avoid and what paths to follow.

Consider a research program, with a set of observational hypotheses, a "hard core" of irrefutable assumptions, and a set of scope conditions. In the course of research, anomalies are bound to appear sooner or later: predictions of the theory will seem to be falsified. For Lakatos, the reaction of scientists developing the research program is to protect the hard core by constructing auxiliary hypotheses that will explain the anomalies. Yet any research program, good or bad, can invent such auxiliary hypotheses on an *ad hoc* basis. The key test for Lakatos of the value of a research program is whether these auxiliary hypotheses are "progressive," that is, whether their invention leads to the discovery of *new facts* (other than the anomalous facts that they were designed to explain). Progressive research programs display "continuous growth": their auxiliary hypotheses increase our capacity to understand reality (Lakatos 1970:116–122, 132–138, 173–180).

Lakatos developed this conception to assess developments in the natural sciences, particularly physics. If we took literally the requirements that he laid down for "progressive" research programs, all actual theories of international politics—and perhaps all conceivable theories—would fail the test. Indeed, it has been argued that much of economics, including oligopoly theory (heavily relied upon by Structural Realists), fails to meet this standard (Latsis 1976). Nevertheless, Lakatos's conception has the great merit of providing clear and sensible criteria for the evaluation of scientific traditions, and of asking penetrating questions that may help us to see Realism in a revealing light. Lakatos's questions are relevant, even if applying them without modification could lead to premature rejection not only of Realism, but of our whole field, or even the entire discipline of political science![7]

The stringency of Lakatos's standards suggests that we should supplement this test with a "softer," more interpretive one. That is, how much insight does Realism provide into contemporary world politics?

For this line of evaluation we can draw inspiration from Clifford Geertz's discussion of the role of theory in anthropology. Geertz argues that culture "is not a power, something to which social events, behaviors, institutions, or processes can be causally attributed; it is a context—something within which they can be intelligibly—that is, thickly—described" (1973:14). The role of theory, he claims, is "not to codify abstract regularities but to make thick description possible, not to generalize across cases but to generalize within them" (ibid., p. 26). This conception is the virtual antithesis of the standards erected by Lakatos, and could all too easily serve as a rationalization for the proliferation of atheoretical case studies. Nevertheless, culture as discussed by Geertz has something in common with the international system as discussed by students of world politics. It is difficult to generalize across systems. We are continually bedeviled by the paucity of comparable cases, particularly when making systemic statements—for example, about the operation of balances of power. Much of what students of world politics do, and what Classical Realism in particular aspires to, is to make the actions of states understandable (despite obfuscatory statements by their spokesmen): that is, in Geertz's words, to provide "a context within which they can be intelligibly described." For example, Morgenthau's discussion of the concept of interest defined in terms of power, quoted at length below, reflects this objective more than the goal of arriving at testable generalizations.

This essay is divided into four major sections. The first of these seeks to establish the basis for a dual evaluation of Realism: as a source of interpretive insights into the operation of world politics, and as a scientific research program that enables the investigator to discover new facts. I examine the argument of Thucydides and Morgenthau to extract the key assumptions of Classical Realism. Then I discuss recent work by Kenneth N. Waltz, whom I regard as the most systematic spokesman for contemporary Structural Realism.

Section II addresses the question of interpretation and puzzle-solving within the Realist tradition. How successful are Realist thinkers in making new contributions to our understanding of world politics? In Section III, I consider the shortcomings of Realism when judged by the standards that Lakatos establishes, or even when evaluated by less rigorous criteria, and begin to ask whether a modified version of Structural Realism could correct some of these faults. Section IV carries this theme further by attempting to outline how a multidimensional research program, including a modified structural theory, might be devised; what its limitations would be; and how it could be relevant, in particular, to problems of peaceful change.

The conclusion emphasizes the issue of peaceful change as both a theoretical and a practical problem. Realism raises the question of how peaceful change could be achieved, but does not resolve it. Understanding the conditions under which peaceful change would be facilitated remains, in my view, the most urgent task facing students of world politics.

I. STRUCTURAL REALISM AS RESEARCH PROGRAM

To explicate the research program of Realism, I begin with two classic works, one ancient, the other modern: *The Peloponnesian War*, by Thucydides, and *Politics Among Nations*, by Morgenthau.[8] The three most fundamental Realist assumptions are evident in these books: that the most important actors in world politics are territorially organized entities (city-states or modern states); that state behavior can be explained rationally; and that states seek power and calculate their interests in terms of power, relative to the nature of the international system that they face.

The Peloponnesian War was written in an attempt to explain the causes of the great war of the Fifth Century B.C. between the coalition led by Athens and its adversaries, led by Sparta. Thucydides assumes that to achieve this purpose, he must explain the behavior of the major city-states involved in the conflict. Likewise, Morgenthau assumes that the subject of a science of international politics is the behavior of states. Realism is "state-centric."[9]

Both authors also believed that observers of world politics could understand events by imagining themselves, as rational individuals, in authoritative positions, and reflecting on what they would do if faced with the problems encountered by the actual decisionmakers. They both, therefore, employ the method of *rational reconstruction*. Thucydides admits that he does not have transcripts of all the major speeches given during the war, but he is undaunted:

> It was in all cases difficult to carry [the speeches] word for word in one's memory, so my habit has been to make the speakers say what was in my opinion demanded of them by the various occasions, of course adhering as closely as possible to the general sense of what they really said. (Thucydides, Book I, paragraph 23 [Chapter I, Modern Library edition, p. 14])

Morgenthau argues that in trying to understand foreign policy,

> We put ourselves in the position of a statesman who must meet a certain problem of foreign policy under certain circumstances, and we ask ourselves what the rational alternatives are from which a statesman may choose . . . and which of these rational alternatives this particular statesman, acting under these circumstances, is likely to choose. It is the testing of this rational hypothesis against the actual facts and their consequences that gives meaning to the facts of international politics and makes a theory of politics possible. (Morgenthau 1966:5)

In reconstructing state calculations, Thucydides and Morgenthau both assume that states will act to protect their power positions, perhaps even to the point of seeking to maximize their power. Thucydides seeks to go beneath the surface of events to the power realities that are fundamental to state action:

> The real cause [of the war] I consider to be the one which was formally most kept out of sight. *The growth in the power of Athens, and the alarm which this inspired in Lacedemon, made war inevitable* (Thucydides, Book I, paragraph 24 [Chapter I, Modern Library edition, p. 15]).[10]

Morgenthau is even more blunt: "International politics, like all politics, is a struggle for power" (1966:25; see also Morgenthau 1946). Political Realism, he argues, understands international politics through the concept of "interest defined as power":

We assume that statesmen think and act in terms of interest defined as power, and the evidence of history bears that assumption out. That assumption allows us to retrace and anticipate, as it were, the steps a statesman—past, present, or future—has taken or will take on the political scene. We look over his shoulder when he writes his dispatches; we listen in on his conversation with other statesmen; we read and anticipate his very thoughts. (1966:5)

The three assumptions just reviewed define the hard core of the Classical Realist research program:

(1) The *state-centric assumption:* states are the most important actors in world politics;

(2) The *rationality assumption:* world politics can be analyzed as if states were unitary rational actors, carefully calculating costs of alternative courses of action and seeking to maximize their expected utility, although doing so under conditions of uncertainty and without necessarily having sufficient information about alternatives or resources (time or otherwise) to conduct a full review of all possible courses of action;[11]

(3) The *power assumption:* states seek power (both the ability to influence others and resources that can be used to exercise influence); and they calculate their interests in terms of power, whether as end or as necessary means to a variety of other ends.

More recently, Kenneth N. Waltz (1959) has attempted to reformulate and systematize Realism on the basis of what he called, in *Man, the State and War,* a "third image" perspective. This form of Realism does not rest on the presumed iniquity of the human race—original sin in one form or another—but on the nature of world politics as an anarchic realm:

Each state pursues its own interests, however defined, in ways it judges best. Force is a means of achieving the external ends of states because there exists no consistent, reliable process of reconciling the conflicts of interests that inevitably arise among similar units in a condition of anarchy. (p. 238)[12]

Even well-intentioned statesmen find that they must use or threaten force to attain their objectives.

Since the actions of states are conceived of as resulting from the nature of international politics, the paramount theoretical task for Realists is to create a *systemic* explanation of international politics. In a systemic theory, as Waltz explains it, the propositions of the theory specify relationships between certain aspects of the system and actor behavior (1979:67–73). Waltz's third-image Realism, for instance, draws connections between the distribution of power in a system and the actions of states: small countries will behave differently than large ones, and in a balance of power system, alliances can be expected to shift in response to changes in power relationships. Any theory will, of course, take into account the attributes of actors, as well as features of the system itself. But the key distinguishing characteristic of a systemic theory is that *the internal attributes of actors are given by assumption rather than treated as variables.* Changes in actor behavior, and system outcomes, are explained not on the basis of variations in these actor characteristics, but on the basis of changes in the attributes of the system itself. A good example of such a systemic theory is microeconomic theory in its standard form. It posits the existence of business firms, with given utility functions (such as profit maximization), and attempts to explain their behavior on the basis of environmental factors such as the competitiveness of markets. It is systemic because its propositions about variations in behavior depend on variations in characteristics of the system, not of the units (Waltz 1979:89–91, 93–95, 98).

To develop a systemic analysis, abstraction is necessary: one has to avoid being distracted by the details and vagaries of domestic politics and other variables at the level of the acting unit. To reconstruct a systemic research program, therefore, Structural Realists must devise a way to explain state behavior on the basis of systemic characteristics, and to account for outcomes in the same manner. This needs to be a coherent explanation, although it need not tell us everything we would like to know about world politics.

Waltz's formulation of Structural Realism as a systemic theory seeks to do this by developing a concept not explicitly used by Morgenthau or Thucydides: the *structure* of the international system. Two elements of international structure are constants: (1) the international system is anarchic rather than hierarchic, and (2) it is characterized by interaction among units with similar functions. These are such enduring background characteristics that they are constitutive of what we mean by "international politics."[14] The third element of structure, the distribution of capabilities across the states in the system, varies from system to system, and over time. Since it is a variable, this element—the distribution of "power"—takes on particular importance in the theory. The most significant capabilities are those of the most powerful actors. Structures "are defined not by all of the actors that flourish within them but by the major ones" (Waltz 1979:93).

According to Waltz, structure is the principal determinant of outcomes at the systems level: structure encourages certain actions and discourages others. It may also lead to unintended consequences, as the ability of states to obtain their objectives is constrained by the power of others (1979:104–111).

For Waltz, understanding the structure of an international system allows us to explain patterns of state behavior, since states determine their interests and strategies on the basis of calculations about their own positions in the system. The link between system structure and actor behavior is forged by the rationality assumption, which enables the theorist to predict that leaders will respond to the incentives and constraints imposed by their environments. Taking rationality as a constant permits one to attribute variations in state behavior to variations in characteristics of the international system. Otherwise, state behavior might have to be accounted for by variations in the calculating ability of states; in that case, the systemic focus of Structural Realism (and much of its explanatory power) would be lost. Thus the rationality assumption—as we will see in examining Waltz's balance of power theory—is essential to the theoretical claims of Structural Realism.[15]

The most parsimonious version of a structural theory would hold that any international system has a single structure of power. In such a conceptualization, power resources are homogeneous and fungible: they can be used to achieve results on any of a variety of issues without significant loss of efficacy. Power in politics becomes like money in economics: "in many respects, power and influence play the same role in international politics as money does in a market economy" (Wolfers 1962:105).

In its strong form, the Structural Realist research program is similar to that of microeconomics. Both use the rationality assumption to permit inferences about actor behavior to be made from system structure. The Realist definition of interests in terms of power and position is like the economist's assumption that firms seek to maximize profits: it provides the utility function of the actor. Through these assumptions, actor characteristics become constant rather than variable, and systemic theory becomes possible.[16] The additional assumption of power fungibility simplifies the theory further: on the basis of a *single* characteristic of the international system (overall power capabilities), *multiple* inferences can be drawn about actor behavior and outcomes. "Foreknowledge"—that aspiration of all theory—is thereby attained (Eckstein 1975:88–89). As we will see below, pure Structural Realism provides an insufficient basis for explaining state interests and behavior, even when the rationality assumption is accepted; and the fungibility assumption is highly questionable. Yet the Structural Realist research program is an impressive intellectual achievement: an elegant, parsimonious, deductively rigorous instrument for scientific discovery. The anomalies that it generates are more interesting than its own predictions; but as Lakatos emphasizes, it is the exploration of anomalies that moves science forward.

Richard K. Ashley has recently argued that Structural Realism—which he calls "technical realism"—actually represents a regression from the classical Realism of Herz or Morgenthau.[17] In his view, contemporary Realist thinkers have forgotten the importance of subjective self-reflection, and the dialectic between subjectivity and objectivity, which are so important in the writings of "practical," or "classical" realists such as Thucydides and Morgenthau. Classical Realism for Ashley is interpretive: "a practical tradition of statesmen is the real subject whose language of experience the interpreter tries to make his own" (1981:221). It is self-reflective and nondeterministic. It treats the concept of balance of power as a dialectical relation: not merely as an objective characterization of the international system but also as a collectively recognized orienting scheme for strategic action. Classical Realism encompasses the unity of opposites, and draws interpretive insight from recognizing the dialectical quality of human experience. Thus its proponents understand that the state system is problematic, and that "strategic artistry" is required to keep it in existence (Ashley 1982:22).

The problem with Classical Realism is that it is difficult to distinguish what Ashley praises as dialectical insight from a refusal to define concepts clearly and consistently, or to develop a systematic set of propositions that could be subjected to empirical tests. Structural Realism seeks to correct these flaws, and thus to construct a more rigorous theoretical framework for the study of world politics, while drawing on the concepts and insights of the older Realism. Structural Realism, as embodied particularly in the work of Waltz, is more systematic and logically more coherent than that of its Classical Realist predecessors. By its own standards, Structural Realism is, in Ashley's words, "a progressive scientific redemption of classical realism" (Ashley 1982:25). That is, it sees itself, and Classical Realism, as elements of a continuous research tradition.

Ashley complains that this form of Realism objectifies reality, and that in particular it regards the state as unproblematic. This leads, in his view, to some pernicious implications: that the interests expressed by dominant elites must be viewed as legitimate, that economic rationality is the highest form of thought, and that individuals are not responsible for the production of insecurity (1982:34–41). But Structural Realists need not make any of these claims. It is true that Structural Realism seeks to understand the limits of, and constraints on, human action in world politics. It emphasizes the strength of these constraints, and in that sense could be considered "conservative." But an analysis of constraints, far from implying an acceptance of the *status quo*, should be seen as a precondition to sensible attempts to change the world. To be self-reflective, human action must take place with an understanding of the context within which it occurs. Structural Realists can be criticized, as we will see, for paying insufficient attention to norms, institutions, and change. But this represents less a fault of Structural Realism as such than a failure of some of its advocates to transcend its categories. Structural Realism's focus on systemic constraints does not contradict classical Realism's concern with action and choice. On the contrary, Classical Realism's emphasis on *praxis* helps us to understand the origins of Structural Realism's search for systematic understanding, and—far from negating the importance of this search—makes it seem all the more important.

I have argued thus far that Structural Realism is at the center of contemporary international relations theory in the United States; that it constitutes an attempt to systematize Classical Realism; and that its degree of success as a theory can be legitimately evaluated in part according to standards such as those laid down by Lakatos, and in part through evaluation of its capacity to generate insightful interpretations of international political behavior. Two distinct tests, each reflecting one aspect of this dualistic evaluative standard, can be devised to evaluate Structural Realism as a research program for international relations:

(1) How "fruitful" is the Realist paradigm for puzzle-solving and interpretation of world politics (Toulmin 1963)? That is, does current work in the Realist tradition make us see issues more clearly, or provide answers to formerly unsolved puzzles? Realism was designed to provide insights into such issues and, if it remains a live tradition, should continue to do so.

(2) Does Realism meet the standards of a scientific research program as enunciated by Lakatos? To answer this question, it is important to remind

ourselves that the hard core of a research program is irrefutable within the terms of the paradigm. When anomalies arise that appear to challenge Realist assumptions, the task of Realist analysts is to create auxiliary theories that defend them. These theories permit explanation of anomalies consistent with Realist assumptions. For Lakatos, the key question about a research program concerns whether the auxiliary hypotheses of Realism are "progressive." That is, do they generate new insights, or predict new facts? If not, they are merely exercises in "patching up" gaps or errors on an ad hoc basis, and the research program is degenerative.

Realism cannot be judged fairly on the basis of only one set of standards. Section II addresses the question of fruitfulness by examining works in the central area of Realist theory: the study of conflict, bargaining, and war. Section II then judges Realism by the more difficult test of Lakatos, which (as noted above) is better at asking trenchant questions than at defining a set of standards appropriate to social science. We will see that in one sense Realilsm survives these tests, since it still appears as a good starting point for analysis. But it does not emerge either as a comprehensive theory or as a progressive research program in the sense employed by Lakatos. Furthermore, it has difficulty interpreting issues, and linkages among issues, outside of the security sphere: it can even be misleading when applied to these issues without sufficient qualification. It also has little to say about the crucially important question of peaceful change. The achievements of Realism, and the prospect that it can be modified further to make it even more useful, should help students of world politics to avoid unnecessary self-deprecation. Yet they certainly do not justify complacency.

II. PROGRESS WITHIN THE REALISM PARADIGM: THREE ACHIEVEMENTS

The fruitfulness of contemporary Realist analysis is best evaluated by considering some of the finest work in the genre. Poor scholarship can derive from even the best research proggram; only the most insightful work reveals the strengths as well as the limits of a theoretical approach. In this section I will consider three outstanding examples of works that begin, at least, from Realist concerns and assumptions: Waltz's construction of balance of power theory in *Theory of International Politics* (1979); the attempt by Glenn Snyder and Paul Diesing in *Conflict Among Nations* (1977) to apply formal game-theoretic models of bargaining to sixteen case studies of major-power crises during the seventy-five years between Fashoda and the Yom Kippur "alert crisis" of 1973; and Robert Gilpin's fine recent work, *War and Change in World Politics* (1981). These works are chosen to provide us with one systematic attempt to develop structural Realist theory, one study of bargaining in specific cases, and one effort to understand broad patterns of international political change. Other recent works could have been chosen instead, such as three books on international conflict and crises published in 1980 or 1981 (Brecher 1980; Bueno de Mesquita 1981; Lebow 1981), or the well-known works by Nazli Choucri and Robert C. North (1975) or by Alexander George and Richard Smoke (1974). But there are limits on what can be done in a single chapter of limited size.

Balance of Power Theory: Waltz

Waltz has explicated balance of power theory as a central element in his Structural Realist synthesis: "If there is any distinctively political theory of international politics, balance of power theory is it" (1979:117). The realization that balances of power periodically form in world politics, is an old one, as are attempts to theorize about it. The puzzle that Waltz addresses is how to "cut through such confusion" as has existed about it: that is, in Kuhn's words, how to "achieve the anticipated in a new way" (1962:36).

Waltz attacks this problem by using the concept of structure, which he has carefully developed earlier in the book, and which he also employs to account for the dreary persistence of patterns of international action (1979:66–72). Balance of power theory applies to "anarchic" realms, which are formally unorganized and in which, therefore, units have to worry about their survival: "Self-help is necessarily the principle of action in an anarchic order" (p. 111). In Waltz's system, states (which are similar to one another in function) are the relevant actors; they use external as well as internal means to achieve their goals. Relative capabilities are (as we saw above) the variable element of structure; as they change, we expect coalitional patterns or patterns of internal effort to be altered as well. From his assumptions, given the condition for the theory's operation (self-help), Waltz deduces "the expected outcome; namely, the formation of balances of power" (p. 118). His solution to the puzzle that he has set for himself is carefully formulated and ingenious.

Nevertheless, Waltz's theory of the balance of power encounters some difficulties. First, it is difficult for him to state precisely the conditions under which coalitions will change. He only forecasts that balances of power will periodically recur. Indeed, his theory is so general that it hardly meets the difficult tests that he himself establishes for theory. In chapter 1 we are told that to test a theory, one must "devise a number of distinct and demanding tests" (1979:13). But such tests are not proposed for balance of power theory: "Because only a loosely defined and inconstant condition of balance is predicted, it is difficult to say that any given distribution of power falsifies the theory" (p. 124). Thus rather than applying demanding tests, Waltz advises that we "should seek *confirmation* through observation of difficult cases" (p. 125, emphasis added). In other words, he counsels that we should search through history to find examples that conform to the predictions of the theory; he then proclaims that "these examples tend to confirm the theory" (p. 125). Two pages later, Waltz appears to change his view, admitting that "we can almost always find confirming cases if we look hard." We should correct for this by looking "for instances of states conforming to common international practices even though for internal reasons they would prefer not to" (p. 127). But Waltz is again making an error against which he warns us. He is not examining a universe of cases, in all of which states would prefer not to conform to "international practice," and asking how often they nevertheless do conform. Instead, he is looking only at the latter cases, chosen *because* they are consistent with his theory. Building grand theory that meets Popperian standards of scientific practice is inherently difficult; even the best scholars, such as Waltz, have trouble simultaneously saying what they want to say and abiding by their canons of scientific practice.

Waltz's theory is also ambiguous with respect to the status of three assumptions that are necessary to a strong form of Structural Realism. I have already mentioned the difficult problem of whether a structural theory must (implausibly) assume fungibility of power resources. Since this problem is less serious with respect to balance of power theory than in a broader context, I will not pursue it here, but will return to it in Section III. Yet Waltz is also, in his discussion of balances of power, unclear on the questions of rationality and interests.

Waltz argues that his assumptions do not include the rationality postulate: "The theory says simply that if some do relatively well, others will emulate them or fall by the wayside" (p. 118). This evolutionary principle, however, can hold only for systems with many actors, experiencing such severe pressure on resources that many will disappear over time. Waltz undermines this argument by pointing out later (p. 137) that "the death rate for states is remarkably low." Furthermore, he relies explicitly on the rationality principle to show that bipolar balances must be stable. "Internal balancing," he says, "is more reliable and precise than external balancing. States are less likely to misjudge their relative strengths than they are to misjudge the strength and reliability of opposing coalitions" (p. 168). I conclude that Waltz does rely on the rationality argument, despite his earlier statement to the contrary.

The other ambiguity in Waltz's balance of power theory has to do with the interests, or motivations, of states. Waltz recognizes that any theory of state behavior must ascribe (by assumption) some motivations to states, just as microeconomic theory ascribes motivations to firms. It is not reductionist to do so as long as these motivations are not taken as varying from state to state as a result of their internal characteristics. Waltz specifies such motivations: states "at a minimum, seek their own preservation, and at a maximum, drive for universal domination" (p. 118).

For his balance of power theory to work, Waltz needs to assume that states seek self-preservation, since if at least some major states did not do so, there would be no reason to expect that roughly equivalent coalitions (i.e., "balances of power") would regularly form. The desire for self-preservation makes states that are behind in a struggle for power try harder, according to Waltz, and leads states allied to a potential hegemon to switch coalitions in order to construct balances of power. Neither of these processes on which Waltz relies to maintain a balance—intensified effort by the weaker country in a bipolar system and coalition formation against potentially dominant states in a multipolar system—could operate reliably without this motivation.

The other aspect of Waltz's motivational assumption—that states "at a maximum, drive for universal domination"—is reminiscent of the implication of Realists such as Morgenthau that states seek to "maximize power." For a third-image Realist theory such as Waltz's, such an assumption is unnecessary. Waltz's defense of it is that the balance of power depends on the possibility that force may be used. But this possibility is an attribute of the self-help international system, for Waltz, rather than a reflection of the actors' characteristics. That some states seek universal domination is not a necessary condition for force to be used.

This ambiguity in Waltz's analysis points toward a broader ambiguity in Realist thinking: *Balance of power theory is inconsistent with the assumption frequently made by Realists that states "maximize power,"* if power is taken to refer to tangible resources that can be used to induce other actors to do what they would not otherwise do, through the threat or infliction of deprivations.[18] States concerned with self-preservation do not seek to maximize their power when they are not in danger. On the contrary, they recognize a trade-off between aggrandizement and self-preservation; they realize that a relentless search for universal domination may jeopardize their own autonomy. Thus they moderate their efforts when their positions are secure. Conversely, they intensify their efforts when danger arises, which assumes that they were not maximizing them under more benign conditions.

One might have thought that Realists would readily recognize this point, yet they seem drawn against their better judgment to the "power maximization" or "universal domination" hypotheses. In part, this may be due to their anxiety to emphasize the significance of force in world politics. Yet there may be theoretical as well as rhetorical reasons for their ambivalence. The assumption of power maximization makes possible strong inferences about behavior that would be impossible if we assumed only that states "sometimes" or "often" sought to aggrandize themselves. In that case, we would have to ask about competing goals, some of which would be generated by the internal social, political, and economic characteristics of the countries concerned. Taking into account these competing goals relegates Structural Realism to the status of partial, incomplete theory.

Waltz's contribution to the study of world politics is conceptual. He helps us think more clearly about the role of systemic theory, the explanatory power of structural models, and how to account deductively for the recurrent formation of balances of power. He shows that the international system shapes state behavior as well as vice versa. These are major contributions. But Waltz does not point out "new ways of seeing" international relations that point toward major novelties. He reformulates and systematizes Realism, and thus develops what I have called Structural Realism, consistently with the fundamental assumptions of his classical predecessors.

Game Theory, Structure, and Bargaining: Snyder and Diesing

Game theory has yielded some insights into issues of negotiations, crises, and limited war, most notably in the early works of Thomas Schelling (1960).

Snyder and Diesing's contribution to this line of analysis, as they put it, is to "distinguish and analyze nine different kinds of bargaining situations, each one a unique combination of power and interest relations between the bargainers, each therefore having its own dynamics and problems" (1977:181–182). They employ their game-theoretic formulations of these nine situations, within an explicit structural context, to analyze sixteen historical cases.

This research design is consistent with the hard core of Realism. Attention is concentrated on the behavior of states. In the initial statement of the problem, the rationality assumption, in suitably modest form, is retained: each actor attempts "to maximize expected value across a given set of consistently ordered objectives, given the information actually available to the actor or which he could reasonably acquire in the time available for decision" (p. 181). Interests are defined to a considerable extent in terms of power: that is, power factors are built into the game structure. In the game of "Protector," for instance, the more powerful state can afford to "go it alone" without its ally, and thus has an interest in doing so under certain conditions, whereas its weaker partner cannot (pp. 145–147). Faced with the game matrix, states, as rational actors, calculate their interests and act accordingly. The structure of world politics, as Waltz defines it, is reflected in the matrices and becomes the basis for action.

If Structural Realism formed a sufficient basis for the understanding of international crises, we could fill in the entries in the matrices solely on the basis of states' positions in the international system, given our knowledge of the fact that they perform "similar functions," including the need to survive as autonomous entities. Interests would indeed be defined in terms of power. This would make game theory a powerful analytic tool, which could even help us predict certain outcomes. Where the game had no unique solution (because of strategic indeterminacy), complete predictability of outcomes could not be achieved, but our expectations about the range of likely action would have been narrowed.

Yet Snyder and Diesing find that even knowledge of the values and goals of top leaders could not permit them to determine the interests of about half the decision-making units in their cases. In the other cases, one needed to understand intragovernmental politics, even when one ignored the impact of wider domestic political factors (pp. 510–511). The "internal-external interaction" is a key to the understanding of crisis bargaining.

As Snyder and Diesing make their analytical framework more complex and move into detailed investigation of their cases, their focus shifts toward concern with cognition and with the effects on policy of ignorance, misperception, and misinformation. In my view, the most creative and insightful of their chapters use ideas developed largely by Robert Jervis (1976) to analyze information processing and decision-making. These chapters shift the focus of attention away from the systemic-level factors reflected in the game-theoretic matrices, toward problems of perception, personal bias, and group decision-making (Snyder and Diesing 1977, chapters 4 and 5).

Thus Snyder and Diesing begin with the hard core of Realism, but their most important contributions depend on their willingness to depart from these assumptions. They are dissatisfied with their initial game-theoretic classificatory scheme. They prefer to explore information processing and decision-making, without a firm deductive theory on which to base their arguments, rather than merely to elucidate neat logical typologies.

Is the work of Snyder and Diesing a triumph of Realism or a defeat? At this point in the argument, perhaps the most that can be said is that it indicates that work in the Realist tradition, analyzing conflict and bargaining with the concepts of interests and power, continues to be fruitful, but it does not give reason for much confidence that adhering strictly to Realist assumptions will lead to important advances in the field.

Cycles of Hegemony and War: Gilpin

In *War and Change in World Politics,* Gilpin uses Realist assumptions to reinterpret the last 2400 years of Western history. Gilpin assumes that states, as the principal actors in world politics, make cost-benefit calculations about alternative courses of action. For instance, states attempt to change the international system as the expected benefits of so doing exceed the costs. Thus, the rationality assumption is applied explicitly, in a strong form, although it is relaxed toward the end of the book (1981b:77, 202). Furthermore, considerations of power, relative to the structure of the international system, are at the core of the calculations made by Gilpin's states: "the distribution of power among states constitutes the principal form of control in every international system" (p. 29). Thus Gilpin accepts the entire hard core of the classical Realist research program as I have defined it.[19]

Gilpin sees world history as an unending series of cycles: "The conclusion of one hegemonic war is the beginning of another cycle of growth, expansion, and eventual decline" (p. 210). As power is redistributed, power relations become inconsistent with the rules governing the system and, in particular, the hierarchy of prestige; war establishes the new hierarchy of prestige and "thereby determines which states will in effect govern the international system" (p. 33).

The view that the rules of a system, and the hierarchy of prestige, must be consistent with underlying power realities is a fundamental proposition of Realism, which follows from its three core assumptions. If states, as the central actors of international relations, calculate their interests in terms of power, they will seek international rules and institutions that are consistent with these interests by maintaining their power. Waltz's conception of structure helps to systematize this argument, but it is essentially static. What Gilpin adds is a proposed solution to the anomalies (for static Realism) that institutions and rules can become inconsistent with power realities over time, and that hegemonic states eventually decline. If, as Realists argue, "the strong do what they can and the weak suffer what they must" (Thucydides, Book V, paragraph 90 [Chapter XVII, Modern Library Edition, p. 331]), why should hegemons ever lose their power? We know that rules do not always reinforce the power of the strong and that hegemons do sometimes lose their hold, but static Realist theory cannot explain this.

In his attempt to explain hegemonic decline, Gilpin formulates a "law of uneven growth":

> According to Realism, the fundamental cause of wars among states and changes in international systems is the uneven growth of power among states. Realist writers from Thucydides and MacKinder to present-day scholars have attributed the dynamics of international relations to the fact that the distribution of power in an international system shifts over a period of time; this shift results in profound changes in the relationships among the states and eventually changes in the nature of the international system itself. (p. 94)

This law, however, restates the problem without resolving it. In accounting for this pattern, Gilpin relies on three sets of processes. One has to do with increasing, and then diminishing, marginal returns from empire. As empires grew, "the economic surplus had to increase faster than cost of war" (p. 115). Yet sooner or later, diminishing returns set in: "the law of diminishing returns has universal applicability and causes the growth of every society to describe an S-shaped curve" (p. 159). Secondly, hegemonic states tend increasingly to consume more and invest less; Gilpin follows the lead of Carlo Cipolla in viewing this as a general pattern in history (Cipolla 1970). Finally, hegemonic states decline because of a process of diffusion of technology to others. In *U.S. Power and the Multinational Corporation* (1975), Gilpin emphasized this process as contributing first to the decline of Britain, then in the 1970s to that of the United States. In *War and Change* he makes the argument more general:

> Through a process of diffusion to other states, the dominant power loses the advantage on which its political, military, or economic success has been based. Thus, by example, and frequently in more direct fashion, the dominant power helps to create challenging powers. (p. 176)

This third argument is systemic, and, therefore, fully consistent with Waltz's Structural Realism. The other two processes, however, reflect the operation of forces within the society as well as international forces. A hegemonic power may suffer diminishing returns as a result of the expansion of its defense perimeter and the increased military costs that result (Gilpin 1981b:191; Luttwak 1976). But whether diminishing returns set in also depends on internal factors such as technological inventiveness of members of the society and the institutions that affect incentives for innovation (North 1981). The tendency of hegemonic states to consume more and invest less is also, in part, a function of their dominant positions in the world system: they can force costs of adjustment to change onto others, at least for some time. But it would be hard to deny that the character of the society affects popular tastes for luxury and, therefore, the tradeoffs between guns and butter that are made. Eighteenth-century Saxony and Prussia were different in this regard; so are contemporary America and Japan. In Gilpin's argument as in Snyder and Diesing's, the "external-internal interaction" becomes a crucial factor in explaining state action, and change.

Gilpin explicitly acknowledges his debt to Classical Realism: "In honesty, one must inquire whether or not twentieth-century students of international relations know anything that Thucydides and his fifth-century [B.C.] compatriots did not know about the behavior of states" (p. 227). For Gilpin as for Thucydides, changes in power lead to changes in relations among states: the *real* cause of the Peloponnesian War, for Thucydides, was the rise of the power of Athens and the fear this evoked in the Spartans and their allies. Gilpin has generalized the theory put forward by Thucydides to explain the Peloponnesian War, and has applied it to the whole course of world history:

> Disequilibrium replaces equilibrium, and the world moves toward a new round of hegemonic conflict. It has always been thus and always will be, until men either destroy themselves or learn to develop an effective mechanism of peaceful change. (p. 210)

This Thucydides-Gilpin theory is a systemic theory of change only in a limited sense. It explains the *reaction* to change systematically, in a rationalistic, equilibrium model. Yet at a more fundamental level, it does not account fully for the sources of change. As we saw above, although it is insightful about systemic factors to hegemonic decline, it also has to rely on internal processes to explain the observed effects. Furthermore, it does not account well for the rise of hegemons in the first place, or for the fact that certain contenders emerge rather than others.[20] Gilpin's systemic theory does not account for the extraordinary bursts of energy that occasionally catapult particular countries into dominant positions on the world scene. Why were the Athenians, in words that Thucydides attributes to Corinthian envoys to Sparta, "addicted to innovation," whereas the Spartans were allegedly characterized by a "total want of invention" (Thucydides, Book I, paragraph 70 [Chapter III, Modern Library edition, p. 40])? Like other structural theories, Gilpin's theory underpredicts outcomes. It contributes to our understanding but (as its author recognizes) does not explain change.

This is particularly true of peaceful change, which Gilpin identifies as a crucial issue: "The fundamental problem of international relations in the contemporary world is the problem of peaceful adjustment to the consequences of the uneven growth of power among states, just as it was in the past" (p. 230).

Gilpin's book, like much contemporary American work on international politics, is informed and propelled by concern with peaceful change under conditions of declining hegemony. Gilpin sympathetically discusses E. H. Carr's "defense of peaceful change as the solution to the problem of hegemonic war," written just before World War II (Gilpin, p. 206; Carr 1939/1946). Yet peaceful change does not fit easily into Gilpin's analytical framework, since it falls, by and large, into the category of "interactions change," which does not entail alteration in the overall hierarchy of power and prestige in a system, and Gilpin deliberately avoids focusing on interactions change (p. 44). Yet after one puts down *War and Change*, the question of how institutions and rules can be developed *within* a given international system, to reduce the probability of war and promote peaceful change, looms even larger than it did before.

Thus Gilpin's sophisticated adaptation of Classical Realism turns us away from Realism. Classical Realism, with its philosophical roots in a tragic conception of the human condition, directs our attention in the twentieth century to the existential situation of modern humanity, doomed apparently to recurrent conflict in a world with weapons that could destroy life on our planet. But Realism, whether classical or structural, has little to say about how to deal with that situation, since it offers few insights into the international rules and institutions that people invent to reduce risk and uncertainty in world affairs, in the hope of ameliorating the security dilemma.[21] Morgenthau put his hopes in diplomacy (1966 ch. 32). This is a practical art, far removed from the abstractions of Structural Realism. But diplomacy takes place within a context of international rules, institutions, and practices, which affect the incentives of the actors (Keohane 1982b). Gilpin realizes this, and his gloomy argument—hardly alleviated by a more optimistic epilogue—helps us to understand their importance, although it does not contribute to an explanation of their creation or demise.

Conclusions

Realism, as developed through a long tradition dating from Thucydides, continues to provide the basis for valuable research in international relations. This point has been made by looking at writers who explicitly draw on the Realist tradition, and it can be reinforced by briefly examining some works of Marxist scholars. If they incorporate elements of Realism despite their general antipathy to its viewpoint, our conclusion that Realism reflects enduring realities of world politics will be reinforced.

For Marxists, the fundamental forces affecting world politics are those of class struggle and uneven development. International history is dynamic and dialectical rather than cyclical. The maneuvers of states, on which Realism focuses, reflect the stages of capitalist development and the contradictions of that development. Nevertheless, in analyzing the surface manifestations of world politics under capitalism, Marxists adopt similar categories to those of Realists. Power is crucial; world systems are periodically dominated by hegemonic powers wielding both economic and military resources.

Lenin defined imperialism differently than do the Realists, but he analyzed its operation in part as a Realist would, arguing that "there can be *no* other conceivable basis under capitalism for the division of spheres of influence, of interests, of colonies, etc. than a calculation of the *strength* of the participants in the division" (Lenin 1916/1939:119).

Immanuel Wallerstein provides another example of my point. He goes to some effort to stress that modern world history should be seen as the history of capitalism as a world system. Apart from "relatively minor accidents" provided by geography, peculiarities of history, or luck—which give one country an edge over others at crucial historical junctures—"it is the operations of the world-market forces which accentuate the differences, institutionalize them, and make them impossible to surmount over the long run" (1979:21). Nevertheless, when his attention turns to particular epochs, Wallerstein emphasizes hegemony and the role of military force. Dutch economic hegemony in the seventeenth century was destroyed, in quintessential Realist fashion, not by the operation of the world-market system, but by the force of British and French arms (Wallerstein 1980:38–39).

The insights of Realism are enduring. They cross ideological lines. Its best contemporary exponents use Realism in insightful ways. Waltz has systematized the basic assumptions of Classical Realism in what I have called Structural Realism. Snyder and Diesing have employed this framework for the analysis of bargaining; Gilpin has used the classical arguments of Thucydides to explore problems of international change. For all of these writers, Realism fruitfully focuses attention on fundamental issues of power, interests, and rationality. But as we have seen, many of the most interesting questions raised by these authors cannot be answered within the Realist framework.

III. EXPLANATIONS OF OUTCOMES FROM POWER: HYPOTHESES AND ANOMALIES

A Structural Realist theory of interests could be used both for explanation and for prescription. If we could deduce a state's interests from its position in the system, via the rationality assumption, its behavior could be explained on the basis of systemic analysis. Efforts to define the national interest on an a priori basis, however, or to use the concept for prediction and explanation, have been unsuccessful. We saw above that the inability to define interests independently of observed state behavior robbed Snyder and Diesing's game-theoretical matrices of predictive power. More generally, efforts to show that external considerations of power and position play a dominant role in determining the "national interest" have failed. Even an analyst as sympathetic to Realism as Stephen D. Krasner has concluded, in studying American foreign economic policy, that the United States was "capable of defining its own autonomous goals" in a nonlogical manner (1978a:333). That is, the systemic constraints emphasized by Structural Realism were not binding on the American government during the first thirty years after the Second World War.

Sophisticated contemporary thinkers in the Realist tradition, such as Gilpin, Krasner, and Waltz, understand that interests cannot be derived, simply on the basis of rational calculation, from the external positions of states, and that this is particularly true for great powers, on which, ironically, Structural Realism focuses its principal attentions (Gilpin 1975; Waltz 1967). Realist analysis has to retreat to a "fall-back position": that, *given state interests*, whose origins are not predicted by the theory, patterns of outcomes in world politics will be determined by the overall distribution of power among states. This represents a major concession for systemically oriented analysts, which it is important not to forget. Sensible Realists are highly cognizant of the role of domestic politics and of actor choices within the constraints and incentives provided by the system. Since systemic theory cannot predict state interests, it cannot support deterministic conclusions (Sprout and Sprout 1971:73–77). This limitation makes it both less powerful as a theory, and less dangerous as an ideology.[22] Despite its importance, it cannot stand alone.

When realist theorists say that, given interests, patterns of outcomes will be determined by the overall distribution of power among states, they are using "power" to refer to resources that can be used to induce other actors to do what they would not otherwise do, in accordance with the desires of the power-wielder. "Outcomes" refer principally to two sets of patterns: (1) the results of conflicts, diplomatic or military, that take place between states; and (2) changes in the rules and institutions that regulate relations among governments in world politics. This section focuses on conflicts, since they pose the central puzzles that Realism seeks to explain. Section IV and the Conclusion consider explanations of changes in rules and institutions.

Recent quantitative work seems to confirm that power capabilities (measured not only in terms of economic resources but with political variables added) are rather good predictors of the outcomes of wars. Bueno de Mesquita finds, for example, that countries with what he calls positive "expected utility" (a measure that uses composite capabilities but adjusts them for distance, alliance relationships, and uncertainty) won 179 conflicts while losing only 54 between 1816 and 1974, for a success ratio of over 75 percent (1981, especially p. 151; Organski and Kugler 1980, ch. 2).

The question of the fungibility of power poses a more troublesome issue. As I have noted earlier (see note 19), Structural Realism is ambiguous on this point; the desire for parsimonious theory impels Realists toward a unitary notion of power as homogeneous and usable for a variety of purposes, but close examination of the complexities of world politics induces caution about such an approach. In his discussion of system structure, for instance, Waltz holds that "the units of an anarchic system are distinguished primarily by their greater or lesser capabilities for performing similar tasks," and that the distribution of capabilities across a system is the principal characteristic differentiating international-political structures from one another (1979:97, 99). Thus each international political system has one structure. Yet in emphasizing the continued role of military power, Waltz admits that military power is not perfectly fungible: "Differences in strength do matter, *although not for every conceivable purpose*"; "military power no longer brings political control, but then it never did" (1979:189, 191, emphasis added). This seems to imply that any given international system is likely to have *several* structures, differing by issue-areas and according to the resources that can be used to affect outcomes. Different sets of capabilities will qualify as "power resources" under different conditions. This leads to a much less parsimonious theory and a much more highly differentiated view of the world, in which what Nye and I called "issue-structure" theories play a major role, and in which military force, although still important, is no longer assumed to be at the top of a hierarchy of power resources (Keohane and Nye 1977, chs. 3 and 6).

The status in a Structural Realist theory of the fungibility assumption affects both its power and the incidence of anomalies. A strong version of Structural Realism that assumed full fungibility of power across issues would predict that when issues arise between great powers and smaller states, the great powers should prevail. This has the advantage of generating a clear prediction and the liability of being wrong much of the time. Certainly it does not fit the American experience of the last two decades. The United States lost a war in Vietnam and was for more than a year unable to secure the return of its diplomats held hostage in Iran. Small allies such as Israel, heavily dependent on the United States, have displayed considerable freedom of action. In the U.S.-Canadian relationship of the 1950s and 1960s, which was virtually free of threats of force, outcomes of conflicts as often favored the Canadian as the American position, although this was not true for relations between Australia and the United States (Keohane and Nye 1977, ch. 7).

In view of power theory in social science, the existence of these anomalies is not surprising. As James G. March observes, "there appears to be general consensus that either potential power is different from actually exerted power or that actually exerted power is variable" (1966:57). That is, what March calls "basic force models," which rely, like Realist theory, on measurable indices of power, are inadequate tools for either prediction or explanation. They are often valuable in suggesting long-term trends and patterns, but they do not account well for specific outcomes: the more that is demanded of them, the less well they are likely to perform.

Lakatos's discussion of scientific research programs leads us to expect that, when confronted with anomalies, theorists will create auxiliary theories that preserve the credibility of their fundamental assumptions. Thus it is not surprising that Realists committed to the fungibility assumption have devised auxiliary hypotheses to protect its "hard core" against challenge. One of these is what David Baldwin calls the "conversion-process explanation" of unanticipated outcomes: "The would-be wielder of power is described as lacking in skill and/or the 'will' to use his power resources effectively: 'The Arabs had the tanks but didn't know how to use them.' 'The Americans had the bombs but lacked the will to use them.'" (1979:163–164)

The conversion-process explanation is a classic auxiliary hypothesis, since it is designed to protect the assumption that power resources are homogeneous and fungible. If we were to accept the conversion-process account, we could continue to believe in a single structure of power, even if outcomes do not favor the "stronger" party. This line of argument encounters serious problems, however, when it tries to account for the discrepancy between anticipated and actual outcomes by the impact of intangible resources (such as intelligence, training, organization, foresight) not recognized until after the fact. The problem with this argument lies in its post hoc quality. It is theoretically degenerate in Lakatos's sense, since it does not add any explanatory power to Structural Realist theory, but merely "explains away" uncomfortable facts.

Thus what March says about "force activation models" applies to Structural Realist theories when the conversion-process explanation relies upon sources of power that can be observed only after the events to be explained have taken place:

> If we observe that power exists and is stable and if we observe that sometimes weak people seem to triumph over strong people, we are tempted to rely on an activation hypothesis to explain the discrepancy. But if we then try to use the activation hypothesis to predict the results of social-choice procedures, we discover that the data requirements of 'plausible' activation models are quite substantial. As a result, we retreat to what are essentially degenerate forms of the activation model—retaining some of the form but little of the substance. This puts us back where we started, looking for some device to explain our failures in prediction. (1966:61)

A second auxiliary hypothesis designed to protect the fungibility assumption must be taken more seriously: that discrepancies between power resources and outcomes are explained by an asymmetry of motivation in favor of the objectively weaker party. Following this logic, John Harsanyi has proposed the notion of power "in a schedule sense," describing how various resources can be translated into social power. An actor with intense preferences on an issue may be willing to use more resources to attain a high probability of a favorable result, than an actor with more resources but lower intensity. As a result, outcomes may not accurately reflect underlying power resources (Harsanyi 1962).

To use this insight progressively rather than in a degenerate way, Realist theory needs to develop indices of intensity of motivation that can be measured independently of the behavior that theorists are trying to explain. Russett, George, and Bueno de Mesquita are among the authors who have attempted, with some success, to do this (Russett 1963; George et al. 1971; Bueno de Mesquita 1981). Insofar as motivation is taken simply as a control, allowing us to test the impact of varying power configurations more successfully, Harsanyi's insights can be incorporated into Structural Realist theory. If it became a key variable, however, the effect could be to transform a systemic theory into a decision-making one.

An alternative approach to relying on such auxiliary hypotheses is to relax the fungibility assumption itself. Failures of great powers to control smaller ones could be explained on the basis of independent evidence that in the relevant issue-areas, the states that are weaker on an overall basis have more power resources than their stronger partners, and that the use of power derived from one area of activity to affect outcomes in other areas (through "linkages") is difficult. Thus Saudi Arabia can be expected to have more impact on world energy issues than on questions of strategic arms control; Israel more influence over the creation of a Palestinian state than on the reconstruction of the international financial and debt regime.

Emphasizing the problematic nature of power fungibility might help to create more discriminating power models, but it will not resolve the inherent problems of power models, as identified by March and others. Furthermore, at the limit, to deny fungibility entirely risks a complete disintegration of predictive power. Baldwin comes close to this when he argues that what he calls the "policy-contingency framework" of an influence attempt must be specified before power explanations are employed. If we defined each issue as existing within a unique "policy-contingency framework," no generalizations would be possible. Waltz could reply, if he accepted Baldwin's view of power, that all of world politics should be considered a single policy-contingency framework, characterized by anarchy and self-help.[23] According to this argument, the parsimony gained by assuming the fungibility of power would compensate for the marginal mispredictions of such a theory.

This is a crucial theoretical issue, which should be addressed more explicitly by theorists of world politics. In my view, the dispute cannot be resolved a priori. The degree to which power resources have to be disaggregated in a structural theory depends both on the purposes of the theory and on the degree to which behavior on distinct issues is linked together through the exercise of influence by actors. The larger the domain of a theory, the less accuracy of detail we expect. Since balance of power theory seeks to explain large-scale patterns of state action over long periods of time, we could hardly expect the precision from it that we demand from theories whose domains have been narrowed.

This assertion suggests that grand systemic theory can be very useful as a basis for further theoretical development in international relations, even if the theory is lacking in precision, and it therefore comprises part of my defense of the Realist research program as a foundation on which scholars should build. Yet this argument needs immediate qualification.

Even if a large-scale theory can be developed and appropriately tested, its predictions will be rather gross. To achieve a more finely tuned understanding of how resources affect behavior in particular situations, one needs to specify the policy-contingency framework more precisely. The domain of theory is narrowed to achieve greater precision. Thus the debate between advocates of parsimony and proponents of contextual subtlety resolves itself into a question of *stages*, rather than an either/or choice. We should seek parsimony first, then add complexity while monitoring the adverse effects that this has on the predictive power of our theory: its ability to make significant inferences on the basis of limited information.

To introduce greater complexity into an initially spare theoretical structure, the conception of an issue-area, developed many years ago by Robert A. Dahl (1961) and adapted for use in international relations by James N. Rosenau (1966), is a useful device. Having tentatively selected an area of activity to investigate, the analyst needs to delineate issue-areas at various levels of aggregation. Initial explanations should seek to account for the main features of behavior at a high level of aggregation—such as the international system as a whole—while subsequent hypotheses are designed to apply only to certain issue-areas.

In some cases, more specific issue-areas are "nested" within larger ones (Aggarwal 1981; Snidal 1981). For instance, North Atlantic fisheries issues constitute a subset of fisheries issues in general, which comprise part of the whole area of oceans policy, or "law of the sea." In other cases, specific issues may belong to two or more broader issues: the question of passage through straits, for example, involves questions of military security as well as the law of the sea.

Definitions of issue-areas depend on the beliefs of participants, as well as on the purposes of the investigator. In general, however, definitions of issue-areas should be made on the basis of empirical judgments about the extent to which governments regard sets of issues as closely interdependent and treat them collectively. Decisions made on one issue must affect others in the issue-area, either through functional links or through regular patterns of bargaining. These relationships of interdependence among issues may change. Some issue-areas, such as international financial relations, have remained fairly closely linked for decades; others, such as oceans, have changed drastically over the past 35 years (Keohane and Nye 1977, ch. 4, especially pp. 64–65; Simon 1969; Haas 1980).

When a hierarchy of issue-areas has been identified, power-structure models employing more highly aggregated measures of power resources can be compared with models that disaggregate resources by issue-areas. How much accuracy is gained, and how much parsimony lost, by each step in the disaggregation process? In my view, a variegated analysis, which takes some specific "snapshots" by issue-area as well as looking at the broader picture, is superior to either monistic strategy, whether assuming perfect fungibility or none at all.

This approach represents an adaptation of Realism. It preserves the basic emphasis on power resources as a source of outcomes in general, but it unambiguously jettisons the assumption that power is fungible across all of world politics. Disaggregated power models are less parsimonious than more aggregated ones, and they remain open to the objections to power models articulated by March and others. But in one important sense disaggregation is progressive rather than degenerative. Disaggregated models call attention to linkages among issue-areas, and raise the question: under what conditions, and with what effects, will such linkages arise? Current research suggests that understanding linkages systematically, rather than merely describing them on an *ad hoc* basis, will add significantly to our comprehension of world politics (Oye 1979, 1983; Stein 1980; Tollison and Willett 1979). It would seem worthwhile, in addition, for more empirical work to be done on this subject, since we know so little about when, and how, linkages are made.

Conclusions

Structural Realism is a good starting-point for explaining the outcomes of conflicts, since it directs attention to fundamental questions of interest and power within a logically coherent and parsimonious theoretical framework. Yet the ambitious attempt of Structural Realist theory to deduce national interests from system structure via the rationality postulate has been unsuccessful. Even if interests are taken as given, the attempt to predict outcomes from interests and power leads to ambiguities and incorrect predictions. The auxiliary theory attributing this failure to conversion-processes often entails unfalsifiable tautology rather than genuine explanation. Ambiguity prevails on the question of the fungibility of power: whether there is a single structure of the international system or several. Thus the research program of Realism reveals signs of degeneration. It certainly does not meet Lakatos's tough standards for progressiveness.

More attention to developing independent measures of intensity of motivation, and greater precision about the concept of power and its relationship to the context of action, may help to correct some of these faults. Careful disaggregation of power-resources by issue-area may help to improve the predictive capability of structural models, at the risk of reducing theoretical parsimony. As I argue in the next section, modified structural models, indebted to Realism although perhaps too different to be considered Realist themselves, may be valuable elements in a multilevel framework for understanding world politics.

Yet to some extent the difficulties encountered by Structural Realism reflect the inherent limitations of structural models, which will not be corrected by mere modifications or the relaxation of assumptions. Domestic politics and decision-making, Snyder and Diesing's "internal-external interactions," and the workings of international institutions all play a role, along with international political structure, in affecting state behavior and outcomes. Merely to catalog these factors, however, is not to contribute to theory but rather to compound the descriptive anarchy that already afflicts the field, with too many independent variables, exogenously determined, chasing too few cases. As Waltz emphasizes, the role of unit-level forces can be properly understood only if we comprehend the structure of the international system within which they operate.

IV. BEYOND STRUCTURAL REALISM

Structural Realism helps us to understand world politics as in part a systemic phenomenon, and provides us with a logically coherent theory that establishes the context for state action. This theory, because it is relatively simple and clear, can be modified progressively to attain closer correspondence with reality. Realism's focus on interests and power is central to an understanding of how nations deal with each other. Its adherents have understood that a systemic theory of international relations must account for state behavior by examining the constraints and incentives provided by the system;

for this purpose to be accomplished, an assumption of rationality (although not of perfect information) must be made. The rationality assumption allows inferences about state behavior to be drawn solely from knowledge of the structure of the system.

Unfortunately, such predictions are often wrong. The concept of power is difficult to measure validly a priori; interests are underspecified by examining the nature of the international system and the position of various states in it; the view of power resources implied by overall structure theories is overaggregated, exaggerating the extent to which power is like money. The problem that students of international politics face is how to construct theories that draw on Realism's strengths without partaking fully of its weaknesses.

To do this we need a multidimensional approach to world politics that incorporates several analytical frameworks or research programs. One of these should be that of Structural Realism, which has the virtues of parsimony and clarity, although the range of phenomena that it encompasses is limited. Another, in my view, should be a modified structural research program, which relaxes some of the assumptions of Structural Realism but retains enough of the hard core to generate a priori predictions on the basis of information about the international environment. Finally, we need better theories of domestic politics, decision-making, and information processing, so that the gap between the external and internal environments can be bridged in a systematic way, rather than by simply adding catalogs of exogenously determined foreign policy facts to theoretically more rigorous structural models. That is, we need more attention to the "internal-external interactions" discussed by Snyder and Diesing.

Too much work in this last category is being done for me to review it in detail here. Mention should be made, however, of some highlights. Peter J. Katzenstein, Peter Gourevitch, and others have done pioneering work on the relationship between domestic political structure and political coalitions, on the one hand, and foreign economic policies, on the other (Katzenstein 1978; Gourevitch 1978). This line of analysis, which draws heavily on the work of Alexander Gerschenkron (1962) and Barrington Moore (1966), argues that the different domestic structures characteristic of various advanced industrialized countries result from different historical patterns of development; in particular, whether development came early or late, and what the position of the country was in the international political system at the time of its economic development (Kurth 1979). Thus it attempts to draw connections both between international and domestic levels of analysis, and across historical time. This research does not provide deductive explanatory models, and it does not account systematically for changes in established structures after the formative developmental period, but its concept of domestic structure brings order into the cacophony of domestic political and economic variables that could affect foreign policy, and therefore suggests the possibility of eventual integration of theories relying on international structure with those focusing on domestic structure.

Katzenstein and his associates focus on broad political, economic, and social patterns within countries, and their relationship to the international division of labor and the world political structure. Fruitful analysis can also be done at the more narrowly intragovernmental level, as Snyder and Diesing show. An emphasis on bureaucratic politics was particularly evident in the 1960s and early 1970s, although Robert J. Art has pointed out in detail a number of difficulties, weaknesses, and contradictions in this literature (1973). At the level of the individual decision-maker, insights can be gained by combining theories of cognitive psychology with a rich knowledge of diplomatic history, as in Jervis's work, as long as the investigator understands the systemic and domestic-structural context within which decision-makers operate.[24] This research program has made decided progress, from the simple-minded notions criticized by Waltz (1959) to the work of Alexander and Juliette George (1964), Alexander George (1980), Ole Holsti (1976) and Jervis (1976).[25]

Despite the importance of this work at the levels of domestic structure, intragovernmental politics, and individual cognition, the rest of my analysis will continue to focus on the concept of international political structure and its relevance to the study of world politics. I will argue that progress could be made by constructing a modified structural research program, retaining some of the parsimony characteristic of Structural Realism and its emphasis on the incentives and constraints of the world system, while adapting it to fit contemporary reality better. Like Realism, this research program would be based on microeconomic theory, particularly oligopoly theory. It would seek to explain actor behavior by specifying a priori utility functions for actors, using the rationality principle as a "trivial animating law" in Popper's sense (Latsis 1976:21), and deducing behavior from the constraints of the system as modeled in the theory.

Developing such a theory would only be worthwhile if there were something particularly satisfactory both about systemic explanations and about the structural forms of such explanations. I believe that this is the case, for two sets of reasons.

First, systemic theory is important because we must understand the context of action before we can understand the action itself. As Waltz (1979) has emphasized, theories of world politics that fail to incorporate a sophisticated understanding of the operation of the system—that is, how systemic attributes affect behavior—are bad theories. Theoretical analysis of the characteristics of an international system is as important for understanding foreign policy as understanding European history is for understanding the history of Germany.

Second, structural theory is important because it provides an irreplaceable *component* for a thorough analysis of action, by states or non-state actors, in world politics. A good structural theory generates testable implications about behavior on an a priori basis and, therefore, comes closer than interpretive description to meeting the requirements for scientific knowledge of neopositivist philosophers of science such as Lakatos. This does not mean, of course, that explanation and rich interpretation—Geertz's "thick description" (1973)—are in any way antithetical to one another. A good analysis of a given problem will include both.[26]

The assumptions of a modified structural research program can be compared to Realist assumptions as follows:

(1) The assumption that the principal actors in world politics are states would remain the same, although more emphasis would be placed on nonstate actors, intergovernmental organizations, and transnational and transgovernmental relations than is the case in Realist analysis (Keohane and Nye 1972).

(2) The rationality assumption would be retained, since without it, as we have seen, inferences from structure to behavior become impossible without heroic assumptions about evolutionary processes or other forces that compel actors to adapt their behavior to their environments. It should be kept in mind, however, as is made clear by sophisticated Realists, that the rationality postulate only assumes that actors make calculations "so as to maximize expected value across a given set of consistently ordered objectives" (Snyder and Diesing 1977:81). It does not assume perfect information, consideration of all possible alternatives, or unchanging actor preferences.

(3) The assumption that states seek power and calculate their interests accordingly, would be qualified severely. Power and influence would still be regarded as important state interests (as ends or necessary means), but the implication that the search for power constitutes an overriding interest in all cases, or that is always takes the same form, would be rejected. Under different systemic conditions states will define their self-interests differently. For instance, where survival is at stake efforts to maintain autonomy may take precedence over all other activities, but where the environment is relatively benign energies will also be directed to fulfilling other goals. Indeed, over the long run, whether an environment is malign or benign can alter the standard operating procedures and sense of identity of the actors themselves.[27]

In addition, this modified structural approach would explicitly modify the assumption of fungibility lurking behind unitary conceptions of "international structure." It would be assumed that the value of power resources for influencing behavior in world politics depends on the goals sought. Power resources that are well-suited to achieve certain purposes are less effective when used for other objectives. Thus power resources are differentially effective across issue-areas, and the usability of a given set of power resources depends on the "policy-contingency frameworks" within which it must be employed.

This research program would pay much more attention to the roles of institutions and rules than does Structural Realism. Indeed, a structural interpretation of the emergence of international rules and procedures, and of obedience to them by states, is one of the rewards that could be expected from this modified structural research program (Krasner 1982; Keohane 1982b; Stein 1982).

This research program would contain a valuable positive heuristic—a set of suggestions about what research should be done and what questions should initially be asked—which would include the following pieces of advice:

(1) When trying to explain a set of outcomes in world politics, always consider the hypothesis that the outcomes reflect underlying power resources, without being limited to it;

(2) When considering different patterns of outcomes in different relationships, or issue-areas, entertain the hypothesis that power resources are differently distributed in these issue-areas, and investigate ways in which these differences promote or constrain actor attempts to link issue-areas in order to use power-resources from one area to affect results in another;

(3) When considering how states define their self-interests, explore the effects of international structure on self-interests, as well as the effects of other international factors and of domestic structure.

Such a modified structural research program could begin to help generate theories that are more discriminating, with respect to the sources of power, than is Structural Realism. It would be less oriented toward reaffirming the orthodox verities of world politics and more inclined to explain variations in patterns of rules and institutions. Its concern with international institutions would facilitate insights into processes of peaceful change. This research program would not solve all of the problems of Realist theory, but it would be a valuable basis for interpreting contemporary world politics.

Yet this form of structural theory still has the weaknesses associated with power analysis. The essential problem is that from a purely systemic point of view, situations of strategic interdependence do not have determinate solutions. No matter how carefully power resources are defined, no power model will be able accurately to predict outcomes under such conditions.[28]

One way to alleviate this problem without moving immediately to the domestic level of analysis (and thus sacrificing the advantages of systemic theory) is to recognize that what it is rational for states to do, and what states' interests are, depend on the institutional context of action as well as on the underlying power realities and state position upon which Realist thought concentrates. Structural approaches should be seen as only a basis for further systemic analysis. They vary the power condition in the system, but they are silent on variations in the frequency of mutual interactions in the system or in the level of information.

The importance of these non-power factors is demonstrated by some recent work on cooperation. In particular, Robert Axelrod has shown that cooperation can emerge among egoists under conditions of strategic interdependence as modeled by the game of prisoners' dilemma. Such a result requires, however, that these egoists expect to continue to interact with each other for the indefinite future, and that these expectations of future interactions be given sufficient weight in their calculations (Axelrod 1981). This argument reinforces the practical wisdom of diplomats and arms controllers, who assume that state strategies, and the degree of eventual cooperation, will depend significantly on expectations about the future. The "double-cross" strategy, for instance, is more attractive when it is expected to lead to a final, winning move, than when a continuing series of actions and reactions is anticipated.

High levels of uncertainty reduce the confidence with which expectations are held, and may therefore lead governments to discount the future heavily. As Axelrod shows, this can inhibit the evolution of cooperation through reciprocity. It can also reduce the ability of actors to make mutually beneficial agreements at any given time, quite apart from their expectations about whether future interactions will occur. That is, it can lead to a form of "political market failure" (Keohane 1982b).

Information that reduces uncertainty is therefore an important factor in world politics. But information is not a systemic constant. Some international systems are rich in institutions and processes that provide information to governments and other actors; in other systems, information is scarce or of low quality. Given a certain distribution of power (Waltz's "international structure"), variations in information may be important in influencing state behavior. If international institutions can evolve that improve the quality of information and reduce uncertainty, they may profoundly affect international political behavior even in the absence of changes either in international structure (defined in terms of the distribution of power) or in the preference functions of actors.

Taking information seriously at the systemic level could stimulate a new look at theories of information-processing within governments, such as those of Axelrod (1976), George (1980), Jervis (1976), and Holsti (1976). It could also help us, however, to understand a dimension of the concept of complex interdependence (Keohane and Nye 1977) that has been largely ignored. Complex interdependence can be seen as a condition under which it is not only difficult to use conventional power resources for certain purposes, but under which information levels are relatively high due to the existence of multiple channels of contact among states. If we focus exclusively on questions of power, the most important feature of complex interdependence—almost its *only* important feature—is the ineffectiveness of military force and the constraints that this implies on fungibility of power across issue-areas. Sensitizing ourselves to the role of information, and information-provision, at the international level brings another aspect of complex interdependence— the presence of multiple channels of contact among societies—back into the picture. Actors behave differently in information-rich environments than in information-poor ones where uncertainty prevails.

This is not a subject that can be explored in depth here.[29] I raise it, however, to clarify the nature of the multidimensional network of theories and research programs that I advocate for the study of world politics. We need both spare, logically tight theories, such as Structural Realism, and rich interpretations, such as those of the historically oriented students of domestic structure and foreign policy. But we also need something in-between: systemic theories that retain some of the parsimony of Structural

Realism, but that are able to deal better with differences between issue-areas, with institutions, and with change. Such theories could be developed on the basis of variations in power (as in Structural Realism), but they could also focus on variations in other systemic characteristics, such as levels and quality of information.

CONCLUSION:
WORLD POLITICS AND PEACEFUL CHANGE

As Gilpin points out, the problem of peaceful change is fundamental to world politics. Thermonuclear weapons have made it even more urgent than it was in the past. Realism demonstrates that peaceful change is more difficult to achieve in international politics than within well-ordered domestic societies, but it does not offer a theory of peaceful change.[30] Nor is such a theory available from other research traditions. The question remains for us to grapple with: under what conditions will adaptations to shifts in power, in available technologies, or in fundamental economic relationships take place without severe economic disruption or warfare?

Recent work on "international regimes" has been addressed to this question, which is part of the broader issue of order in world politics (*International Organization*, Spring 1982). Structural Realist approaches to understanding the origins and maintenance of international regimes are useful (Krasner 1982), but since they ignore cognitive issues and quesitons of information, they comprise only part of the story (Haas 1982).

Realism, furthermore, is better at telling us why we are in such trouble than how to get out of it. It argues that order can be created from anarchy by the exercise of superordinate power: periods of peace follow establishment of dominance in Gilpin's "hegemonic wars." Realism sometimes seems to imply, pessimistically, that order can *only* be created by hegemony. If the latter conclusion were correct, not only would the world economy soon become chaotic (barring a sudden resurgence of American power), but at some time in the foreseeable future, global nuclear war would ensue.

Complacency in the face of this prospect is morally unacceptable. No serious thinker could, therefore, be satisfied with Realism as the correct theory of world politics, even if the scientific status of the theory were stronger than it is. Our concern for humanity requires us to do what Gilpin does in the epilogue to *War and Change* (1981), where he holds out the hope of a "new and more stable international order" in the final decades of the twentieth century, despite his theory's contention that such a benign outcome is highly unlikely. Although Gilpin could be criticized for inconsistency, this would be beside the point: the conditions of terror under which we live compel us to search for a way out of the trap.

The need to find a way out of the trap means that international relations must be a policy science as well as a theoretical activity.[31] We should be seeking to link theory with practice, bringing insights from Structural Realism, modified structural theories, other systemic approaches, and actor-level analyses to bear on contemporary issues in a sophisticated way. This does not mean that the social scientist should adopt the policymaker's framework, much less his normative values or blinders about the range of available alternatives. On the contrary, independent observers often do their most valuable work when they reject the normative or analytic framework of those in power, and the best theorists may be those who maintain their distance from those at the center of events. Nevertheless, foreign policy and world politics are too important to be left to bureaucrats, generals, and lawyers—or even to journalists and clergymen.

Realism helps us determine the strength of the trap, but does not give us much assistance in seeking to escape. If we are to promote peaceful change, we need to focus not only on basic long-term forces that determine the shape of world politics independently of the actions of particular decision-makers, but also on variables that to some extent can be manipulated by human action. Since international institutions, rules, and patterns of cooperation can affect calculations of interest, and can also be affected incrementally by contemporary political action, they provide a natural focus for scholarly attention as well as policy concern.[32] Unlike Realism, theories that attempt to explain rules, norms, and institutions help us to understand how to create patterns of cooperation that could be essential to our survival. We need to respond to the questions that Realism poses but fails to answer: How can order be created out of anarchy *without* superordinate power; how can peaceful change occur?

To be reminded of the significance of international relations as policy analysis, and the pressing problem of order, is to recall the tradition of Classical Realism. Classical Realism, as epitomized by the work of John Herz (1981), has recognized that no matter how deterministic our theoretical aspirations may be, there remains a human interest in autonomy and self-reflection. As Ashley puts it, the Realism of a thinker such as Herz is committed to an "emancipatory cognitive interest—an interest in securing freedom from unacknowledged constraints, relations of domination, and conditions of distorted communication and understanding that deny humans the capacity to make their future with full will and consciousness" (1981:227).[33] We think about world politics not because it is aesthetically beautiful, because we believe that it is governed by simple, knowable laws, or because it provides rich, easily accessible data for the testing of empirical hypotheses. Were those concerns paramount, we would look elsewhere. We study world politics because we think it will determine the fate of the earth (Schell 1982). Realism makes us aware of the odds against us. What we need to do now is to understand peaceful change by combining multidimensional scholarly analysis with more visionary ways of seeing the future.

ACKNOWLEDGMENTS

I am grateful to Raymond Hopkins for inviting me to prepare the original version of this paper for the American Political Science Association Annual

Meeting in Denver, September 1982. A number of ideas presented here were developed with the help of discussions in the graduate international relations field seminar at Brandeis University during the spring semester, 1982, which I taught with my colleague, Robert J. Art. I have also received extremely valuable comments from a number of friends and colleagues on an earlier draft of this paper, in particular from Vinod Aggarwal, David Baldwin, Seyom Brown, Ben Dickinson, Alexander George, Robert Gilpin, Ernst Haas, Thomas Ilgen, Robert Jervis, Peter Katzenstein, Stephen Krasner, Timothy McKeown, Helen Milner, Joseph Nye, and Kenneth Waltz.

NOTES

1. An unfortunate limitation of this chapter is that its scope is restricted to work published in English, principally in the United States. I recognize that this reflects the Americanocentrism of scholarship in the United States, and I regret it. But I am not sufficiently well-read in works published elsewhere to comment intelligently on them. For recent discussions of the distinctively American stamp that has been placed on the international relations field see Hoffmann (1977) and Lyons (1982).

2. Nye and I, in effect, conceded this in our later work, which was more cautious about the drawbacks of conventional "state-centric" theory (see Keohane and Nye 1977).

3. For a discussion of "theory as a set of questions," see Hoffmann (1960:1–12).

4. For a complementary account of developments in international relations theory, which originally appeared in the same volume as this essay, see Bruce Russett, "International Interactions and Processes: The Internal versus External Debate Revisited," in Finifter (1983):541–568.

5. Stanley J. Michalak, Jr. pointed out correctly that our characterization of Realism in *Power and Interdependence* was unfair when taken literally, although he also seems to me to have missed the Realist basis of our structural models. (See Michalak 1979.)

6. It has often been noted that Kuhn's definition of a paradigm was vague: one sympathetic critic identified 21 distinct meanings of the term in Kuhn's relatively brief book (Masterman 1970). But Lakatos particularly objected to what he regarded as Kuhn's relativism, which in his view interpreted major changes in science as the result of essentially irrational forces. (See Lakatos 1970:178.)

7. Lakatos's comments on Marxism and psychology were biting, and a colleague of his reports that he doubted the applicability of the methodology of scientific research programs to the social sciences. (See Latsis 1976:2.)

8. Robert Jervis and Ann Tickner have both reminded me that Morgenthau and John H. Herz, another major proponent of Realist views in the 1950s, later severely qualified their adherence to what has generally been taken as Realist doctrine. (See Herz 1981, and Boyle 1980:218.) I am particularly grateful to Dr. Tickner for obtaining a copy of the relevant pages of the latter article for me.

9. For commentary on this assumption, see Keohane and Nye (1972), and Mansbach, Ferguson, and Lampert (1976). In *Power and Interdependence*, Nye and I were less critical than we had been earlier of the state-centric assumption. In view of the continued importance of governments in world affairs, for many purposes it seems justified on grounds of parsimony. Waltz's rather acerbic critique of our earlier position seems to me essentially correct (see Waltz 1979:7).

10. Emphasis added. Thucydides also follows this "positive heuristic" of looking for underlying power realities in discussions of the Athenian-Corcyrean alliance

(chapter II), the decision of the Lacedemonians to vote that Athens had broken the treaty between them (chapter III), and Pericles' Funeral Oration (chapter IV). In the Modern Library edition, the passages in question are on pp. 28, 49–50, and 83.

11. Bruce Bueno de Mesquita (1981:29–33) has an excellent discussion of the rationality assumption as used in the study of world politics.

12. As Waltz points out, Morgenthau's writings reflect the "first image" Realist view that the evil inherent in man is at the root of war and conflict.

13. Sustained earlier critiques of the fungibility assumption can be found in Keohane and Nye (1977:49–52) and in Baldwin (1979).

14. In an illuminating recent review essay, John Gerard Ruggie has criticized Waltz's assumption that the second dimension of structure, referring to the degree of differentiation of units, can be regarded as a constant (undifferentiated units with similar functions) in world politics. Ruggie argues that "when the concept 'differentiation' is properly defined, the second structural level of Waltz's model . . . serves to depict the kind of institutional transformation illustrated by the shift from the medieval to the modern international system."

15. Waltz denies that he relies on the rationality assumption; but I argue in section II that he requires it for his theory of the balance of power to hold.

16. For a brilliant discussion of this theoretical strategy in microeconomics, see Latsis (1976 esp. pp. 16–23).

17. Since the principal purpose of Realist analysis in the hands of Waltz and others is to develop an explanation of international political reality, rather than to offer specific advice to those in power, the label "technical realism" seems too narrow. It also carries a pejorative intent that I do not share. "Structural Realism" captures the focus on explanation through an examination of the structure of the international system. Capitalization is used to indicate that Realism is a specific school, and that it would be possible to be a realist—in the sense of examining reality as it really is—without subscribing to Realist assumptions. For a good discussion, see Krasner (1982).

18. This is the common-sense view of power, as discussed, for example, by Arnold Wolfers (1962:103). As indicated in section III, any such definition conceals a large number of conceptual problems.

19. My reading of Gilpin's argument on pp. 29–34 led me originally to believe that he also accepted the notion that power is fungible, since he argues that hegemonic war creates a hierarchy of prestige in an international system, which is based on the hegemon's "demonstrated ability to enforce its will on other states" (p. 34), and which appears to imply that a single structure of power resources exists, usable for a wide variety of issues. But in letters sent to the author commenting on an earlier draft of this paper, both Gilpin and Waltz explicitly disavowed the assumption that power resources are necessarily fungible. In *War and Change*, Gilpin is very careful to disclaim the notion, which he ascribes to Political Realists but which I have not included in the hard core of Realism, that states seek to maximize their power: "Acquisition of power entails an opportunity cost to a society; some other desired good must be abandoned" (p. 5).

20. A similar issue is posed in chapter 3 of part II of *Lineages of the Absolutist State* (1974). Its author, Perry Anderson, addresses the puzzle of why it was Prussia, rather than Bavaria or Saxony, that eventually gained predominance in Germany. Despite his inclinations, Anderson has to rely on a variety of conjunctural, if not accidental, factors to account for the observed result.

21. For a lucid discussion of the security dilemma, see Jervis (1978).

22. The fact that sensitive Realists are aware of the limitations of Realism makes me less worried than Ashley about the policy consequences of Realist analysis. (See above, pp. 168–169.)

23. Waltz does not accept Baldwin's (and Dahl's) definition of power in terms of causality, arguing that "power is one cause among others, from which it cannot be isolated." But this makes it impossible to falsify any power theory; one can always claim that other factors (not specified a priori) were at work. Waltz's discussion of power (1979:191–192) does not separate power-as-outcome properly from power-as-resources; it does not distinguish between resources that the observer can assess a priori from those only assessable post hoc; it does not relate probabilistic thinking properly to power theory; and it takes refuge in a notion of power as "affecting others more than they affect him," which would result (if taken literally) in the absurdity of attributing maximum power to the person or government that is least responsive to outside stimuli, regardless of its ability to achieve its purposes.

24. Jervis (1976, ch. 1) has an excellent discussion of levels of analysis and the relationship between perceptual theories and other theories of international relations. Snyder and Diesing discuss similar issues in chapter 6 on "Crises and International Systems" (1977).

25. Waltz commented perceptively in *Man, the State and War* that contributions of behavioral scientists had often been "rendered ineffective by a failure to comprehend the significance of the political framework of international action" (1959:78).

26. Thorough description—what Alexander George has called "process-tracing"—may be necessary to evaluate a structural explanation, since correlations are not reliable where only a small number of comparable cases is involved. (See George 1979.)

27. I am indebted for this point to a conversation with Hayward Alker.

28. Latsis (1976) discusses the difference between "single-exit" and "multiple-exit" situations in his critique of oligopoly theory. What he calls the research program of "situational determinism"—structural theory, in my terms—works well for single-exit situations, where only one sensible course of action is possible. (The building is burning down and there is only one way out: regardless of my personal characteristics, one can expect that I will leave through that exit.) It does not apply to multiple-exit situations, where more than one plausible choice can be made. (The building is burning, but I have to choose between trying the smoky stairs or jumping into a fireman's net: my choice may depend on deep-seated personal fears.) In foreign policy, the prevalence of multiple-exit situations reinforces the importance of decision-making analysis at the national level.

29. For a more detailed discussion of some aspects of this notion, and for citations to some of the literature in economics on which my thinking is based, see Keohane (1982b). Discussions with Vinod Aggarwal have been important in formulating some of the points in the previous two paragraphs.

30. Morgenthau devotes a chapter of *Politics Among Nations* to peaceful change, but after a review of the reasons why legalistic approaches will not succeed, he eschews general statements for descriptions of a number of United Nations actions affecting peace and security. No theory of peaceful change is put forward. In *Politics Among Nations* Morgenthau put whatever faith he had in diplomacy. The chapter on peaceful change is chapter 26 of the fourth edition (1966).

31. For a suggestive discussion of international relations as policy science, see George and Smoke (1974), Appendix, "Theory for Policy in International Relations," pp. 616–642.

32. Recall Weber's aphorism in "Politics as a Vocation": "Politics is the strong and slow boring of hard boards." Although much of Weber's work analyzed broad

historical forces beyond the control of single individuals or groups, he remained acutely aware of "the truth that man would not have attained the possible unless time and again he had reached out for the impossible" (Gerth and Mills 1958:128). For a visionary, value-laden discourse on future international politics by a scholar "reaching out for the impossible," see North (1976, ch. 7).

33. Ernst B. Haas, who has studied how political actors learn throughout his distinguished career, makes a similar point in a recent essay, where he espouses a "cognitive-evolutionary view" of change and argues that such a view "cannot settle for a concept of hegemony imposed by the analyst. . . . It makes fewer claims about basic directions, purposes, laws and trends than do other lines of thought. It is agnostic about the finality of social laws" (1982:242–243). The difference between Haas and me is that he seems to reject structural analysis in favor of an emphasis on cognitive evolution and learning, whereas I believe that modified structural analysis (more modest in its claims than Structural Realism) can provide a context within which analysis of cognition is politically more meaningful.

REFERENCES

Aggarwal, Vinod. *Hanging by a thread: International regime change in the textile apparel system, 1950–1979.* Unpublished doctoral dissertation, Stanford University, 1981.

Anderson, Perry. *Lineages of the absolutist state.* London: New Left Books, 1974.

Art, Robert J. Bureaucratic politics and American foreign policy: A critique. *Policy Sciences*, 1973, 4, 467–490.

Ashley, Richard K. Political realism and human interests. *International Studies Quarterly*, 1981, 25, 204–236.

Ashley, Richard K. Realistic dialectics: Toward a critical theory of world politics. Paper presented at the Annual Meeting of the American Political Science Association, Denver, Colorado, September 1982.

Axelrod, Robert (Ed.). *The structure of decision: The cognitive maps of political elites.* Princeton, N.J.: Princeton University Press, 1976.

Axelrod, Robert. The emergence of cooperation among egoists. *American Political Science Review*, 1981, 25, 306–318.

Baldwin, David A. Power analysis and world politics: New trends versus old tendencies. *World Politics*, 1979, 31, 161–194.

Boyle, Francis A. The irrelevance of international law: The schism between international law and international politics. *California Western International Law Journal*, 1980, 10.

Brecher, Michael, with Geist, Benjamin. *Decisions in crisis: Israel 1967–1973.* Berkeley: University of California Press, 1980.

Bueno de Mesquita, Bruce. *The war trap.* New Haven: Yale University Press, 1981.

Carr, E. H. *The twenty years' crisis, 1919–1939* (1st ed.). London: Macmillan, 1946. (Originally published, 1939.)

Choucri, Nazli, & North, Robert C. *Nations in conflict: National growth and international violence.* San Francisco: W. H. Freeman & Co., 1975.

Cipolla, Carlo. *The economic decline of empires.* London: Methuen, 1970.

Dahl, Robert A. *Who governs? Democracy and power in an American city.* New Haven: Yale University Press, 1961.

Eckstein, Harry. Case study and theory in political science. In Fred I. Greenstein & Nelson W. Polsby (Eds.), *Handbook of political science* (Vol. 7) *Strategies of inquiry.* Reading, MA: Addison-Wesley, 1975.

Geertz, Clifford. *The interpretation of cultures.* New York: Basic Books, 1973.

George, Alexander L. Case studies and theory development: The method of structured, focused comparison. In Paul Gordon Lauren (Ed.), *Diplomacy: New approaches in history, theory and policy.* New York: Free Press, 1979.

George, Alexander L. *Presidential decisionmaking in foreign policy: The effective use of information and advice.* Boulder: Westview, 1980.

George, Alexander L., & George, Juliette. *Woodrow Wilson and Colonel House.* New York: Dover, 1964.

George, Alexander L., Hall, D. K., & Simons, W. E. *The limits of coercive diplomacy.* Boston: Little, Brown, 1971.

George, Alexander L., & Smoke, Richard. *Deterrence in American foreign policy.* New York: Columbia University Press, 1974.

Gerschenkron, Alexander: *Economic backwardness in historical perspective.* Cambridge: The Belknap Press of Harvard University Press, 1962.

Gerth, H. H., & Mills, C. Wright. *From Max Weber: Essays in Sociology.* New York: Oxford University Press, 1958.

Gilpin, Robert. *U.S. power and the multinational corporation.* New York: Basic Books, 1975.

Gilpin, Robert. *War and change in world politics.* New York: Cambridge University Press, 1981.

Gourevitch, Peter A. The second image reversed: The international sources of domestic politics. *International Organization,* 1978, *32,* 881–913.

Haas, Ernst B. Why collaborate? Issue-linkage and international regimes. *World Politics,* 1980, *32,* 357–405.

Haas, Ernst B. Words can hurt you: Or who said what to whom about regimes. *International Organization,* 1982, *36,* 207–244.

Harsanyi, John. Measurement of social power, opportunity costs, and the theory of two-person bargaining games. *Behavioral Science,* 1962, *7,* 67–80.

Herz, John H. Political realism revisited. *International Studies Quarterly,* 1981, *25,* 182–197.

Hoffmann, Stanley. *Contemporary theory in international relations.* Englewood Cliffs, N.J.: Prentice-Hall, 1960.

Hoffmann, Stanley. An American social science: International relations. *Daedalus,* Summer 1977, 41–60.

Holsti, Ole. Foreign policy viewed cognitively. In Robert Axelrod (Ed.), *The structure of decision: The cognitive maps of political elites.* Princeton, N.J.: Princeton University Press, 1976.

International Organization, 1982, *36.* Special issue on international regimes edited by Stephen D. Krasner.

Jervis, Robert. *Perception and misperception in international politics.* Princeton, N.J.: Princeton University Press, 1976.

Jervis, Robert. Cooperation under the security dilemma. *World Politics,* 1978, *30,* 167–214.

Katzenstein, Peter J. *Between power and plenty: Foreign economic policies of advanced industrial states.* Madison: University of Wisconsin Press, 1978.

Keohane, Robert O. The demand for international regimes. *International Organization,* 1982, *36,* 325–356.

Keohane, Robert O., & Nye, Joseph (Eds.). *Transnational relations and world politics.* Cambridge, MA: Harvard University Press, 1972.

Keohane, Robert O., & Nye, Joseph. *Power and interdependence: World politics in transition.* Boston: Little, Brown, 1977.

Krasner, Stephen D. *Defending the national interest: Raw materials investments and U.S. foreign policy.* Princeton: Princeton University Press, 1978.

Krasner, Stephen D. Structural causes and regime consequences: Regimes as intervening variables. *International Organization,* 1982, *36,* 185–206.

Kuhn, Thomas S. *The structure of scientific revolutions.* Chicago: University of Chicago Press, 1962.

Kurth, James R. The political consequences of the product cycle: Industrial history and political outcomes. *International Organization,* 1979, *33,* 1–34.

Lakatos, Imre. Falsification and the methodology of scientific research programmes. In Imre Lakatos & Alan Musgrave (Eds.), *Criticism and the growth of knowledge.* Cambridge: Cambridge University Press, 1970.

Latsis, Spiro J. A research programme in economics. In Latsis (Ed.), *Method and appraisal in economics.* Cambridge: Cambridge University Press, 1976.

Lebow, Richard Ned. *Between peace and war: The nature of international crisis.* Baltimore: Johns Hopkins University Press, 1981.

Lenin, V. I. *Imperialism: The highest stage of capitalism.* New York: International Publishers, 1939. (Originally written, 1916.)

Luttwak, Edward. *The grand strategy of the Roman Empire—from the first century A.D. to the third.* Baltimore: Johns Hopkins University Press, 1976.

Lyons, Gene M. Expanding the study of international relations: The French connection. *World Politics,* 1982, *35,* 135–149.

Mansbach, Richard, Ferguson, Yale H., & Lampert, Donald E. *The web of world politics.* Englewood Cliffs, N.J.: Prentice-Hall, 1976.

Mansbach, Richard, & Vasquez, John A. *In search of theory: A new paradigm for global politics.* New York: Columbia University Press, 1981.

March, James G. The power of power. In David Easton (Ed.), *Varieties of political theory.* New York: Prentice-Hall, 1966.

Masterman, Margaret. The nature of a paradigm. In Lakatos & Musgrave (Eds.), *Criticism and the growth of knowledge.* Cambridge: Cambridge University Press, 1970.

Michalak, Stanley J., Jr. Theoretical perspectives for understanding international interdependence. *World Politics,* 1979, *32,* 136–150.

Moore, Barrington, Jr. *Social origins of dictatorship and democracy: Lord and peasant in the making of the modern world.* Boston: Beacon Press, 1966.

Morgenthau, Hans J. *Scientific man versus power politics.* Chicago: University of Chicago Press, 1946.

Morgenthau, Hans J. *Politics among nations* (4th ed.). New York: Knopf, 1966. (Originally published, 1948.)

North, Douglass C. *Structure and change in economic history.* New York: W. W. Norton, 1981.

North, Robert C. *The world that could be.* (The Portable Stanford: Stanford Alumni Association.) Palo Alto: Stanford University, 1976.

Organski, A.F.K., & Kugler, Jacek. *The war ledger.* Chicago: University of Chicago Press, 1980.

Oye, Kenneth A. The domain of choice. In Kenneth A. Oye, Donald Rothchild, & Robert J. Lieber (Eds.), *Eagle entangled: U.S. foreign policy in a complex world.* New York: Longman, 1979, pp. 3–33.

Oye, Kenneth A. *Belief systems, bargaining and breakdown: International political economy 1929–1934.* Unpublished doctoral dissertation, Harvard University, 1983.

Rosenau, James N. Pre-theories and theories of foreign policy. In R. Barry Farrell (Ed.), *Approaches to comparative and international politics.* Evanston: Northwestern University Press, 1966.

Ruggie, John Gerard. Continuity and transformation in the world polity: Toward a neo-realist synthesis. *World Politics,* 1983, *35,* 261–285.

Russett, Bruce M. The calculus of deterrence. *Journal of Conflict Resolution,* 1963, *7,* 97–109.

Schell, Jonathan. *The fate of the earth.* New York: Knopf, 1982.

Schelling, Thomas. *The strategy of conflict.* New York: Oxford University Press, 1960.

Simon, Herbert A. The architecture of complexity. In Simon (Ed.), *The sciences of the artificial.* Cambridge: MIT Press, 1969.

Snidal, Duncan. *Interdependence, regimes, and international cooperation.* Unpublished manuscript, University of Chicago, 1981.

Snyder, Glenn H., & Diesing, Paul. *Conflict among nations: Bargaining, decisionmaking and system structure in international crises.* Princeton, N.J.: Princeton University Press, 1977.

Sprout, Harold, & Sprout, Margaret. *Toward a politics of the planet earth.* New York: Van Nostrand Reinhold, 1971.

Stein, Arthur. The politics of linkage. *World Politics,* 1980, *33,* 62–81.

Stein, Arthur. Coordination and collaboration: Regimes in an anarchic world. *International Organization,* 1982, *36,* 299–324.

Thucydides. *The Peloponnesian War* (John H. Finley, Jr., trans.). New York: Modern Library, 1951. (Originally written c. 400 B.C.)

Tollison, Robert D., & Willett, Thomas D. An economic theory of mutually advantageous issue linkage in international negotiations. *International Organization,* 1979, *33,* 425–450.

Toulmin, Stephen. *Foresight and understanding: An enquiry into the aims of science.* New York: Harper Torchbooks, 1963.

Wallerstein, Immanuel. The rise and future demise of the world capitalist system: Concepts for comparative analysis. In Wallerstein, *The capitalist world-economy.* Cambridge: Cambridge University Press, 1979. (This essay was originally printed in *Comparative Studies in Society and History,* 1974, *16.*)

Wallerstein, Immanuel. *The modern world-system II: Mercantilism and the consolidation of the European world-economy, 1600–1750.* New York: Academic Press, 1980.

Waltz, Kenneth N. *Man, the state and war.* New York: Columbia University Press, 1959.

Waltz, Kenneth N. *Foreign policy and democratic politics: The American and British experience.* Boston: Little, Brown, 1967.

Waltz, Kenneth N. *Theory of international politics.* Reading, MA: Addison-Wesley, 1979.

Wolfers, Arnold. *Discord and collaboration: Essays on international politics.* Baltimore: Johns Hopkins University Press, 1962.

CHAPTER 4

The Theory of
Hegemonic Stability and Changes
in International Economic Regimes,
1967–1977

In 1967 the world capitalist system, led by the United States, appeared to be working smoothly. Europe and Japan had recovered impressively from World War II and during the 1960s the United States had been enjoying strong, sustained economic growth as well. Both unemployment and inflation in seven major industrialized countries stood at an average of only 2.8 percent. International trade had been growing even faster than output, which was expanding at about 5 percent annually; and direct investment abroad was increasing at an even faster rate.[1] The Kennedy round of trade talks was successfully completed in June 1967; in the same month, the threat of an oil embargo by Arab countries in the wake of an Israeli-Arab war had been laughed off by the Western industrialized states. Fixed exchange rates prevailed; gold could still be obtained from the United States in exchange for dollars; and a prospective "international money," Special Drawing Rights (SDRs), was created in 1967 under the auspices of the International Monetary Fund (IMF). The United States, "astride the world like a colossus," felt confident enough of its power and position to deploy half a million men to settle the affairs of Vietnam. U.S. power and dynamism constituted the problem or the promise; "the American challenge" was global. Conservative and radical commentators alike regarded U.S. dominance as the central reality of contemporary world politics, although they differed as to whether its implications were benign or malign.[2]

A decade later the situation was very different. Unemployment rates in the West had almost doubled while inflation rates had increased almost threefold. Surplus capacity had appeared in the steel, textiles, and shipbuilding industries, and was feared in others.[3] Confidence that Keynesian policies could ensure uninterrupted growth had been undermined if not shattered. Meanwhile, the United States had been defeated in Vietnam and no longer seemed to have either the capability or inclination to extend its military domination to the far corners of the world. The inability of the United

States to prevent or counteract the oil price increases of 1973–1974 seemed to symbolize the drastic changes that had taken place.

The decade after 1967 therefore provides an appropriate historical context for exploring recent developments in the world's political economy, and for testing some explanations of change.

What changes are observed, and how can they be accounted for in a politically sophisticated way? As the question suggests, this chapter has both a descriptive and an explanatory aspect. Descriptively, it examines changes between 1967 and 1977 in three issue areas: trade in manufactured goods, international monetary relations, and petroleum trade. The focus in each issue area is on the character of its *international regime*—that is, with the norms, rules, and procedures that guide the behavior of states and other important actors.[4] In each issue area an international regime can be identified as of 1967; and in each area identifiable changes in that regime took place during the following decade. These changes in regimes constitute the dependent variable of this study.

The explanatory portion of this chapter attempts to test a theory of "hegemonic stability," which posits that changes in the relative power resources available to major states will explain changes in international regimes. Specifically, it holds that hegemonic structures of power, dominated by a single country, are most conducive to the develoment of strong international regimes whose rules are relatively precise and well obeyed. According to the theory, the decline of hegemonic structes of power can be expected to presage a decline in the strength of corresponding international economic regimes.

It is necessary to explain more fully what is meant in this chapter by an "international regime," and to specify the criteria used here for the selection of a theory to account for regime change. The major changes that took place in each of the three regimes during the decade after 1967 will be briefly described before turning to the problem of explanation.

THE CONCEPT OF INTERNATIONAL REGIME

The concept of international regime can be relatively narrow and precise or quite elastic. Regimes in the narrow sense are defined by explicit rules, usually agreed to by governments at international conferences and often associated with formal international organizations. The International Telecommunications Union, for instance, supervises rules governing radio broadcasting. International commodity agreements have sometimes been characterized by explicit agreements about international price maintenance arrangements. The international monetary regime agreed to at Bretton Woods, which came fully into force at the end of 1958, was characterized by explicit rules mandating pegged exchange rates and procedures for consultation if exchange rates were to be changed. With some exceptions these rules were respected by governments during the early- to mid-1960s. The nondiscriminatory reciprocal trade regime of the General Agreement on Tariffs and

Trade (GATT) contains rules about which governmental measures affecting trade are permitted, and which are prohibited, by international agreement. Each successive trade negotiation adds to the list of rules, although some of the old rules have decayed over time.

The definition of regime employed in this chapter, however, is more elastic than this relatively precise and rule-oriented version. The focus is less on institutionalization and rule development than on patterns of regularized cooperative behavior in world politics. Therefore, this chapter includes as regimes those arrangements for issue areas that embody implicit rules and norms insofar as they actually guide behavior of important actors in a particular issue area. The distinction between explicit and implicit rules is less important than the distinction between strong regimes—in which predictable, orderly behavior takes place according to a set of standards understood by participants—and weak ones—in which rules are interpreted differently or broken by participants. Explicit regimes may be stronger than implicit ones, but this is not always the case, as indicated by the weakness of the international monetary regime between 1971 and 1976 despite the fact that the rules of Bretton Woods still remained nominally in force.

By this definition, there have not only been international regimes for money and trade during the postwar period, but there has also been an international regime governing the production for export, and the pricing, of oil. In 1967 this regime was dominated by the major international oil companies and their home governments, and the norms emphasized maintaining cooperation among the companies (through a variety of joint agreements, especially with respect to production), acting to maintain barriers to entry by new producers, limiting price competition (with increasing difficutly as the industry became somewhat less concentrated), and refraining from competing with one another vis à vis the host governments, in order to avoid bidding up the price of concessions or the host governments' share of the profits.[5] In 1977 the regime for oil was quite different: its norms had been developed by oil-producing governments largely within the framework of the Organization of Petroleum Exporting Countries (OPEC), with the strongest norm being the injunction not to sell oil so far, or so massively, below the official OPEC price that the cartel structure would be threatened. For both 1967 and 1977 operative norms can be identified and therefore it can be asserted that an international regime existed, although patterns of behavior may have been more orderly and predictable in 1967 than in 1977.

The concept of international regime enables a coherent analysis of changes in world politics. Rather than on an explanation of particular events, in which idiosyncratic and frequently random factors have played a role, the focus is on a pattern of events—not on particular bargaining outcomes but on what a pattern of bargaining outcomes reveals about implicit norms and rules in world politics. Fragments of political behavior take on additional meaning when thought of in terms of regimes: they are part of a larger mosaic, a context within which they become intelligible.[6] In this larger mosaic, accidental factors and improbable events become less important, since the focus is on a pattern of behavior and overall trends rather than on one particular event or another. Having identified the international regime and described how it has changed, we can then proceed to the second, more difficult analytical task—to account for these changes in terms of deeper political and economic forces. Describing changes in regimes provides interpretive richness for the analysis of political behavior; attempts to explain these changes may lead to insights about causal patterns.

The emphasis in the study of international regimes has usually been on their creation—how and under what conditions they developed. Here, however, stress must necessarily be placed on the dis-integration of international regimes. Can their collapse in theoretically interesting ways be explained? For policymakers, periods of stress are threatening and difficult; for students of world politics, however, they provide opportunities for insights into change.

EXPLAINING CHANGES
IN INTERNATIONAL REGIMES

This chapter attempts to account for changes in international regimes over time. It therefore poses different questions from those of the literature on comparative foreign policy, particularly comparative foreign economic policy, which seeks to account for cross-national variation in policy historically as well as at similar points in time.[7] Assuming that such policy variation exists without trying to explain it, we focus here on the international regimes that result from political bargaining among governments.

Changes in international economic regimes could in principle be explained by either domestic or international developments or by some combination of the two. Shifts in the policies or constitutional status of national governments can be extremely important—elections, coups d'état, and social revolutions may change the orientation of major states toward the world economy and therefore affect international economic regimes. The coming to power of fascist regimes in Italy, Japan, and Germany during the interwar period certainly helped (along with other factors) to push the world toward autarchic and semiautarchic arrangements during the 1930s. The Iranian revolution of 1978–1979 has exerted significant effects, at least in the short run, on the international petroleum regime; and there is little doubt that a nationalist-fundamentalist revolution or coup in Saudi Arabia would have more profound and far-reaching implications.

From a theoretical standpoint, however, explanations of regime change based on domestic politics would encounter serious problems. So many potentially important causal factors become potentially important that one can no longer construct a parsimonious model that facilitates interpretation and anticipation (if not prediction) of events. Sickness or assassination of a ruler, the revival of fundamentalist values, or failure in war can lead to changes in national policies affecting international regimes. Since many of these phenomena represent unique events involving large elements of chance they cannot be intelligently incorporated into a theory. In principle, therefore, it is impossible to obtain a complete theory of international economic regimes without developing an integrated theory of national and international politics.

The search for theoretical completeness would therefore lead to descriptive anarchy: investigation of domestic political reasons for international regime change could easily lead to an increasingly diffuse set of ad hoc observations about particular cases. The result would be a theoretical inductivism in which "additional variables" were added to the account at will. If we wish to build theory, it makes more sense to proceed in the opposite way, by constructing a relatively parsimonious theory that purports to explain relevant phenomena through the use of propositions linking a small number of variables to one another. Such a theory will not account perfectly for the observed changes—after all, the independent variables will not include the personalities of either a de Gaulle or an Ayatollah Khomeini—but it should correctly explain tendencies and directions of change. Whether it does so— not whether it accounts for every perturbation or crisis—is the test of its theoretical adequacy.[8]

A parsimonious theory of international regime change has recently been developed by a number of authors, notably Charles Kindleberger, Robert Gilpin, and Stephen Krasner. According to this theory, strong international economic regimes depend on hegemonic power. Fragmentation of power between competing countries leads to fragmentation of the international economic regime; concentration of power contributes to stability.[9] Hegemonic powers have the capabilities to maintain international regimes that they favor. They may use coercion to enforce adherence to rules; or they may rely largely on positive sanctions—the provision of benefits to those who cooperate. Both hegemonic powers and the smaller states may have incentives to collaborate in maintaining a regime—the hegemonic power gains the ability to shape and dominate its international environment, while providing a sufficient flow of benefits to small and middle powers to persuade them to acquiesce. Some international regimes can be seen partially as collective goods, whose benefits (such as stable money) can be consumed by all participants without detracting from others' enjoyment of them. Insofar as this is the case, economic theory leads us to expect that extremely large, dominant countries will be particularly willing to provide these goods, while relatively small participants will attempt to secure "free rides" by avoiding proportionate shares of payment. International systems with highly skewed distributions of capabilities will therefore tend to be more amply supplied with such collective goods than systems characterized by equality among actors.[10]

The particular concern of this chapter is the erosion of international economic regimes. The hegemonic stability theory seeks sources of erosion in changes in the relative capabilities of states. As the distribution of tangible resources, especially economic resources, becomes more equal, international regimes should weaken. One reason for this is that the capabilities of the hegemonial power will decline—it will become less capable of enforcing rules against unwilling participants, and it will have fewer resources with which to entice or bribe other states into remaining within the confines of the regime. Yet the incentives facing governments will also change. As the hegemonial state's margin of resource superiority over its partners declines, the costs of leadership will become more burdensome. Enforcement of rules will be more difficult and side payments will seem less justifiable. Should other states—now increasingly strong economic rivals—not have to contribute their "fair shares" to the collective enterprise? The hegemon (or former hegemon) is likely to seek to place additional burdens on its allies. At the same time, the incentives of the formerly subordinate secondary states will change. They will not only become more capable of reducing their support for the regime; they may acquire new interests in doing so. On the one hand, they will perceive the possibility of rising above their subordinate status, and they may even glimpse the prospect of reshaping the international regime in order better to suit their own interests. On the other hand, they may begin to worry that their efforts (and those of others) in chipping away at the hegemonial power and its regime may be too successful—that the regime itself may collapse. This fear, however, may lead them to take further action to hedge their bets, reducing their reliance on the hegemonial regime and perhaps attempting to set up alternative arrangements of their own.

As applied to the last century and a half, this theory—which will be referred to as the "hegemonic stability" theory—does well at identifying apparently necessary conditions for strong international economic regimes, but poorly at establishing sufficient conditions. International economic regimes have been most orderly and predictable where there was a single hegemonic state in the world system: Britain during the mid-nineteenth century in trade and until 1914 in international financial affairs; the United States after 1945. Yet although tangible U.S. power resources were large during the interwar period, international economic regimes were anything but orderly. High inequality of capabilities was not, therefore, a sufficient condition for strong international regimes; there was in the case of the United States a lag between its attainment of capabilities and its acquisition of a willingness to exert leadership, or of a taste for domination depending on point of view.[11]

The concern here is not with the validity of the hegemonic stability theory throughout the last 150 years, but with its ability to account for changes in international economic regimes during the decade between 1967 and 1977. Since the United States remained active during those years as the leading capitalist country, the problem of "leadership lag" does not exist, which raises difficulties for the interpretation of the interwar period. Thus the theory should apply to the 1967–1977 period. Insofar as "potential economic power" (Krasner's term) became more equally distributed—reducing the share of the United States—during the 1960s and early to mid-1970s, U.S.-created and U.S.-centered international economic regimes should also have suffered erosion or decline.

The hegemonic stability thesis is a power-as-resources theory, which attempts to link tangible state capabilities (conceptualized as "power resources") to behavior. In its simplest form, it is what James G. March calls a "basic force model" in which outcomes reflect the potential power (tangible and known capabilities) of actors. Basic force models typically fail to predict accurately particular political outcomes, in part because differential opportunity costs often lead competing actors to use different proportions of their potential power. Yet they offer clearer and more easily interpretable explanations than "force activation models," which incorporate assumptions about differential exercise of power.[12] Regarding tendencies rather than particular decisions, they are especially useful in establishing a baseline, a measure of what can be accounted for by the very parsimonious theory that tangible resources are directly related to outcomes, in this case to the nature of international regimes. The hegemonic stability theory, which is systemic and parsimonious, therefore seems to constitute a useful starting point for analysis, on the assumption that it is valuable to see how much can be learned from simple explanations before proceeding to more complex theoretical formulations.

Ultimately, it will be necessary to integrate systemic analysis with explanations at the level of foreign policy. Domestic forces help to explain changes in the international political structure; changes in the international political structure affect domestic institutions and preferences.[13] This chapter focuses only on one part of the overall research problem: the relationship between international structure and international regimes. It examines to what extent changes in recent international economic regimes can be accounted for by changes in international power distributions within the relevant issue areas.

CHANGES IN INTERNATIONAL ECONOMIC REGIMES, 1967–1977

The dependent variable in this analysis is international regime change between 1967 and 1977 in three issue areas: international monetary relations, trade in manufactured goods, and the production and sale of petroleum. These are not the only important areas of international economic activity—for example, foreign investment is not included—but they are among the most important.[14] Descriptive contentions about international regime change in the three chosen areas that are (1) all three international regimes existing in 1967 became weaker during the subsequent decade; (2) this weakening was most pronounced in the petroleum area and in monetary relations, where the old norms were destroyed and very different practices emerged—it was less sudden and less decisive in the field of trade; and (3) in the areas of trade and money, the dominant political coalitions supporting the regime remained largely the same, although in money certain countries (especially Saudi Arabia) were added to the inner "club," whereas in the petroleum issue area, power shifted decisively from multinational oil companies and governments of major industrialized countries to producing governments. Taking all three dimensions into account, it is clear that regime change was most pronounced during the decade in oil and least pronounced in trade in manufactured goods, with the international monetary regime occupying an intermediate position.

These descriptive contentions will now be briefly documented and then interpreted, inquiring about the extent to which the hegemonic stability theory accounts for these changes in international economic regimes.

The international trade regime of the General Agreement on Tariffs and Trade was premised on the principles of reciprocity, liberalization, and nondiscrimination. Partly as a result of its success, world trade had increased since 1950 at a much more rapid rate than world production. Furthermore, tariff liberalization was continuing: in mid-1967 the Kennedy round was successfully completed, substantially reducing tariffs on a wide range of industrial products. Yet despite its obvious successes, the GATT trade regime in 1967 was already showing signs of stress. The reciprocity and nondiscrimination provisions of GATT were already breaking down. Tolerance for illegal trade restrictions had grown, few formal complaints were being processed, and by 1967 GATT did not even require states maintaining illegal quantitative restrictions to obtain formal waivers of the rules. The "general breakdown in GATT legal affairs" had gone very far indeed, largely as a result of toleration of illegal restrictions such as the variable levy of the European Economic Community (EEC), EEC association agreements, and export subsidies.[15] In addition, nontariff barriers, which were not dealt with effectively by GATT codes, were becoming more important. The trade regime in 1967 was thus strongest in the area of tariff liberalization, but less effective on nontariff barriers or in dealing with discrimination.

In the decade ending in 1967 the international monetary regime was explicit, formally institutionalized, and highly stable. Governments belonging to the International Monetary Fund were to maintain official par values for their currencies, which could be changed only to correct a "fundamental disequilibrium" and only in consultation with IMF. During these nine years, the rules were largely followed; parity changes for major currencies were few and minor.[16] In response to large U.S. deficits in its overall liquidity balance of payments, the U.S. government introduced an Interest Equalization Tax in 1963 and voluntary capital controls in 1965; in addition, a variety of ingenious if somewhat ephemeral expedients had been devised, both to improve official U.S. balance of payment statements and to provide for cooperative actions by central banks or treasuries to counteract the effects of destabilizing capital flows. Until November 1967 even British devaluation (seen by many as imminent in 1964) had been avoided. Nevertheless, as in trade, signs of weakness in the system were apparent. U.S. deficits had to a limited extent already undermined confidence in the dollar; and the United States was fighting a costly war in Vietnam which it was attempting to finance without tax increases at home. Consequently, inflation was increasing in the United States.[17]

The international regime for oil was not explicitly defined by intergovernmental agreement in 1967. There was no global international organization supervising the energy regime. Yet, as mentioned above, the governing arrangements for international oil production and trade were rather clear. With the support of their home governments, the major international oil companies cooperated to control production and, within limits, price. The companies were unpopular in the host countries, and these host country governments put the companies on the defensive on particular issues, seeking increased revenue or increased control. However, as Turner puts it, "the critical fact is that the companies did not really lose control of their relationship with host governments until the 1970s, when the concessionary system finally came close to being swept away. The long preceding decade of the 1960s had seen only minimal improvement for the host governments in the terms under which the majors did business with them."[18] The companies retained superior financial resources and capabilities in production, transportation, and marketing that the countries could not attain. Furthermore, the companies possessed superior information: "Whatever the weakness of company defences which is apparent in retrospect, the host governments did not realize it at the time. Their knowledge of the complexities of the industry was scanty, their experience of serious bargaining with the companies was limited and their awe of the companies was great."[19]

In addition, and perhaps most important, the feudal and semifeudal elites that controlled many oil-producing countries until the end of the 1960s were more often concerned with their personal and family interests than with modernization or national interests on a larger scale.

Although the U.S. government did not participate directly in oil production or trade, it was the most influential actor in the system. The United States had moved decisively during and after World War II to ensure that U.S. companies would continue to control Saudi Arabian oil.[20] Later, when the Anglo-Iranian Oil Company became unwelcome as sole concessionaire in Iran, the United States sponsored an arrangement by which U.S. firms received 40 percent of the consortium established in the wake of the U.S.-sponsored coup that overthrew Premier Mossadegh and restored the shah to his throne.[21] U.S. tax policy was changed in 1950 to permit U.S. oil companies to increase payments to producing governments without sacrificing profits, thus solidifying the U.S. position in the Middle East and Venezuela.[22] The United States had provided military aid and political support to the rulers of Saudi Arabia and Iran, maintaining close relations with them throughout the first two postwar decades (except for the Mossadegh period in Iran). And in case of trouble—as in 1956–1957—the United States was willing to use its own reserves to supply Europe with petroleum.[23] The governing arrangements for oil thus reflected the U.S. government's interests in an ample supply of oil at stable or declining prices, close political ties with conservative Middle Eastern governments, and profits for U.S.-based multinational companies.

The international economic regime of 1977 looked very different. Least affected was trade regime, although even here important changes had taken place. Between 1967 and 1977, nontariff barriers to trade continued to proliferate, and the principle of nondiscrimination was further undermined. Restrictions on textile imports from less developed countries, orginally limited to cotton textiles, were extended to woolen and manmade fabrics in 1974.[24] Nontariff barriers affecting world steel trade in the early 1970s included import licensing, foreign exchange restrictions, quotas, export limitations, domestic-biased procurement, subsidies, import surcharges, and antidumping measures.[25] During the 1970s, "voluntary" export restraints, which had covered about one-eighth of U.S. imports in 1971, were further extended.[26] In late 1977, the United States devised a "trigger price system" to help protect the U.S. steel industry from low-priced imports. Contemporaneously, the European Economic Community launched an ambitious program to protect and rationalize some of its basic industries afflicted with surplus but relatively inefficient capacity, such as steel and shipbuilding. On the basis of a general survey, the GATT secretariat estimated tentatively in 1977 that import restrictions introduced or seriously threatened by industrially advanced countries since 1974 would affect 3–5 percent of world trade— $30 to $50 billion. The stresses on the international trade system, according to the director-general of GATT, "have now become such that they seriously threaten the whole fabric of postwar cooperation in international trade policy."[27]

Nevertheless, the weakening of some aspects of the international trade regime had not led, by the end of 1977, to reductions in trade or to trade wars; in fact, after a 4 percent decline in 1975, the volume of world trade rose 11 percent in 1976 and 4 percent in 1977.[28] Furthermore, by 1977 the Tokyo round of trade negotiations was well under way; in 1979 agreement was reached on trade liberalizing measures that not only would (if put into effect) reduce tariffs on industrial products, but that would also limit or prohibit a wide range of nontariff barriers, including export subsidies, national preferences on government procurement, and excessively complex import licensing procedures.[29] The weakening of elements of the old regime was therefore accompanied both by expanding trade (although at a lower rate than before 1973) and by efforts to strengthen the rules in a variety of areas.

By 1977 the international monetary regime had changed much more dramatically. The pegged-rate regime devised at Bretton Woods had collapsed in 1971, and its jerry-built successor had failed in 1973. Since then, major currencies had been floating against one another, their values affected both by market forces and frequently extensive governmental intervention. In 1976 international agreement was reached on amendments to the Articles of Agreement of the International Monetary Fund, yet this did not return the world to stable international exchange rates or multilateral rule making but merely provided for vaguely defined "multilateral surveillance" of floating exchange rates. Exchange rates have fluctuated quite sharply at times, and have certainly been more unpredictable than they were in the 1960s. Substantial secular changes have also taken place; nominal effective exchange rates on 15 May 1978, as a percentage of the rates prevailing in March

1973, ranged from 58.6 for Italy to 130.0 for Germany and 154.2 for Switzerland.[30]

In the oil area, the rules of the old regime were shattered between 1967 and 1977, as power shifted dramatically from the multinational oil companies and home governments (especially the United States and Britain), on the one hand, to producing countries' governments, on the other. The latter, organized since 1960 in the Organization of Petroleum Exporting Countries, secured as a substantial price rise in negotiations at Teheran in 1971, then virtually quadrupled prices without negotiation after the Yom Kippur War of October 1973. Despite some blustering and various vague threats the United States could do little directly about this, although high rates of inflation in industrial countries and the decline of the dollar in 1977 helped to reduce substantially the real price of oil between 1974 and 1977.[31] By 1977 the United States had apparently conceded control of the regime for oil pricing and production to OPEC, and particularly to its key member, Saudi Arabia. OPEC made the rules in 1977, influenced (but not controlled) by the United States. Only in case of a crippling supply embargo would the United States be likely to act. The United States was still, with its military and economic strength, an influential actor, but it was no longer dominant.

Reviewing this evidence about three international economic regimes supports the generalizations offered earlier. Although all three old regimes became weaker during the decade, this was most pronounced for oil and money, least for trade. In oil, furthermore, dominant coalitions changed as well, so that by 1977 the regime that existed, dominated by OPEC countries, was essentially a *new regime*. The old petroleum regime had disappeared. By contrast, the 1977 trade regime was still a recognizable version of the regime existing in 1967; and the international monetary regime of 1977, although vastly different than in 1967, retained the same core of supportive states along with the same international organization, the IMF, as its monitoring agent. Since the rules had changed, the function of the IMF had also changed; but it persisted as an element, as well as a symbol, of continuity. In the oil area, the emergence of the International Energy Agency (IEA) after the oil embargo symbolized discontinuity: only after losing control of the pricing-production regime did it become necessary for the industrialized countries to construct their own formal international organization.

THE THEORY OF HEGEMONIC STABILITY AND INTERNATIONAL REGIME CHANGE

It shoud be apparent from the above account that a theory purporting to explain international economic regime change between 1967 and 1977 faces two tasks: first, to account for the *general pattern* of increasing weakness, and second, to explain why the oil regime experienced the most serious changes, followed by money and trade. Furthermore, the hegemonic stability theory must show not only a correspondence between patterns of regime

TABLE [4.1]
Distribution of Overall Economic Resources Among the Five Major Market-Economy Countries, 1960-1975
(Gross Domestic Product in Billions of Current U.S. Dollars)

Year	United States	Germany	Britain	France	Japan	U.S. as Percent of Top Five Countries
1960	507	72	71	61	43	67
1963	594	95	85	83	68	64
1970	981	185	122	141	197	60
1975	1,526	419	229	335	491	51

Source: *United Nations Statistical Yearbook*, 1977, pp. 742-744.
Last column calculated from these figures.

change and changes in tangible power resources, but it must be possible to provide at least a plausible account of how those resource changes could have caused the regime changes that we observe.

The most parsimonious version of a hegemonic stability theory would be that changes in the *overall* international economic structure account for the changes in international regimes that we have described. Under this interpretation, a decline in U.S. economic power (as measured crudely by gross domestic product) would be held responsible for changes in international economic regimes. Power in this view would be seen as a fungible set of tangible economic resources that can be used for a variety of purposes in world politics.

There are conceptual as well as empirical problems with this parsimonious overall structure theory. The notion that power resources are fungible—that they can be allocated to issues as policymakers choose, without losing efficacy—is not very plausible in world political economy. As David Baldwin has recently argued, this theory fails to specify the context within which specific resources may be useful: "What functions as a power resource in one policy-contingency framework may be irrelevant in another. The only way to determine whether something is a power resource or not is to place it in the context of a real of hypothetical policy-contingency framework."[32] A second problem with the overall structure version of the hegemonic stability thesis is itself contextual: since we have to account not only for the general pattern of increasing weakness but also the differential patterns by issue area, focusing on a single independent variable will clearly not suffice. Changes in the overall U.S. economic position will clearly not explain different patterns of regime change in different issue areas.

Table [4.1] indicates the gross domestic product of the United States and the five other major market economy countries. As the last column indicates the U.S. share of gross domestic product (GDP) of all five countries fell between 1960 and 1975 from about two-thirds to about one-half of the total five-country GDP. This is consistent with the hegemonic stability thesis, although one can question whether such a moderate decline (leaving the United States more than triple the economic size of its nearest competitor) accounts very convincingly for the regime changes that have been observed.

To explain different patterns of regime change in different issue areas, a differentiated, issue-specific version of the hegemonic stability thesis has greater value than the overall structure version. According to this view, declines in resources available to the United States for use in a given issue area should be closely related to the weakening of the international regime (*circa* 1967) in that area. Specifically, the least evidence of structural change should be found in the trade area, an intermediate amount in international monetary relations, and the most in petroleum. This correspondence between changes in the independent and dependent variable would lend support to the theory. To establish the theory of a firmer basis, however, it would be necessary to develop a plausible causal argument based on the hegemonic stability theory for the issue areas and regimes under scrutiny here.

Table [4.2] summarizes the evidence about changes in the distribution of economic power resources in the areas of trade, money, and petroleum. For trade and money the same comparative measures are used, similar to those used in Table [4.1]: the U.S. proportion of resources is compared to that of the top five market-economy countries taken as a group. This measure can be justified on the grounds that only Germany, Britain, France and Japan were strong enough during this period to consider challenging the United States or attempting to thwart it in significant ways; they are the potential rivals against whom it is significant to measure U.S. resources. The measures have to be somewhat different for petroleum. The relevant resources here appear to be U.S. imports vs. excess production capacity (since in 1956–1957 and 1967 the United States helped to maintain the existing regime by shipping oil to Europe from its own wells), and oil imports as a percentage of energy supply, giving a measure of relative U.S. and European dependence on imports.[33]

None of these measures of "economic power" is perfect; indeed, they are quite crude. Often the composition of exports, for instance, may be as important as the amount; and the balance of trade may in some cases weigh as heavily as the combination of imports and exports. Probably most deficient is the monetary measure, since reserves are not necessarily an indication of a country's *net* position. Measures of the U.S. net liquidity position, however, would also show a sharp decline.[34]

The figures on economic resources provide prima facie support for the hegemonic stabilty thesis. The U.S. proportion of trade, for the top five market-economy countries, fell only slightly between 1960 and 1975—much less than its proportion of gross domestic product, reflecting the rapid increases during these years in U.S. trade as a proportion of total product. As we saw, the international trade regime—already under pressure in 1967—changed less in the subsequent decade than the regimes for money and oil. U.S. financial resources in the form of reserves fell sharply, reflecting the shift from U.S. dominance in 1960 to the struggles over exchange rates of the 1970s. In view of the continued ability of the United States to finance its deficits with newly printed dollars and treasury bills rather than with reserves, Table [4.2B] should not be overinterpreted: it does *not* mean that

TABLE [4.2]
Distribution of Economic Resources, by Issue Area, Among the Five Major Market-Economy Countries,
1960-1975

A. Trade Resources (exports plus imports as percentage of world trade)

Year	United States	Germany	Britain	France	Japan	U.S. as Percent of Top Five Countries
1960	13.4	8.1	8.7	4.9	3.3	35
1965	14.4	9.4	8.0	5.7	4.2	35
1970	15.0	11.0	6.9	6.3	6.2	33
1975	13.0	10.0	5.8	6.4	6.6	31

Source: Kenneth N. Waltz, Theory of International Politics (Reading, Mass.: Addison-Wesley, 1979),
Appendix Table IV, p. 215.
Last column calculated from these figures.

- -

B. Monetary Resources (reserves as percentage of world reserves)

Year	United States	Germany	Britain	France	Japan	U.S. as Percent of Top Five Countries
1960	32.4	11.8	6.2	3.8	3.3	56
1965	21.8	10.5	4.2	9.0	3.0	45
1970	15.5	10.7	3.0	5.3	5.2	39
1975	7.0	13.6	2.4	5.5	5.6	21

Source: Calculated from International Financial Statistics (Washington: IMF), Volume XXXI-5 (May 1978),
1978 Supplement, pp. 34-35.
Last column calculated from these percentages.

- -

C. Petroleum Resources
    1. United States imports and excess production capacity in three crisis years

Year	U.S. Oil Imports as Percent of Oil Consumption	U.S. Excess Production Capacity as Percent of Oil Consumption	Net U.S. Position
1956	11	25	+14
1967	19	25	+6
1973	35	10	-25

Source: Joel Darmstadter and Hans H. Landsberg, "The Economic Background," in
Raymond Vernon, ed., The Oil Crisis, special issue of Daedalus (Fall 1975), pp. 30-31.

    2. Oil Imports as percentage of energy supply

Year	United States	Western Europe	Japan	Ratio of U.S. to European Dependence
1967	9	50	62	.18
1970	10	57	73	.18
1973	17	60	80	.28
1976	20	54	74	.37

Source: Kenneth N. Waltz, Theory of International Politics (Reading, Mass.: Addison-Wesley, 1979),
Appendix Table X, p. 221.
Last column calculated from these figures.

Germany was "twice as powerful as the United States" in the monetary area by 1975. Yet it does, as indicated above, signal a very strong shift in the resource situation of the United States. Finally, the petroleum figures—especially in Table [4.2], C-1—are dramatic: the United States went from a large positive position in 1956 and a small positive position in 1967 to a very large petroleum deficit by 1973. The hegemonic stability theory accurately predicts from this data that U.S. power in the oil area and the stability of the old international oil regime world decline sharply during the 1970s.

These findings lend plausibility to the hegemonic stability theory by not disconfirming its predictions. They do not, however, establish its validity, even for this lmited set of issues over one decade. It is also necessary, before concluding that the theory accounts for the observed changes, to see whether plausible causal sequences can be constructed linking shifts in the international distribution of power to changes in international regimes. The following sections of this paper therefore consider the most plausible and well-founded particular accounts of changes in our three issue areas, to see whether the causal arguments in these accounts are consistent with the hegemonic stability theory. The ensuing discussion begins with oil, since it fits the theory so well, and then addresses the more difficult cases.

Interpreting Changes in the Petroleum Regime

The transformation in oil politics between 1967 and 1977 resulted from a change in the hegemonic coalition making the rules and supporting the regime: OPEC countries, particularly Saudi Arabia, replaced the Western powers, led by the United States. OPEC members had previously lacked the ability to capture monopolistic profits by forming a producers' cartel. In part, this reflected low self-confidence. Poor communications and a low level of information about one another also played a role, although both were already being corrected by greater elite sophistication and more intensive contacts among OPEC members. Yet OPEC's impotence was also a result, in the 1950s and 1960s, of overwhelming U.S. power. Until the huge asymmetry between U.S. power and that of the OPEC members was reduced or reversed, massive changes in the implicit regime could not be expected to occur. Without these changes, neither foolish U.S. tactics nor an Israeli-Arab war could have led to the price rises observed in February 1971, or October–December 1973.[35]

U.S. military power vis-à-vis Middle Eastern members of OPEC was lower in the late 1960s and early 1970s than it had been before the entry of Russia into the Middle East in 1955; but it is not clear that U.S. military power declined dramatically between 1967 and the oil crisis of 1973. Yet fundamental shifts in available petroleum supplies were taking place. When previous oil crises had threatened in the wake of Arab-Israeli wars in 1956 and 1967, the United States was able to compensate by increasing domestic production, since about 25 percent of its oil-producing capacity was not being used prior to each crisis. In 1973 U.S. spare capacity had declined to about 10 percent of the total. In 1956 U.S. imports were only about 11 percent of consumption, mostly from Venezuela and Canada; in 1967 they constituted 19 percent; but by 1973 they amounted to over 35 percent, a substantial proportion of which came from the Middle East. U.S. proved reserves had fallen from 18.2 to 6.4 percent of world proved reserves.[36] In the earlier situations, the United States could be "part of the solution"; in 1973, it was "part of the problem." Its fundamental petroleum resource base had been greatly weakened.

The hegemonic stability model leads us to expect a change in international petroleum arrangements during the mid-1970s: The dominance of the United States and other industrialized countries was increasingly being undermined, as OPEC members gained potential power resources at their expense. What the Yom Kippur War did was to make the Arab members of OPEC willing to take greater risks. When their actions succeeded in quadrupling the price of oil almost overnight, mutual confidence rose that members of the cartel who cut back production would not be "double-crossed" by other producers, but would rather benefit from the externalities (high prices as a result of supply shortages) created by others' similar actions. Calculations about externalities became positive and risks fell. A self-reinforcing cycle of underlying resource strength leading to success, to increased incentives to cooperate, and to greater strength was launched.

Interpreting Changes in the International Monetary Regime

The breakdown of the Bretton Woods pegged-rate monetary system is usually attributed by economists principally to two factors. First is the inherent instability of a gold-exchange standard, which Benjamin J. Cohen describes, with reference to the 1960s, as follows:

> A gold-exchange standard is built on the illusion of convertibility of its fiduciary element into gold at a fixed price. The Bretton Woods system, though, was relying on deficits in the U.S. balance of payments to avert a world liquidity shortage. Already, America's "overhang" of overseas liabilities to private and official foreigners was growing larger than its gold stock at home. The progressive deterioration of the U.S. net reserve position, therefore, was bound in time to undermine global confidence in the dollar's continued convertibility. In effect, governments were caught on the horns of a dilemma. To forestall speculation against the dollar, U.S. deficits would have to cease. But this would confront governments with the liquidity problem. To forestall the liquidity problem, U.S. deficits would have to continue. But this would confront goverments with the confidence problem. Governments could not have their cake and eat it too.[37]

This situation would have made the international monetary system of the 1960s quite delicate under the best of circumstances. As a response to it during the 1960s, negotiations took place to create Special Drawing Rights, designed to provide a source of international liquidity to serve in lieu of dollars when the U.S. deficit came to an end. Whether this reform would have been effective, however, is unclear because the conditions that it was meant to deal with never came into being. Rather than eliminating its deficit, the United States let its balance of payments on current account deteriorate sharply in the last half of the 1960s, as a result of increased military spending to fight the Vietnam War, coupled with a large fiscal deficit, excess demand in the United Sates, and the inflationary momentum that resulted. When U.S. monetary policy turned from restriction to ease in 1970, in reaction to a recession, huge capital outflows took place. The U.S. decision of August 1971 to suspend the convertibility of the dollar into gold and thus to force a change in the Bretton Woods regime followed. An agreement reached in December 1971 to restore fixed exchange rates collapsed under the pressure of monetary expansion in the United States and abroad and large continuing U.S. deficits, which reached a total (on an official settlements basis) of over \$50 billion during the years 1970-1973.[38]

As this account suggests, the collapse of the international monetary regime in 1971-1973 was in part a result of the inherent instability of gold-exchange systems; but the proximate cause was U.S. economic policy, devised in response to the exigencies of fighting an unpopular and costly war in Vietnam. The hegemonic stability theory does not account for either the long-run entropy of regimes resting on both gold and foreign exchange or policy failures by the U.S. governments. Yet in at least a narrow sense the theory is consistent with events: the Bretton Woods regime collapsed only after U.S. reserves had fallen sharply, which contributed to the difficulty of maintaining the value of the dollar at the old exchange rates.

The hegemonic stability theory is thus not disconfirmed by the monetary case. For several reasons, however, it functions as a highly unsatisfactory explanation of regime change in the monetary area. In the first place, the resources that were most important to the United States to maintain the regime were not tangible resources (emphasized by the theory) but the symbolic resources that go under the name of "confidence" in discussion of international financial affairs. U.S. reserves were less important than confidence in U.S. policy: as a reserve-currency country, the United States could generate more international money (dollars), as long as holders of dollars believed that the dollar would retain value compared to alternative assets, such as other currencies or gold. By 1970-1971, however, confidence in U.S. economic policy, and hence in the dollar, had become severely undermined, and after August 1971 became impossible to restore.

The second major problem with the hegemonic stability theory's explanation of the monetary case is that it focuses on a variable—U.S. resources in the monetary area—which was itself largely a result of U.S. policy. the theory, as indicated earlier, is systemic: but the most important sources of change (*reflected* in resource shifts) lay within the U.S. polity. To some extent, of course, this was true in the oil areas as well, since the United States could have conserved its oil resources during the 1950s and 1960s; but it is particularly important in monetary politics, since confidence depended on evaluations of U.S.-policy and expectations about it. Perceptions of U.S.

economic policy as inflationary thus translated directly into loss of intangible U.S. resources (confidence on the part of foreigners) through changes in the expectations of holders, or potential holders, of dollars.

The final problem with the explanation offered by the hegemonic stability theory is that it does not capture the *dual* nature of the U.S. power position in 1971. On the one hand, as we have seen, the U.S. position was eroding. Yet to a considerable extent the scope of U.S. weakness was the *result* of the rules of the old regime: within these rules the United States, not being able to force creditor nations such as Germany and Japan to revalue their currencies, thus was in the position of having to defend the dollar by a variety of short-term expedients. Only by breaking the rules explicitly—by suspending convertibility of the dollar into gold—could the United States transform the bargaining position and make its creditors offer concessions of their own. As Henry Aubrey had pointed out in 1969, "surely a creditor's influence over the United States rests on American willingness to play the game according to the old concepts and rules. If the United States ever seriously decided to challenge them, the game would take a very different course."[39] The United States thus had a strong political incentive to smash the old regime, and it also had the political power to do so. Once the regime had been destroyed, other governments had to heed U.S. wishes, since the active participation of the United States was the sine qua non of a viable international monetary regime.

As we have seen, the hegemonic stability theory is helpful in accounting for the collapse of the Bretton Woods regime, and its proposition linking potential power resources to regime outcomes is not disconfirmed by events. Yet the causal sequences that it suggests are not adequate; one has to take into account the symbolic nature of power resources, direct effects of U.S. policy, and the dual nature of the U.S. power position in 1971.

On the basis of the hegemonic stability theory, one would predict that the major financial powers would have had great difficulty reconstructing the international monetary regime after the events of 1971. Yet the theory's precise prediction would have been ambiguous. As Table [4.1] indicates, in the early 1970s the gross domestic product of the United States still exceeded the combined total of the four next largest market-economy countries. Unilateral U.S. actions, furthermore, had strengthened the U.S. position and made its weak official reserve position less relevant. Thus there was some reason to believe that it might have been possible to reconstruct a stable international monetary regime under U.S. leadership in 1971.

This, of course, failed to occur. The exchange rates established at the Smithsonian Institution in December 1971 collapsed within fifteen months. The United States was no more willing after 1971 to play a responsible, constrained international role than it had been during the six years before the destruction of the Bretton Woods regime. Indeed, the U.S. monetary expansion of 1972, which helped to secure Richard Nixon's reelection, implied a decision by the administration to abandon that role.[40] Had its own economic policies been tailored to international demands, the United States could probably in 1971 have resumed leadership of a reconstructed international monetary system; but the United States did not have sufficient power to compel others to accept a regime in which only it would have monetary autonomy. Between 1971 and 1976, the United States was the most influential actor in international monetary negotiations, and secured a weak flexible exchange rate regime that was closer to its own preferences than to those of its partners; but given its own penchant for monetary autonomy, it could not construct a strong, stable new regime.

Interpreting Changes in the International Trade Regime

As has been seen, changes in the trade regime between 1967 and 1977 were broadly consistent with changes in potential power resources in the issue area. Power resources (as measured by shares of world trade among the industrialized countries) changed less in trade than in money or oil; and the regime changed less as well. So once again, the hegemonic stability theory is not disconfirmed.

The causal argument of the hegemonic stability theory, however, implies that the changes we do observe in trade (which are less than those in money and oil but are by no means insignificant) should be ascribable to changes in international political structure. Yet this does not appear to be the case. Protectionism is largely a grass-roots phenomenon, reflecting the desire of individuals for economic security and stability and of privileged groups for higher incomes than they would command in a free market. Adam Smith excoriated guilds for protecting the wages of their members at the expense of society (although to the advantage, he thought, of the towns).[41] Officials of the GATT now criticize labor unions and inefficient industries for seeking similar protection and attempt to refute their arguments that such actions would increase national as well as group income. Most governments of advanced capitalist states show little enthusiasm for protectionist policies, but have been increasingly goaded into them by domestic interests.

A recent GATT study identifies as a key source of protectionism "structural weaknesses and maladjustments" in the countries of the Organization for Economic Cooperation and Development (OECD). Its authors focus particularly on the recent tendency in Europe for wages to rise at similar rates across sectors, regardless of labor productivity. Yet industries that are old in one country, faced by dynamic, low-cost competitors from abroad, can only adjust effectively either by paying lower wages than higher-productivity industries or by reducing employment: "To maintain *both* the wage differential and the absolute size of employment in the industry, protection is necessary." Yet the workers affected and the political leaders may prevent steps to widen wage differentials or to reduce employment. This resistance to change leads both to inflation and to pressures for protection. According to this view, governments share the responsibility for inflation and protectionism insofar as they tolerate and accommodate these pressures.[42]

It may be true that for reasons internal to advanced industrial societies—or to certain societies, since some seem to be affected more than others—people of these countries are more resistant to adjustment than they once were.[43] This may not just be a problem of the masses. More emphasis could be placed on insufficient levels of research and development by governments and firms, thus contributing to failure to innovate; or one could attempt to account for stagnation by reference to managerial inadequacy on the part of leaders of established oligopolistic industries.[44] In either case, however, explanations from domestic politics or political culture would appear necessary to account for changes in international regimes. Shifts in preference functions—from profit maximization to the quiet life, as Charles Kindleberger has put it—are not accounted for by the hegemonic stability model.[45]

Most explanations of increased protectionism also focus on the recession of the 1970s and the rise of manufactured exports from less developed countries. Between the end of 1973 and the end of 1977, rates of growth in industrial production lagged throughout the OECD area, and in Western Europe and Japan industrial production hardly grew at all. Unemployment rates in Europe in 1977 were three times as high as average unemployment rates between 1957 and 1973. At the same time, recessionary pressure was accentuated by the rapid growth of exports of manufactured goods from developing countries, which increased by about 150 percent in volume terms between 1970 and 1977, while manufacturing output in the developed market economy countries increased by only about 30 percent. Although developing countries still account for barely more than 10 perent of the combined manufacturing output of developing countries and developed market economy countries, that proportion has been rising and in some sectors (textiles; processed food, drink, and tobacco; and clothing, leather, and footwear) it exceeds or approaches 20 percent.[46] Some recent restrictive measures, particularly the progressive tightening of export restraints on textiles, reflect these pressures from dynamic developing country exporters.

To some extent, difficulties in maintaining liberal trade among the OECD countries do reflect erosion of U.S. hegemony, although this is more pronounced as compared with the 1950s than with the late 1960s. In the 1950s the United States was willing to open its markets to Japanese goods in order to integrate Japan into the world economic system, even when most European states refused to do so promptly or fully. This has been much less the case in recent years. Until the European Common Market came into existence, the United States dominated trade negotiations; but since the EEC has been active, it has successfully demanded numerous exceptions to GATT rules. Relative equality in trade-related power resources between the EEC and the United States seems to have been a necessary, if not sufficient, condition for this shift.[47]

On the whole, the hegemonic stability theory does not explain recent changes in international trade regimes as well as it explains changes in money or oil. The theory is not disconfirmed by the trade evidence, and correctly anticipates less regime change in trade than in money or oil; but

TABLE [4.3]
Hegemonic Stability and International Economic Regimes, 1966-1977: An Analytical Summary

	Issue Areas		
	Oil	Money	Trade
Correspondence Between Changes in Power Resources and Changes in International Regimes:			
Extent of change in tangible power resources, 1965-1975 (rank orders)	1	2	3
Extent of change in regime, 1967-1977 (rank orders)	1	2	3
Causal Links:			
Plausibility of causal argument linking tangible resource changes to changes in the regime	high	medium	low

it is also not very helpful in interpreting the changes that we do observe. Most major forces affecting the trade regime have little to do with the decline of U.S. power. For an adequate explanation of changes in trade, domestic political and economic patterns, and the strategies of domestic political actors, would have to be taken into account.

HEGEMONIC STABILITY
AND COMPLEX INTERDEPENDENCE:
A CONCLUSION

A structural approach to international regime change, differentiated by issue area, takes us some distance toward a sophisticated understanding of recent changes in the international politics of oil, money, and trade. Eroding U.S. hegemony helps to account for political reversals in petroleum politics, to a lesser extent for the disintegration of the Bretton Woods international monetary regime, and to a still lesser extent for the continuing decay of the GATT-based trade regime.

Table [4.3] summarizes the results of the analysis. There is a definite correspondence between the expectations of a hegemonic stability theory and the evidence presented here. Changes in tangible power resources by issue area and changes in regimes tend to go together. In terms of causal analysis, however, the results are more mixed. In the petroleum area a plausible and compelling argument links changes in potential economic power resources directly with outcomes. With some significant caveats and qualifications, this is also true in international monetary politics; but in trade, the observed changes do not seem causally related to shifts in international political structure.

On the basis of this evidence, we should be cautious about putting the hegemonic stability theory forward as a powerful explanation of events. It is clearly useful as a first step; to ignore its congruence with reality, and its considerable explanatory power, would be foolish. Nevertheless, it carries with it the conceptual difficulties and ambiguities characteristic of power analysis. Power is viewed in terms of resources; if the theory is to be operationalized, these resources have to be tangible. Gross domestic product, oil import dependence, international monetary reserves, and share of world trade are crude indicators of power in this sense. Less tangible resources such as confidence (in oneself or in a currency) or political position relative to other actors are not taken into account. Yet these sources of influence would seem to be conceptually as close to what is meant by "power resources" as are the more tangible and measurable factors listed above. Tangible resource models, therefore, are inherently crude and can hardly serve as more than first-cut approximations—very rough models that indicate the range of possible behavior or the probable path of change, rather than offering precise predictions.

The version of the hegemonic stability theory that best explains international economic regime change between 1967 and 1977 is an "issue structure" rather than "overall structure" model.[48] That is, changes in power resources specific to particular issue areas are used to explain regime change. Issue structure models such as this one assume the separateness of issue areas in world politics; yet functional linkages exist between issue areas, and bargaining linkages are often drawn by policymakers between issue areas that are not functionally linked. The decline in the value of the dollar from 1971–1973, after the conclusion of the Teheran Agreements in February 1971, contributed strongly to dissatisfaction by OPEC states with oil prices, since it adversely affected their share of the rewards.[49] Sudden oil price rises had a major impact on the international financial system during 1974; if floating exchange rates had not already been in place, they would almost certainly have had to be implemented. And the inflationary effects of monetary disorder and oil price rises, as well as the recessionary effects of those price increases, certainly had an impact on the international trade regime, although the effects are more difficult to trace.

The existence of interissue linkages limits the explanatory power of issue structure models. To solve this problem would require a strong and sophisticated theory of linkage, which would indicate under what conditions linkages between issue areas would be important and what their impact on outcomes would be.[50] No issue-specific explanation of events can be completely satisfactory in a world of multiple issues linked in a variety of ways.

Despite all the limitations on power structure analysis, beginning with it has the great advantage of setting up some very general predictions based on a theory that requires only small amounts of information. A remarkable portion of the observed changes rely only on this parsimonious, indeed almost simple-minded, theory. Furthermore, its very inadequacies indicate where other explanations and other levels of analysis must be considered.

Having examined the explanatory strengths and weaknesses of a hegemonic stability theory, we understand better what puzzles remain to be solved by investigating other systemic theories or by focusing on domestic politics and its relationship to foreign economic policy. Beginning with a simple, international-level theory clarifies the issues. It helps to bring some analytical rigor and order into the analysis of international economic regimes. Without employing a structural model as a starting point, it is difficult to progress beyond potentially rich but analytically unsatisfactory description, which allows recognition of complexity to become a veil hiding our ignorance of the forces producing change in a world political economy. To limit ambitions to such description would be a premature confession of failure.

ACKNOWLEDGMENTS

I have benefited from comments by numerous colleagues on earlier drafts of this chapter. I am particularly obliged for extensive comments to Benjamin J. Cohen, Peter J. Katzenstein, Stephen D. Krasner, and David Laitin; and to three graduate students at Stanford University, Vinod Aggarwal, Linda Cahn, and David Yoffie. My greatest debt is to Alexander George, who went beyond an editor's call of duty by thoroughly pointing out the lacunae and non sequiturs in two earlier drafts. The first draft of this chapter was written when I was a fellow at the Center for Advanced Study in the Behavioral Sciences. There I benefited from the research assistance of Shannon Salmon and from research support from the German Marshall Fund of the United States and the National Science Foundation, the latter through a grant to the Center for Advanced Study (BNS 76-22943).

NOTES

1. For figures relating to these points, see Paul McCracken et al., *Towards Full Employment and Price Stability* (Paris: Organization for Economic Cooperation and Development, 1977), esp. pp. 41–42. Cited below as "McCracken Report."

2. See, for instance, George Liska, *Imperial America: The International Politics of Primacy*, no. 2 (Washington, D.C.: Johns Hopkins Studies in International Affairs, 1967); J. J. Servan-Schreiber, *The American Challenge*, trans. Ronald Steel (New York: Avon Books, 1969); and Harry Magdoff, *The Age of Imperialism* (New York: Monthly Review Press, 1969).

3. Susan Strange, "The Management of Surplus Capacity," *International Organization* 33 (Summer 1979).

4. For a similar earlier definition, see Robert O. Keohane and Joseph S. Nye, Jr., *Power and Interdependence: World Politics in Transition* (Boston: Little, Brown and Co., 1977), pp. 19–22.

5. Edith T. Penrose, *The Large International Film in Developing Countries: The International Petroleum Industry* (Cambridge, Mass.: M.I.T. Press, 1968), pp. 150–165, 183–197; and Morris A. Adelman, *The World Petroleum Market* (Baltimore, Md.: Johns Hopkins University Press, 1971), pp. 78–100.

6. This way of thinking about international regimes was suggested by the work of Clifford Geertz, especially his essay, "Thick Description: Toward an Interpretive

Theory of Culture," in Clifford Geertz, *The Interpretation of Cultures* (New York: Basic Books, 1973). Geertz, however, is principally concerned with meaning and symbolism, whereas the explanatory theory tested in this paper emphasizes tangible power resources. Thus, apart from the suggestiveness of Geertz's concept of culture for the concept of regime, this chapter has little in common with Geertz's model of analysis.

7. See especially Peter J. Katzenstein, ed., *Between Power and Plenty: Foreign Economic Policies of Advanced Industrial States* (Madison: University of Wisconsin Press, 1978). As noted in the text, the dependent variable of this study is national political strategy, not change in international regimes.

8. For a lucid discussion of these issues, see Kenneth N. Waltz, *Theory of International Politics* (Reading, Mass.: Addison-Wesley Publishing Co., 1979), chap. 1.

9. For analysis along these lines, see the following: Charles P. Kindleberger, *The World In Depression, 1929–1939* (Berkeley: University of California Press, 1974; Robert Gilpin, *U.S. Power and the Multinational Corporation* (New York: Basic Books, 1975); and Stephen D. Krasner, "State Power and the Structure of International Trade," *World Politics* 28 (April 1976):317–347.

10. Kindleberger relies most heavily on the theory of collective goods. See his "Systems of International Economic Organization." in David P. Calleo, ed., *Money and the Coming World Order* (New York University Press for the Lehrman Institute, 1976), pp. 19–20; and Kindleberger, *The World in Depression*, chap. 14. It is necessary to be cautious in viewing international regimes as "collective goods," since in many cases rivalry may exist (everyone may benefit from stable money but not everyone can benefit noncompetitively from an open U.S. market for imported electronic products) and countries can be excluded from many international regimes (as the debate over whether to give most-favored-nation status to the Soviet Union illustrates). On the provision of collective goods, a useful article is Mancur Olson, Jr., and Richard Zeckhauser, "An Economic Theory of Alliances," *Review of Economics and Statistics* 48 (1966):266–279, reprinted in Bruce Russett, ed., *Economic Theories of International Politics* (Chicago: Markham Publishing Co., 1968). See also John Gerard Ruggie, "Collective Goods and Future International Collaboration," *American Political Science Review* 66 (September 1972):874–893.

11. Both Krasner, "State Power," and Kindleberger, *World In Depression*, make this admission. The hegemonic stability theory is criticized by David P. Calleo in his concluding essay in Benjamin Rowland, ed., *Balance of Power or Hegemony: The Interwar Monetary System* (New York: New York University Press, published for the Lehrman Institute, 1976). Calleo dislikes hegemony and seems reluctant to admit its association with economic order; he therefore seeks both to reinterpret the pre-1914 period as not "imperial," and to characterize the bloc system of the 1930s as having "worked relatively well." Harold van B. Cleveland and Benjamin Rowland make better differentiated arguments in the same volume that critique or qualify the hegemonic stability thesis.

12. The problem with "force activiation models" is that such models can "save" virtually any hypothesis, since one can always think of reasons, after the fact, why an actor may not have used all available potential power. See James G. March, "The Power of Power," in David Easton, ed., *Varieties of Political Theory* (New York: Prentice-Hall, 1966), esp. pp. 54–61. See also John C. Harsanyi, "Measurement of Social Power, Opportunity Costs, and the Theory of Two-Person Bargaining Games," *Behavioral Science* 7 (1962):67–80.

13. Peter A. Gourevitch, "The Second Image Reversed," *International Organization* 32 (Autumn 1978):881–912.

14. Recent work on foreign investment indicates that international regimes in this area have also changed since 1967. See Stephen D. Krasner, *Defending the National Interest: Raw Materials Investment and U.S. Foreign Policy* (Princeton, N.J.: Princeton University Press, 1978); and Charles Lipson, *Standing Guard: The Protection of Foreign Investment* (Berkeley: University of California Press, forthcoming).

15. Robert E. Hudec, *The GATT Legal System and World Trade Diplomacy* (New York: Praeger Publishers, 1975), p. 256. See also Gardner C. Patterson, *Discrimination in International Trade* (Princeton, N.J.: Princeton University Press, 1965).

16. For good discussions, see Benjamin J. Cohen, *Organizing the World's Money: The Political Economy of International Monetary Relations* (New York: Basic Books, 1977); C. Fred Bergsten, *Dilemmas of the Dollar* (New York: New York University Press, 1975); Alfred E. Eckes, Jr., *A Search for Solvency: Bretton Woods and the International Monetary System, 1941–1971* (Austin: University of Texas Press, 1975); and Fred Hirsch, *Money International* (London: Penguin Press, 1967).

17. Harold T. Shapiro, "Inflation in the United States," in Lawrence B. Krause and Walter S. Salant, eds., *Worldwide Inflation: Theory and Recent Experience* (Washington, D.C.: Brookings Institution, 1977).

18. Louis Turner, *Oil Companies in the International System* (London: George Allen & Unwin for the Royal Institute of International Affairs, 1978), p. 70.

19. Ibid., pp. 94–95.

20. Gabriel Kolko, *The Politics of War: 1943–45* (New York: Vintage Books, 1968), pp. 294–307; Krasner, *Defending the National Interest*, pp. 190–205; Herbert Feis, *Petroleum and American Foreign Policy* (Stanford, Calif.: Food Research Institute, Stanford University, March 1944); Herbert Feis, *Seen From E.A.: Three International Episodes* (New York: Alfred A. Knopf, 1947), pp. 104ff.; and Benjamin Shwadran, *The Middle East, Oil and the Great Powers* (New York: Praeger Publishers, 1955), pp. 302–309. See also *Foreign Relations of the United States* (Washington, D.C.: U.S. Government Printing Office, 1943 and 1944), vol. 4, pp. 941–948, vol. 3, pp. 94–111.

21. See Krasner, *Defending the National Interest*, pp. 119–128; Joyce and Gabriel Kolko, *The Limits of Power: The World and American Foreign Policy, 1946–1954* (New York: Harper & Row, 1972), pp. 413–420; John M. Blair, *The Control of Oil* (New York: Pantheon Books, 1976), pp. 43–47, 78–80; U.S., Congress, Senate, Committee on Foreign Relations, Subcommittee on Multinational Corporations, *The International Petroleum Cartel, The Iranian Consortium and U.S. National Security*, Committee Print, 93d Cong., 2d sess., 21 February 1974.

22. U.S., Congress, Senate, Committee on Foreign Relations, Subcommittee on Multinational Corporations, *Multinational Corporations and United States Foreign Policy*, Part 4, Hearings, 93d Cong., 2d sess., 30 January 1974, pp. 84–110. See also Glenn P. Jenkins and Brian D. Wright, "Taxation of Income of Multinational Corporations: The Case of the United States Petroleum Industry," *Review of Economics and Statistics* 17 (February 1975); and Krasner, *Defending the National Interest*, pp. 205–213.

23. U.S. Congress, Senate, Committee on the Judiciary and on Interior and Insular Affairs, *Emergency Oil Lift Program*, Hearings, 85th Cong., 1st sess., February 1957; OECD, *Europe's Need for Oil: Implications and Lessons of the Suez Crisis* (Paris, 1958); and News Conference of President Eisenhower, 6 February 1957 (*Public Papers of the President*, 1957), p. 124.

24. This was accomplished by the Arrangement Regarding International Trade in Textiles, known as the "Multifiber Agreement," or MFA. For the text, see "Arrangement Regarding International Trade in Textiles" (GATT publication, 1974). UNCTAD has commented on implementation of the agreement in "International Trade in Textiles," Report by UNCTAD secretariat, 12 May 1977.

25. Craig R. MacPhee, *Restrictions on International Trade in Steel* (Lexington, Mass.: Lexington Books, 1974).

26. C. Fred Bergsten, "On the Non-Equivalence of Import Quotas and 'Voluntary' Export Restraints," in C. Fred Bergsten, ed., *Toward a New World Trade Policy: The Maidenhead Papers* (Lexington, Mass.: Lexington Books, 1975).

27. *IMF Survey*, 12 December 1977, p. 373.

28. *IMF Survey*, 20 March 1978, p. 81; and 18 September 1978, p. 285.

29. *New York Times*, 12 April 1979.

30. Morgan Guaranty Trust Company, *World Financial Markets*, May 1978.

31. On the basis of an index with 1974 as 100, OPEC's terms of trade had declined by 1977 to 91.0 (and by 1978 to 81.0). In 1977 this reflected import prices that were 25 percent higher, compared with oil prices that had only increased by 14 percent. Morgan Guaranty Trust Company, *World Financial Markets*, December 1978.

32. As an argument against the overall structural version of a hegemonic stability theory, this is convincing, since it is hard to see how undifferentiated economic power resources (as measured by gross domestic product) would be equally efficacious in a variety of issue areas. As a general criticism of much international relations literature, the criticism is too harsh. Those who use the notion of undifferentiated power in world politics have rather clear assumptions about the nature of world politics, which help to set (admittedly broad) scope conditions on their generalizations. For what these authors regard as the essential core of world politics (adversary relations among competitive states), aggregate economic resources, and the military capabilities for which economic resources are essential preconditions, play an extremely large role. For the quotation in the text and the policy-contingency argument, see David A. Baldwin, "Power Analysis and World Politics: New Trends vs. Old Tendencies," *World Politics* (January 1979):165. For a carefully worked-out overall structure argument, see Waltz, *Theory of International Politics*.

33. Since excess U.S. capacity fell between 1967 and 1976, the figures in Table [4.2], part C-2, actually understate the increase in U.S. dependence on foreign oil during that nine-year period. In 1967 the United States could have withstood a complete embargo quite comfortably (apart from any obligations or desire it might have had to export oil), simply by increasing production from shut-in wells. In a sense, then, its real energy dependence increased from zero to 20 percent during the 1967–1976 period.

34. U.S. liquid liabilities to all foreigners began to exceed reserve assets in 1959 (not alarming for a country acting in many ways like a bank), and had reached five times reserve assets by 1971. *The United States in the Changing World Economy*, statistical background material (Washington, D.C.: U.S. Government Printing Office, 1971), chart 53, p. 40. However, total U.S. assets abroad remained about 50 percent higher than foreign assets in the United States in 1975 [*International Economic Report of the President* (January 1977), p. 161].

35. For discussions of U.S. tactics at Teheran in 1971, see Henry M. Schuler, "The International Oil Negotiations," in I. William Zartman, ed., *The 50% Solution* (New York: Doubleday & Co., 1976), pp. 124–207; John M. Blair, *The Control of Oil*, pp. 223–227; and Edith T. Penrose, "The Development of Crisis," in Raymond Vernon, ed., *The Oil Crisis*, Special issue of *Daedalus* (Fall 1975):39–57. *The Oil Crisis* also contains a number of accounts of other aspects of the events in 1973–1974.

36. Joel Darmstadter and Hans H. Landberg, "The Economic Background," in Raymond Vernon, ed., *The Oil Crisis*, special issue of *Daedalus* (Fall 1975):30–32.

37. Benjamin J. Cohen, *Organizing the World's Money*, p. 99.

38. "McCracken Report," pp. 52–56; charts 14B (p. 83) and 12 (p. 71). See also Cohen, *Organizing the World's Money*, pp. 103–104.

39. Henry Aubrey, "Behind the Veil of International Money," *Princeton Essays in International Finance*, no. 71 (January 1969):9.

40. For a discussion of President Nixon's manipulation of U.S. monetary policy for electoral purposes in 1971–1972, see Edward R. Tufte, *Political Control of the Economy* (Princeton, N.J.: Princeton University Press, 1978), pp. 45–55.

41. Adam Smith, *An Inquiry into the Nature and Causes of the Wealth of Nations*, book 1, part 2, chap. 10 (Chicago: University of Chicago Press, 1976), pp. 132ff.

42. Richard Blackhurst, Nicolas Marian, and Jan Tumlir, *Trade Liberalization, Protectionism and Interdependence*, GATT Studies in International Trade, no. 5 (Geneva: GATT, November 1977), esp. pp. 44–52. For a discussion along similar lines, see the "McCracken Report," esp. chaps. 5, 8.

43. William Diebold, Jr., "Adaptation to Structural Change," *International Affairs* (October 1978).

44. The emphasis on innovation and technological development is suggested by Schumpeter's theory of economic development and has been the subject of substantial recent comment in the business press in the United States. See Joseph A. Schumpeter, *The Theory of Economic Development: An Inquiry into Profits, Capital, Credit Interest and the Business Cycle*, translated from the German by Redvers Opie, 1934 (Cambridge, Mass.: Harvard University Press, 1951); and Schumpeter, *Business Cycles* 2 vols. (New York: McGraw-Hill Book Co., 1939). A critique of attempts to attribute Britain's poor economic performance in the last quarter of the nineteenth century to low-quality managerial and entrepreneurial skills can be found in Donald N. McCloskey, *Economic Maturity and Entrepreneurial Decline: British Iron and Steel, 1870–1913* (Cambridge, Mass.: Harvard University Press, 1973).

45. Kindleberger, *Economic Response*, chap. 7.

46. For the figures, see United Nations Conference on Trade and Development, *Review of Recent Trends and Developments in Trade in Manufactures and Semi-Manufactures*, Report by the secretariat, 21 March 1978, chart 1, p. 4 and chart 3, p. 24.

47. On discrimination against Japan, see Gardner C. Patterson, *Discrimination in International Trade*, chap. 6, pp. 271–322; on the EEC and the United States in trade negotiations, see Robert E. Hudec, *The GATT Legal System and World Trade Diplomacy*.

48. The distinction between "issue structure" and "overall structure" models is drawn in Keohane and Nye, *Power and Interdependence*, chap. 3.

49. Edith T. Penrose, "The Development of Crisis," in Vernon, ed., *The Oil Crisis*, pp. 39–58.

50. Kenneth A. Oye has made some useful distinctions that may help to contribute to such a theory. See "Towards Disentangling Linkage: Issue Interdependence and Regime Change," mimeo (Berkeley, Calif.: Institute of International Studies, April 1979).

CHAPTER 5

The Demand for International Regimes

W e study international regimes because we are interested in understanding order in world politics. Conflict may be the rule; if so, institutionalized patterns of cooperation are particularly in need of explanation. The theoretical analysis of international regimes begins with what is at least an apparent anomaly from the standpoint of Realist theory: the existence of many "sets of implicit or explicit principles, norms, rules, and decision-making procedures around which actor expectations converge," in a variety of areas of international relations.

This article constitutes an attempt to improve our understanding of international order, and international cooperation, through an interpretation of international regime-formation that relies heavily on rational-choice analysis in the utilitarian social contract tradition. I explore why self-interested actors in world politics should seek, under certain circumstances, to establish international regimes through mutual agreement; and how we can account for fluctuations over time in the number, extent, and strength of international regimes, on the basis of rational calculation under varying circumstances.

Previous work on this subject in the rational-choice tradition has emphasized the "theory of hegemonic stability": that is, the view that concentration of power in one dominant state facilitates the development of strong regimes, and that fragmentation of power is associated with regime collapse.[1] This theory, however, fails to explain lags between changes in power structures and changes in international regimes; does not account well for the differential durability of different institutions within a given issue-area; and avoids addressing the question of why international regimes seem so much more extensive now in world politics than during earlier periods (such as the late 19th century) of supposed hegemonic leadership.[2]

The argument of this article seeks to correct some of these faults of the hegemonic stability theory by incorporating it within a supply-demand approach that borrows extensively from microeconomic theory. The theory of hegemonic stability can be viewed as focusing only on the supply of international regimes: according to the theory, the more concentrated power is in an international system, the greater the supply of international regimes at any level of demand.[3] But fluctuations in demand for international regimes are not taken into account by the theory; thus it is necessarily incomplete.

This article focuses principally on the demand for international regimes in order to provide the basis for a more comprehensive and balanced interpretation.

Emphasizing the demand for international regimes focuses our attention on why we should want them in the first place, rather than taking their desirability as a given. I do not assume that "demand" and "supply" can be specified independently and operationalized as in microeconomics. The same actors are likely to be the "demanders" and the "suppliers." Furthermore, factors affecting the demand for international regimes are likely simultaneously to affect their supply as well. Yet supply and demand language allows us to make a distinction that is useful in distinguishing phenomena that, in the first instance, affect the desire for regimes, on the one hand, or the ease of supplying them, on the other. "Supply and demand" should be seen in this analysis as a metaphor, rather than an attempt artificially to separate, or to reify, different aspects of an interrelated process.[4]

Before proceeding to the argument, two caveats are in order. First, the focus of this article is principally on the *strength* and *extent* of international regimes, rather than on their *content* or *effects*. I hope to contribute to understanding why international regimes wax and wane, leaving to others the analysis of what ideologies they encompass or how much they affect ultimate, value-laden outcomes. The only significant exception to this avoidance of questions of content comes in Section 5, which distinguishes between control-oriented and insurance-oriented regimes. Second, no claim is made here that rational-choice analysis is the only valid way to understand international regimes, or even that it is preferable to others. On the contrary, I view rational-choice analysis as one way to generate an insightful interpretation of international regimes that complements interpretations derived from analyses of conventions and of learning. My analysis is designed to be neither comprehensive nor exclusive: I suggest hypotheses and try to make what we know more intelligible, rather than seeking to put forward a definitive theory of international regimes.

The major arguments of this article are grouped in five sections. First, I outline the analytical approach by discussing the virtues and limitations of "systemic constraint-choice analysis." Section 2 lays the basis for the development of a constraint-choice theory of international regimes by specifying the context within which international regimes operate and the functions they perform. In Section 3 elements of a theory of the demand for international regimes are presented, emphasizing the role of regimes in reducing transactions costs and coping with uncertainty. In Section 4, I use insights from theories of information and uncertainty to discuss issues of closure and communication. Section 5 suggests that control-oriented regimes are likely to be increasingly supplemented in the 1980s by insurance regimes as the dominance of the advanced industrial countries in the world political economy declines.

1. SYSTEMIC CONSTRAINT-CHOICE ANALYSIS: VIRTUES AND LIMITATIONS

The argument developed here is deliberately limited to the *systemic* level of analysis. In a systemic theory, the actors' characteristics are given by assumption, rather than treated as variables; changes in outcomes are explained not on the basis of variations in these actor characteristics, but on the basis of changes in the attributes of the system itself. Microeconomic theory, for instance, posits the existence of business firms, with given utility functions, and attempts to explain their behavior on the basis of environmental factors such as the competitiveness of markets. It is therefore a systemic theory, unlike the so-called "behavioral theory of the firm," which examines the actors for internal variations that could account for behavior not predicted by microeconomic theory.

A systemic focus permits a limitation of the number of variables that need to be considered. In the initial steps of theory-building, this is a great advantage: attempting to take into account at the outset factors at the foreign policy as well as the systemic level would lead quickly to descriptive complexity and theoretical anarchy. Beginning the analysis at the systemic level establishes a baseline for future work. By seeing how well a simple model accounts for behavior, we understand better the value of introducing more variables and greater complexity into the analysis. Without the systemic microeconomic theory of the firm, for instance, it would not have been clear what puzzles needed to be solved by an actor-oriented behavioral theory.

A systems-level examination of changes in the strength and extent of international regimes over time could proceed through historical description. We could examine a large number of cases, attempting to extract generalizations about patterns from the data. Our analysis could be explicitly comparative, analyzing different regimes within a common analytical framework, employing a methodology such as George's "focused comparison."[5] Such a systematic comparative description could be quite useful, but it would not provide a theoretical framework for posing questions of why, and under what conditions, regimes should be expected to develop or become stronger. Posing such fundamental issues is greatly facilitated by *a priori* reasoning that makes specific predictions to be compared with empirical findings. Such reasoning helps us to reinterpret previously observed patterns of behavior as well as suggesting new questions about behavior or distinctions that have been ignored: it has the potential of "discovering new facts."[6] This can be useful even in a subject such as international politics, where the variety of relevant variables is likely to confound any comprehensive effort to build deductive theory. Deductive analysis can thus be used in interpretation as well as in a traditional strategy of theory-building and hypothesis-testing.

This analysis follows the tradition of microeconomic theory by focusing on constraints and incentives that affect the choices made by actors.[7] We assume that, in general, actors in world politics tend to respond rationally to constraints and incentives. Changes in the characteristics of the international system will alter the opportunity costs to actors of various courses of action, and will therefore lead to changes in behavior. In particular, decisions about creating or joining international regimes will be affected by system-level changes in this way; in this model the demand for international regimes is a function of system characteristics.

This article therefore employs a form of rational-choice analysis, which I prefer to term "constraint-choice" analysis to indicate that I do not make some of the extreme assumptions often found in the relevant literature. I assume a prior context of power, expectations, values, and conventions; I do not argue that rational-choice analysis can derive international regimes from a "state of nature" through logic alone.[8] This paper also eschews deterministic claims, or the hubris of believing that a complete explanation can be developed through resort to deductive models. To believe this would commit one to a narrowly rationalistic form of analysis in which expectations of gain provide both necessary and sufficient explanations of behavior.[9] Such beliefs in the power of Benthamite calculation have been undermined by the insufficiency of microeconomic theories of the firm—despite their great value as initial approximations—as shown by the work of organization theorists such as Simon, Cyert, and March.[10]

Rational-choice theory is not advanced here as a magic key to unlock the secrets of international regime change, much less as a comprehensive way of interpreting reality. Nor do I employ it as a means of explaining particular actions of specific actors. Rather, I use rational-choice theory to develop models that help to explain trends or tendencies toward which patterns of behavior tend to converge. That is, I seek to account for typical, or modal, behavior. This analysis will not accurately predict the decisions of all actors, or what will happen to all regimes; but it should help to account for overall trends in the formation, growth, decay, and dissolution of regimes. The deductive logic of this approach makes it possible to generate hypotheses about international regime change on an a priori basis. In this article several such hypotheses will be suggested, although their testing will have to await further specification. We shall therefore be drawing on microeconomic theories and rational-choice approaches heuristically, to help us construct nontrivial hypotheses about international regime change that can guide future research.

The use of rational-choice theory implies that we must view decisions involving international regimes as in some meaningful sense voluntary. Yet we know that world politics is a realm in which power is exercised regularly and in which inequalities are great. How, then, can we analyze international regimes with a voluntaristic mode of analysis?

My answer is to distinguish two aspects of the process by which international regimes come into being: the imposition of constraints, and decision making. Constraints are dictated not only by environmental factors but also by powerful actors. Thus when we speak of an "imposed regime," we are speaking (in my terminology) of a regime agreed upon within constraints that are mandated by powerful actors.[11] Any agreement that results from bargaining will be affected by the opportunity costs of alternatives faced by the various actors: that is, by which party has the greater need for agreement with the other.[12] Relationships of power and dependence in world politics will therefore be important determinants of the characteristics of international regimes. Actor choices will be constrained in such a way that the preferences of more powerful actors will be accorded greater weight. Thus in applying rational-choice theory to the formation and maintenance of international regimes, we have to be continually sensitive to the structural context within which agreements are made. Voluntary choice does not imply equality of situation or outcome.

We do not necessarily sacrifice realism when we analyze international regimes as the products of voluntary agreements among independent actors within the context of prior constraints. Constraint-choice analysis effectively captures the nonhierarchical nature of world politics without ignoring the role played by power and inequality. Within this analytical framework, a systemic analysis that emphasizes constraints on choice and effects of system characteristics on collective outcomes provides an appropriate way to address the question of regime formation.

Constraint-choice analysis emphasizes that international regimes should not be seen as quasi-governments—imperfect attempts to institutionalize centralized authority relationships in world politics. Regimes are more like contracts, when these involve actors with long-term objectives who seek to structure their relationships in stable and mutually beneficial ways.[13] In some respects, regimes resemble the "quasi-agreements" that Fellner discusses when analyzing the behavior of oligopolistic firms.[14] In both contracts and quasi-agreements, there may be specific rules having to do with prices, quantities, delivery dates, and the like; for contracts, some of these rules may be legally enforceable. the most important functions of these arrangements, however, are not to preclude further negotiations, but to establish stable mutual expectations about others' patterns of behavior and to develop working relationships that will allow the parties to adapt their practices to new situations. Rules of international regimes are frequently changed, bent, or broken to meet the exigencies of the moment. They are rarely enforced automatically, and they are not self-executing. Indeed, they are often matters for negotiation and renegotiation; as Puchala has argued, "attempts to enforce EEC regulations open political cleavages up and down the supranational-to-local continuum and spark intense politicking along the cleavage lines."[15]

This lack of binding authority associated with international regimes has important implications for our selection of analytical approaches within a constraint-choice framework: it leads us to rely more heavily on microeconomic, market-oriented theory than on theories of public choice. Most public-choice theory is not applicable to international regime change because it focuses on the processes by which authoritative, binding decisions, are made within states.[16] Yet in international politics, binding decisions, arrived at through highly institutionalized, rule-oriented processes, are relatively rare and unimportant, and such decisions do not constitute the essence of international regimes. Traditional microeconomic supply and demand analysis, by contrast, assumes a situation in which choices are made continuously over a period of time by actors for whom "exit"—refusal to purchase goods or services that are offered—is an ever-present option. This conforms more closely to the situation faced by states contemplating whether to create, join, remain members of, or leave international regimes. Since no binding decisions can be made, it is possible to imagine a market for international regimes as one thinks of an economic market: on the basis of an analysis of relative prices and cost-benefit calculations, actors decide which regimes to "buy." In general, we expect states to join those regimes in which they expect the benefits of membership to outweigh the costs. In such an analysis, observed changes in the extent and strength of international regimes may be explained by reference to changes either in the characteristics of the international system (the context within which actors make choices) or of the international regimes themselves (about which the choices are made).

This constraint-choice approach draws attention to the question of why disadvantaged actors join international regimes even when they receive fewer benefits than other members—an issue ignored by arguments that regard certain regimes as simply imposed. Weak actors as well as more powerful actors make choices, even if they make them within more severe constraints. (Whether such choices, made under severe constraint, imply obligations for the future is another question, one not addressed here.)[17]

2. THE CONTEXT AND FUNCTIONS OF INTERNATIONAL REGIMES

Analysis of international regime-formation within a constraint-choice framework requires that one specify the nature of the context within which actors make choices and the functions of the institutions whose patterns of growth and decay are being explained. Two features of the international context are particularly important: world politics lacks authoritative governmental institutions, and is characterized by pervasive uncertainty. Within this setting, a major function of international regimes is to facilitate the making of mutually beneficial agreements among governments, so that the structural condition of anarchy does not lead to a complete "war of all against all."

The actors in our model operate within what Waltz has called a "self-help system," in which they cannot call on higher authority to resolve difficulties or provide protection.[18] Negative externalities are common: states are forever impinging on one another's interests.[19] In the absence of authoritative global institutions, these conflicts of interest produce uncertainty and risk: possible future evils are often even more terrifying than present ones. All too obvious with respect to matters of war and peace, this is also characteristic of the international economic environment.

Actors in world politics may seek to reduce conflicts of interest and risk by coordinating their behavior. Yet coordination has many of the characteristics of a public good, which leads us to expect that its production will be too low.[20] That is, increased production of these goods, which would yield net benefits, is not undertaken. This insight is the basis of the major "supply-side" argument about international regimes, epitomized by the theory of hegemonic stability. According to this line of argument, hegemonic international systems should be characterized by levels of public goods production higher than in fragmented systems; and, if international regimes provide public goods, by stronger and more extensive international regimes.[21]

This argument, important though it is, ignores what I have called the "demand" side of the problem of international regimes: why should governments desire to institute international regimes in the first place, and how much will they be willing to contribute to maintain them? Addressing these issues will help to correct some of the deficiencies of the theory of hegemonic stability, which derive from its one-sidedness, and will contribute to a more comprehensive interpretation of international regime change. The familiar context of world politics—its competitiveness, uncertainty, and conflicts of interest—not only sets limits on the supply of international regimes, but provides a basis for understanding why they are demanded.

Before we can understand why regimes are demanded, however, it is necessary to establish what the functions of international regimes, from the perspective of states, might be.[22]

At the most specific level, students of international cooperation are interested in myriads of particular agreements made by governments: to maintain their exchange rates within certain limits, to refrain from trade discrimination, to reduce their imports of petroleum, or progressively to reduce tariffs. These agreements are made despite the fact that, compared to domestic political institutions, the institutions of world politics are extremely weak: an authoritative legal framework is lacking and regularized institutions for conducting transactions (such as markets backed by state authority or binding procedures for making and enforcing contracts) are often poorly developed.

Investigation of the sources of specific agreements reveals that they are not, in general, made on an *ad hoc* basis, nor do they follow a random pattern. Instead, they are "nested" within more comprehensive agreements, covering more issues. An agreement among the United States, Japan, and the European Community in the Multilateral Trade Negotiations to reduce a particular tariff is affected by the rules, norms, principles, and procedures of the General Agreement on Tariffs and Trade (GATT)—that is, by the trade regime. The trade regime, in turn, is nested within a set of other arrangements—including those for monetary relations, energy, foreign investment, aid to developing countries, and other issues—that together constitute a complex and interlinked pattern of relations among the advanced market-economy countries. These, in turn, are related to military-security relations among the major states.[23]

Within this multilayered system, a major function of international regimes is to facilitate the making of specific agreements on matters of substantive significance within the issue-area covered by the regime. International regimes help to make governments' expectations consistent with one another. Regimes are developed in part because actors in world politics believe that with such arrangements they will be able to make mutually beneficial agreements that would otherwise be difficult or impossible to attain. In other words, regimes are valuable to governments where, in their absence, certain mutually beneficial agreements would be impossible to consummate. In such situations, *ad hoc* joint action would be inferior to results of negotiation within a regime context.

Yet this characterization of regimes immediately suggests an explanatory puzzle. Why should it be worthwhile to construct regimes (themselves requiring agreement) in order to make specific agreements within the regime frameworks? Why is it not more efficient simply to avoid the regime stage and make the agreements on an *ad hoc* basis? In short, why is there any demand for international regimes apart from a demand for international agreements on particular questions?

An answer to this question is suggested by theories of "market failure" in economics. Market failure refers to situations in which the outcomes of market-mediated interaction are suboptimal (given the utility functions of actors and the resources at their disposal). Agreements that would be beneficial to all parties are not made. In situations of market failure, economic activities uncoordinated by hierarchical authority lead to *in*efficient results, rather than to the efficient outcomes expected under conditions of perfect competition. In the theory of market failure, the problems are attributed not to inadequacies of the actors themselves (who are presumed to be rational utility-maximizers) but rather to the structure of the system and the institutions, or lack thereof, that characterize.[24] Specific attributes of the system impose transactions costs (including information costs) that create barriers to effective cooperation among the actors. Thus institutional defects are responsible for failures of coordination. To correct these defects, conscious institutional innovation may be necessary, although a good economist will always compare the costs of institutional innovation with the costs of market failure before recommending tampering with the market.

Like imperfect markets, world politics is characterized by institutional deficiencies that inhibit mutually advantageous coordination. Some of the deficiencies revolve around problems of transactions costs and uncertainty that have been cogently analyzed by students of market failure. Theories of market failure specify types of institutional imperfections that may inhibit agreement; international regimes may be interpreted as helping to correct similar institutional defects in world politics. Insofar as regimes are established through voluntary agreement among a number of states, we can interpret them, at least in part, as devices to overcome the barriers to more efficient coordination identified by theories of market failure.[25]

The analysis that follows is based on two theoretical assumptions. First, the actors whose behavior we analyze act, in general, as rational utility-maximizers in that they display consistent tendencies to adjust to external changes in ways that are calculated to increase the expected value of outcomes to them. Second, the international regimes with which we are concerned are devices to facilitate the making of agreements among these actors. From these assumptions it follows that the demand for international regimes at any given price will vary directly with the desirability of agreements to states and with the ability of international regimes actually to facilitate the making of such agreements. The condition for the theory's operation (that is, for regimes to be formed) is that sufficient complementary or common interests exist so that agreeements benefiting all essential regime members can be made.

The value of theories of market failure for this analysis rests on the fact that they allow us to identify more precisely barriers to agreements. They therefore suggest insights into how international regimes help to reduce those barriers, and they provide richer interpretations of previously observed, but unexplained, phenomena associated with international regimes and international policy coordination. In addition, concepts of market failure help to explain the strength and extent of international regimes by identifying characteristics of international systems, or of international regimes themselves, that affect the demand for such regimes and therefore, given a supply schedule, their quantity. Insights from the market-failure literature therefore take us beyond the trivial cost-benefit or supply-demand propositions with which we began, to hypotheses about relationships that are less familiar.

The emphasis on efficiency in the market-failure literature is consistent with our constraint-choice analysis of the decision-making processes leading to the formation and maintenance of international regimes. Each actor must be as well or better off with the regime than without it—given the prior structure of constraints. This does not imply, of course, that the whole process leading to the formation of a new international regime will yield overall welfare benefits. Outsiders may suffer; indeed, some international regimes (such as alliances or cartel-type regimes) are specifically designed to impose costs on them. These costs to outsiders may well outweigh the benefits to members. In addition, powerful actors may manipulate constraints prior to the formation of a new regime. In that case, although the regime *per se* may achieve overall welfare improvements compared to the immediately preceding situation, the results of the joint process may be inferior to those that existed before the constraints were imposed.

3. ELEMENTS OF A THEORY OF THE DEMAND
FOR INTERNATIONAL REGIMES

We are now in a position to address our central puzzle—why is there any demand for international regimes?—and to outline a theory to explain why this demand exists. First, it is necessary to use our distinction between "agreements" and "regimes" to pose the issue precisely: given a certain level of demand for international agreements, what will affect the demand for international regimes? The Coase theorem, from the market-failure literature, will then be used to develop a list of conditions under which international regimes are of potential value for facilitating agreements in world politics. This typological analysis turns our attention toward two central problems, *transactions cost* and *informational imperfections*. Questions of information, involving uncertainty and risk, will receive particular attention, since their exploration has rich implications for interpretation and future research.

The Demand for Agreements and
the Demand for Regimes

It is crucial to distinguish clearly between international regimes, on the one hand, and mere *ad hoc* substantive agreements, on the other. Regimes, as argued above, facilitate the making of substantive agreements by providing a framework of rules, norms, principles, and procedures for negotiation. A theory of international regimes must explain why these intermediate arrangements are necessary.

In our analysis, the demand for agreements will be regarded as exogenous. It may be influenced by many factors, particularly by the perceptions that leaders of governments have about their interests in agreement or non-agreement. These perceptions will, in turn, be influenced by domestic politics, ideology, and other factors not encompassed by a systemic, constraint-choice approach. In the United States, "internationalists" have been attracted to international agreements and international organizations as useful devices for implementing American foreign policy; "isolationists" and "nationalists" have not. Clearly, such differences cannot be accounted for by our theory. We therefore assume a given desire for agreements and ask: under these conditions, what will be the demand for international regimes?

Under certain circumstances defining the demand and supply of agreements, there will be no need for regimes and we should expect none to form. This will be the situation in two extreme cases, where demand for agreements is nil and where the supply of agreements is infinitely elastic and free (so that all conceivable agreements can be made costlessly). But where the demand for agreements is positive at some level of feasible cost, and the supply of agreements is not infinitely elastic and free, there may be a demand for international regimes *if* they actually make possible agreements yielding net benefits that would not be possible on an *ad hoc* basis. In such a situation regimes can be regarded as "efficient." We can now ask: under what specific conditions will international regimes be efficient?

One way to address this question is to pose its converse. To ask about the conditions under which international regimes will be *worthless* enables us to draw on work in social choice, particularly by Ronald Coase. Coase was able to show that the presence of externalities alone does not necessarily prevent Pareto-optimal coordination among independent actors: under certain conditions, bargaining among these actors could lead to Pareto-optimal solutions. The key conditions isolated by Coase were (a) a legal framework establishing liability for actions, presumably supported by governmental authority; (b) perfect information; and (c) zero transactions costs (including organization costs and costs of making side-payments).[26] If all these conditions were met in world politics, *ad hoc* agreements would be costless and regimes unnecessary. *At least one of them must not be fulfilled if international regimes are to be of value, as facilitators of agreement, to independent utility-maximizing actors in world politics.* Inverting the Coase theorem provides us, therefore, with a list of conditions, at least one of which must apply if regimes are to be of value in facilitating agreements among governments:[27]

    (a) lack of a clear legal framework establishing liability for actions;
    (b) information imperfections (information is costly);
    (c) positive transactions costs.[28]

In world politics, of course, *all* of these conditions are met all of the time: world government does not exist; information is extremely costly and often impossible to obtain; transactions costs, including costs of organization and side-payments, are often very high. Yet the Coase theorem is useful not merely as a way of categorizing these familiar problems, but because it suggests how international regimes can improve actors' abilities to make mutually beneficial agreements. Regimes can make agreement easier if they provide frameworks for establishing legal liability (even if these are not perfect); improve the quantity and quality of information available to actors; or reduce other transactions costs, such as costs of organization or of making side-payments. This typology allows us to specify regime functions—as devices to make agreements possible—more precisely, and therefore to understand demand for international regimes. Insofar as international regimes can correct institutional defects in world politics along any of these three dimensions (liability, information, transactions costs), they may become efficient devices for the achievement of state purposes.

Regimes do not establish binding and enforceable legal liabilities in any strict or ultimately reliable sense, although the lack of a hierarchical structure does not prevent the development of bits and pieces of law.[29] Regimes are much more important in providing established negotiating frameworks (reducing transactions costs) and in helping to coordinate actor expectations (improving the quality and quantity of information available to states). An explanation of these two functions of international regimes, with the help of microeconomic analysis, will lead to hypotheses about how the demand for international regimes should be expected to vary with changes in the nature of the international system (in the case of transactions costs) and about effects of characteristics of the international regime itself (in the case of information).

International Regimes and Transactions Costs

Neither international agreements nor international regimes are created spontaneously. Political entrepreneurs must exist who see a potential profit;

in organizing collaboration. For entrepreneurship to develop, not only must there be a potential social gain to be derived from the formation of an international arrangement, but the entrepreneur (usually, in world politics, a government) must expect to be able to gain more itself from the regime than it invests in organizing the activity. Thus organizational costs to the entrepreneur must be lower than the net discounted value of the benefits that the entrepreneur expects to capture for itself.[30] As a result, international cooperation that would have a positive social payoff may not be initiated unless a potential entrepreneur would profit sufficiently. This leads us back into questions of supply and the theory of hegemonic stability, since such a situation is most likely to exist where no potential entrepreneur is large relative to the whole set of potential beneficiaries, and where "free riders" cannot be prevented from benefiting from cooperation without paying proportionately.

Our attention here, however, is on the demand side: we focus on the efficiency of constructing international regimes, as opposed simply to making *ad hoc* agreements. We only expect regimes to develop where the costs of making *ad hoc* agreements on particular substantive matters are higher than the sum of the costs of making such agreements within a regime framework and the costs of establishing that framework.

With respect to transactions costs, where do we expect these conditions to be met? To answer this question, it is useful to introduce the concept of *issue density* to refer to the number and importance of issues arising within a given policy space. The denser the policy space, the more highly inter-dependent are the different issues, and therefore the agreements made about them. Where issue density is low, *ad hoc* agreements are quite likely to be adequate: different agreements will not impinge on one another significantly, and there will be few economies of scale associated with establishing international regimes (each of which would encompass only one or a few agreements). Where issue density is high, on the other hand, one substantive objective may well impinge on another and regimes will achieve economies of scale, for instance in establishing negotiating procedures that are applicable to a variety of potential agreements within similar substantive areas of activity.[31]

Furthermore, in dense policy spaces, complex linkages will develop among substantive issues. Reducing industrial tariffs without damaging one's own economy may depend on agricultural tariff reductions from others; obtaining passage through straits for one's own warships may depend on wider decisions taken about territorial waters; the sale of food to one country may be more or less advantageous depending on other food-supply contracts being made at the same time. As linkages such as these develop, the organizational costs involved in reconciling distinct objectives will rise and demands for overall frameworks of rules, norms, principles, and procedures to cover certain clusters of issues—that is, for international regimes—will increase.

International regimes therefore seem often to facilitate side-payments among actors within issue-areas covered by comprehensive regimes, since they bring together negotiators to consider a whole complex of issues. Side-payments in general are difficult in world politics and raise serious issues of transaction costs: in the absence of a price system for the exchange of favors, these institutional imperfections will hinder cooperation.[32] International regimes may provide a partial corrective.[33] The well-known literature on "spillover" in bargaining, relating to the European Community and other integration schemes, can also be interpreted as being concerned with side-payments. In this literature, expectations that an integration arrangement can be expanded to new issue-areas permit the broadening of potential side-payments, thus facilitating agreement.[34]

It should be noted, however, that regimes may make it more difficult to link issues that are clustered separately. Governments tend to organize themselves consistently with how issues are treated internationally, as well as vice versa; issues considered by different regimes are often dealt with by different bureaucracies at home. Linkages and side-payments become difficult under these conditions, since they always involve losses as well as gains. Organizational subunits that would lose, on issues that matter to them, from a proposed side-payment are unlikely to support it on the basis of another agency's claim that it is in the national interest. Insofar as the dividing lines between international regimes place related issues in different jurisdictions, they may well make side-payments and linkages between these issues less feasible.

The crucial point about regimes to be derived from this discussion of transactions costs can be stated succinctly: the optimal size of a regime will increase if there are increasing rather than diminishing returns to regime-scale (reflecting the high costs of making separate agreements in a dense policy space), or if the marginal costs of organization decline as regime size grows. The point about increasing returns suggests an analogy with the theory of imperfect competition among firms. As Samuelson notes, "increasing returns is the prime case of deviations from perfect competition."[35] In world politics, increasing returns to scale lead to more extensive international regimes.

The research hypothesis to be derived from this analysis is that increased issue density will lead to greater demand for international regimes and to more extensive regimes. Since greater issue density is likely to be a feature of situations of high interdependence, this forges a link between interdependence and international regimes: increases in the former can be expected to lead to increases in demand for the latter.[36]

The Demand for Principles and Norms

The definition of international regimes provided in the introduction to this volume stipulates that regimes must embody principles ("beliefs of fact, causation, and rectitude") and norms ("standards of behavior defined in terms of rights and obligations") as well as rules and decision-making procedures.[37] Otherwise, international regimes would be difficult to distinguish from any regular patterns of action in world politics that create common expectations about behavior: even hostile patterns of interactions could be seen as embodying regimes if the observer could infer implied rules and decision-making procedures from behavior.

Arguments about definitions are often tedious. What is important is not whether this definition is "correct," but that principles and norms are integral parts of many, if not all, of the arrangements that we regard as international regimes. This raises the question of why, in interactions (such as those of world politics) characterized by conflict arising from self-interest, norms and principles should play any role at all.

The constraint-choice framework used in this article is not the best approach for describing how principles and norms of state behavior evolve over time. The legal and sociological approaches discussed in this volume by Young are better adapted to the task of historical interpretation of norm-development. Nevertheless, a brief analysis of the function of principles and norms in an uncertain environment will suggest why they are important for fulfilling the overall function of international regimes: to facilitate mutually advantageous international agreements.

An important principle that is shared by most, if not all, international regimes is what Jervis calls "reciprocation": the belief that if one helps others or fails to hurt them, even at some opportunity cost to oneself, they will reciprocate when the tables are turned. In the Concert of Europe, this became a norm specific to the regime, a standard of behavior providing that statesmen should avoid maximizing their interests in the short term for the sake of expected long-run gains.[38]

This norm requires action that does not reflect specific calculations of self-interest: the actor making a short-run sacrifice does not know that future benefits will flow from comparable restraint by others, and can hardly be regarded as making precise calculations of expected utility. What Jervis calls the norm of reciprocation—or (to avoid confusion with the concept of reciprocity in international law) what I shall call a norm of generalized commitment—precisely forbids specific interest calculations. It rests on the premise that a veil of ignorance stands between us and the future, but that we should nevertheless assume that regime-supporting behavior will be beneficial to us even though we have no convincing evidence to that effect.

At first glance, it may seem puzzling that governments ever subscribe either to the principle of generalized commitment (that regime-supporting behavior will yield better results than self-help in the long run) or to the corresponding norm in a given regime (that they should act in a regime-supporting fashion). But if we think about international regimes as devices to facilitate mutually beneficial agreements the puzzle can be readily resolved. Without such a norm, each agreement would have to provide net gains for every essential actor, or side-payments would have to be arranged so that the net gains of the package were positive for all. Yet as we have seen, side-payments are difficult to organize. Thus, packages of agreements will usually be difficult if not impossible to construct, particularly when time is short, as in a balance of payments crisis or a sudden military threat. The principle of generalized commitment, however, removes the necessity for specific clusters of agreements, each of which is mutually beneficial. Within the context of a regime, help can be extended by those in a position to do so, on the assumption that such regime-supporting behavior will be reciprocated in the future. States may demand that others follow the norm of generalized commitment even if they are thereby required to supply it themselves, because the result will facilitate agreements that in the long run can be expected to be beneficial for all concerned.

The Demand for Specific Information

The problems of organization costs discussed earlier arise even in situations where actors have entirely consistent interests (pure coordination games with stable equilibria). In such situations, however, severe information problems are not embedded in the structure of relationships, since actors have incentives to reveal information and their own preferences fully to one another. In these games the problem is to reach some agreement point; but it may not matter much which of several is chosen.[39] Conventions are important and ingenuity may be required, but serious systemic impediments to the acquisition and exchange of information are lacking.[40]

The norm of generalized commitment can be seen as a device for coping with the conflictual implications of uncertainty by imposing favorable assumptions about others' future behavior. The norm of generalized commitment requires that one accept the veil of ignorance but act *as if* one will benefit from others' behavior in the future if one behaves now in a regime-supporting way. Thus it creates a coordination game by ruling out potentially antagonistic calculations.

Yet in many situations in world politics, specific and calculable conflicts of interest exist among the actors. In such situations, they all have an interest in agreement (the situation is not zero-sum), but they prefer different types of agreement or different patterns of behavior (e.g., one may prefer to cheat without the other being allowed to do so). As Stein points out, . . . these situations are characterized typically by unstable equilibria. Without enforcement, actors have incentives to deviate from the agreement point:

> [Each] actor requires assurances that the other will also eschew its rational choice [and will not cheat, and] such collaboration requires a degree of formalization. The regime must specify what constitutes cooperation and what constitutes cheating.[41]

In such situations of strategic interaction, as in oligopolistic competition and world politics, systemic constraint-choice theory yields no determinate results or stable equilibria. Indeed, discussions of "blackmailing" or games such as "prisoners' dilemma" indicate that, under certain conditions, suboptimal equilibria are quite likely to appear. Game theory, as Simon has commented, only illustrates the severity of the problem; it does not solve it.[42]

Under these circumstances, power factors are important. They are particularly relevant to the supply of international regimes: regimes involving enforcement can only be supplied if there is authority backed by coercive resources. As we have seen, regimes themselves do not possess such resources. For the means necessary to uphold sanctions, one has to look to the states belonging to the regime.

Yet even under conditions of strategic interaction and unstable equilibria, regimes may be of value to actors by providing information. Since high-quality information reduces uncertainty, we can expect that there will be a demand for international regimes that provide such information.

Firms that consider relying on the behavior of other firms within a context of strategic interaction—for instance, in oligopolistic competition—face similar information problems. They also do not understand reality fully. Students of market failure have pointed out that risk-averse firms will make fewer and less far-reaching agreements than they would under conditions of perfect information. Indeed, they will eschew agreements that would produce mutual benefits. Three specific problems facing firms in such a context are also serious for governments in world politics and give rise to demands for international regimes to ameliorate them.

(1) *Asymmetric information.* Some actors may have more information about a situation than others. Expecting that the resulting bargains would be unfair, "outsiders" may therefore be reluctant to make agreements with "insiders."[43] One aspect of this in the microeconomic literature is "quality uncertainty," in which a buyer is uncertain about the real value of goods being offered. In such a situation (typified by the market for used cars when sellers are seen as unscrupulous), no exchange may take place despite the fact that with perfect information, there would be extensive trading.[44]

(2) *Moral hazard.* Agreements may alter incentives in such a way as to encourage less cooperative behavior. Insurance companies face this problem of "moral hazard." Property insurance, for instance, may make people less careful with their property and therefore increase the risk of loss.[45]

(3) *Deception and irresponsibility.* Some actors may be dishonest, and enter into agreements that they have no intention of fulfilling. Others may be "irresponsible," and make commitments that they are unlikely to be able to carry out. Governments or firms may enter into agreements that they intend to keep, assuming that the environment will continue to be benign; if adversity sets in, they may be unable to keep their commitments. Banks regularly face this problem, leading them to devise standards of "credit-worthiness." Large governments trying to gain adherents to international agreements may face similar difficulties: countries that are enthusiastic about cooperation are likely to be those that expect to gain more, proportionately, than they contribute. This is analogous to problems of self-selection in the market-failure literature. For instance, if rates are not properly adjusted, people with high risks of heart attack will seek life insurance more avidly than those with longer life expectancies; people who purchased "lemons" will tend to sell them earlier on the used-car market than people with

"creampuffs."[46] In international politics, self-selection means that for certain types of activities—for example, sharing research and development information—weak states (with much to gain but little to give) may have greater incentives to participate than strong ones. But without the strong states, the enterprise as a whole will fail. From the perspective of the outside observer, irresponsibility is an aspect of the problem of public goods and free-riding;[47] but from the standpoint of the actor trying to determine whether to rely on a potentially irresponsible partner, it is a problem of uncertainty and risk. Either way, information costs may prevent mutually beneficial agreement, and the presence of these costs will provide incentives to states to demand international regimes (either new regimes or the maintenance of existing ones) that will ameliorate problems of uncertainty and risk.

4. INFORMATION, OPENNESS, AND COMMUNICATION IN INTERNATIONAL REGIMES

International regimes, and the institutions and procedures that develop in conjunction with them, perform the function of reducing uncertainty and risk by linking discrete issues to one another and by improving the quantity and quality of information available to participants. Linking issues is important as a way to deal with potential deception. Deception is less profitable in a continuing "game," involving many issues, in which the cheater's behavior is closely monitored by others and in which those actors retaliate for deception with actions in other areas, than in a "single-shot" game. The larger the number of issues in a regime, or linked to it, and the less important each issue is in proportion to the whole, the less serious is the problem of deception likely to be.

Another means of reducing problems of uncertainty is to increase the quantity and quality of communication, thus alleviating the information problems that create risk and uncertainty in the first place. Williamson argues on the basis of the organization theory literature that communication tends to increase adherence to group goals: "Although the precise statement of the relation varies slightly, the general proposition that intragroup communication promotes shared goals appears to be a well-established empirical finding."[48] Yet not all communication is of equal value: after all, communication may lead to asymmetrical or unfair bargaining outcomes, deception, or agreements entered into irresponsibly. And in world politics, governmental officials and diplomats are carefully trained to communicate precisely what they wish to convey rather than fully to reveal their preferences and evaluations. Effective communication is not measured well by the amount of talking that used-car salespersons do to customers or that governmental officials do to one another in negotiating international regimes. Strange has commented, perhaps with some exaggeration:

> One of the paradoxes of international economic relations in the 1970s has been that the soft words exchanged in trade organizations have coexisted with hard deeds perpetuated by national governments. The reversion to economic na-

tionalism has been accompanied by constant reiterations of continued commitment to international cooperation and consultation. The international bureaucracies of Geneva, New York, Paris and Brussels have been kept busier than ever exchanging papers and proposals and patiently concocting endless draft documents to which, it is hoped, even deeply divided states might subscribe. But the reality has increasingly been one of unilateral action, even where policy is supposedly subject to multilateral agreement.[49]

The information that is required in entering into an international regime is not merely information about other governments' resources and formal negotiating positions, but rather knowledge of their internal evaluations of the situation, their intentions, the intensity of their preferences, and their willingness to adhere to an agreement even in adverse future circumstances. As Hirsch points out with respect to the "Bagehot Problem" in banking, lenders need to know the moral as well as the financial character of borrowers.[50] Likewise, governments contemplating international cooperation need to *know* their partners, not merely know *about* them.

This line of argument suggests that governments that successfully maintain "closure," protecting the autonomy of their decision-making processes from outside penetration, will have more difficulty participating in international regimes than more open, apparently disorganized governments. "Closed" governments will be viewed with more skepticism by potential partners, who will anticipate more serious problems of bounded rationality in relations with these closed governments than toward their more open counterparts. Similarly, among given governments, politicization of issues and increases in the power of political appointees are likely to reduce the quality of information and will therefore tend to reduce cooperation. Thus as an issue gains salience in domestic politics, other governments will begin to anticipate more problems of bounded rationality and will therefore perceive greater risks in cooperation. International cooperation may therefore decline quite apart from the real intentions or objectives of the policy makers involved.

This conclusion is important: international policy coordination and the development of international regimes depend not merely on interests and power, or on the negotiating skills of diplomats, but also on expectations and information, which themselves are in part functions of the political structures of governments and their openness to one another. Intergovernmental relationships that are characterized by ongoing communication among working-level officials, "unauthorized" as well as authorized, are inherently more conducive to information-exchange and agreements that are traditional relationships between internally coherent bureaucracies that effectively control their communications with the external world.[51]

Focusing on information and risk can help us to understand the performance of international regimes over time, and therefore to comprehend better the sources of demands for such regimes. Again, reference to theories of oligopoly, as in Williamson's work, is helpful. Williamson assumes that cooperation—which he refers to as "adherence to group goals"—will be a function both of communication and of the past performance of the oligopoly;

reciprocally, communication levels will be a function of cooperation. In addition, performance will be affected by the condition of the environment. Using these assumptions, Williamson derives a model that has two points of equilibrium, one at high levels and one at low levels of cooperation. His oligopolies are characterized by substantial inertia. Once a given equilibrium has been reached, substantial environmental changes are necessary to alter it:

> If the system is operating at a low level of adherence and communication (i.e., the competitive solution), a substantial improvement in the environment will be necessary before the system will shift to a high level of adherence and communication. *Indeed, the condition of the environment required to drive the system to the collusive solution is much higher than the level required to maintain it once it has achieved this position. Similarly, a much more unfavorable condition of the environment is required to move the system from a high to a low level equilibrium than is required to maintain it there.*[52]

It seems reasonable to suppose that Williamson's assumptions about relationships among communication, cooperation or adherence, and performance have considerable validity for international regimes as well as for cartels. If so, his emphasis on the role of information, for explaining persistent behavior (competitive or oligopolistic) by groups of firms, helps us to understand the lags between structural change and regime change that are so puzzling to students of international regimes. In our earlier work, Nye and I observed discrepancies between the predictions of structural models (such as what I later called the "theory of hegemonic stability") and actual patterns of change; in particular, changes in international regimes tend to lag behind changes in structure.[53] But our explanation for this phenomenon was essentially *ad hoc*: we simply posited the existence of inertia, assuming that "a set of networks, norms, and institutions, once established, will be difficult either to eradicate or drastically to rearrange."[54] Understanding the role of communication and information in the formation and maintenance of international regimes helps locate this observation in a theoretical context. The institutions and procedures that develop around international regimes acquire value as arrangements permitting communication, and therefore facilitating the exchange of information. As they prove themselves in this way, demand for them increases. Thus, even if the structure of a system becomes more fragmented—presumably increasing the costs of providing regime-related collective goods (as suggested by public goods theory)— increased demand for a particular, well-established, information-providing international regime may, at least for a time, outweigh the effects of increasing costs on supply.

These arguments about information suggest two novel interpretations of puzzling contemporary phenomena in world politics, as well as providing the basis for hypotheses that could guide research on fluctuations in the strength and extent of international regimes.

Understanding the value of governmental openness for making mutually beneficial agreements helps to account for the often-observed fact that effective international regimes—such as the GATT in its heyday, or the Bretton Woods international monetary regime[55]—are often associated with a great deal of informal contact and communication among officials. Governments no longer act within such regimes as unitary, self-contained actors. "Transgovernmental" networks of acquaintance and friendship develop, with the consequences that supposedly confidential internal documents of one government may be seen by officials of another; informal coalitions of like-minded officials develop to achieve common purposes; and critical discussions by professionals probe the assumptions and assertions of state policies.[56] These transgovernmental relationships increase opportunities for cooperation in world politics by providing policy makers with high-quality information about what their counterparts are likely to do. Insofar as they are valued by policy makers, they help to generate demand for international regimes.

The information-producing "technology" that becomes embedded in a particular international regime also helps us to understand why the erosion of American hegemony during the 1970s has not been accompanied by an immediate collapse of international regimes, as a theory based entirely on supply-side public goods analysis would have predicted. Since the level of institutionalization of postwar regimes was exceptionally high, with intricate and extensive networks of communication among working-level officials, we should expect the lag between the decline of American hegemony and the disruption of international regimes to be quite long and the "inertia" of the existing regimes relatively great.

The major hypothesis to be derived from this discussion of information is that demand for international regimes should be in part a function of the effectiveness of the regimes themselves in providing high-quality information to policy makers. The success of the institutions associated with a regime in providing such information will itself be a source of regime persistence.

Three inferences can be made from this hypothesis. First, regimes accompanied by highly regularized procedures and rules will provide more information to participants than less regularized regimes and will therefore, on information grounds, be in greater demand. Thus, considerations of high-quality information will help to counteract the normal tendencies of states to create vague rules and poorly specified procedures as a way of preventing conflict or maintaining freedom of action where interests differ.

Second, regimes that develop norms internalized by participants—in particular, norms of honesty and straightforwardness—will be in greater demand and will be valued more than regimes that fail to develop such norms.

Third, regimes that are accompanied by open governmental arrangements and are characterized by extensive transgovernmental relations will be in greater demand and will be valued more than regimes whose relationships are limited to traditional state-to-state ties.[57]

Perhaps other nontrivial inferences can also be drawn from the basic hypothesis linking a regime's information-provision with actors' demands for it. In any event, this emphasis on information turns our attention back toward the regime, and the process of institutionalization that accompanies regime formation, and away from an exclusive concern with the power structure of world politics. The extent to which institutionalized cooperation has been developed will be an important determinant, along with power-structural conditions and issue density, of the extent and strength of international regimes.

From a future-oriented or policy perspective, this argument introduces the question of whether governments (particularly those of the advanced industrial countries) could compensate for the increasing fragmentation of power among them by building communication-facilitating institutions that are rich in information. The answer depends in part on whether hegemony is really a necessary condition for effective international cooperation or only a facilitative one. Kindleberger claims the former, but the evidence is inconclusive.[58] Analysis of the demand for international regimes, focusing on questions of information and transactions costs, suggests the possibility that international institutions could help to compensate for eroding hegemony. International regimes could not only reduce the organization costs and other transactions costs associated with international negotiations; they could also provide information that would make bargains easier to strike.

How effectively international regimes could compensate for the erosion of hegemony is unknown. Neither the development of a theory of international regimes nor the testing of hypotheses derived from such a theory is likely to resolve the question in definitive terms. But from a contemporary policy standpoint, both theory development and theory testing would at least help to define the dimensions of the problem and provide some guidance for thinking about the future consequences of present actions.

5. COPING WITH UNCERTAINTIES: INSURANCE REGIMES

Creating international regimes hardly disposes of risks or uncertainty. Indeed, participating in schemes for international cooperation entails risk for the cooperating state. If others fail to carry out their commitments, it may suffer. If (as part of an international growth scheme) it reflates its economy and others do not, it may run a larger-than-desired current-account deficit; if it liberalizes trade in particular sectors and its partners fail to reciprocate, import-competing industries may become less competitive without compensation being received elsewhere; if it curbs bribery by its multinational corporations without comparable action by others, its firms may lose markets abroad. In world politics, therefore, governments frequently find themselves comparing the risks they would run from lack of regulation of particular issue-areas (i.e., the absence of international regimes) with the risks of entering into such regimes. International regimes are designed to mitigate the effects on individual states of uncertainty deriving from rapid and often unpredictable changes in world politics. Yet they create another kind of uncertainty, uncertainty about whether other governments will keep their commitments.

In one sense, this is simply the old question of dependence: dependence on an international regime may expose one to risks, just as dependence on any given state may. Governments always need to compare the risks they run by being outside a regime with the risks they run by being within one. If the price of achieving short-term stability by constructing a regime is increasing one's dependence on the future decisions of others, that price may be too high.

Yet the question of coping with risk also suggests the possibility of different types of international regimes. Most international regimes are *control-oriented*. Through a set of more or less institutionalized arrangements, members maintain some degree of control over each other's behavior, thus decreasing harmful externalities arising from independent action as well as reducing uncertainty stemming from uncoordinated activity. A necessary condition for this type of regime is that the benefits of the regularity achieved thereby must exceed the organizational and autonomy costs of submitting to the rules, both for the membership as a whole and for each necessary member.

Control-oriented regimes typically seek to ensure two kinds of regularity, internal and environmental. Internal regularity refers to orderly patterns of behavior among members of the regime. The Bretton Woods international monetary regime and the GATT trade regime have focused, first of all, on members' obligations, assuming that, if members behaved according to the rules, the international monetary and trade systems would be orderly. Where all significant actors within an issue-area are members of the regime, this assumption is warranted and mutual-control regimes tend to be effective.

Yet there are probably few, if any, pure cases of mutual-control regimes. Typically, an international regime is established to regularize behavior not only among the members but also between them and outsiders. This is a side-benefit of stable international monetary regimes involving convertible currencies.[59] It was an explicit purpose of the nonproliferation regime of the 1970s, in particular the "suppliers' club," designed to keep nuclear material and knowledge from diffusing rapidly to potential nuclear powers. Military alliances can be viewed as an extreme case of attempts at environmental control, in which the crucial benefits of collaboration stem not from the direct results of cooperation but from their effects on the behavior of outsiders. Alliances seek to induce particular states of minds in non-members, to deter or to intimidate.

Observers of world politics have often assumed implicitly that all significant international regimes are control-oriented. The economic literature, however, suggests another approach to the problem of risk. Instead of expanding to control the market, firms or individuals may diversify to reduce risk or may attempt to purchase insurance against unlikely but costly contingencies.

Portfolio diversification and insurance thus compensate for deficiencies in markets that lack these institutions. Insurance and diversification are appropriate strategies where actors cannot exercise control over their environment at reasonable cost, but where, in the absence of such strategies, economic activity would be suboptimal.[60]

In world politics, such strategies are appropriate under similar conditions. The group of states forming the insurance or diversification "pool" is only likely to resort to this course of action if it cannot control its environment effectively. Second, for insurance regimes to make sense, the risks insured against must be specific to individual members of the group. If the catastrophic events against which one wishes to insure are likely (should they occur at all) to affect all members simultaneously and with equal severity, risk sharing will make little sense.[61]

International regimes designed to share risks are less common than those designed to control events, but three examples from the 1970s can be cited that contain elements of this sort of regime:

(1) The STABEX scheme of the Lomé Convention, concluded between the European Community and forty-six African, Caribbean, and Pacific states in 1975. "Under the STABEX scheme, any of the 46 ACP countries dependent for more than 7.5 percent (2.5 percent for the poorest members of the ACP) of their export earnings on one of a list of commodities, such as tea, cocoa, coffee, bananas, cotton, and iron ore, will be eligible for financial help if these earnings fall below a certain level."[62] STABEX, of course, is not a genuine mutual-insurance regime because the guarantee is made by one set of actors to another set.

(2) The emergency sharing arrangements of the International Energy Agency, which provide for the mandatory sharing of oil supplies in emergencies, under allocation rules devised and administered by the IEA.[63]

(3) The Financial Support Fund of the OECD, agreed on in April 1975 but never put into effect, which would have provided a "lender of last resort" at the internatinal level, so that risks on loans to particular countries in difficulty would have been "shared among all members, in proportion to their quotas and subject to the limits of their quotas, however the loans are financed."[64]

Control-oriented and insurance strategies for coping with risk and uncertainty have different advantages and liabilities. Control-oriented approaches are more ambitious; when effective, they may eliminate adversity rather than simply spread risks around. After all, it is more satisfactory to prevent floods than merely to insure against them; likewise, it would be preferable for consumers to be able to forestall commodity embargoes rather than simply to share their meager supplies fairly if such an embargo should take place.

Yet the conditions for an effective control-oriented regime are more stringent than those for insurance arrangements. An effective control-oriented regime must be supported by a coalition that has effective power in the issue-area being regulated, and whose members have sufficient incentives to exercise such power.[65] Where these conditions are not met, insurance regimes may be "second-best" strategies, but they are better than no strategies at all. Under conditions of eroding hegemony, one can expect the increasing emergence of insurance regimes, in some cases as a result of the unwillingness of powerful states to adopt control-oriented strategies (as in the case of STABEX), in other cases as replacements for control-oriented regimes that have collapsed (as in the cases of the IEA emergency sharing arrangements and the OECD Financial Support Fund or "safety net"). Economic theories of risk and uncertainty suggest that as power conditions shift, so will strategies to manage risk, and therefore the nature of international regimes.

6. CONCLUSIONS

The argument of this paper can be summarized under six headings. First, international regimes can be interpreted, in part, as devices to facilitate the making of substantive agreements in world politics, particularly among states. Regimes facilitate agreements by providing rules, norms, principles, and procedures that help actors to overcome barriers to agreement identified by economic theories of market failure. That is, regimes make it easier for actors to realize their interests collectively.

Second, public goods problems affect the supply of international regimes, as the "theory of hegemonic stability" suggests. But they also give rise to demand for international regimes, which can ameliorate problems of transactions costs and information imperfections that hinder effective decentralized responses to problems of providing public goods.

Third, two major research hypotheses are suggested by the demand-side analysis of this article.

(a) Increased issue density will lead to increased demand for international regimes.
(b) The demand for international regimes will be in part a function of the effectiveness of the regimes themselves in developing norms of generalized commitment and in providing high-quality information to policymakers.

Fourth, our analysis helps us to interpret certain otherwise puzzling phenomena, since our constraint-choice approach allows us to see how demands for such behavior would be generated. We can better understand transgovernmental relations, as well as the lags observed between structural change and regime change in general, and between the decline of the United States' hegemony and regime disruption in particular.

Fifth, in the light of our analysis, several assertions of structural theories appear problematic. In particular, it is less clear that hegemony is a necessary condition for stable international regimes under all circumstances. Past patterns of institutionalized cooperation may be able to compensate, to some extent, for increasing fragmentation of power.

Sixth, distinguishing between conventional control-oriented international regimes, on the one hand, and insurance regimes, on the other, may help us to understand emerging adaptations of advanced industrialized countries to a global situation in which their capacity for control over events is much less than it was during the postwar quarter-century.

None of these observations implies an underlying harmony of interests in world politics. Regimes can be used to pursue particularistic and parochial interests, as well as more widely shared objectives. They do not necessarily increase overall levels of welfare. Even when they do, conflicts among units will continue. States will attempt to force the burdens of adapting to change onto one another. Nevertheless, as long as the situations involved are not constant-sum, actors will have incentives to coordinate their behavior, implicitly or explicitly, in order to achieve greater collective benefits without reducing the utility of any unit. When such incentives exist, and when sufficient interdependence exists that *ad hoc* agreements are insufficient, opportunities will arise for the development of international regimes. If international regimes did not exist, they would surely have to be invented.

ACKNOWLEDGMENTS

The original idea for this paper germinated in discussions at a National Science Foundation–sponsored conference on International Politics and International Economics held in Minneapolis, Minnesota, in June 1978.

I am indebted to Robert Holt and Anne Krueger for organizing and to the NSF for funding that meeting. Several knowledgeable friends, particularly Charles Kindleberger, Timothy J. McKeown, James N. Rosse, and Laura Tyson, provided bibliographical suggestions that helped me think about the issues discussed here. For written comments on earlier versions of this article I am especially grateful to Robert Bates, John Chubb, John Conybeare, Colin Day, Alex Field, Albert Fishlow, Alexander George, Ernst B. Haas, Gerald Helleiner, Harold K. Jacobson, Robert Jervis, Stephen D. Krasner, Helen Milner, Timothy J. McKeown, Robert C. North, John Ruggie, Ken Shepsle, Arthur Stein, Susan Strange, Harrison Wagner, and David Yoffie. I also benefited from discussions of earlier drafts at meetings held at Los Angeles in October 1980 and at Palm Springs in February 1981, and from colloquia in Berkeley, California, and Cambridge, Massachusetts.

NOTES

1. See especially Robert O. Keohane, "The Theory of Hegemonic Stablity and Changes in International Economic Regimes, 1967–1977," in Ole R. Holsti, Randolph Siverson, and Alexander George, eds., *Changes in the International System* (Boulder: Westview, 1980); and Linda Cahn, "National Power and International Regimes: The United States and International Commodity Markets," Ph.D. diss., Stanford University, 1980.

2. Current research on the nineteenth century is beginning to question the assumption that Britain was hegemonic in a meaningful sense. See Timothy J.

McKeown, "Hegemony Theory and Trade in the Nineteenth Century," paper presented to the International Studies Association convention, Philadelphia, 18–21 March 1981; and Arthur A. Stein, "The Hegemon's Dilemma: Great Britain, the United States, and the International Economic Order," paper presented to the American Political Science Association annual meeting, New York, 3–6 September 1981.

3. The essential reason for this (discussed below) is that actors that are large relative to the whole set of actors have greater incentives both to provide collective goods themselves and to organize their provision, than do actors that are small relative to the whole set. The classic discussion of this phenomenon appears in Mancur Olson Jr., *The Logic of Collective Action: Political Goods and the Theory of Groups* (Cambridge: Harvard University Press, 1965).

4. I am indebted to Albert Fishlow for clarifying this point for me.

5. Alexander L. George, "Case Studies and Theory Development: The Method of Structured, Focused Comparison," in Paul Lauren, ed., *Diplomacy: New Approaches in History, Theory, and Policy* (New York: Free Press, 1979).

6. Imre Lakatos, "Falsification and the Methodology of Scientific Research Programmes," in Lakatos and Alan Musgrave, eds., *Criticism and the Growth of Scientific Knowledge* (Cambridge: Cambridge University Press, 1970).

7. Stimulating discussions of microeconomic theory can be found in Martin Shubik, "A Curmudgeon's Guide to Microeconomics," *Journal of Economic Literature* 8 (1970): 405–34; and Spiro J. Latsis, "A Research Programme in Economics," in Latsis, ed., *Method and Appraisal in Economics* (Cambridge: Cambridge University Press, 1976).

8. I am indebted to Alexander J. Field for making the importance of this point clear to me. See his paper, "The Problem with Neoclassical Institutional Economics: A Critique with Special Reference to the North/Thomas Model of Pre-1500 Europe," *Explorations in Economic History* 18 (April 1981).

9. Lance E. Davis and Douglass C. North adopt this strong form of rationalistic explanation when they argue that "an institutional arrangement will be innovated if the expected net gains exceed the expected costs." See their volume, *Institutional Change and American Economic Growth* (Cambridge: Cambridge University Press, 1971).

10. Two of the classic works are James March and Herbert Simon, *Organizations* (New York: Wiley, 1958); and Richard Cyert and James March, *The Behavioral Theory of the Firm* (Englewood Cliffs, N.J.: Prentice-Hall, 1963).

11. For a discussion of "spontaneous," "negotiated," and "imposed" regimes, see [Oran Young, "Regime Dynamics: The Rise and Fall of International Regimes," *International Organization* 36,2 (Spring 1982): 93–113].

12. For a lucid and original discussion based on this obvious but important point, see John Harsanyi, "Measurement of Social Power, Opportunity Costs and the Theory of Two-Person Bargaining Games," *Behavioral Science* 7, 1 (1962): 67–80. See also Albert O. Hirschman, *National Power and the Structure of Foreign Trade* (1945; Berkeley: University of California Press, 1980), especially pp. 45–48.

13. S. Todd Lowry, "Bargain and Contract Theory in Law and Economics," in Warren J. Samuels, ed., *The Economy as a System of Power* (New Brunswick, N.J.: Transaction Books, 1979), p. 276.

14. William Fellner, *Competition Among the Few* (New York: Knopf, 1949).

15. Donald J. Puchala, "Domestic Politics and Regional Harmonization in the European Communities," *World Politics* 27,4 (July 1975), p. 509.

16. There are exceptions to this generalization, such as Tiebout's "voting with the feet" models of population movements among communities. Yet only one chapter

of fourteen in a recent survey of the public-choice literature is devoted to such models, which do not focus on authoritative decision-making processes. See Dennis C. Mueller, *Public Choice* (Cambridge: Cambridge University Press, 1980). For a brilliantly innovative work on "exit" versus "voice" processes, see Albert O. Hirschman, *Exit, Voice, and Loyalty* (Cambridge: Harvard University Press, 1970).

17. Anyone who has thought about Hobbes's tendentious discussion of "voluntary" agreements in *Leviathan* realizes the dangers of casuistry entailed in applying voluntaristic analysis to politics, especially when obligations are inferred from choices. This article follows Hobbes's distinction between the structure of constraints in a situation, on the one hand, and actor choices, on the other; but it does not adopt his view that even severely constrained choices ("your freedom or your life") create moral or political obligations.

18. Kenneth N. Waltz, *Theory of International Politics* (Reading, Mass.: Addison-Wesley, 1979).

19. Externalities exist whenever an acting unit does not bear all of the costs, or fails to reap all of the benefits, that result from its behavior. See Davis and North, *Institutional Change and American Economic Growth*, p. 16.

20. Olson, *The Logic of Collective Action*; Bruce M. Russett and John D. Sullivan, "Collective Goods and International Organization," with a comment by Mancur Olson Jr., *International Organization* 25,4 (Autumn 1971); John Gerard Ruggie, "Collective Goods and Future International Collaboration," *American Political Science Review* 66,3 (September 1972); Duncan Snidal, "Public Goods, Property Rights, and Political Organization," *International Studies Quarterly* 23,4 (December 1979), p. 544.

21. Keohane, "The Theory of Hegemonic Stability"; Charles P. Kindleberger, *The World in Depression, 1929-1939* (Berkeley: University of California Press, 1974); Mancur Olson and Richard Zeckhauser, "An Economic Theory of Alliances," *Review of Economics and Statistics* 48,3 (August 1966), reprinted in Bruce M. Russett, ed., *Economic Theories of International Politics* (Chicago: Markham, 1968). For a critical appraisal of work placing emphasis on public goods as a rationale for forming international organizations, see John A. C. Conybeare, "International Organizations and the Theory of Property Rights," *International Organization* 34,3 (Summer 1980), especially pp. 329-32.

22. My use of the word "functions" here is meant to designate consequences of a certain pattern of activity, particularly in terms of the utility of the activity; it is not to be interpreted as an explanation of the behavior in question, since there is no teleological premise, or assumption that necessity is involved. Understanding the function of international regimes helps, however, to explain why actors have an incentive to create them, and may therefore help to make behavior intelligible within a rational-choice mode of analysis that emphasizes the role of incentives and constraints. For useful distinctions on functionalism, see Ernest Nagel, *The Structure of Scientific Explanation* (New York: Harcourt, Brace, 1961), especially "Functionalism and Social Science," pp. 520-35. I am grateful to Robert Packenham for this reference and discussions of this point.

23. Vinod Aggarwal has developed the concept of "nesting" in his work on international regimes in textiles since World War II. I am indebted to him for this idea, which has been elaborated in his "Hanging by a Thread: International Regime Change in the Textile/Apparel System, 1950-1979," Ph.D. diss., Stanford University, 1981.

24. Of particular value for understanding market failure is Kenneth J. Arrow, *Essays in the Theory of Risk-Bearing* (New York: North Holland/American Elsevier, 1974).

25. Helen Milner suggested to me that international regimes were in this respect like credit markets, and that the history of the development of credit markets could be informative for students of international regimes. The analogy seems to hold. Richard Ehrenberg reports that the development of credit arrangements in medieval European Bourses reduced transaction costs (since money did not need to be transported in the form of specie) and provided high-quality information in the form of merchants' newsletters and exchanges of information at fairs: "during the Middle Ages the best information as to the course of events in the world was regularly to be obtained in the fairs and the Bourses" (p. 317). The Bourses also provided credit ratings, which provided information but also served as a crude substitute for effective systems of legal liability. Although the descriptions of credit market development in works such as that by Ehrenberg are fascinating, I have not been able to find a historically-grounded theory of these events. See Richard Ehrenberg, *Capital and Finance in the Age of the Renaissance: A Study of the Fuggers and Their Connections*, translated from the German by H. M. Lucas (New York: Harcourt, Brace, no date), especially chap. 3 (pp. 307–33).

26. Ronald Coase, "The Problem of Social Cost," *Journal of Law and Economics* 3 (October 1960). For a discussion, see James Buchanan and Gordon Tullock, *The Calculus of Consent: Logical Foundations of Constitutional Democracy* (Ann Arbor: University of Michigan Press, 1962), p. 186.

27. If we were to drop the assumption that actors are strictly self-interested utility-maximizers, regimes could be important in another way: they would help to develop norms that are internalized by actors as part of their own utility functions. This is important in real-world political-economic systems, as works by Schumpeter, Polanyi, and Hirsch on the moral underpinnings of a market system indicate. It is likely to be important in many international systems as well. But it is outside the scope of the analytical approach taken in this article—which is designed to illuminate some issues, but not to provide a comprehensive account of international regime change. See Joseph Schumpeter, *Capitalism, Socialism, and Democracy* (New York: Harper & Row, 1942), especially Part II, "Can Capitalism Survive?"; Karl Polanyi, *The Great Transformation: The Political and Economic Origins of Our Time* (1944; Boston: Beacon Press, 1957); and Fred Hirsch, *Social Limits to Growth* (Cambridge: Harvard University Press, 1976).

28. Information costs could be considered under the category of transaction costs, but they are so important that I categorize them separately in order to give them special attention.

29. For a discussion of "the varieties of international law," see Louis Henkin, *How Nations Behave: Law and Foreign Policy*, 2d ed. (New York: Columbia University Press for the Council on Foreign Relations, 1979), pp. 13–22.

30. Davis and North, *Institutional Change and American Economic Growth*, especially pp. 51–57.

31. The concept of issue density bears some relationship to Herbert Simon's notion of "decomposability," in *The Sciences of the Artificial* (Cambridge: MIT Press, 1969). In both cases, problems that can be conceived of as separate are closely linked to one another functionally, so that it is difficult to affect one without also affecting others. Issue density is difficult to operationalize, since the universe (the "issue-area" or "policy space") whose area forms the denominator of the term cannot easily be specified precisely. But given a certain definition of the issue-area, it is possible to trace the increasing density of issues within it over time. See, for example, Robert O. Keohane and Joseph S. Nye, *Power and Interdependence: World Politics in Transition* (Boston: Little, Brown, 1977), chap. 4.

32. On questions of linkage, see Arthur A. Stein, "The Politics of Linkage," *World Politics* 33,1 (October 1980): 62–81; Kenneth Oye, "The Domain of Choice," in Oye et al., *Eagle Entangled: U.S. Foreign Policy in a Complex World* (New York: Longmans, 1979), pp. 3–33; and Robert D. Tollison and Thomas D. Willett, "An Economic Theory of Mutually Advantageous Issue Linkage in International Negotiations," *International Organization* 33,4 (Autumn 1979).

33. GATT negotiations and deliberations on the international monetary system have been characterized by extensive bargaining over side-payments and complex politics of issue-linkage. For a discussion see Nicholas Hutton, "The Salience of Linkage in International Economic Negotiations," *Journal of Common Market Studies* 13, 1–2 (1975): 136–60.

34. Ernst B. Haas, *The Uniting of Europe* (Stanford: Stanford University Press, 1958).

35. Paul A. Samuelson, "The Monopolistic Competition Revolution," in R. E. Kuenne, ed., *Monopolistic Competition Theory* (New York: Wiley, 1967), p. 117.

36. Increases in issue density could make it more difficult to supply regimes; the costs of providing regimes could grow, for instance, as a result of multiple linkages across issues. The 1970s Law of the Sea negotiations illustrate this problem. As a result, it will not necessarily be the case that increases in interdependence will lead to increases in the number, extensiveness, and strength of international regimes.

37. Stephen D. Krasner, ["Structural Causes and Regime Consequences: Regimes as Intervening Variables," *International Organization*, 36,2 (Spring 1982): 2.]

38. Robert Jervis, ["Security Regimes," *International Organization*, 36,2 (Spring 1982): 180.]

39. The classic discussion is in Thomas C. Schelling, *The Strategy of Conflict* (1960; Cambridge: Harvard University Press, 1980), chap. 4, "Toward a Theory of Interdependent Decision." See also Schelling, *Micromotives and Macrobehavior* (New York: Norton, 1978).

40. For an interesting discussion of regimes in these terms, see Young, "Regime Dynamics." On conventions, see David K. Lewis, *Convention: A Philosophical Study* (Cambridge: Cambridge University Press, 1969).

41. Arthur A. Stein, ["Coordination and Collaboration: Regimes in an Anarchic World," *International Organization*, 36,2 (Spring 1982): 128.]

42. Herbert Simon, "From Substantive to Procedural Rationality," in Latsis, ed., *Method and Appraisal in Economics*; Spiro J. Latsis, "A Research Programme in Economics," in ibid.; and on blackmailing, Oye, "The Domain of Choice."

43. Oliver E. Williamson, *Markets and Hierarchies: Analysis and Anti-Trust Implications* (New York: Free Press, 1975).

44. George A. Ackerlof, "The Market for 'Lemons': Qualitative Uncertainty and the Market Mechanism," *Quarterly Journal of Economics* 84,3 (August 1970).

45. Arrow, *Essays in the Theory of Risk-Bearing*.

46. Ackerlof, "The Market for 'Lemons'"; Arrow, *Essays in the Theory of Risk-Bearing*.

47. For an analysis along these lines, see Davis B. Bobrow and Robert T. Kudrle, "Energy R&D: In Tepid Pursuit of Collective Goods," *International Organization* 33,2 (Spring 1979): 149–76.

48. Oliver E. Williamson, "A Dynamic Theory of Interfirm Behavior," *Quarterly Journal of Economics* 79 (1965), p. 584.

49. Susan Strange, "The Management of Surplus Capacity: or How Does Theory Stand Up to Protectionism 1970s Style?" *International Organization* 33,3 (Summer 1979): 303–34.

50. Fred Hirsch, "The Bagehot Problem," *The Manchester School* 45,3 (1977): 241–57.

51. Notice that here, through a functional logic, a systemic analysis has implications for the performance of different governmental structures at the level of the actor. The value of high-quality information in making agreements does not force governments to become more open, but it gives advantages to those that do.

52. Williamson, "A Dynamic Theory of Interfirm Behavior," p. 592, original italics.

53. *Power and Interdependence*, especially pp. 54–58 and 146–53. Linda Cahn also found lags, particularly in the wheat regime; see "National Power and International Regimes."

54. *Power and Interdependence*, p. 55.

55. On the GATT, see Gardner Patterson, *Discrimination in International Trade: The Policy Issues* (Princeton: Princeton University Press, 1966); on the international monetary regime, see Robert W. Russell, "Transgovernmental Interaction in the International Monetary System, 1960–1972," *International Organization* 27,4 (Autumn 1973) and Fred Hirsch, *Money International*, rev. ed. (Harmondsworth, England: Pelican Books, 1969), especially chap. 11, "Central Bankers International."

56. Robert O. Keohane and Joseph S. Nye, "Transgovernmental Relations and International Organizations," *World Politics* 27,1 (October 1974): 39–62.

57. These first three inferences focus only on the *demand* side. To understand the degree to which norms, for example, will develop, one needs also to look at supply considerations. Problems of organization, such as those discussed in the public goods literature and the theory of hegemonic stability, may prevent even strongly desired regimes from materializing.

58. Kindleberger has asserted that "for the world economy to be stabilized, there has to be a stabilizer, one stabilizer." *The World in Depression*, p. 305.

59. Charles P. Kindleberger, "Systems of International Economic Organization," in David P. Calleo, ed., *Money and the Coming World Order* (New York: New York University Press for the Lehrman Institute, 1978); Ronald McKinnon, *Money in International Exchange: The Convertible Currency System* (New York: Oxford University Press, 1979).

60. Arrow, *Essays in the Theory of Risk-Bearing*, pp. 134–43.

61. In personal correspondence, Robert Jervis has suggested an interesting qualification to this argument. He writes: "If we look at relations that involve at least the potential for high conflict, then schemes that tie the fates of all the actors together may have utility even if the actors are concerned about catastrophic events which will affect them all. They can worry that if some states are not affected, the latter will be much stronger than the ones who have been injured. So it would make sense for them to work out a scheme which would insure that a disaster would not affect their relative positions, even though this would not mean that they would all not be worse off in absolute terms." The point is certainly well taken, although one may wonder whether such an agreement would in fact be implemented by the states that would make large relative gains in the absence of insurance payments.

62. Isebill V. Gruhn, "The Lomé Convention: Inching toward Interdependence," *International Organization* 30,2 (Spring 1976), pp. 255–56.

63. Robert O. Keohane, "The International Energy Agency: State Influence and Transgovernmental Politics," *International Organization* 32,4 (Autumn 1978): 929–52.

64. OECD *Observer*, no. 74 (March–April 1975), pp. 9–13.

65. The optimal condition under which such a coalition may emerge could be called the "paper tiger condition": a potential external threat to the coalition exists but is too weak to frighten or persuade coalition members to defect or to desist from effective action. OPEC has been viewed by western policy makers since 1973 as a real rather than paper tiger, although some observers keep insisting that there is less to the organization than meets the eye.

CHAPTER 6

Reciprocity in
International Relations

W orld politics is commonly referred to as anarchic, meaning that it lacks a common government. Yet a Hobbesian "war of all against all" does not usually ensue: even sovereign governments that recognize no common authority may engage in limited cooperation. The anarchic structure of world politics does mean, however, that the achievement of cooperation can depend neither on deference to hierarchical authority nor on centralized enforcement. On the contrary, if cooperation is to emerge, whatever produces it must be consistent with the principles of sovereignty and self-help.[1]

Reciprocity is consistent with these principles: as Elizabeth Zoller declares, it "is a condition theoretically attached to every legal norm of international law."[2] Reciprocity is also often invoked as an appropriate standard of behavior which can produce cooperation among sovereign states. This is true in international trade, where reciprocity is a central norm of the General Agreement on Tariffs and Trade (GATT),[3] as well as in political relations between the superpowers. The Basic Principles Agreement signed in Moscow in May 1972 by Richard Nixon and Leonid Brezhnev provided that "discussions and negotiations on outstanding issues" between the United States and the Soviet Union would "be conducted in a spirit of reciprocity, mutual accommodation and mutual benefit."[4] Nine years later, President Ronald Reagan declared that the Soviet-American relationship must be based upon "restraint and reciprocity."[5] In a speech to the Chicago Council on Foreign Relations in March 1984, Senator Gary Hart, campaigning for the Democratic presidential nomination, declared that reciprocity would be one of three major foreign-policy themes for his administration.[6]

This praise for reciprocity by political leaders has recently been echoed by scholars. Robert Axelrod has advised people and governments to practice and teach reciprocity in order to foster cooperation.[7] Convinced by his arguments, I declared two years ago that reciprocity "seems to be the most effective strategy for maintaining cooperation among egoists."[8]

This applause for reciprocity by politicians and scholars may seem impressive. Yet whenever a concept in international relations becomes popular, particularly as a remedy for conflict, we should be cautious. The current enthusiasm for reciprocity resembles the revival of balance-of-power thinking in the United States after World War II. At that time scholars such as Ernst

B. Haas and Inis Claude pointed out that the balance of power could be a useful tool for understanding international relations, or a worthwhile guide for determining policy, only if analysts distinguished its various meanings clearly from one another. As Claude put it, "'Balance of power' is to writers on international relations as 'a pinch of salt' is to cooks, 'stellar southpaw' to baseball writers, and 'dialectical materialism' to Marxist theoreticians."[9] The concept of balance of power had by then lost much analytical value because it had been used in many confusing ways: like "national security," it had become, in Arnold Wolfers's words, an "ambiguous symbol." Wolfers pointed out that "when political formulas such as 'national interest' or 'national security' gain popularity they need to be scrutinized with particular care."[10]

Reciprocity is an ambiguous term, in part because it appears in so many different literatures. Each school of thought defines reciprocity in accordance with its own theoretical purposes, with little regard for its other definitions and little comprehension of the conceptual progress that other disciplines may have made. The fact that reciprocity can refer either to a policy pursued by a single actor or to a systemic pattern of action futher confounds its meaning. But the political uses to which the concept has been put are primarily responsible for the confusion. Reciprocity is both a symbol in politics and a concept for scholars.

To illustrate this point, let us consider how the term has been used in American debates on international trade policy. In American foreign economic policy, reciprocity has been put forward as an appropriate standard of behavior since the early years of the Republic. The first commercial treaty signed by the United States, the treaty with France of 1778, contained a provision for reciprocal trade concessions between the two countries.[11] Later, American threats of retaliation led Britain to enact the Reciprocity of Duties Act in 1823, and retaliatory actions by both countries regarding trade with the West Indies culminated in what Americans called "the Reciprocity of 1830," a compromise Anglo-American agreement dealing with that issue.[12] Throughout the antebellum period, "the notion of reciprocity, as a policy, received considerable attention," although it was espoused toward the end of the century less by liberal traders than by those who sought to restrict imports.[13] The Republican platform of 1896 declared that "Protection and Reciprocity are twin measures of Republican policy and go hand in hand"; the Harding administration later claimed to base its protectionist foreign-trade policy on reciprocity.[14]

Since passage of the Trade Agreements Act of 1934, reciprocity has been associated with liberal trade policies. In the United States, the virtue of reciprocity has been so widely assumed that contemporary opponents of liberalization seek to capture the concept for their own purposes. They define it to mean that "a U.S. trading partner should accord American goods, services and investments essentially the same treatment as the partner's goods, services and investments are accorded in the U.S. market."[15] In hearings on reciprocity legislation held in 1983, officials of the Reagan administration defined reciprocity as a strategy for opening foreign markets, but Senator Russell Long (D.-Louisiana) declared that reciprocity to him meant "moving toward a balance with Japan rather than the big surplus in their account trading with us."[16] For Senator Long reciprocity meant a bilateral balance of trade—exactly what the liberal architects of GATT sought to displace. Not surprisingly, two commentators have characterized some proponents of reciprocity as seeking unilaterally to repeal the law of comparative advantage,[17] and others have written about new tendencies toward "aggressive reciprocity" in American discussions of trade policy.[18]

In debates on foreign trade, as well as in the academic literature, reciprocity has two quite distinct meanings. I will use *specific* reciprocity here to refer to situations in which specified partners exchange items of equivalent value in a strictly delimited sequence. If any obligations exist, they are clearly specified in terms of rights and duties of particular actors. This is the typical meaning of reciprocity in economics and game theory. In situations characterized by *diffuse* reciprocity, by contrast, the definition of equivalence is less precise, one's partners may be viewed as a group rather than as particular actors, and the sequence of events is less narrowly bounded. Obligations are important. Diffuse reciprocity involves conforming to generally accepted standards of behavior. In the field of trade, as we will see in more detail below, demands for aggressive reciprocity, or what used to be known as conditional most-favored-nation (MFN) treatment, reflect the concept of specific reciprocity, while unconditional MFN treatment embodies diffuse reciprocity.

Concepts similar to that of diffuse reciprocity appear in an extensive literature on social exchange, whose intellectual leaders include such scholars as Peter Blau, Alvin Gouldner, George Homans, and Marshall Sahlins. This school emphasizes that reciprocal obligations hold societies together. Participants typically view diffuse reciprocity as an ongoing series of sequential actions which may continue indefinitely, never balancing but continuing to entail mutual concessions within the context of shared commitments and values. In personal life, bargaining over the price of a house reflects specific reciprocity; groups of close friends practice diffuse reciprocity.[19]

Throughout this article, I will illustrate my arguments about reciprocity with examples from international politics. I will pay special attention to international trade, since reciprocity has been an important principle in trade negotiations for at least 150 years, and abundant experience with its operation in trade therefore exists.

Section 1 offers a general definition that seeks to capture what is common to specific and diffuse reciprocity. Section 2 analyzes the meaning of reciprocity in the game-theoretic literature and explores the strengths and weaknesses of specific reciprocity as a principle of action designed to elicit mutually beneficial cooperation in world politics. Section 3 pursues the less familiar concept of diffuse reciprocity, as suggested by the sociological and anthropological literature on social exchange. Diffuse reciprocity also has advantages and liabilities as a principle of action in world politics, but these are quite different from those of specific reciprocity. In the final section I briefly investigate how specific and diffuse reciprocity are related in practice, and how they could be combined to gain some of the advantages of both. This discussion emphasizes the importance of institutional innovations that can facilitate international cooperation.

1. RECIPROCITY AS A GENERAL CONCEPT

Despite the ambiguities that bedevil it, the concept of reciprocity does have a core meaning and thus can be defined in a way that is consistent with the notions both of specific and diffuse reciprocity. I focus on two aspects of reciprocity that constitute, at least in qualified form, essential dimensions of the concept: *contingency* and *equivalence*.

Contingency. Gouldner observed twenty-five years ago that sociologists had often failed to define reciprocity, and that "few concepts in sociology remain more obscure and ambiguous."[20] In seeking to rectify this situation, Gouldner emphasized that reciprocity implies conditional action, and other social exchange theorists have followed his lead. Reciprocity implies "actions that are contingent on rewarding reactions from others and that cease when these expected reactions are not forthcoming."[21] Reciprocal behavior returns ill for ill as well as good for good: "people should meet smiles with smiles and lies with treachery."[22] Unconditionality "would be at variance with the basic character of the reciprocity norm which imposes obligations only contingently, that is, in response to the benefits conferred by others."[23] In game theory, contingency is also a central component of reciprocity: actors behaving in a reciprocal fashion respond to cooperation with cooperation and to defection with defection.

Equivalence. The social exchange literature is careful not to define reciprocity as the strict equivalence of benefits. Among equals, rough equivalence is the usual expectation: the man who gives a dinner party does not bargain with his guests about what they will do for him in return, but "he expects them not simply to ask him for a quick lunch if he has given a formal dinner for them."[24] Reciprocity can also characterize relations among un-equals, for instance, between a patron and his client, when there is little prospect of equivalent exchange. Patron-client relationships are characterized by exchanges of mutually valued but noncomparable goods and services. Marc Bloch refers to "reciprocity in unequal obligations" as the "really distinctive feature of European vassalage."[25]

Nevertheless, at least rough equivalence is essential to our usual un-derstanding of reciprocity. When we observe one-sided and unrequited exploitation, which cannot under any circumstances be considered an ex-change of equivalents, we do not describe the relationship as reciprocal. As Barrington Moore, Jr. has commented, a pattern of reciprocity is "one where services and favors, trust and affection, in the course of mutual exchanges are ideally expected to find some rough balancing out."[26] Specific reciprocity emphasizes an overall balance within a group.

The literature on reciprocity in international relations emphatically associates reciprocity with equivalence of benefits. Axelrod views "the insistence on no more than equity" as a common property of many rules based on reciprocity. Reciprocity is not defined in the General Agreement on Tariffs and Trade, but the director-general of GATT defines it as "the equivalence of concessions."[27] Both of these definitions allow rough equivalence to qualify as reciprocity, but some usages are more strict. Reciprocity has been defined, under fixed exchange rates, as "an insistence that other countries simultaneously reduce their tariffs by the amount required to produce a balanced expansion of trade at the given exchange rate"; for a number of writers "reciprocal concessions" are those that result in projected increases in each country's exports equal to the increments in its imports.[28]

Although reciprocity clearly entails at least rough equivalence of benefits, in international relations as in personal social relations precise measurement is often impossible. States in reciprocal relationships with one another often do not have identical obligations.[29] How is one to ascertain the relative value of a superpower's pledge to protect an ally from attack, on the one hand, and the ally's willingness to accept stationing of the superpower's troops in its territory, on the other? Without market prices, determining whether an exchange involves equivalent values may be difficult. When the Chicago White Sox in 1951 traded Gus Zernial in order to obtain Minnie Minoso, I initially believed that the exchange had been disadvantageous (although I soon changed my mind and my hero). No one could have proved at the time—to me or any other skeptic—that the trade was equal, or beneficial, any more than one could have reliably so characterized the terms of Britain's entry into the European Economic Community in 1973, or the "50/50" profit-sharing agreements between governments of oil-producing countries and companies that prevailed for roughly two decades after 1950.

Despite the impossibility of determining exact equivalence, some degree of rough equivalence is integral to the meaning of reciprocity. Reciprocity refers to *exchanges of roughly equivalent values in which the actions of each party are contingent on the prior actions of the others in such a way that good is returned for good, and bad for bad.* These exchanges are often, but not necessarily, mutually beneficial; they may be based on self-interest as well as on shared concepts of rights and obligations; and the value of what is exchanged may or may not be comparable.

The requirement of rough equivalence means that many relationships in world politics are not reciprocal. Claims of reciprocity may be fraudulent, hiding domination and exploitation. Furthermore, even genuinely reciprocal relationships are not power-free: strong and weak actors practicing reciprocity face different opportunity costs, and the international structure of power helps to establish what values are regarding as equivalent. Nothing in this article should be interpreted as suggesting that reciprocity is a universal principle of world politics or that it insulates its practitioners from considerations of power.

2. SPECIFIC RECIPROCITY

In his elegantly argued and influential book, Robert Axelrod develops a theory of cooperation which relies heavily on specific reciprocity. Axelrod focuses on the game of Prisoner's Dilemma. In plays of this game, both players benefit more from cooperation than from mutual defection, but each player achieves the most successful outcome by defecting, provided that her partner cooperates.[30] In single plays of this game, players lack any way of enforcing promises; therefore, it is always rational for an egoistic player to defect. Yet defection by both players yields lower payoffs than do mutual cooperation. Paradoxically, "stupid" but nice players who cooperate without calculating succeed more often at Prisoner's Dilemma than do more rational counterparts.

Axelrod is concerned not with single plays of Prisoner's Dilemma but with an indefinite number of interactions. He follows the argument of Michael Taylor, who showed that when an indefinite sequence of such games is played, cooperation may become rational for the players.[31] Axelrod then demonstrates that the rationality of cooperation depends not only on the immediate payoff facing the players but also on what he calls "the shadow of the future." The more important outcomes of future plays are, the more sensible it is for players to forgo maximal current payoffs (by defecting), but instead to cooperate; such a strategy fosters cooperation on future moves.

Axelrod uses an ingenious computer simulation to pit various strategies against one another. As the strategy of reciprocity, he uses Tit for Tat. A player following Tit for Tat cooperates on the first move of a sequence, then does on a subsequent move what the other player did on the previous one. In Axelrod's simulation, given the mix of strategies submitted, Tit for Tat not only induced cooperation more effectively than alternatives but also reaped the highest overall payoff. Axelrod's simulation thus adds a new dimension to the already impressive experimental evidence indicating that reciprocity is an effective strategy in Prisoner's Dilemma.[32]

Of course, not all situations characterized by potential conflict as well as incentives for cooperation resemble the situation in Prisoner's Dilemma. Other games with somewhat different structures have not been analyzed as carefully. Nevertheless, the appeal of specific reciprocity is not strictly limited to Prisoner's Dilemma. On the contrary, reciprocity often seems to be an attractive strategy for players of bilateral games in which mutual cooperation can yield more satisfying results than mutual defection but in which temptations for defection also exist.[33]

As an additional virtue, specific reciprocity may create incentives for otherwise passive interests within countries to oppose discordant unilateral action by their own governments. In trade, for instance, specific reciprocity creates incentives for export interests within countries to resist protective tariffs on other products, for fear that retaliation could be directed at them. In 1984, for instance, American farmers opposed steel quotas, anticipating retaliation against agricultural exports. Thus when we consider the complexity of international trade as contrasted with the simplicity of game-theoretic models, the appeal of specific reciprocity seems to be reinforced.

Difficulties of Reciprocity in Bilateral Situations

As we have seen, valid reasons exist to believe that under some conditions specific reciprocity can facilitate cooperation in world politics. Yet reciprocity is clearly not a sufficient condition for cooperation; indeed, it need not entail cooperation of any kind. We are all familiar with the chilling phrase, "a reciprocal exchange of nuclear weapons." Because reciprocity implies returning ill for ill as well as good for good, its moral status is ambiguous. Because it can lead to mutually harmful conflict, its political value may also be questionable. If either of two parties practicing specific reciprocity begins with a malign move, cooperation can never be achieved as long as both persist in this strategty. Axelrod points out that what he calls "echo effects" can produce conflict: "the trouble with TIT FOR TAT is that once a feud gets started, it can continue indefinitely."[34]

Mark Twain discussed this problem in *Adventures of Huckleberry Finn*. In chapter 18, Huck tries to discover the reasons for the feud between the Grangerfords and the Shepherdsons:

> "What was the trouble about, Buck?—land?"
> "I reckon maybe—I don't know."
> "Well, who done the shooting? Was it a Grangerford or a Shepherdson?"
> "Laws, how do *I* know? It was so long ago."
> "Don't anybody know?"
> "Oh, yes, pa knows, I reckon, and some of the other old people, but they don't know now what the row was about in the first place."

This defect of Tit for Tat is compounded by two others, even when the situation being faced is structurally comparable to Prisoner's Dilemma. First, governments tend to evaluate "equivalence" in biased ways. Insofar as governments, being partial to their own interests, demand to be overcompensated in the name of equivalence, abuse of reciprocity can lead to escalating cycles of discord and conflict. Second, even when many shared interests exist and judgments of equivalence are not distorted, strategies of reciprocity may lead to deadlock. John W. Evans points out that in tariff negotiations conducted through exchanges of equivalent concessions, potential concessions may become "bargaining chips" to be hoarded: "Tariffs that have no intrinsic economic value for a country that maintains them have acquired value because of the insistence of other countries on reciprocity in the bargaining process." As a result, "tariff levels may be maintained in spite of the fact that a lower level would raise the country's real income."[35]

These problems with specific reciprocity are illustrated by Soviet-American détente during the 1970s. George Breslauer argues that what he calls "collaborative competition" requires a "mutual commitment to reciprocity," as well as mutual restraint. Yet in the 1970s the Soviet Union and the United States interpreted the meaning of such a commitment in incompatible ways. The Soviets sought "the maximization of reciprocal exchanges *within* policy realms," and "forms of collaboration that would increase Soviet leverage where there previously had been little," but resisted American attempts at linkage. The United States, in contrast, "defined collaborative reciprocity as Soviet forebearance from exploiting targets of opportunity when U.S. efforts to control a local situation were failing and the United States was in retreat." Both sides were too ambitious.[36]

The key ambiguity of détente involved how far specific reciprocity would extend beyond the terms of particular agreements. Neither the United States nor the Soviet Union was willing to make substantial unrequited concessions in the hope of eventually achieving reciprocity. This is not surprising since their relationship remained highly competitive, they disagreed about what constituted equivalence, and neither could be confident that détente would continue for long. With the existence of only minimal common standards to indicate a basis for legitimate action, each nation therefore had an incentive to reinterpret the Basic Principles Agreement to its own advantage. Biased interpretations of equivalence contributed to deadlock and in the early 1980s to what would even be viewed as a feud between the superpowers.

Axelrod's remedy for such problems is a modification of specific reciprocity in which players "return only nine-tenths of a tit for a tat. This would help dampen the echoing of conflict and still provide an incentive to the other player not to try any gratuitous defections."[37] This solution acknowledges that reciprocity is no panacea even in bilateral relationship. Feuds, biased judgments of equivalence, and deadlock that results from hoarded bargaining chips undermine the value of specific reciprocity. But these problems only point out pitfalls along the path of reciprocity rather than indicating an alternative route.

Difficulties of Reciprocity in Multilateral Situations

One of the most frequent objections to specific reciprocity pertains to a multilateral situation involving a large number of actors, in which collective, or public, goods are involved. (Public goods are indivisible and cannot be denied to any member of a group, regardless of whether that member contributed to their provision.) Such multilateral situations offer substantial incentives to behave as a "free-rider"—not to pay for the good but to gain from its provision by others. In such a situation, public choice theory predicts less cooperation (in producing the public good) than in an otherwise comparable bilateral or small-group context.

Under these conditions enforcement of reciprocal agreements may prove problematic. Incentives to police an agreement by retaliating against defectors are likely to be much lower than in bilateral games, since the "policeman" will suffer the opprobrium of other actors, while gaining only a small portion of the benefits of enforcing the rules. Thus if a given actor's violation of a particular rule does not directly threaten the benefits received by the group, retaliation is unlikely to be severe. As a consequence, the incentive to cooperate provided by reciprocity—that defection will lead to punishment by one's partners—may not prove compelling in a multilateral situation.[38]

Although public good arguments are important, they do not constitute strong objections to the use of specific reciprocity to induce cooperation in world politics. Many opportunities for cooperation in international relations involve relatively few states of unequal capabilities which can monitor each other's behavior. Even when large numbers of actors are involved, specific reciprocity may be used to prevent free-riding. Undifferentiated multilateral groups can be broken down into smaller clusters, within which specific reciprocity can be pursued effectively: that is, institutional arrangements are established that make it possible to exclude actors from benefits. In this sense, what would otherwise have been public goods are privatized.[39]

Because the use of specific reciprocity may be an effective device for dealing with free-riding and sanctioning problems, we might expect the concept to be institutionalized. And indeed, this inference appears to be confirmed in the field of international trade, where bargaining—mixing cooperation and discord—has a long history. As we have seen, American and British attempts to pursue reciprocity in trade go back very far, and are clearly manifest in the early 19th century.

Yet a closer look raises doubts about whether the evidence from trade negotiations supports the proposition that specific reciprocity facilitates international cooperation. Although Britain in the 1830s, and the United States around the turn of the century sought to implement trade policies embodying specific reciprocity, both later abandoned the attempt. A review of these endeavors and why they were given up raises questions about the usefulness of specific reciprocity, especially when sequential negotiations take place in the context of extensive interdependence.

Britain and Trade Reciprocity

Great Britain enacted the Reciprocity of Duties Act in 1823, under the leadership of William Huskisson, the president of the Board of Trade. Under this act, Britain entered into bilateral treaties that provided MFN treatment for both countries' exports and equality of treatment with respect to port charges on shipping. MFN treatment did not, however, put outsiders on and equal footing with Britain's colonies, which continued to receive preferences on their exports to the mother country. Nor did equality of treatment for shipping cancel out extensive British restrictions on imports into Britain carried by non-British ships.[40] Nevertheless, the Reciprocity of Duties Act did constitute a significant change from the old system of the Navigation Acts, under which Britain had acted unilaterally.

Huskisson later made it clear that his acceptance of reciprocity had been based neither on belief in principles of fair trade nor on altruism, but rather on concern about foreign retaliation:

> If the system of discriminating Duties for the encouragement of Shipping were a secret known to this country alone; if a similar system were not, or could

not be, put in force in every other country, I should not be standing here to vindicate the measure to which I have just referred, and the present policy of his Majesty's Government. So long as, in fact, no independent trading community existed out of Europe, and so long as the old Governments of Europe looked upon these matters,—if they looked to them at all,—as little deserving their attention and were content, either from ignorance or indifference, not to thwart our System, it would have been wrong to disturb any part of it.[41]

In other words, as long as Britain could exploit other countries through unilateral action, little reason existed to adopt a policy of reciprocity. Just as in Prisoner's Dilemma, one player benefits from defecting if the other player ignores her actions.

The treaties negotiated under the Reciprocity of Duties Act accomplished little. Although Britain sought vigorously to negotiate a reciprocity treaty with France in the 1830s—even to the point of seeking to stir up French public opinion against the French government—this effort was unsuccessful. The French feared that liberalizing their duties on iron, coal, cotton, and wool would hurt these industries more than Britain's liberalization of wine duties would help the wine industry; and Britain refused to lower its duty on silk.[42]

In 1840 Parliament provided for the appointment of a Select Committee on Import Duties, most of whose members turned out to be advocates of free trade. This committee argued for abandonment of reciprocity in favor of unilateral free trade, on the grounds that this policy would provide other countries with resources to purchase British exports; reduce food costs and therefore costs of British production for export; reduce retaliation from abroad; and induce other countries to copy British free trade policy.[43] Influenced by these arguments, Parliament in 1842 adopted free trade legislation; within a few years it repealed the Corn Laws and abandoned the Navigation Acts.

Why was reciprocity abandoned, when in Prisoner's Dilemma, as Axelrod has shown, it has such clear bargaining advantages over unilateral renunciation of tariffs? The answer to this question seems to be that the situation facing Britain was not that of Prisoner's Dilemma, in which arrangements must be made to prevent cheating, but an example of what Arthur Stein calls a "dilemma of common aversions," in which stable equilibria exist and in which, therefore, problems of cheating and compliance do not emerge.[44] British leaders made it clear that they preferred to abandon their tariffs even if others retained theirs. James Deacon Hume, joint secretary to the Board of Trade in 1840, expressed this view as follows: "I think it is unwise to do that upon stipulation, upon certain terms, which upon any terms it would be better for you to do yourself."[45] Sir James Graham declared in 1849 that the principle of reciprocity made "the interest of others the measure of our interest—I had almost said it makes the folly of others the limit of our wisdom."[46]

In game-theoretic terms, Britain did not face Prisoner's Dilemma in dealing with France, since the British government preferred to abolish its tariffs unilaterally rather than to continue high tariffs on both sides. The payoff matrix was as follows, with 4 as the best payoff:

FRANCE

		low tariffs	high tariffs
BRITAIN	low tariffs	4, 2	3, 4
	high tariffs	2, 1	1, 3

For Britain, a continuation of mutual high tariffs was least desirable. But Britain could not induce France to move to reciprocal lower tariffs because France preferred to maintain high tariffs regardless of what Britain did. The equilibrium position was thus at the upper right: low British tariffs and high French ones. As long as their conceptions of self-interest remained the same, and no linkages were drawn to other issues (as was done in the Cobden-Chevalier Treaty of 1860), neither party had an incentive to alter its choice.

The United States and Trade Reciprocity

U.S. tariff policy between 1890 and 1923 incorporated specific reciprocity in two different ways: in so-called reciprocity provisions, used between 1890 and 1894 and again between 1897 and 1909; and in the form of conditional MFN clauses inserted into commercial treaties. Of these two manifestations of specific reciprocity, the latter is more significant, but the reciprocity provisions deserve some comment as well.

The Tariff Act of 1890 provided for imposition of duties on certain agricultural products when the country exporting those products imposed duties that the U.S. president declared "reciprocally unjust or unreasonable." A Democratic Congress repealed this provision in 1894, for reasons similar to those argued by the British a half-century earlier—that tariffs damaged the interests of a nation's own people, regardless of the response of the other side. In 1897, the Republicans reinstituted reciprocity and included the carrot as well as the stick by providing for concessions on brandies, champagne, wine, paintings, and statuary, in return for "reciprocal and reasonable concessions." Not surprisingly, this provision was designed to promote a reciprocal trade agreement with France. The Tariff Act of 1909, however, abolished these reciprocity arrangements.[47]

Scholars generally agree that these provisions for reciprocity did not lead to significant results, largely because the Republicans regarded reciprocity as supplementary to a protective tariff rather than as a means of moving toward liberalization.[48] The United States offered few concessions, and Congress demanded that the president submit trade agreements in the form

of treaties. Indeed, of the thirteen reciprocity treaties negotiated by the
American government between 1844 and 1902, only three became effective.
Two of these were with virtual dependencies of the United States: Hawaii
(until annexation in 1900) and Cuba; the other was a short-lived agreement
with Canada (1854–66).[49]

More significant was the commitment of the United States to the conditional
rather than unconditional MFN clause. An unconditional MFN clause obliges
a country to refrain from discriminating against any country with which it
has an agreement. Thus, if A and B have a reciprocal trade agreement, and
A makes a new agreement with C, concessions made by A to C are
automatically applicable to B as well. Under a conditional MFN clause,
however, B only receives those concessions if it provides "equivalent"
compensation to A.[50]

It is important to note that a country cannot simultaneously follow a
conditional MFN policy toward some countries and an unconditional MFN
policy toward others. As Jacob Viner explains:

> The existence of a single unconditional most-favored-nation pledge in a country's
> treaties makes all the other pledges, whatever their form, unconditional in
> effect. Suppose that A has most-favored-nation treaties with countries C, D
> and E, of which [those with] C and D are conditional and E unconditional,
> and that A grants to B for compensation, reduction in tariff duties. C and D
> cannot claim from A the benefit of this tariff reduction for their own commodities
> on the ground that it has been given to B, unless they offer compensation for
> the reduction equivalent to that given by B. But E can claim the reduction
> unconditionally, and once it has been given to E freely, it must then be extended
> to C and D also.[51]

The conditional MFN clause is an American invention, and for some
time only the United States, among the major trading powers, adopted it.
This put the United States in the position of a free-rider: "Dealing mainly
with countries who were extending unconditional most-favored-nation treatment to other countries, the United States received, by virtue of her conditional
most-favored-nation treatment, everything which she would have received
if they had all been unconditional. But she gave nothing in return."[52] In
game-theoretic terms, the United States was defecting, while its partners
were continuing to cooperate.

Nevertheless, the United States exchanged the conditional MFN clause
for the unconditional one in 1923, under the Harding administration.
According to Viner, American adherence to the conditional MFN clause
resulted from the impossibility of negotiating commercial treaties with several
important countries, as a consequence of which American exports were
seriously discriminated against. The one-sided advantages gained from
conditional MFN agreements by the United States made it difficult to negotiate
commercial agreements at all.

The alternative to a change in U.S. policy would have been a move
toward conditional MFN treatment by its trading partners. Had such a move

been made, what Adam Smith excoriated as "the sneaking arts of underling tradesmen" would have been elevated into political maxims for the conduct not merely of a great empire but of world trade in general.[53] Perhaps influenced by Smith's famous rhetoric, contemporary observers recognized that conditional MFN policy was also encumbered by the two defects of specific reciprocity noted above: the difficulty of establishing equivalence and the temptation to erect barriers for bargaining purposes. Equivalence is impossible to ascertain reliably, since "the relations between nations are so widely disparate that no two can offer precisely the same price." As the acting chairman of the U.S. Tariff Commission wrote to the secretary of state in 1922, it was "almost impossible to arrive at any agreement upon the equivalent concessions to be made by the third party." Furthermore, conditional MFN policy invites countries to pad tariff rates and raise trade barriers, in order to improve their bargaining positions when called upon to make equivalent concessions.[54]

An even more serious difficulty with conditional MFN policy was created by the combination of sequential negotiations and interdependence among the trading partners. In such a situation the terms of even mutually advantageous bilateral agreements can be altered by the consummation of new bargains between one of those trading partners and another country. The partner to the original agreement that is disadvantaged by this shift is naturally inclined to renegotiate the original pact. Suppose that in 1905 the United States had granted a concession on French wines in return for a concession by France on imports of American machinery, and that in due course the United States had offered Italy a similar concession on its wines, in return for, say, a reciprocal concession on American grain. France could claim that the value of the concession it received on wine had been reduced, since much of the benefit of the concession to France would have depended on the discrimination against Italian and in favor of French wines. France could then demand further concessions from the United States.

Reflecting on this problem, contemporary leaders saw that the result of an active policy of negotiating trade agreements under conditional MFN would be, at best, an infinite series of inconclusive bargains, perpetuating rather than removing discrimination among countries. Each new bargain would undermine previous ones; the more agreements made, the worse the tangle would become. They concluded that what I have called specific reciprocity, as provided in the conditional MFN clause, "involves unceasing and difficult negotiations which are quite unnecessary and often costly." Such bargaining "is at best complicated and dilatory and seldom, if ever, produces results which are commensurate with the irritation which it engenders among excluded nations."[55] Such considerations—advanced by a Republican tariff commissioner (William Culbertson) in the 1920s and by a Democratic assistant secretary of state (Francis Sayre) during the New Deal, contributed to the adoption of the unconditional form of the MFN clause by the United States in 1923 and to its incorporation in the Trade Agreements Act of 1934.

Where many issues and many countries are involved, insisting on specific reciprocity can create administrative and diplomatic nightmares. Even in the Kennedy Round of negotiations of 1967, insistence on reciprocity could have led to difficulties. Compensatory withdrawals of concessions threatened by governments in reaction to bargaining difficulties "affected third parties, and their efforts to redress the balance further widened the circle of those who felt that reciprocity could be preserved by still further withdrawals by them."[56] In this case, however, the institutional arrangements of the Kennedy Round, including the provision for simultaneous final agreement and the involvement of the GATT secretariat, prevented the feared chain reaction of retaliation.

Specific reciprocity can lead to internal administrative tangles as well as negotiating perversities. An example of this is provided by U.S. policy with respect to the Tokyo Round code on subsidies and countervailing duties. In adhering to this code, the United States accepted an obligation to apply an injury test to subsidized exports from those signatories and countries that have accepted similar obligations. Yet only about thirty countries have fully subscribed to this code. If the United States were to practice specific reciprocity, it would have to apply different tests to identically subsidized exports of identical products from different countries: for instance, it could impose countervailing duties on Indian exports without determining that American producers had been injured, but it could not do so with respect to Pakistani exports.[57] This would complicate procedures enormously and make "the interest of others the measure of our interest."

The practical difficulties of specific reciprocity extend beyond trade. Consider, for instance, issues of bank regulation. Specific reciprocity might seem to be a reasonable principle to apply to bank regulation: permission for a bank from country A to establish a branch in country B would be contingent on A's willingness to permit a branch bank for B to establish itself in A's territory. Yet although a few members of the Organization for Economic Cooperation and Development (OECD) apply this principle, the largest advanced industrialized countries have abandoned it. As a recent OECD report indicates, practicing reciprocity in this form leads to negotiating difficulties, since equivalence is difficult to establish. Each case is likely to be somewhat different. Furthermore, countries that are prepared to accept large foreign banking sectors cannot, in practice, enforce reciprocity, since to do so would "entail a fragmentation of the national regulatory framework to embody the different regulations applied in the home country of the foreign banks, thereby giving rise to a large range of competitive inequalities within the national banking system."[58]

The failure of the conditional MFN clause should make us cautious about specific reciprocity. Often such reciprocity can contribution to cooperation; but in complex multilateral situations perhaps involving domestic politics as well as international relations, its results may frustrate those who seek stable, beneficial agreements.

3. DIFFUSE RECIPROCITY

Governments that rely solely on specific reciprocity in international relations need not accept any obligations toward one another. They may play Tit for Tat on the basis of self-interest alone. Thus writers on international relations hardly mention obligation when discussing reciprocity. Axelrod, for instance, does not discuss reciprocity in terms of obligation; nor does the literature on reciprocity in trade policy emphasize obligation. Governments certainly cannot be counted on to behave benignly toward one another on the basis of a vague sense of global public interest. Within societies, on the other hand, actions that enhance social solidarity cannot be accounted for solely on the basis of specific reciprocity. To account for these actions, social scientists have introduced what I refer to here as the concept of diffuse reciprocity.

Consider the following example. Egoistic rational-choice theory predicts that individuals will not contribute voluntarily to the production of public goods, yet in societies such as the United States and Great Britain, they often do. Robert Sugden argues for the existence of a reciprocity principle in some societies which "says, with certain qualifications, that if everyone else contributes a particular level of effort to the production of a public good, you must do the same." That is, "you must not take a free ride when other people are contributing."[59] This interpretation of reciprocity clearly cannot be derived from specific reciprocity: a contribution to the lifeboat service in the United Kingdom or to the Wilderness Society in the United States will not increase one's own chances of being rescued at sea or enjoying public wilderness. Although the notion of diffuse reciprocity rests on an untested assumption about norms, Sugden incorporates it into his argument because specific reciprocity alone cannot account for voluntary cooperation.

Obviously such strong principles of reciprocity are not widely shared in contemporary international relations.[60] Yet as we have also seen, the "sneaking arts" of specific reciprocity are often inadequate to promote mutually beneficial cooperation. To expand the range of cooperation in world politics, it may be necessary to go beyond the practice of specific reciprocity and to engage in diffuse reciprocity: that is, to contribute one's share, or behave well toward others, not because of ensuing rewards from specific actors, but in the interests of continuing satisfactory overall results for the group of which one is a part, as a whole.

Since practitioners of diffuse reciprocity do not receive direct rewards for their cooperative actions, a pattern of diffuse reciprocity can be maintained only by a widespread sense of obligation. The social exchange literature helps us to think about obligation, since works in this tradition distinguish reciprocity from simple bargaining or exchange by stipulating that reciprocity always entails obligations of one actor toward another.[61] Indeed, in the sociological and anthropological literature the language of reciprocity is the language of obligation. Moore, for instance, identifies reciprocity with mutual obligation. Gouldner declares that reciprocity connotes that each party has rights and duties. He defines norms of reciprocity as beliefs that "people should help those who have helped them, and people should not injure those who have helped them," and holds that such norms "impose obligations."[62] Such norms need not imply altruism. Norms can consist of standards of behavior which are widely regarded as legitimate; they do not necessarily embody ethical principles that override self-interest.[63]

Specific reciprocity, based on egoism, can help to limit conflicts in primitive socieites as well as in international relations.[64] Even egoistic actors realize that limited cooperation is necessary if they are to engage in social exchange. In Blau's words, "it is a necessary condition of exchange that individuals, in the interest of continuing to receive needed services, discharge their obligations for having received them in the past." In turn, obligations and a pattern of compliance "contribute substantially to the stability of social systems. It is obviously inexpedient for creditors to break off relationships with those who have outstanding obligations to them. It may also be inexpedient for *debtors* to do so because their creditors may not again allow them to run up a bill of social indebtedness." In the long run, reciprocity based on self-interest can generate trust based on mutual experience as a result of the "recurrent and gradually expanding character" of processes of social exchange. That is, by engaging successfully in specific reciprocity over a period of time, governments may create suitable conditions for the operation of diffuse reciprocity.[65]

For specific reciprocity to become successfully institutionalized, much less to lead to diffuse reciprocity, exchange must take place sequentially rather than simultaneously. Both game theory and social exchange theory stress that reliance on simultaneous exchange alone provides an unsatisfactory basis for long-term relationships. If simultaneous exchange alone were possible, few agreements could be made, since issues frequently arise sequentially and an appropriate "quid" for a "quo" may be impossible to find at any given time. Furthermore, in simultaneous exchange, obligations never exist, since the exchange is balanced at every moment. There is never a "debt" or a "credit." Yet as Blau observes, the existence of debts and credits can in the long run increase confidence among members of a social system. Sahlins comments that among primitive tribes, "a measure of imbalance sustains the trade partnership, compelling as it does another meeting." Likewise, Gouldner argues that we should expect to find mechanisms in society which not only promote repayment of obligations but which "induce people to *remain* socially indebted to each other and which *inhibit* their complete repayment."[66] In chapters 42 and 43 of Herman Melville's novel, *The Confidence-Man*, this association between simultaneous exchange and lack of confidence is epitomized by the sign that the riverboat barber uses to indicate his demand for immediate cash payment: "No Trust." From a game-theoretic point of view, it is significant that the action of Melville's novel takes place aboard a large boat that makes frequent stops and that characters continually appear and disappear. Since no one can count on seeing anyone else again, each game of Prisoner's Dilemma must be played in isolation—that is, conflictually.

Sequential reciprocity promotes long-term cooperation much more effectively than does simultaneous exchange. Conversely, when simultaneous
exchange takes place, it often reflect a breakdown of confidence. Extreme
examples of purely simultaneous exchange indicate hostility and distrust.
Such an instance occurred in 1981, when American diplomats held hostage
by Iran were liberated in return for the release of Iranian financial assets
held in the United States. Detailed arrangements involving third-party
guarantors were made to ensure that neither side could double-cross the
other.

In practice, specific reciprocity in world politics combines elements of
simultaneity and sequentiality. When the Soviet Union and the United States
endorsed reciprocity as a valuable principle for their relationship, as in the
strategic arms agreements, they surely had in mind simultaneous concessions.
Likewise, "reciprocal trade negotiations" such as the Tokyo Round are
designed to lead to simultaneous commitments by the parties involved. Yet
in both instances, these commitments are made against the background of
past sequences of action and reaction and in the context of expectations
that other actions, such as the enactment of legislation and its implementation
by governments, will follow.

Both game theories and theories of social exchange emphasize the
importance of sequences of action in enabling reciprocity to contribute to
cooperation. The social exchange literature carries the emphasis even further,
however, by alerting us to the importance, for the development of institutionalized patterns of reciprocity, of temporarily unbalanced exchange and
the obligations that such imbalances create. That unbalanced exchanges are
common in the world political economy is thus significant. As in primitive
societies and credit markets under capitalism, such exchanges may create
mutual confidence, since repayment over a period of time provides information
to lenders about the habits and character of borrowers.

Stable patterns of specific reciprocity are often the most one can expect
in world politics: genuinely diffuse reciprocity is rare. The latter only occurs
within cooperative international regimes that link countries with extensive
shared interest and is never as solidary as family or small-group ties. Perhaps
the closest approximations to diffuse reciprocity on a global level are found
in international integration processes involving "upgrading the common
interest," such as Haas discovered in the early years of European integration
efforts.[67] In such international regimes, actors recognize that a "veil of
ignorance" separates them from the future but nevertheless offer benefits
to others on the assumption that these will rebound to their own advantage
in the end.[68]

The experience of European integration shows that diffuse reciprocity
can be transformed into specific reciprocity as well as vice versa. Haas has
pointed out that in the early period of European integration, between 1955
and 1965, "the parties expected reciprocal benefits of a sequential nature,
i.e., they expected these to be realized in the medium to long term and

therefore were quite prepared to offer one-sided concessions as down payments, banking on the development of a *process* of reciprocal response to satisfy their individual interests and values. . . . Equivalence was soft-pedaled." This changed after 1965: "equivalence is now highly valued and benefits are not deferred."[69] The current emphasis on a specific reciprocity by the British and others, including the French, constitutes a violation of the older, more integrative diffuse norm.

To analyze the virtues and defects of diffuse reciprocity, let us return to our international trade example. Unconditional MFN treatment constitutes diffuse reciprocity. Third parties no longer demand reciprocity for concessions given to others: these are extended automatically. The demand for equivalent contingent concessions is abandoned provided that each partner remains sufficiently loyal to the norms of the regime to be "in good standing." In GATT, for instance the legal obligation to reciprocate is the obligation to extend MFN treatment to other GATT members, subject to various exceptions such as those for customs unions and free-trade areas (Article 24) and for less developed countries (Article 36).

Yet unconditional MFN treatment can render countries that continue to make trade concessions vulnerable to exploitation by others. Imagine a situation in which a number of countries have made reciprocal trade agreements with one another, thus forming a network of such arrangements all of which incorporate unconditional MFN. Now suppose that one of these countries refuses to make any additional concessions, but simply acts as a free-rider, taking advantage of any future concessions made among its partners. Insofar as this recalcitrant country is an important trader, its policy will confront its partners with a distasteful choice: continue to liberalize, providing the defecting state with uncompensated benefits and thus rewarding it for its intransigence; or limit the scope or extent of otherwise rewarding liberalization to avoid this result.[70]

As a result of this free-rider problem, unconditional MFN treatment does not necessarily lead to lower trade barriers than does the specific reciprocity of conditional MFN. In his defense of unconditional MFN, Viner asserts flatly that it afforded no remedy for "exaggerated tariffs."[71] As Blackhurst points out, unconditional MFN treatment may retard or accelerate liberalization: "Do the pro-liberalization countries pull along the unenthusiastic countries, with the result that the overall pace of liberalization is speeded up, or do the recalcitrant countries act as such a drag that the overall pace is slower than it would be if the pro-liberalization countries acted unilaterally?"[72] The government procurement and safeguards codes of the Tokyo Round, which permit nonsignatories to be excluded from their benefits, suggest second thoughts about unconditional MFN treatment by the United States and some other countries. Diffuse reciprocity, in the absence of strong norms of obligation, exposes its practitioners to the threat of exploitation. In the absence of strong norms of obligation, specific reciprocity may provide an antidote to the abuse of diffuse reciprocity.

4. RECIPROCITY AND
INSTITUTIONAL INNOVATION

Specific reciprocity is an appropriate principle of behavior when norms of obligation are weak—the usual case in world politics—but when the occurrence of mutually beneficial cooperation seems possible. Three conditions principally determine whether the exercise of specific reciprocity leads to cooperation: the extent to which the players have interests in common, the "shadow of the future," and the number of players in any given game. In addition, international regimes may make specific reciprocity more effective by providing information to the players, reducing transaction costs, and limiting strategic options.[73]

Diffuse reciprocity, on the other hand, is only feasible when some norms of obligation exist: that is, when international regimes are relatively strong. These norms may express the actors' conceptions of their self-interest, but their conceptions of self-interest must be broad and their confidence in the good faith of others fairly great. An important contribution of the social exchange literature is the suggestion that the successful pursuit of specific reciprocity may lead to the development of diffuse reciprocity. In other words, repayment of political and economic debts in a strictly bilateral context may increase confidence, enabling actors to take a broader view of their common interests. Conversely, the decay of diffuse reciprocity may lead actors to revert to conditional exchanges on a quid pro quo basis. Thus specific and diffuse reciprocity are closely interrelated. They can be located on a continuum, although the relationships between them are as much dialectical as linear.

This discussion of specific and diffuse reciprocity points up the connections between international regimes and governments' interests. International regimes are fundamentally affected by state interest, but how governments define these interests is not self-evident. The institutions that link states together, and the forms of reciprocal behavior in which states engage, can affect the conceptions of self-interest that guide behavior.

Policy makers often try to combine specific and diffuse reciprocity in order to get the best of both worlds. Such attempts can create ambiguity and lead to further difficulty. Properly structured, however, institutions that embody combinations of the two forms of reciprocity can facilitate cooperation in world politics. International trade policy since World War II illustrates this point well.

Neither diffuse nor specific reciprocity has provided a fully satisfactory principle of behavior in international trade. Over the last forty years, governments of the major market-economy countries have responded accordingly by devising a new, intermediate form of reciprocity, institutionalized in the GATT. This hybrid invention is built on the principle of diffuse reciprocity: the adoption of unconditional MFN clauses means that each bilateral relationship need not be characterized by a balance of equivalent concessions. On the contrary, GATT relies on indefinite obligations and expectations of achieving a rough balance at a higher level of welfare for everyone.

As we have seen, however, simple adoption of unconditional MFN clauses would create serious free-rider problems. To forestall these problems, GATT first adopted the "principal supplier rule" as a supplement to unconditional MFN clauses. This rule provided that compensation for concessions on a given product was demanded from all countries supplying at least a certain proportion of the market. Thus only quite small suppliers (in the Dillon Round, 1960–62, only those with less than 10% of a market) could be free-riders.[74] Beginning with the Kennedy Round in the mid-1960s, and continuing with the Tokyo Round ending in 1979, negotiations on tariff-cutting formulas and exceptions to these formulas replaced item-by-item negotiations. The primary negotiations took place among the major trading powers in each round, but care was taken to extract concessions on a reciprocal basis from other countries before the signing of a final accord. As GATT ministers declared in preparing for the Kennedy Round, "in the trade negotiations it shall be open to each country to request additional trade concessions or to modify its own offers . . . to obtain a balance of advantages between it and the other participating countries."[75]

Thus the actual principles of contemporary "reciprocal trade" incorporate a compromise. The emphasis in tariff negotiations on formula reductions and negotiations among major trading countries, with these concessions generalized to other members of GATT, avoids the complex problem of attaining item-by-item reciprocity. Yet specific reciprocity still comes into play at the end of negotiations, as a way of forestalling the free-rider problem.

Specific reciprocity as applied in these multilateral trade negotiations differs in two important ways from the conditional MFN treatment employed by the United States in 1900: first, it is applied within the context of an international regime whose norms emphasize liberalization and nondiscrimination; and second, it is employed in simultaneous rather than sequential negotiations. Agreements do not unravel, because they are not made until the related pieces are in place; indeed, it is precisely the threat that everything will fall apart that propels participants toward last-minute concessions. At the same time diffuse reciprocity plays a greater role than before, based on a shared belief in the importance of the overall balance of concessions and the resultant effect on trade and welfare. Ultimately, neither specific nor diffuse reciprocity alone constitutes a satisfactory principle of action.

The successful synthesis of specific and diffuse reciprocity in the Kennedy and Tokyo rounds exemplifies the significance of institutional innovation in world politics. The forms of reciprocity adopted made a difference. As the social exchange literature suggests, sequences of action, both within negotiating rounds and between them, help to create obligations and solidify ties among the participants. Yet the resulting norms remain weak enough that specific reciprocity persists as an essential element of the tariff reduction process.

CONCLUSION

Specific reciprocity has much to commend it as a principle of action in international relations: it can permit cooperation to emerge in a situation of anarchy; it tends to deter defection; and it provides a standard of behavior—expressed well in Axelrod's Tit for Tat strategy—that bureaucrats and politicians can easily understand and explain. It may also create conditions for the growth of diffuse reciprocity.

Yet specific reciprocity is not a sure-fire recipe for promoting cooperation. It protects its users against exploitation by focusing responses on identifiable actors but thereby restricts the possible bargains that can be reached, makes multilateral negotiations extremely complex, and may provoke feuds even in bilateral relationships. Diffuse reciprocity, on the other hand, may reduce the chances of unnecessary conflict where interests are compatible but exposes its practitioners to the danger of exploitation.

Given that neither type of reciprocity is entirely satisfactory, it is not surprising that governments have sought to devise strategies for capitalizing on the benefits of each while compensating for their defects. Institutional innovations in trade are particularly interesting. Negotiations conducted on the basis of simultaneous specific reciprocity were embedded in a larger pattern of sequential trade negotiations. These negotiations were incorporated, in turn, in a set of norms and rules which emphasized diffuse reciprocity (unconditional MFN treatment). The effect was to encourage agreement by avoiding the perversities of sequential specific reciprocity, yet still limiting opportunities for exploitation.

We know that the anarchy of international politics is consistent with a wide range of conflict and cooperation. Without altering the basic structure of anarchy, governments can make the world safer, or more dangerous, through the strategies they follow. The feasibility of alternative strategies can be affected in turn by prevailing institutional arrangements, as embodied in international regimes. Thinking about reciprocity reminds us of the significance of the international regimes that provide the context for strategic interaction in much of contemporary world politics. To understand the conditions under which international cooperation can occur, we need to think further about strategies and institutions in world politics, and how they are linked.

ACKNOWLEDGMENTS

A much earlier version of this article was presented to a seminar at the University of Minnesota, 24 April 1984. I am grateful for comments on earlier versions and for citations to Robert J. Art, David Baldwin, John A. C. Conybeare, Peter Cowhey, Alexander L. George, Joanne Gowa, Joseph Grieco, Ernst B. Haas, Stanley Hoffmann, Peter J. Katzenstein, Charles P. Kindleberger, Deborah Larson, Helen Milner, Joseph S. Nye, Susan Moller Okin, Louis W. Pauly, Carolyn Rhodes-Jones, Howard Silverman, Raymond Vernon, and two anonymous referees for this journal.

NOTES

1. For discussions see Barry Buzan, *People, States, and Fear: The National Security Problem in International Relations* (Chapel Hill: University of North Carolina Press, 1983), especially chap. 3; Robert O. Keohane, *After Hegemony: Cooperation and Discord in the World Political Economy* (Princeton: Princeton University Press, 1984); and Kenneth Waltz, *Theory of World Politics* (Reading, Mass.: Addison-Wesley, 1979).

2. Elizabeth Zoller, *Peacetime Unilateral Remedies* (Dobbs Ferry, N.Y.: Transnational, 1984), p. 15.

3. Jock A. Finlayson and Mark Zacher, "The GATT and the Regulation of Trade Barriers: Regime Dynamics and Functions," in Stephen D. Krasner, ed., *International Regimes* (Ithaca: Cornell University Press), p. 286. The provisions of the General System of Preferences (GSP) make exceptions to this principle for developing countries, although the impact of the reciprocity norm is evident in debates about when certain newly industrializing countries should "graduate" to full reciprocal status.

4. Alexander L. George, "The Basic Principles Agreement of 1972: Origins and Expectations," in George, ed., *Managing U.S.-Soviet Rivalry: Problems of Crisis Prevention* (Boulder: Westview, 1983), p. 108.

5. Alexander L. George, "Political Crises," in Joseph S. Nye, ed., *The Making of America's Soviet Policy* (New Haven: Yale University Press for the Council on Foreign Relations, 1984), p. 155.

6. *New York Times*, 17 March 1984.

7. Robert Axelrod, *The Evolution of Cooperation* (New York: Basic, 1984), pp. 136–39.

8. Keohane, *After Hegemony*, p. 214.

9. Inis L. Claude, Jr., *Power and International Relations* (New York: Random House, 1962), p. 12. See also Ernst B. Haas, "The Balance of Power: Prescription, Concept or Propaganda?" *World Politics* 5 (July 1953).

10. Arnold Wolfers, "National Security as an Ambiguous Symbol," in Wolfers, *Discord and Collaboration: Essays on International Politics* (Baltimore: Johns Hopkins University Press, 1962), p. 147.

11. Jacob Viner, "The Most-Favored-Nation Clause," in Viner, *International Economics* (Glencoe, Ill.: Free, 1951), p. 103.

12. Lucy Brown, *The Board of Trade and the Free-Trade Movement, 1830–1842* (Oxford: Clarendon, 1958), p. 2; Robert Livingston Schuyler, *The Fall of the Old Colonial System: A Study in British Free Trade, 1770–1870* (London: Oxford University Press, 1945), pp. 114–15.

13. J. Laurence Laughlin and H. Parker Willis, *Reciprocity* (New York: Baker & Taylor, 1903), p. 7.

14. William S. Culbertson, *Reciprocity: A National Policy for Foreign Trade* (New York: McGraw-Hill, 1937), p. 159.

15. Keith J. Hay and B. Andrei Sulzenko, "U.S. Trade Policy and 'Reciprocity,'" *Journal of World Trade Law* 16 (November-December 1982), p. 472.

16. U.S. Senate, Committee on Finance, Subcommittee on International Trade, *Hearing on S. 144, The Reciprocal Trade and Investment Act of 1982*, 98th Cong., 1st sess. (4 March 1983). The statement of administration policy is on p. 19, the quotation from Senator Long on p. 33.

17. Bart S. Fisher and Ralph G. Steinhardt III, "Section 301 of the Trade Act of 1974: Protection for U.S. Exporters of Goods, Services and Capital," *Law and Policy in International Business* 14 (1982), p. 688.

18. William R. Cline, "'Reciprocity': A New Approach to World Trade Policy?" Institute for International Economics, Policy Analyses in International Economics no. 2 (Washington, September 1982), and R. J. Wonnacott, "Aggressive U.S. Reciprocity Evaluated with a New Analytical Approach to Trade Conflicts," Institute for Research on Public Policy, Essays in International Economics (Montreal, 1984).

19. My distinction between specific and diffuse reciprocity was suggested by Peter Blau's distinction between social and economic exchange. Social exchange involves somewhat indefinite, sequential exchanges within the context of a general pattern of obligation. In economic exchange, however, the benefits to be exchanged are precisely specified and no trust is required. The distinction between specific and diffuse reciprocity also bears some similarity to Marshall Sahlins's distinction between "balanced" and "generalized" reciprocity. Sahlins, however, views generalized exchange as "putatively altruistic." See Blau, *Exchange and Power in Social Life* (New York: Wiley, 1964), pp. 8, 93–97, and Sahlins, *Stone Age Economics* (Chicago: Aldine-Atherton, 1972), p. 194.

20. Alvin W. Gouldner, "The Norm of Reciprocity: A Preliminary Statement," *American Sociological Review* 25 (April 1960), p. 161.

21. Blau, *Exchange and Power in Social Life*, p. 6.

22. Marcel Mauss, *The Gift* (1925; reprint, New York: Norton, 1967), p. xiv.

23. Gouldner, "Norm of Reciprocity," p. 171. In the case of what I have called diffuse reciprocity, cooperation is contingent not on the behavior of particular individuals but on the continued successful functioning of the group.

24. Peter M. Blau, *On the Nature of Organizations* (New York: Wiley, 1974), pp. 208–9.

25. Marc Bloch, *Feudal Society* (1940; reprint, Chicago: University of Chicago Press, 1968). This quotation is from selections from *Feudal Society* in Steffen W. Schmidt et al., *Friends, Followers and Factions: A Reader in Political Clientelism* (Berkeley: University of California Press, 1977), p. 205. On patron-client relations see two other articles in the Schmidt volume: John Duncan Powell, "Peasant Society and Clientelist Politics," and James C. Scott, "Patron-Client Politics and Political Change in Southeast Asia." Imbalances in favor of the patron may be accounted for by the resources, sometimes including force, at the patron's disposal: that is, the patron's bargaining power may be greater than that of the client. Sometimes, however, the observable material flow of goods favors the client, which poses a potential paradox for exchange theory: why should a patron enter into an exchange relationship in which surrendered resources are greater in value than those received? Social exchange theory answers that the political deference of the client toward the patron balances the exchange. This deference may be used to extract resources indirectly, from the client and from other similarly placed people in the society, through the operation of the political system. Thus the eventual material rewards to the patron may be quite considerable. See George C. Homans, *Soical Behavior: Its Elementary Forms* (New York: Harcourt Brace & World, 1961), and Blau, *Exchange and Power in Social Life.*

26. Barrington Moore, Jr., *Injustice: The Social Bases of Obedience and Revolt* (White Plains, N.Y.: Sharpe, 1978), p. 509.

27. Axelrod, *Evolution of Cooperation*, p. 137, and Arthur Dunkel, "GATT: Its Evolution and Role in the 1980s," Li and Fung Lecture, Chinese University of Hong Kong, 23 March 1984, mimeo (Geneva: GATT), p. 6.

28. Richard Blackhurst, "Reciprocity in Trade Negotiations under Flexible Exchange Rates," in John P. Martin and Alasdair Smith, eds., *Trade and Payments Adjustment Under Flexible Exchange Rates* (London: Macmillan for the Trade Policy Research Centre, 1979), quotation on p. 215, discussion of reciprocal concessions on p. 225.

On the latter see also Finlayson and Zacher, "GATT and the Regulation of Trade Barriers," p. 286. A related article that helped stimulate my thinking on this subject is Frieder Roessler, "The Rationale for Reciprocity in Trade Negotiations under Floating Currencies," *Kyklos* 31, 2 (1978), pp. 258–74.

29. Zoller, *Peacetime Unilateral Remedies*, p. 20.

30. If C represents a cooperative move and D an uncooperative "defection," the order of preferences for player A is as follows, listing A's move first: DC>CC>DD>CD. For a detailed account see Axelrod, *Evolution of Cooperation*, or the special issue of *World Politics* 38 (October 1985).

31. Michael Taylor, *Anarchy and Cooperation* (New York: Wiley, 1976). As Axelrod points out, it has long been argued in the game-theoretic literature that in Prisoner's Dilemma with a finite number of plays, a rational player will defect continually: "On the next-to-last move neither player will have an incentive to cooperate since they can both anticipate a defection by the other player on the very last move. Such a line of reasoning implies that the game will unravel all the way back to mutual defection on the first move of any sequence of plays that is of known finite length" (*Evolution of Cooperation*, p. 10). However, this finding is highly sensitive to the assumption of perfect information embedded in it. In finite Prisoner's Dilemma even a small amount of uncertainty involving asymmetrical information can make it rational to follow a strategy of reciprocity, which yields higher payoffs than the "rational" strategy of defection under perfect information. A certain amount of ignorance is indeed bliss! See D. Kreps and R. Wilson, "Rational Cooperation in the Finitely Repeated Prisoners' Dilemma," *Journal of Economic Theory* 27 (1982), pp. 245–52, and other articles in the same issue.

32. On Prisoner's Dilemma see Stuart Oskamp, "Effects of Programmed Strategies on Cooperation in the Prisoner's Dilemma and Other Mixed-Motive Games," *Journal of Conflict Resolution* 15 (June 1971), pp. 225–59; Warner Wilson, "Reciprocation and Other Techniques for Inducing Cooperation in the Prisoner's Dilemma Game," ibid., pp. 167–95; and Hayward R. Alker, Jr., and Rober Hurwitz, *Resolving Prisoner's Dilemma* (Teaching Module) (Washington, D.C.: APSA, 1981).

33. For some experimental evidence about the effects of reciprocity in a bargaining game that is quite different from Prisoner's Dilemma, see James K. Esser and S. S. Komorita, "Reciprocity and Concession Making in Bargaining," *Journal of Personality and Social Psychology* 31, 5 (1975), pp. 864–72; and S. S. Komorita and James K. Esser, "Frequency of Reciprocated Concessions in Bargaining," *Journal of Personality and Social Psychology* 32, 4 (1975), pp. 699–705. See also Robert Axelrod and Robert O. Keohane, "Achieving Cooperation under Anarchy: Strategies and Institutions," *World Politics* 38 (October 1985).

34. Axelrod, *Evolution of Cooperation*, p. 138. Reciprocity may be regarded as morally wrong even when it could be expected to lead to an agreement rather than to a feud. For instance, many ethical doctrines would consider it wrong for the United States to have seized innocent Shiite Moslem hostages in retaliation for the Shiite hijacking of a TWA airliner in June 1985. When adversaries hold themselves to very different ethical standards, one side may be unwilling to behave as the other does, making reciprocity unattainable.

35. John W. Evans, *The Kennedy Round in American Trade Policy: The Twilight of the GATT?* (Cambridge: Harvard University Press, 1971), pp. 31–32. On problems of biased equivalence in implementing "aggresssive reciprocity," see Wonnacott, "Aggressive U.S. Reciprocity," especially pp. 11–12.

36. George Breslauer, "Why Detente Failed: An Interpretation," in George, ed., *Managing U.S.-Soviet Rivalry*, pp. 319–40. The quotations appear on pp. 321, 327,

334, and 335, respectively. Without focusing on reciprocity per se, Stanley Hoffmann also emphasizes the overambitiouness of American's détente policy—its lack of "modesty"—as a key reason for its failure. See Hoffmann, "Detente," in Nye, ed., *The Making of America's Soviet Policy,* p. 259.

37. Axelrod, *Evolution of Cooperation,* p. 138.

38. This constitutes what Axelrod and I in "Achieving Cooperation under Anarchy" call the "sanctioning problem."

39. See Keohane, *After Hegemony,* chap. 3; Bruce M. Russett, "The Mysterious Case of Vanishing Hegemony: or, Is Mark Twain Really Dead?" *International Organization* 39 (Spring 1985), pp. 207–32; and the special issue of *World Politics* 38 (October 1985) on cooperation under anarchy. In the last see especially the contributions by Kenneth Oye, who developed the concept of privatization, and Charles Lipson's "Bankers' Dilemmas," which discusses the breakdown of large groups.

40. Brown, *Board of Trade,* pp. 116–17.

41. Schuyler, *Fall of the Old Colonial System,* p. 119.

42. Brown, *Board of Trade,* pp. 123, 138–39.

43. Ibid., chap. 12.

44. Arthur A. Stein, "Coordination and Collaboration: Regimes in an Anarchic World," in Krasner, ed., *International Regimes,* p. 130. See also Stein, "The Hegemon's Dilemma: Great Britain, the United States, and the International Economic Order," *International Organization* 38 (Spring 1984), p. 130.

45. Brown, *Board of Trade,* p. 206.

46. Quoted in Albert Imlah, *Economic Elements in the Pax Brittanica* (New York: Russell & Russell, 1958), pp. 14–15. The director-general of the GATT expressed the same sentiment 135 years later. He argued that the search for reciprocity "now threatens to set back the process [of trade liberalization]." In his view, "it makes no economic sense for [a country involved in world trade] to react to barriers in its export markets by imposing on itself the additional burden of inefficiency and price distortion." Yet what does not make economic sense may be prudent politically: "It may pay to postpone one's liberalization if other countries can thus be induced to bring forward their own." See Dunkel, "GATT: Its Evolution and Role," p. 7.

47. Frank W. Taussig, *The Tariff History of the United States,* 8th ed. (New York: Putnam, 1931), pp. 279 and 353.

48. David A. Lake, "Structure and Strategy: The International Sources of American Trade Policy, 1887–1939" (Ph.D. diss., Cornell University, 1983), pp. 3–19.

49. Francis Bowes Sayre, *The Way Forward: The American Trade Agreements Program* (New York: Macmillan, 1939), p. 50.

50. Henry J. Tasca, *The Reciprocal Trade Policy of the United States: A Study in Trade Philosophy* (Philadelphia: University of Pennsylvania Press, 1938), p. 102.

51. Viner, "Most-Favored-Nation Clause," p. 104.

52. Ibid., p. 105.

53. Adam Smith, *An Inquiry into the Nature and Causes of the Wealth of Nations* (1776; reprint, Chicago: University of Chicago Press, 1976), 1:518. This passage appears in bk. 4, chap. 3, pt. 2.

54. Sayre, *Way Forward,* p. 108; Culbertson, *Reciprocity,* p. 246; Sayre, *Way Forward,* p. 109.

55. Sayre, *Way Forward,* p. 109; Culbertson, *Reciprocity,* p. 249.

56. Evans, *Kennedy Round,* p. 275.

57. Gary Clyde Hufbauer and Joanna Shelton Erb, *Subsidies in International Trade* (Washington: Institute for International Economics, 1984), pp. 120–23.

58. R. M. Peccioli, *The Internationalization of Banking: The Policy Issues* (Paris: OECD, 1983), p. 78.

59. Robert Sugden, "Reciprocity: The Supply of Public Goods through Voluntary Contributions," *Economic Journal* 94 (December 1984), pp. 775 and 776.

60. Nevertheless, what I have elsewhere called "empathetic interdependence" should not be excluded a priori as irrelevant to world politics. See Keohane, *After Hegemony,* pp. 123ff.

61. Charles E. Lindblom, *The Intelligence of Democracy* (New York: Free, 1965), p. 63.

62. Moore, *Injustice,* p. 506; Gouldner, "Norm of Reciprocity," 169–71.

63. Blau defines norms as involving not merely standards of behavior but moral codes that supersede self-interest. He therefore refuses to associate reciprocity with norms, on the ground that this would make reciprocity inconsistent with self-interest. Like Blau, I think that a valuable conception of reciprocity must be consistent with self-interested practice; but since obligations may be undertaken by egoists, it seems clearest to define norms as standards of behavior to some of which even egoists could conform. See Keohane, *After Hegemony,* p. 57.

64. Roger D. Masters, "World Politics as a Primitive International System," *World Politics* 16 (July 1964), pp. 595–619.

65. The quotations are, respectively, from Blau, *Exchange and Power in Social Life,* p. 92; Gouldner, "Norm of Reciprocity," p. 175; and Blau, *Exchange and Power,* p. 94. In some cases, of course, reciprocity may reflect solidaristic social norms. Edward Schlieffen, for instance, accounts for reciprocity among the Kaluli, a New Guinea tribe with about 1,200 members, by pointing out that for this tribe reciprocity embodies a "socially shared sense of proportion, an ideology and a set of assumptions and expectations which form the basis upon which Kaluli approach and deal with many kinds of situations, both inside and outside the context of exchange." See Schlieffen, "Reciprocity and the Construction of Reality," *Man* 15 (September 1980), pp. 502–17.

66. Sahlins, *Stone Age Economics,* p. 201; Gouldner, "Norm of Reciprocity," p. 175, his emphases.

67. Ernst B. Haas, *The Uniting of Europe: Political, Social and Economic Forces, 1950–57* (Stanford: Stanford University Press, 1958).

68. Robert O. Keohane, "The Demand for International Regimes," in Krasner, *International Regimes,* p. 158.

69. Ernst Haas, personal communication.

70. This, of course, is similar to the situation faced by major trading partners of the United States before 1923, as described above, insofar as they had made commercial agreements with the United States.

71. Viner, "Most-Favored-Nation Clause," p. 107.

72. Blackhurst, "Reciprocity," p. 231.

73. These three dimensions of situations, which affect cooperation, are discussed by Kenneth Oye and others in the special issue of *World Politics* 38 (October 1985). Keohane, *After Hegemony,* discusses how regimes facilitiate cooperation.

74. Blackhurst, "Reciprocity," p. 224.

75. Evans, *Kennedy Round,* p. 185.

CHAPTER 7

International Institutions:
Two Approaches

Contemporary world politics is a matter of wealth and poverty, life and death. [The members of the International Studies Association] have chosen to study it because it is so important to our lives and those of other people—not because it is either aesthetically attractive or amenable to successful theory-formulation and testing. Indeed, we would be foolish if we studied world politics in search of beauty or lasting truth. Beauty is absent because much that we observe is horrible, and many of the issues that we study involve dilemmas whose contemplation no sane person would find pleasing. Deterministic laws elude us, since we are studying the purposive behavior of relatively small numbers of actors engaged in strategic bargaining. In situations involving strategic bargaining, even formal theories, with highly restrictive assumptions, fail to specify which of many possible equilibrium outcomes will emerge (Kreps, 1984:16). This suggests that no general theory of international politics may be feasible. It makes sense to seek to develop cumulative verifiable knowledge, but we must understand that we can aspire only to formulate conditional, context-specific generalizations rather than to discover universal laws, and that our understanding of world politics will always be incomplete.

The ways in which members of this Association study international relations are profoundly affected by their values. Most of us are children of the Enlightenment, insofar as we believe that human life can be improved through human action guided by knowledge. We therefore seek knowledge in order to improve the quality of human action. Many of us, myself included, begin with a commitment to promote human progress, defined in terms of the welfare, liberty, and security of individuals, with special attention to principles of justice (Haas, 1986; Rawls, 1971). With this commitment in mind, we seek to analyze how the legal concept of state sovereignty and the practical fact of substantial state autonomy coexist with the realities of strategic and economic interdependence.

Robert O. Keohane [was] President of the International Studies Association, 1988–89. This article is an edited version of his presidential address, delivered at the 29th Annual Convention of the International Studies Association, St. Louis, Missouri, March 31, 1988.

These value commitments help to account for the topic of this essay: the study of international institutions. I focus on institutions because I share K. J. Holsti's desire to "open intellectual doors to peer in on international collaboration, cooperation, and welfare" (Holsti, 1986:356). To understand the conditions under which international cooperation can take place, it is necessary to understand how international institutions operate and the conditions under which they come into being. This is not to say that international institutions always facilitate cooperation on a global basis: on the contrary, a variety of international institutions, including most obviously military alliances, are designed as means for prevailing in military and political conflict. Conversely, instances of cooperation can take place with only minimal institutional structures to support them. But all efforts at international cooperation take place within an institutional context of some kind, which may or may not facilitate cooperative endeavors. To understand cooperation and discord better, we need to investigate the sources and nature of international institutions, and how institutional change takes place.

"Cooperation" is a contested term. As I use it, it is sharply distinguished from both harmony and discord. When harmony prevails, actors' policies *automatically* facilitate the attainment of others' goals. When there is discord, actors' policies hinder the realization of others' goals, and are not adjusted to make them more compatible. In both harmony and discord, neither actor has an incentive to change his or her behavior. Cooperation, however, "requires that the actions of separate individuals or organizations—which are not in pre-existent harmony—be brought into conformity with one another through a process of policy coordination" (Keohane, 1984:51). This means that when cooperation takes place, each party changes his or her behavior *contingent* on changes in the other's behavior. We can evaluate the impact of cooperation by measuring the difference between the actual outcome and the situation that would have obtained in the absence of coordination: that is, the myopic self-enforcing equilibrium of the game. Genuine cooperation improves the rewards of both players.

International cooperation does not necessarily depend on altruism, idealism, personal honor, common purposes, internalized norms, or a shared belief in a set of values embedded in a culture. At various times and places any of these features of human motivation may indeed play an important role in processes of international cooperation; but cooperation can be understood without reference to any of them. This is not surprising, since international cooperation is not necessarily benign from an ethical standpoint. Rich countries can devise joint actions to extract resources from poor ones, predatory governments can form aggressive alliances, and privileged industries can induce their governments to protect them against competition from more efficient producers abroad. The analysis of international cooperation should not be confused with its celebration. As Hedley Bull said about order, "while order in world politics is something valuable, . . . it should not be taken to be a commanding value, and to show that a particular institution or course of action is conducive of order is not to have established a presumption that that institution is desirable or that that course of action should be carried out" (Bull, 1977:98).

Cooperation is in a dialectical relationship with discord, and they must be understood together. Thus to understand cooperation, one must also understand the frequent absence of, or failure of, cooperation, so incessantly stressed by realist writers. But our awareness of cooperation's fragility does not require us to accept dogmatic forms of realism, which see international relations as inherently doomed to persistent zero-sum conflict and warfare. As Stanley Hoffmann has put it, realism "does not, and cannot, prove that one is doomed to repeat the past and that there is no middle ground, however narrow, between the limited and fragile moderation of the past and the impossible abolition of the game" (Hoffmann, 1987:74).

Realist and neorealist theories are avowedly rationalistic, accepting what Herbert Simon has referred to as a "substantive" conception of rationality, characterizing "behavior that can be adjudged objectively to be optimally adapted to the situation" (Simon, 1985:294). But adopting the assumption of substantive rationality does not commit the analyst to gloomy deterministic conclusions about the inevitability of warfare. On the contrary, rationalistic theory can be used to explore the conditions under which cooperation takes place, and it seeks to explain why international institutions are constructed by states (Axelrod, 1984; Keohane, 1984; Oye, 1986).

That rationalistic theory can lead to many different conclusions in international relations reflects a wider indeterminacy of the rationality principle as such. As Simon has argued, the principle of substantive rationality generates hypotheses about actual human behavior only when it is combined with auxiliary assumptions about the structure of utility functions and the formation of expectations. Furthermore, rationality is always contextual, so a great deal depends on the situation posited at the beginning of the analysis. Considerable variation in outcomes is therefore consistent with the assumption of substantive rationality. When limitations on the cognitive capacities of decision-makers are also taken into account—as in the concept of bounded rationality—the range of possible variation expands even further.

Even though the assumption of substantive rationality does not compel a particular set of conclusions about the nature or evolution of international institutions, it has been used in fruitful ways to explain behavior, including institutionalized behavior, in international relations. Its adherents are often highly self-conscious about their analytical perspective, and they have been highly successful in gaining legitimacy for their arguments.

Traditionally counterposed to rationalistic theory is the sociological approach to the study of institutions, which stresses the role of impersonal social forces as well as the impact of cultural practices, norms, and values that are not derived from calculations of interests (Barry, 1970; Gilpin, 1981). Yet the sociological approach has recently been in some disarray, at least in international relations: its adherents have neither the coherence nor the self-confidence of the rationalists. Rather than try in this essay to discuss this diffuse set of views about international relations, I will focus on the work of several scholars with a distinctive and similar point of view who have recently directly challenged the predominant rationalistic analysis of international politics. These authors, of whom the best-known include Hayward Alker, Richard Ashley, Friedrich Kratochwil, and John Ruggie, emphasize the importance of the "intersubjective meanings" of international institutional activity (Kratochwil and Ruggie, 1986:765). In their view, understanding how people think about institutional norms and rules, and the discourse they engage in, is as important in evaluating the significance of these norms as measuring the behavior that changes in response to their invocation.

These writers emphasize that individuals, local organizations, and even states develop within the context of more encompassing institutions. Institutions do not merely reflect the preferences and power of the units constituting them; the institutions themselves shape those preferences and that power. Institutions are therefore *constitutive* of actors as well as vice versa. It is not sufficient in this view to treat the preferences of individuals as given exogenously: they are affected by institutional arrangements, by prevailing norms, and by historically contingent discourse among people seeking to pursue their purposes and solve their self-defined problems.

In order to emphasize the importance of this perspective, and to focus a dialogue with rationalistic theory, I will treat the writers on world politics who have stressed these themes as members of a school of thought. I recognize, of course, that regarding them as members of a group or school obscures the many differences of view among them, and the substantial evolution that has taken place in the thought of each of them. Yet to make my point, I will even give them a label. In choosing such a label, it would be fair to refer to them as "interpretive" scholars, since they all emphasize the importance of historical and textual interpretation and the limitations of scientific models in studying world politics. But other approaches, such as strongly materialist historical-sociological approaches indebted to Marxism, or political-theoretical arguments emphasizing classical political philosophy or international law, also have a right to be considered interpretive. I have therefore coined a phrase for these writers, calling them "reflective," since all of them emphasize the importance of human reflection for the nature of institutions and ultimately for the character of world politics.

My chief argument in this essay is that students of international institutions should direct their attention to the relative merits of two approaches, the rationalistic and the reflective. Until we understand the strengths and weaknesses of each, we will be unable to design research strategies that are sufficiently multifaceted to encompass our subject-matter, and our empirical work will suffer accordingly.

The next section of this essay will define what I mean by "institutions," and introduce some distinctions that I hope will help us to understand international institutions better. Defining institutions entails drawing a distinction between specific institutions and the underlying practices within which they are embedded, of which the most fundamental in world politics are those associated with the concept of sovereignty. I will then attempt to evaluate the strengths and weaknesses of the rationalistic approach, taking into account the criticisms put forward by scholars who emphasize how actors are constituted by institutions and how subjective self-awareness of actors, and the ideas at their disposal, shape their activities. Throughout the essay I will emphasize the critical importance, for the further advance of knowledge, of undertaking empirical research, guided by these theoretical ideas. It will not be fruitful, in my view, indefinitely to conduct a debate at the purely theoretical level, much less simply to argue about epistemological and ontological issues in the abstract. Such an argument would take us away from the study of our subject matter, world politics, toward what would probably become an intellectually derivative and programmatically diversionary philosophical discussion.

INTERNATIONAL INSTITUTIONS:
DEFINITIONS AND DISTINCTIONS

"Institution" is an even fuzzier concept than cooperation. Institutions are often discussed without being defined at all, or after having been defined only casually. Yet it sometimes seems, as a sociologist lamented half a century ago, that "the only idea common to all usages of the term 'institution' is that of some sort of establishment of relative permanence of a distinctly social sort" (Hughes, 1936:180, quoted in Zucker, 1977:726). In the international relations literature, this vagueness persists. We speak of the United Nations and the World Bank (part of the "United Nations System"), IBM and Exxon, as institutions; but we also consider "the international monetary regime" and "the international trade regime" to be institutions. Hedley Bull refers to "the balance of power, international law, the diplomatic mechanism, the managerial system of the great powers, and war" as "the institutions of international society" (Bull, 1977:74).[1] John Ruggie discusses "the institutional framework of sovereignty" (Ruggie, 1986:147), and Stephen Krasner writes about "the particular institutional structures of sovereignty" (Krasner, 1987:11).

It may help in sorting out some of these troubling confusions to point out that "institution" may refer to a *general pattern* or *categorization* of activity or to a *particular* human-constructed arrangement, formally or informally organized. Examples of institutions as general patterns include Bull's "institutions of international society," as well as such varied patterns of behavior as marriage and religion, sovereign statehood, diplomacy, and neutrality. Sometimes norms such as that of reciprocity, which can apply to a variety of situations, are referred to as institutions. When we speak of patterns or categorizations of activity as institutions, the particular instances are often not regarded themselves as institutions: we do not speak of the marriage of the Duke and Duchess of Windsor, international negotiations over the status of the Panama Canal, or the neutrality of Sweden in World War II as institutions. What these general patterns of activity have in common with specific institutions is that they both meet the criteria for a broad definition of institutions: both involve persistent and connected sets of rules (formal or informal) that prescribe behavioral roles, constrain activity, and shape expectations.

Specific institutions, such as the French state, the Roman Catholic church, the international nonproliferation regime, or the General Agreement on Tariffs and Trade, are discrete entities, identifiable in space and time. Specific institutions may be exemplars of general patterns of activity—the United Nations exemplifies multilateral diplomacy; the French state, sovereign statehood; the Roman Catholic church, organized religion. But unlike general patterns of activity, specific institutions have unique life-histories, which depend on the decisions of particular individuals.

General patterns of "institutionalized" activity are more heterogeneous. Some of these institutions are only sets of entities, with each member of the set being an institution. Bull's institution of international law, for instance, can be seen as including a variety of institutions codified in legal form. In this sense, all formal international regimes are parts of international law, as are formal bilateral treaties and conventions. Likewise, the institution of religion includes a variety of quite different specific institutions, including the Roman Catholic church, Islam, and Congregationalism. Other general patterns of activity can be seen as norms that are applicable to a wide variety of situations, such as the norm of reciprocity (Keohane, 1986b).

It is difficult to work analytically with the broad ordinary-language definition of institutions with which I have started, since it includes such a variety of different entities and activities. In the rest of this essay, therefore, I will focus on institutions that can be identified as related complexes of rules and norms, identifiable in space and time. This conception of the scope of my analytical enterprise deliberately omits institutions that are merely categories of activity, as well as general norms that can be attached to any of a number of rule-complexes. It allows me to focus on *specific institutions* and on *practices*. As explained below, it is the mark of a practice that the behavior of those engaged in it can be corrected by an appeal to its own rules. This means that practices are deeply embedded—highly institutionalized in the sociological sense of being taken for granted by participants as social facts that are not to be challenged although their implications for behavior can be explicated.

Specific institutions can be defined in terms of their rules. Douglass North (1987:6) defines institutions as "rules, enforcement characteristics of rules, and norms of behavior that structure repeated human interaction." Institutions can be seen as "frozen decisions," or "history encoded into rules" (March and Olson, 1984:741). These rules may be informal or implicit rather than codified: in fact, some very strong institutions, such as the British constitution, rely principally on unwritten rules. To be institutionalized in the sense in which I will use the term, the rules must be durable, and must prescribe behavioral roles for actors, besides constraining activity and shaping expectations. That is, institutions differentiate among actors according to the roles that they are expected to perform, and institutions can be identified by asking whether patterns of behavior are indeed differentiated by role. When we ask whether X is an institution, we ask whether we can identify persistent sets of rules that constrain activity, shape expectations, and prescribe roles. In international relations, some of these institutions are formal organizations, with prescribed hierarchies and the capacity for purposive action. Others, such as the international regimes for money and trade, are complexes of rules and organizations, the core elements of which have been negotiated and explicitly agreed upon by states.[2]

This definition of specific institutions incorporates what John Rawls has called the "summary view" of rules, in which "rules are pictured as summaries of past decisions," which allow the observer to predict future behavior (Rawls, 1955:19). Rules such as these can be changed by participants on utilitarian grounds without engaging in self-contradictory behavior. This definition is useful as far as it goes, but it does not capture what Rawls calls "the practice conception" of rules. A practice in the sense used by Rawls is analogous to a game such as baseball or chess: "It is the mark of a practice that being taught how to engage in it involves being instructed in the rules that define it, and that appeal is made to those rules to correct the behavior of those engaged in it. Those engaged in a practice recognize the rules as defining it" (Rawls, 1955:24). Were the rules of a practice to change, so would the fundamental nature of the activity in question.

Someone engaged in a practice has to explain her action by showing that it is in accord with the practice. Otherwise, the behavior itself is self-contradictory. As Oran Young points out, "It just does not make sense for a chess player to refuse to accept the concept of checkmate, for a speaker of English to assert that it makes no difference whether subjects and predicates agree, or for an actor in the existing international society to disregard the rules regarding the nationality of citizens." In international relations, the "menu of available practices" is limited: "a 'new' state, for example, has little choice but to join the basic institutional arrangements of the states system" (1986:120).[3]

The concept of a practice is particularly applicable to certain general patterns of activity such as sovereignty and multilateral diplomacy. Their rules, many of which are not codified, define what it means to be sovereign or to engage in multilateral diplomacy.[4] Like the rules of chess and the grammar of the English language, respect for state sovereignty and multilateral diplomacy are taken for granted by most of those who participate in them. When fundamental practices are violated, as in the seizure of the American Embassy in Teheran in 1979, disapproval is virtually universal. This is not surprising, because such practices are based on what Hans J. Morgenthau referred to as "the permanent interests of states to put their normal relations on a stable basis by providing for predictable and enforceable conduct with respect to these relations" (Morgenthau, 1940:279).[5]

Rawls's distinction helps us to see the specific institutions of world politics, with their challengeable rules, as embedded in more fundamental practices.

Just as the actors in world politics are constrained by existing institutions, so are institutions, and prospects for institutional change, constrained by the practices taken for granted by their members. For each set of entities that we investigate, we can identify institutionalized constraints at a more fundamental and enduring level.

Consider, for instance, the practice of sovereign statehood, which has been fundamental to world politics for over three hundred years. At its core is the principle of sovereignty: that the state "is subject to no other state and has full and exclusive powers within its jurisdiction without prejudice to the limits set by applicable law" (*Wimbledon* case, Permanent Court of International Justice, series A, no. 1, 1923; cited in Hoffmann, 1987:172–73). Sovereignty is thus a relatively precise legal concept: a question of law, not of fact, of authority, not sheer power. As a legal concept, the principle of sovereignty should not be confused with the empirical claim that a given state in fact makes its decisions autonomously. Sovereignty refers to a legal status, a property of an organized entity in world politics. It does not imply that the sovereign entity possesses de facto independence, although as a political matter, the fact that an entity is sovereign can be expected to have implications for its power and its autonomy.[6]

Sovereign statehood is a practice in Rawls's sense because it contains a set of rules that define it and that can be used to correct states' behavior. These rules are fundamental to the conduct of modern international relations. Extraterritorial jurisdiction for embassies is such a central rule, implied by the modern conception of sovereignty; immunity from ordinary criminal prosecution for a state's accredited diplomats is a corollary of this principle. More generally, as Martin Wight has argued, the norm of reciprocity is implied by that of sovereignty, and respect for reciprocity is therefore part of the practice of sovereign statehood: "It would be impossible to have a society of sovereign states unless each state, while claiming sovereignty for itself, recognized that every other state had the right to claim and enjoy its own sovereignty as well. This reciprocity was inherent in the Western conception of sovereignty" (Wight, 1977:135).

Treating sovereign statehood as a practice does not imply that the process of recognizing entities as sovereign is automatic: on the contrary, states follow political convenience as well as law in deciding which entities to regard as sovereign. But once an entity has been generally accepted by states as sovereign, certain rights and responsibilities are entailed. Furthermore, acceptance of the principle of sovereignty creates well-defined roles. Only sovereign states or entities such as international organizations created by states can make treaties and enforce them on subjects within their jurisdictions, declare and wage wars recognized by international law, and join international organizations that are part of the United Nations System.

Definitions are not interesting in themselves, but they may be more or less clear, and lead to the identification of more or less tractable problems. I have begun with a broad definition of institutions as persistent and connected sets of rules that prescribe behavioral roles, constrain activity, and shape expectations. I have focused my attention, however, on specific institutions and practices. Specific institutions can be defined in the first instance in terms of rules; but we must recognize that specific institutions are embedded in practices. In modern world politics, the most important practice is that of sovereignty. To understand institutions and institutional change in world politics, it is necessary to understand not only how specific institutions are formulated, change, and die, but how their evolution is affected by the practice of sovereignty.

THE RATIONALISTIC STUDY
OF INTERNATIONAL INSTITUTIONS

Rationalistic research on international institutions focuses almost entirely on specific institutions. It emphasizes international regimes and formal international organizations. Since this research program is rooted in exchange theory, it assumes scarcity and competition as well as rationality on the part of the actors. It therefore begins with the premise that if there were no potential gains from agreements to be captured in world politics—that is, if no agreements among actors could be mutually beneficial—there would be no need for specific international institutions. But there are evidently considerable benefits to be secured from mutual agreement—as evidenced for millenia by trade agreements, rules of war, and peace treaties, and for the last century by international organizations. Conversely, if cooperation were easy—that is, if all mutually beneficial bargains could be made without cost—there would be no need for institutions to facilitate cooperation. Yet such an assumption would be equally as false as the assumption that no potential gains from agreements exist. it is the combination of the potential *value* of agreements and the *difficulty* of making them that renders international regimes significant. In order to cooperate in world politics on more than a sporadic basis, human beings have to use institutions.

Rationalistic theories of institutions view institutions as affecting patterns of costs. Specifically, institutions reduce certain forms of uncertainty and alter transaction costs: that is, the "costs of specifying and enforcing the contracts that underlie exchange" (North, 1984:256). Even in the absence of hierarchical authority, institutions provide information (through monitoring) and stabilize expectations. They may also make decentralized enforcement feasible, for example by creating conditions under which reciprocity can operate (North, 1981; Williamson, 1981, 1985; Keohane, 1984; Moe, 1987). At any point in time, transaction costs are to a substantial degree the result of the institutional context. Dynamically, the relationship between these institutionally affected transaction costs and the formation of new institutions will, according to the theory, be curvilinear. If transaction costs are negligible, it will not be necessary to create new institutions to facilitate mutually beneficial exchange; if transaction costs are extremely high, it will not be feasible to build institutions—which may even be unimaginable.

In world politics, sovereignty and state autonomy mean that transaction costs are never negligible, since it is always difficult to communicate, to monitor performance, and especially to enforce compliance with rules. Therefore, according to this theory, one should expect international institutions to appear whenever the costs of communication, monitoring, and enforcement are relatively low compared to the benefits to be derived from political exchange. Institutions should persist as long as, but only so long as, their members have incentives to maintain them. But the effects of these institutions will not be politically neutral: they can be expected to confer advantages on those to whom their rules grant access and a share in political authority; and insofar as the transaction costs of making agreements outside of an established institution are high, governments disadvantaged within an institution will find themselves at a disadvantage in the issue area as a whole. More generally, the rules of any institution will reflect the relative power positions of its actual and potential members, which constrain the feasible bargaining space and affect transaction costs.[7]

These transaction-cost arguments have been applied in qualitative terms to international relations. As anticipated by the theory, effective international regimes include arrangements to share information and to monitor compliance, according to standards established by the regime; and they adapt to shifts in capabilities among their members (Finlayson and Zacher, 1983; Keohane, 1984: chapter 10; Aggarwal, 1985; Lipson, 1986; Haggard and Simmons, 1987). Furthermore, the access rules of different international regimes affect the success of governments in the related issue areas (Krasner, 1985:123). As a general descriptive model, therefore, this approach seems to do quite well: international regimes work as we expect them to.

However, the rationalistic theory has not been used to explain why international institutions exist in some issue areas rather than in others. Nor has this theory been employed systematically to account for the creation or demise of such institutions. Yet the theory implies hypotheses about these questions: hypotheses that could be submitted to systematic, even quantitative, examination. For instance, this theory predicts that the incidence of specific international institutions should be related to the ratio of benefits anticipated from exchange to the transaction costs of establishing the institutions necessary to facilitate the negotiation, monitoring, and enforcement costs of agreements specifying the terms of exchange. It also predicts that in the absence of anticipated gains from agreements, specific institutions will not be created, and that most specific institutions in world politics will in fact perform the function of reducing transaction costs. Since the theory acknowledges the significance of sunk costs in perpetuating extant institutions, and since its advocates recognize that organizational processes modify the pure dictates of rationality (Keohane, 1984:chapter 7), its predictions about the demise of specific institutions are less clear.

The rationalistic theory could also help us develop a theory of compliance or noncompliance with commitments.[8] For international regimes to be effective, their injunctions must be obeyed; yet sovereignty precludes hierarchical enforcement. The game-theoretic literature suggests that reputation may provide a strong incentive for compliance (Kreps and Wilson, 1982).

But we do not know how strong the reputational basis for enforcement of agreements is in world politics, since we have not done the necessary empirical work. What Oliver Williamson calls "opportunism" is still possible: reputations can be differentiated among partners and violations of agreements can often be concealed. Historically, it is not entirely clear to what extent governments that renege on their commitments are in fact punished for such actions. Indeed, governments that have defaulted on their debts have, it appears, not been punished via higher interest rates in subsequent periods for their defections (Eichengreen, 1987; Lindert and Morton, 1987).

Rationalistic theory can often help us understand the direction of change in world politics, if not always its precise extent or the form that it takes. For instance, there are good reasons to believe that a diffusion of power away from a hegemonic state, which sponsored extant international regimes, will create pressures on these regimes and weaken their rules—even though it is dubious that hegemony is either a necessary or a sufficient condition for the maintenance of a pattern of order in international relations (Keohane, 1984). That is, if we are able to specify the characteristics of a given institutional situation, rationalistic theory may help us anticipate the path that change will take. As Alexander Wendt points out, rationalistic theory has "proved useful in generating insights into the emergence of and re-production of social institutions as the unintended consequences of strategic interactions" (Wendt, 1987:368).

Yet even on its own terms, rationalistic theory encounters some inherent limitations. The so-called Folk Theorem of game theory states that for a class of games that includes 2×2 repeated Prisoner's Dilemma, there are many feasible equilibria above the maximin points of both players (Kreps, 1984:16). We cannot predict which one will emerge without knowing more about the structure of a situation—that is, about the prior institutional context in which the situation is embedded. This means that the conclusions of formal models of cooperation are often highly dependent on the as-sumptions with which the investigations begin—that they are context-dependent. To be sure, once we understand the context, it may be possible to model strategies used by players to devise equilibrium-inducing institutions (Shepsle, 1986). The literatures on bureaucratic politics and agency theory complicate matters further by suggesting that the organizational "actor" will not necessarily act as "its" interests specify, if people within it have different interests (Moe, 1984; Arrow, 1985). Thus even on its own terms rationalistic theory seems to leave open the issue of what kinds of institutions will develop, to whose benefit, and how effective they will be.

Even within the confines of the rationalistic research program, therefore, formal theory alone is unlikely to yield answers to our explanatory puzzles. Rationalistic theory is good at posing questions and suggesting lines of inquiry, but it does not furnish us with answers.[9] Creative uses of simulation, as in Robert Axelrod's work (1984, 1986) are helpful; but most of all we need more empirical research, guided by theory. Such research could begin to delineate the specific conditions under which cooperation takes place. It should seek to map out patterns of interests, information flows and barriers, and anticipated long-term relationships in order to understand more specifically under what conditions cooperation will or will not take place. Brent Sutton and Mark Zacher have illustrated the value of such research in their recent analysis of the international shipping regime (Sutton and Zacher, 1987). They explore in depth six issue-areas within shipping, on the basis of a hypothesis that cooperation will be greatest where market imperfections and failures, hence possibilities for global welfare gains, exist. Unfortunately, there has so far been relatively little of this type of work done; but I hope and expect that we will see more during the next few years.[10]

Rationalistic theory also needs to extend its vision back into history. To do so in a sophisticated way entails a departure from the equilibrium models emphasized by neoclassical economic theory. It requires intellectual contortions to view the evolution of institutions over time as the product of a deterministic equilibrium logic in which rational adaptation to the environment plays the key role. Institutional development is affected by particular leaders and by exogenous shocks—chance events from the perspective of a systemic theory. Theories of "path-dependence" in economics demonstrate that under specified conditions, accumulated random variations can lead an institution into a state that could not have been predicted in advance (David, 1985; Arthur, Ermoliev and Kaniovski, 1987; see also March and Olson, 1984:745). From a technological standpoint, path-dependence occurs under conditions of increasing rather than decreasing returns—resulting for instance from positive externalities that give established networks advantages over their competitors, from learning effects, and from the convergence of expectations around an established standard. Examples include the development of the typewriter keyboard, competition between different railroad gauges or between Betamax and VHS types of video recorders, and between gasoline and steam-powered cars. Viewed from a more strictly institutional perspective, path-dependence can be a result of sunk costs. Arthur Stinchcombe (1968:120–21) points out that if "sunk costs make a traditional pattern of action cheaper, and if new patterns are not enough more profitable to justify throwing away the resource, the sunk costs tend to preserve a pattern of action from one year to the next."

Surely the General Agreement on Tariffs and Trade (GATT), the International Monetary Fund (IMF) and the United Nations are not optimally efficient, and they would not be invented in their present forms today; but they persist. In some cases, this may be a matter of sunk costs making it rational to continue involvement with an old institution. Sometimes the increasing returns pointed to by path-dependence theorists may account for this persistence. Or considerations of power and status may be more important than the functions performed by the institutions. In politics, where institutional innovators may be punished, existing institutions may have an additional advantage. Even in Congress, "it is risky to try to change institutional arrangements in a manner adverse to the interests of those currently in control" (Shepsle, 1986:69). At the very least, theories of path-dependence demonstrate once again that history not only matters, but that historical investigation is consistent with a rationalistic research program.

REFLECTIVE APPROACHES

Scholars imbued with a sociological perspective on institutions emphasize that institutions are often not created consciously by human beings but rather emerge slowly through a less deliberative process, and that they are frequently taken for granted by the people who are affected by them. In this view the assumption of utility maximization often does not tell us much about the origins of institutions; and it also does not take us very far in understanding the variations in institutional arrangements in different cultures and political systems. Ronald Dore, for instance, suggests that Oliver Williamson's attempt to construct "timeless generalizations" perhaps "merely reflects the tendency of American economists to write as if all the world were America. Or perhaps [Williamson] does not have much evidence about America either, and just assumes that 'Man' is a hard-nosed short-run profit maximizer suspicious of everyone he deals with" (Dore, 1983:469).

Values, norms and practices vary across cultures, and such variations will affect the efficacy of institutional arrangements. This point can be put into the language of rationalistic theory: institutions that are consistent with culturally accepted practices are likely to entail lower transaction costs than those that conflict with those practices. But such a statement merely begs the question of where the practices, or the preferences that they reflect, came from in the first place. The most ambitious form of rationalistic theory, which takes fundamental preferences as uniform and constant, is contradicted by cultural variation if preferences are meaningfully operationalized. The more modest form of this theory, which treats variations in preferences as exogenous, thereby avoids seeking to explain them.

Similar problems arise with explanations of changes in institutions over time. Rationalistic theories of specific institutions can be applied historically, as we have seen. Each set of institutions to be explained is viewed within an institutional as well as material context: prior institutions create incentives and constraints that affect the emergence or evolution of later ones. Change is then explained by changes in opportunity costs at the margin, as a result of environmental changes.

Such an approach has been highly revealing, as the literature on institutional change in economics demonstrates (North, 1981). However, these rationalistic theories of specific institutions have to be contextualized before they are empirically useful: that is, they must be put into a prior framework of institutions and practices. Only with this prior knowledge of the situation at one point in time to guide us, can we use this theory effectively to improve our knowledge of what is likely to happen next. We can then work our way back through the various levels of analysis—explaining actor behavior by reference to institutional constraints and opportunities, explaining specific institutions by reference to prior institutions, explaining those institutions by reference to fundamental practices. Up to a point, rationalistic theory can pursue its analysis backwards in time; and it can only gain by becoming more historically sensitive. But as Field (1981) pointed out and as North (1981) has recognized in the field of economic history, at some point one must embed the analysis in institutions that are not plausibly viewed as the product of human calculation and bargaining. And ultimately, the analysis has to come to grips with the structures of social interaction that "constitute or empower those agents in the first place" (Wendt, 1987:369).

International institutions are not created *de novo* any more than are economic institutions. On the contrary, they emerge from prior institutionalized contexts, the most fundamental of which cannot be explained as if they were contracts among rational individuals maximizing some utility function. These fundamental practices seem to reflect historically distinctive combinations of material circumstances, social patterns of thought, and individual initiative—combinations which reflect "conjunctures" rather than deterministic outcomes (Hirschman, 1970), and which are themselves shaped over time by path-dependent processes. Rationalistic theory can help to illuminate these practices, but it cannot stand alone. Despite the ambitions of some of its enthusiasts, it has little prospect of becoming a comprehensive deductive explanation of international institutions.

Quite apart from this limitation, the writers whom I have labeled "reflective" have emphasized that rationalistic theories of institutions contain no *endogenous* dynamic. Individual and social reflection leading to changes in preferences or in views of causality—what Hayward Alker refers to as *historicity* (Alker, 1986) and what Ernst Haas discusses under the rubric of *learning* (Haas, 1987)—is ignored. That is, preferences are assumed to be fixed. But this assumption of fixed preferences seems to preclude understanding of some major changes in human institutions. For example, as Douglass North points out, "the demise of slavery, one of the landmarks in the history of freedom, is simply not explicable in an interest group model" (North, 1987:12). Nor, in the view of Robert Cox, is American hegemony explicable simply in power terms: on the contrary, it implies a "coherent conjunction or fit between a configuration of material power, a prevalent collective image of world order (including certain norms) and a set of institutions which administer the order with a certain semblance of university" (Cox, 1986:223).

From this perspective, rationalistic theories seem only to deal with one dimension of a multidimensional reality: they are incomplete, since they ignore changes taking place in consciousness. They do not enable us to understand how interests change as a result of changes in belief systems. They obscure rather than illuminate the sources of states' policy preferences. The result, according to Richard Ashley, has been a fundamentally unhistorical approach to world politics, which has reified contemporary political arrangements by denying "history as process" and "the historical significance of practice" (Ashley, 1986:290; see also Alker, 1986; Kratochwil, 1986).

Some analysts in the reflective camp have sought to correct this lack of attention to historicity and learning. In analyzing Prisoner's Dilemma, Alker

(1985) emphasizes not merely the structure of payoff matrices but the sequential patterns of learning taking place between actors over the course of a sequence of games. And Ruggie (1986) has argued that only by understanding how individuals think about their world can we understand changes in how the world is organized—for instance, the shift from medieval to modern international politics. Socially influenced patterns of learning are crucial, as Karl Deutsch and Ernst Haas—the teachers, respectively, of Alker and Ruggie—have always emphasized.

Reflective critics of the rationalistic research program have emphasized the inadequacies of rationalism in analyzing the fundamental practice of sovereign statehood, which has been instituted not by agreement but as a result of the elaboration over time of the principle of sovereignty. Sovereignty seems to be *prior* to the kinds of calculations on which rationalistic theory focuses: governments' strategies assume the principle of sovereignty, and the practice of sovereign statehood, as givens. Indeed, according to some critics of rationalistic thinking, sovereignty is of even more far-reaching significance, since it defines the very nature of the actors in world politics. Ruggie conceptualizes sovereignty as a "form of legitimation" that "differentiates units in terms of juridically mutually exclusive and morally self-entailed domains." Like private property rights, it divides space in terms of exclusive rights, and establishes patterns of social relationships among the resulting "possessive individualists," whose character as agents is fundamentally shaped by sovereignty itself (Ruggie, 1986:144–47).

Ruggie's critical analysis of sovereignty calls our attention once again to the significance of practices such as sovereign statehood for our understanding of the specific institutions of world politics. The international monetary or nonproliferation regimes of the 1980s, for example, can be understood only against the background of the constraints and opportunities provided by the practice of sovereign statehood. We are reminded again of the partial nature of rationalistic theory and the need to contextualize it if we are to derive meaningful insights from its analytical techniques.

The criticisms of rationalistic theory, both from within the framework of its assumptions and outside of them, are extensive and telling. The assumption of equilibrium is often misleading, and can lead to mechanical or contorted analysis. Rationalistic theory accounts better for shifts in the strength of institutions than in the values that they serve to promote. Cultural variations create anomalies for the theory. It does not take into account the impact of social processes of reflection or learning on the preferences of individuals or on the organizations that they direct. Finally, rationalistic theory has had little to say about the origins and evolution of practices, and it has often overlooked the impact of such practices as sovereignty on the specific institutions that it studies.[11]

Yet the critics have by no means demolished the rationalistic research program on institutions, although taking their argument seriously requires us to doubt the legitimacy of rationalism's intellectual hegemony. To show that rationalistic theory cannot account for changes in preferences because it has omitted important potential explanatory factors is important, but it is not devastating, since no social science theory is complete. Limiting the number of variables that a theory considers can increase both its explanatory content and its capacity to concentrate the scholarly mind. Indeed, the rationalistic program is heuristically so powerful precisely because it does not easily accept accounts based on post hoc observation of values or ideology: regarding states as rational actors with specified utility functions forces the analyst to look below the surface for interests that provide incentives to behave in apparently anomalous ways. In quite a short time, research stimulated by rationalistic theory has posed new questions and proposed new hypotheses about why governments create and join international regimes, and the conditions under which these institutions wax or wane. A research program with such a record of accomplishment, and a considerable number of interesting but still untested hypotheses about reasons for persistence, change, and compliance, cannot be readily dismissed.

Indeed, the greatest weakness of the reflective school lies not in deficiencies in their critical arguments but in the lack of a clear reflective research program that could be employed by students of world politics. Waltzian neorealism has such a research program; so does neoliberal institutionalism, which has focused on the evolution and impact of international regimes. Until the reflective scholars or others sympathetic to their arguments have delineated such a research program and shown in particular studies that it can illuminate important issues in world politics, they will remain on the margins of the field, largely invisible to the preponderance of empirical researchers, most of whom explicitly or implicitly accept one or another version of rationalistic premises. Such invisibility would be a shame, since the reflective perspective has much to contribute.

As formulated to date, both rationalistic and what I have called reflective approaches share a common blind spot: neither pays sufficient attention to domestic politics. It is all too obvious that domestic politics is neglected by much game-theoretic strategic analysis and by structural explanations of international regime change. However, this deficiency is not inherent in the nature of rationalistic analysis: it is quite possible to use game theory heuristically to analyze the "two-level games" linking domestic and international politics, as Robert Putnam (1988) has done. At one level reflective theory questions, in its discussion of sovereignty, the existence of a clear boundary between domestic and international politics. But at another level it critiques the reification of the state in neorealist theory and contemporary practice, and should therefore be driven to an analysis of how such reification has taken place historically and how it is reproduced within the confines of the domestic-international dichotomy. Such an analysis could lead to a fruitful reexamination of shifts in preferences that emerge from complex interactions between the operation of international institutions and the processes of domestic politics. Both Kenneth Waltz's "second image"—the impact of domestic politics on international relations—and Peter Gourevitch's "second image reversed" need to be taken account of, in their different ways, by the rationalist and reflective approaches (Waltz, 1959; Gourevitch, 1978).[12]

CONCLUSION

I believe that international institutions are worth studying because they are pervasive and important in world politics and because their operation and evolution are difficult to understand. But I also urge attention to them on normative grounds. International institutions have the *potential* to facilitate cooperation, and without international cooperation, I believe that the prospects for our species would be very poor indeed. Cooperation is not always benign; but without cooperation, we will be lost. Without institutions there will be little cooperation. And without a knowledge of how institutions work—and what makes them work well—there are likely to be fewer, and worse, institutions than if such knowledge is widespread.

A major challenge for students of international relations is to obtain such knowledge of institutions, through theory and the application of theory to practice, but especially through empirical research. Neither pure rationalistic theory nor pure criticism is likely to provide such knowledge. We should demand that advocates of both rationalistic and reflective theory create genuine research programs: not dogmatic assertions of epistemological or ontological superiority, but ways of discovering new facts and developing insightful interpretations of international institutions.

Both rationalistic and reflective approaches need further work if they are to become well-developed research programs. Rationalistic theories of institutions need to be historically contextualized: we need to see specific institutions as embedded in practices that are not entirely explicable through rationalistic analysis. And the many hypotheses generated by rationalistic theory need to be tested empirically. Reflective approaches are less well specified as theories: their advocates have been more adept at pointing out what is omitted in rationalistic theory than in developing theories of their own with *a priori* content. Supporters of this research program need to develop testable theories, and to be explicit about their scope. Are these theories confined to practices or do they also illuminate the operations of specific institutions? Above all, students of world politics who are sympathetic to this position need to carry out systematic empirical investigations, guided by their ideas. Without such detailed studies, it will be impossible to evaluate their research program.

Eventually, we may hope for a synthesis between the rationalistic and reflective approaches—a synthesis that will help us to understand both practices and specific institutions and the relationships between them. Such a synthesis, however, will not emerge full-blown, like Athena from the head of Zeus. On the contrary, it will require constructive competition and dialogue between these two research programs—and the theoretically informed investigation of facts. Thus equipped with our new knowledge, we can intervene more persuasively in the policy process, by drawing connections between institutional choices and those practices of cooperation that will be essential to human survival, and progress, in the twenty-first century.

ACKNOWLEDGMENTS

This essay was written while the author was a fellow at the Center for Advanced Study in the Behavioral Sciences, 1987–88. I am grateful for financial support to the Social Science Research Council Foreign Policy Program and to National Science Foundation grant #BNS-8700864 to the Center. My colleagues in the institutional theory seminar at the Center provided inspiration, advice, and literature references; and helpful comments on earlier drafts were received from James A. Caporaso, Glenn Carroll, Lawrence Finkelstein, Ernst B. Haas, Peter J. Katzenstein, Nannerl O. Keohane, John Kingdon, Stephen D. Krasner, Douglass C. North, Claus Offe, John Gerard Ruggie, Barry Weingast, and two editors of *International Studies Quarterly*, Richard K. Ashley and Patrick McGowan.

NOTES

1. Bull also declares that "states themselves are the principal institutions of the society of states" (1977:71), which implies that he subscribed to the view, discussed below, that the international institution of sovereignty is prior to the state.

2. *International regimes* are specific institutions involving states and/or transnational actors, which apply to particular issues in international relations. This is similar to the definition given by Krasner (1983), but makes it clearer that regimes are institutions, taking advantage of the definition of institutions given above. *Formal international organizations* are purposive institutions with explicit rules, specific assignments of roles to individuals and groups, and the capacity for action. Unlike international regimes, international organizations can engage in goal-directed activities such as raising and spending money, promulgating policies, and making discretionary choices.

3. Young defines institutions in terms of practices: "Social institutions are recognized practices consisting of easily identifiable roles, coupled with collections of rules or conventions governing relations among the occupants of these roles" (1986:107). This is quite an acceptable definition, although it does not emphasize the distinctions among different types of "institutions" that I wish to make.

4. These practices have evolved over the course of decades or centuries and can therefore be considered in Young's terminology to be *spontaneous* orders: "the product of the action of many men but . . . not the result of human design" (Young, 1983:98, quoting Hayek, 1973:37).

5. Morgenthau's language is remarkably close to the language of transaction costs employed by rationalistic theorists discussed in the next section.

6. McIlwain (1939) is particularly good on this point; see also James (1986). Waltz confuses this issue by stating that "to say that a state is sovereign means that it decides for itself how it will cope with its internal and external problems, including whether or not to seek assistance from others and in so doing to limit its freedom by making commitments to them" (Waltz, 1979:96).

7. The assertion that hegemony is necessary for institutionalized cooperation, and the less extreme view that hegemony facilitates cooperation, can both be interpreted

within this framework as declaring transaction costs to be lower when a hegemon exists than when power resources are more fragmented.

8. For a pioneering exploration of these issues, see Young (1979).

9. The theoretical indeterminacy of rationalistic theory suggests that in international relations, as in the economics of institutions, "theory is now outstripping empirical research to an excessive extent" (Matthews, 1986:917).

10. Some work by sociologists, although not applied to international relations, seems relevant here since it focuses on the role played by professional and personal networks in facilitating social cooperation. See Dore (1983), Granovetter (1985), and Powell (1987).

11. This does not mean, however, that rationalistic theory is incapable of contributing to our understanding of the evolution of practices. As Wendt argues, "there is no a priori reason why we cannot extend the logic of [rationalistic] analysis to the analysis of generative structures" (Wendt, 1987:368). In notes to the author, Barry Weingast has illustrated this point by sketching a functional, transaction-cost argument for the existence of sovereignty, as a set of relatively unambiguous conventions, known to all players and not revisable ex post, which facilitate coordination and signaling.

12. Recently major work has been done on links between domestic and international politics, by scholars trained in comparative politics. Unlike the critics of rationalistic theory discussed above, however, these writers emphasize international structure, material interests, and state organization as well as the role of ideas and social patterns of learning. Also unlike the critics of rationalist international relations theory, these writers have engaged in extensive and detailed empirical research. See Zysman (1983), Katzenstein (1985), Gourevitch (1986), and Alt (1987).

REFERENCES

Aggarwal, V. K. (1985) *Liberal Protectionism: The International Politics of Organized Textile Trade.* Berkeley: University of California Press.

Alker, H. R. Jr. (1985) From Quantity to Quality: A New Research Program on Resolving Sequential Prisoner's Dilemmas. Paper delivered at the August meeting of the American Political Science Association.

Alker, H. R. Jr. (1986) The Presumption of Anarchy in World Politics. Draft manuscript, Department of Political Science, M.I.T., August.

Alt, J. A. (1987) Crude Politics: Oil and the Political Economy of Unemployment in Britain and Norway, 1970–85. *British Journal of Political Science* 17:149–99.

Arrow, K. J. (1985) The Economics of Agency. In *Principals and Agents: The Structure of Business,* edited by J. W. Pratt and R. J. Zeckhauser, pp. 37–51. Boston: Harvard Business School Press.

Arthur, W. B., Y. M. Ermoliev, and Y. M. Kaniovski (1987) Path-dependent Processes and the Emergence of Macro-Structure. *European Journal of Operational Research,* 30:294–303.

Ashley, R. K. (1986) The Poverty of Neorealism. In *Neorealism and Its Critics,* edited by R. O. Keohane. New York: Columbia University Press.

Axelrod, R. (1984) *The Evolution of Cooperation.* New York: Basic Books.

Axelrod, R. (1986) An Evolutionary Approach to Norms. *American Political Science Review* 80:1095–1111.

Barry, B. (1970) *Sociologists, Economists and Democracy.* London: Macmillan.

Bull, H. (1977) *The Anarchical Society.* New York: Columbia University Press.

Cox, R. W. (1986) Social Forces, States and World Orders: Beyond International Relations Theory. In *Neorealism and Its Critics*, edited by R. O. Keohane, pp. 204–55. New York: Columbia University Press.

David, P. A. (1985) Clio and the Economics of QWERTY. *American Economic Review Proceedings* 75:332–37.

Dore, R. (1983) Goodwill and the Spirit of Market Capitalism. *British Journal of Sociology* 34:459–82.

Eichengreen, B. (1987) Till Debt Do Us Part: The U.S. Capital Market and Foreign Lending. 1920–1955. Cambridge: NBER Working Paper no. 2394 (October).

Field, A. J. (1981) The Problem with Neoclassical Institutional Economics: A Critique with Special Reference to the North/Thomas model of pre-1500 Europe. *Explorations in Economic History* 18:174–98.

Finlayson, J. A., and M. W. Zacher (1983) The Gatt and the Regulation of Trade Barriers: Regime Dynamics and Functions. In *International Regimes*, edited by S. D. Krasner, pp. 273–315. Ithaca: Cornell University Press.

Gilpin, R. (1981) *War and Change in World Politics*. New York: Cambridge University Press.

Gourevitch, P. A. (1978) The Second Image Reversed: International Sources of Domestic Politics. *International Organization* 32:881–912.

Gourevitch, P. A. (1986) *Politics in Hard Times*. Ithaca: Cornell University Press.

Granovetter, M. (1985) Economic Action and Social Structure: The Problem of Embeddedness. *American Journal of Sociology* 91:481–510.

Haas, E. B. (1986) Progress and International Relations. Manuscript. Berkeley: Institute of International Studies.

Haas, E. B. (1987) Adaptation and Learning in International Organizations. Manuscript. Berkeley: Institute of International Studies.

Haggard, S., and B. A. Simmons (1987) Theories of International Regimes. *International Organization* 41:491–517.

Hayek, F. A. (1973) *Rules and Order*. Vol. 1 of *Law, Legislation and Liberty*. Chicago: University of Chicago Press.

Hirschman, A. D. (1970) The Search for Paradigms as a Hinderance to Understanding. *World Politics* 22(3):329–343.

Hoffmann, S. (1987) Hans Morgenthau: The Limits and Influence of "Realism." In *Janus and Minerva: Essays in the Theory and Practice of International Politics*, edited by S. Hoffmann, pp. 70–81. Boulder: Westview.

Holsti, K. J. (1986) The Horseman of the Apocalypse: At the Gate, Detoured, or Retreating? *International Studies Quarterly* 30:355–72.

Hughes, E. C. (1936) The Ecological Aspect of Institutions. *American Sociological Review* 1:180–89.

James, A. (1986) *Sovereign Statehood*. London: Allen and Unwin.

Katzenstein, P. J. (1984) *Small States in World Markets*. Ithaca: Cornell University Press.

Keohane, R. O. (1984) *After Hegemony: Cooperation and Discord in the World Political Economy*. Princeton University Press.

Keohane, R. O., ED. (1986a) *Neorealism and Its Critics*. New York: Columbia University Press.

Keohane, R. O. (1986b) Reciprocity in International Relations. *International Organization* 40:1–27.

Krasner, S. D., ED. (1983) *International Regimes*. Ithaca: Cornell University Press.

Krasner, S. D. (1985) *Structural Conflict: The Third World Against Global Liberalism*. Berkeley: University of California Press.

Krasner, S. D. (1987) Sovereignty: An Institutional Perspective. Manuscript. Stanford, Calif.: Center for Advanced Study in the Behavioral Sciences, October.

Kratochwil, F. (1986) Of Systems, Boundaries and Territoriality: An Inquiry into the Formation of the State System. *World Politics* 39:27–52.

Kratochwil, F., and J. G. Ruggie (1986) International Organization: A State of the Art on an Art of the State. *International Organization* 40:753–76.

Kreps, D. M. (1984) Corporate Culture and Economic Theory. Manuscript. Stanford, Calif.: Graduate School of Business, Stanford University.

Kreps, D., and R. Wilson (1982) Reputation and Imperfect Information. *Journal of Economic Theory* 27:253–79.

Lindert, P. H., and P. J. Morton (1987) How Sovereign Debt Has Worked. University of California, Davis, Institute of Governmental Affairs, Research Program in Applied Macroeconomics and Macro Policy, Working Paper series no. 45, August.

Lipson, C. (1986) Bankers' Dilemmas: Private Cooperation in Rescheduling Sovereign Debts. In *Cooperation Under Anarchy*, edited by K. Oye, pp. 200–25. Princeton University Press.

McIlwain, C. H. (1939) *Constitutionalism and the Changing World*. New York: Macmillan; and Cambridge: Cambridge University Press.

March, J., and J. Olson (1984) The New Institutionalism: Organizational Factors in Political Life. *American Political Science Review* 79:734–49.

Matthews, R.C.O. (1986) The Economics of Institutions and the Sources of Growth. *Economic Journal* 96:903–18.

Moe, T. M. (1984) The New Economics of Organization. *American Journal of Political Science* 28:739–77.

Moe, T. M. (1987) Interests, Institutions and Positive Theory: The Politics of the NLRB. *Studies in American Political Development* 2:236–99.

Morgenthau, H. J. (1940) Positivism, Functionalism and International Law. *American Journal of International Law* 34:260–84.

North, D. C. (1981) *Structure and Change in Economic History*. New York: W. W. Norton.

North, D. C. (1984) Government and the Cost of Exchange in History. *Journal of Economic History* 44:255–64.

North, D. C. (1987) Institutions and Economic Growth: An Historical Introduction. Paper prepared for the Conference on Knowledge and Institutional Change sponsored by the University of Minnesota, Minn., November.

Oye, K. A., ED. (1986) *Cooperation under Anarchy*. Princeton: Princeton University Press.

Powell, W. W. (1987) Hybrid Organizational Arrangements: New Form or Transitional Development? *California Management Review* 30:67–87.

Putnam, R. D. (1988) Diplomacy and Domestic Politics: The Logic of Two-Level Games. *International Organization* 42:427–60.

Rawls, J. (1955) Two Concepts of Rules. *Philosophical Review* 64:3–32.

Rawls, J. (1971) *A Theory of Justice*. Cambridge, Mass.: Harvard University Press.

Ruggie, J. G. (1986) Continuity and Transformation in the World Polity: Toward a Neorealist Synthesis. In *Neorealism and Its Critics*, edited by R. O. Keohane, pp. 131–57. New York: Columbia University Press.

Shepsle, K. (1986) Institutional Equilibrium and Equilibrium Institutions. In *Political Science: The Science of Politics*. New York: Agathon Press, edited by H. F. Weisberg, pp. 51–81.

Simon, H. A. (1985) Human Nature in Politics: The Dialogue of Psychology with Political Science. *American Political Science Review* 79:293–304.

Stinchcombe, A. L. (1968) *Constructing Social Theories.* New York: Harcourt, Brace and World.

Sutton, B. A., and M. W. Zacher (1987) The Calculus and Conditions of International Collaboration: Evolution of the International Shipping Regime. Prepared for delivery at the Annual Meeting of the American Political Science Association, Chicago, September.

Waltz, K. N. (1959) *Man, the State and War.* New York: Columbia University Press.

Waltz, K. N. (1979) *Theory of International Politics.* Reading, Mass.: Addison-Wesley.

Wendt, A. E. (1987) The Agent-Structure Problem in International Relations Theory. *International Organization* 41:335–70.

Wight, M. (1977) *Systems of States,* edited with an introduction by H. Bull. Leicester: Leicester University Press.

Williamson, O. E. (1981) The Modern Corporation: Origins, Evolution, Attributes. *Journal of Economic Literature* 19:1537–68.

Williamson, O. E. (1985) *The Economic Institutions of Capitalism.* New York: Free Press.

Young, O. R. (1979) *Compliance and Public Authority.* Washington: Resources for the Future.

Young, O. R. (1983) Regime Dynamics: The Rise and Fall of International Regimes. In *International Regimes,* edited by S. D. Krasner, pp. 93–114. Ithaca: Cornell University Press.

Young, O. R. (1986) International Regimes: Toward a New Theory of Institutions. *World Politics* 39:104–22.

Zucker, L. G. (1977) The Role of Institutionalization in Cultural Persistence. *American Sociological Review* 42:726–43.

Zysman, J. (1983) *Governments, Markets and Growth.* Ithaca: Cornell University Press.

PART TWO

Policy Choices
and State Power

Associative American Development, 1776–1860: Economic Growth and Political Disintegration

Observers of the world political economy have often been concerned with the effects on less developed countries (LDCs) of international economic interdependence, and the responses of governments to the constraints and opportunities posed by the operation of the world system. To what extent can these countries achieve sociopolitical as well as economic development by adopting policies of "association," which link them closely to the major capitalist centers through trade, capital flows, and the operations of multinational corporations? Or, on the contrary, is it necessary for them to "delink," following strategies of "dissociation," in order to achieve genuine development and to fulfill the basic human needs of their people?

Proponents of associative strategies emphasize the contribution of these policies to global welfare, as explained by Ricardo and generations of classical and neoclassical economists. In the absence of barriers to trade, countries (or regions) will specialize in areas where they have comparative advantages. Undistorted price signals will direct factors of production toward their most efficient uses. Advocates of dissociation, on the other hand, argue that the gains of pursuing comparative advantage are outweighed by economic, political, and social costs. In particular, countries may run the risk of becoming "enclave economies," specializing in one or two staple crops and failing to develop manufacturing capabilities or even diversified agriculture. The result may be a short-lived boom, followed by disastrous decline as a result of loss of demand for the staple. The country or region may stagnate, as technological advances and the benefits of "learning by doing" are captured by areas with more balanced economic structures. Furthermore, if staple production is carried on with plantation agriculture, social inequality and political authoritarianism are likely to result.

There is no general answer to the question of "whether 'tis better to associate or dissociate." Almost no one would advocate association with the world political economy regardless of the terms; but neither is total self-sufficiency, or autarky, widely regarded as a viable option. In practice, however, few countries *choose* between the ideal types of complete openness and autarky. Strategies emerge from sequences of decisions taken not merely on the basis of abstract principles but also in the light of specific historical conditions. Decisions often depend on the particular areas of activity considered: different policies may be followed on technology-transfer questions than on language issues. Choices are also affected by characteristics of the international political economy (such as patterns of comparative advantage) and by domestic social and political structures.

This chapter will consider strategies of association and dissociation in an historically specific, rather than abstract, context. Rather than focusing on contemporary developing countries—not my own area of comparative advantage—I propose to shed some light on these issues by examining how the United States dealt with issues of association and dissociation between 1776 and 1860. Far from being the superpower of today, the United States was in the early part of this period a relatively weak, overwhelmingly agricultural country, whose economy and polity were strongly affected by the policies of the great powers of the day, particularly Britain and France. Students of the contemporary international political economy often fail sufficiently to recognize the extent to which—albeit under very different international and domestic conditions—the United States dealt with issues similar to those that face less-developed countries today.

Yet the United States was not merely an ordinary little country. It was already "imperial-sized—difficult to get at and heavily self-sufficient in fact (if not always in policy). At the time of the adoption of the Constitution, in fact, James Monroe referred to this as a frame of government for organizing an empire; and he was not alone."[1] Furthermore, the United States grew remarkably fast, so that by 1840 its per capita income was almost the same as that of Britain, and by 1860 its population was larger than that of the United Kingdom.[2] Even within the period under review, therefore, its situation changed, from a postcolonial fragment to an important country undergoing self-sustaining economic growth. Furthermore, the American experience was distinctive in the magnitude of immigration. In the decade 1845–1854 alone, almost three million immigrants arrived—amounting to 14.5 percent of the population in 1845.[3]

These differences between the antebellum United States and contemporary Third World countries imply that one should be cautious about drawing conclusions about the present from America's historical experience. Lessons cannot be learned that easily. Yet it may be worthwhile to examine the experience of the United States—both its successes and its failures—in order to understand to what extent the problems facing less-developed countries today are the product of distinctive times and circumstances, and to what extent, on the contrary, they have recurred, for countries on the periphery of the world system, in other international systems at other times.[4]

The following discussion will be divided into three major sections. In the first, I will investigate the position of the United States in the international division of labor between 1776 and 1860. This period divides rather evenly into two: 1776–1815, when the focus of United States activity was on gaining and then consolidating national control over policy and opposing attempts by Britain and France to restrict and dominate American commerce; and 1815–1860, when the United States economy grew impressively, but the nation failed to avert the eruption of a deadly civil war. In the first period the United States desperately tried to protect its commerce, and its political autonomy, from the impact of the Napoleonic Wars, even to the point of declaring a general embargo on shipping. American policies, however, were divisive at home and ineffective abroad, although the basic self-sufficiency of an agricultural economy prevented the economic collapse. After 1815, the northern and western sections of the country embarked on a path of self-sustaining growth, in which foreign trade became relatively less important. The South, however, experienced "growth without development" as an export economy. The uneven development of the United States—the growth of industrial capitalism in the Northeast, linked to homestead agriculture in the West and juxtaposed to a Southern plantation economy employing slave labor to produce cotton for export—contributed to the sectional conflict leading to the Civil War.

The second section of the essay asks in more detail about the economic and social effects of United States policies; or rather about the effects of the *absence* of coherent policies for most of the period under review. The tendency of the federal government to permit forces of comparative advantage to operate seems to have contributed to American economic growth, although this growth was accompanied by increased social inequality. Dissociative policies were sporadic and provided minor benefits at best: the Embargo probably damaged more sectors of the economy than it assisted, and protective tariffs were on balance insignificant as stimulants to growth or industrialization. In narrowly economic terms, over the short run, association "worked."

Yet despite the benefits for economic welfare, pursuing the logic of the market had tragic effects in the long run. The economic impact on the South of growth without diversification or industrialization was harmful enough. Much more serious were the social and political results of making cotton king: slavery was entrenched and civil war became increasingly likely. The third section suggests that from a long-term political-economic standpoint it might have been worthwhile to limit cotton exports and thereby make slavery less profitable. Yet the economic interests and political importance of the South rendered any such policies politically unfeasible. Antebellum history therefore resembles a Greek tragedy: slavery, America's fatal flaw, was reinforced by the economic position of the South in the international division of labor and its political standing in the United States. Since this flaw could not be corrected by the exercise of choice, it led, despite sometimes desperate efforts to thwart Fate, to the disaster of the Civil War.

The conclusion returns to issues of Third World development. It is difficult to draw from the world system of the nineteenth century lessons that apply to the late twentieth century. Nevertheless, the American experience is sobering, since it implies that countries with comparative advantages in the export of raw materials may be "doomed to association." Incentives to take advantage of export markets may be too attractive for even the most farsighted leadership to resist. Antebellum American foreign economic policy suggests that even where economic success beckons, the dangers of associative policies should not be underestimated.

THE UNITED STATES IN THE
WORLD POLITICAL ECONOMY, 1776–1860

American economic growth, and American politics, were profoundly affected by the evolution of the world political economy throughout the period between the Declaration of Independence and the Civil War. The impact of external conditions on the political economy of the United States during this period can be conveniently discussed under three headings: 1) the struggle between 1776 and 1815 against European domination, whether in the form of overt political control or economic mercantilism and naval harassment; 2) the contribution of the world economy to American growth, particularly through cotton exports after 1815; and 3) the effects of the external demand for cotton on slavery, and ultimately on the collapse of the ties binding the North and South together, leading to the Civil War. Although the second and third topics both focus on the 1815–1860 period, the second is concerned with effects of external events on economic growth, the third with effects on political cohesion. If the former effects were benign, the latter most assuredly were not.

European Mercantilism and
the American Reaction, 1776–1815

In a sense, British mercantilism, by stimulating a process of antagonistic imitation, brought the United States into being as a country. Especially after 1763, the British government sought to restrict competition from North America through a series of measures that affected American commerce and also increased the burden of taxation in the colonies.[5] Resistance to these measures was a major factor in the eventual movement for independence. One of the grievances expressed in the Declaration of Independence states that King George III gave his consent to acts of "pretended legislation" including actions "cutting off our trade with all parts of the world."

The constraints imposed on North American commerce did not end with the successful completion of the War of Independence. After the peace treaty was signed, the United States economy entered a difficult period of postwar depression. Having won its independence, the United States found that it had lost its special privileges in the British market, and that the British, Spanish, and Portuguese West Indies were closed to American ships.[6] As a result, although shipping was a major American industry, almost half of American foreign trade was carried in foreign vessels in 1789–90.[7] As Jefferson complained in December 1793, American shipping stood at the mercy of British whim:

> We can carry no article, not of our own production, to the British ports in Europe. Nor even our own produce to her American possessions. Our ships,

though purchased and navigated by their own subjects, are not permitted to be used, even in their trade with us. While the vessels of other nations are secured by standing laws, which cannot be altered but by the concurrent will of the three branches of the British Legislature, in carrying thither any produce or manufacture of the country to which they belong, which may be lawfully carried in any vessels, ours, with the same prohibition of what is foreign, are further prohibited by a standing law (12 Car. 2, 18, Sec. 3) from carrying thither all and any of our own domestic productions and manufactures. A subsequent act, indeed, has authorized their Executive to permit the carriage of our own productions in our own bottoms *at its sole discretion;* and the permission has been given, from year to year, by proclamation, but subject every moment to being withdrawn *on that single will,* in which event our vessels, having anything on board, stand interdicted from entry of all British ports. . . .

The greater part of what they receive from us is reexported to other countries, under the useless charges of an intermediate deposite, and double voyage.[8]

In 1790, U.S. exports to Britain were less than those of the colonies at the beginning of the Revolution. As Douglass North comments:

The problem of United States foreign economic relationships in 1790 was that, in those goods and services where it enjoyed a distinct comparative advantage, the commercial policies of England and Europe effectively prevented U.S. competition. In other major exports, predominantly agricultural, the advantage was not sufficient to overcome high transport costs and assure an expanding market in a Europe at peace, still largely agricultural and self-sufficient in most primary products.[9]

To some extent, the disabilities imposed by other governments on the American economy reflected the weakness of the American government during the period of the Articles of Confederation and provided a major reason for the enactment of the Constitution and establishment of a federal government. In the monetary field, as well as in trade, the absence of strong national authority was debilitating. The postwar depression in the United States had its immediate causes in the outflow of specie, as a result of an uncontrolled surge in imports after the cessation of hostilities, and in export difficulties. Credit formerly offered by British firms could not be repaid; firms in both the United States and Britain failed, and a liquidity crisis resulted.[10]

The experience of the United States between 1783 and 1789 illustrates the severe costs of an uncontrolled associative policy in an international economy dominated by a great power following mercantilist policies. The United States in this period did not have a sufficiently strong government to be able to devise dissociative policies, even if its leaders had wished to do so. British policy imposed dissociation in trade, but not in finance: the hegemonic power was able to be selective, but not the peripheral country. It is not clear that Britain was helped as a result; but the United States was certainly harmed.[11] Britain did not practice either benign or malign neglect toward her former colony, but rather a policy of active discrimination. Had the global political-economic situation remained indefinitely as it was in 1789, prospects for rapid United States commercial development would have been bleak indeed.

In 1793 the situation changed dramatically with the outbreak of warfare between Britain and France—a war that was to continue, except for inter-mittent periods of peace, until 1815. Until 1807 the economic effects of the Anglo-French war were extremely positive for the United States. War increased demand for American products and was even more important in promoting the re-export trade, in which American ships brought goods from the West Indian possessions of France and its allies to the United States, then re-exported them to the mother countries, thus exploiting a loophole in British blockade regulations.[12] Domestic exports doubled between 1790 and 1807, but re-exports increased two-hundredfold to constitute about 55 percent of all exports. Furthermore, strong wartime demand increased commodity prices, so that the export price index for the United States more than doubled between 1793 and 1798–99 and remained above its 1793 level throughout the Napoleonic Wars. Meanwhile, import prices increased much less so that U.S. terms of trade, after falling until 1794, remained well above the 1790 level throughout the 1795–1807 period.[13] During this period, as in the colonial period, shipping and agriculture were the major industries. Agri-cultural products were sent to the West Indies, and manufactured goods were purchased principally from Britain. Although Alexander Hamilton produced his famous *Report on Manufactures* in 1791, it had little immediate effect on policy.[14]

These favorable international economic developments had positive effects in the economy as a whole, although they were not spectacular. The sharp improvement in U.S. terms of trade after 1793 led to modest increases in national income. Growth rates in per capita income appear to have been around 1 percent per year. "Improved trading conditions led to an increase in the per capita income growth rate of about a quarter of a percentage point."[15]

Politically, the effects of the Anglo-French wars were much less benign, since they brought the United States into military conflict with both bel-ligerents and led to severe domestic partisan disputes. Early in the war, Great Britain began seizing American vessels; by March 1794, Britain held 250 American vessels in the West Indies alone. The Washington administration responded by ratifying a treaty negotiated with Britain in 1794 by John Jay; in so doing, the United States abandoned a strict interpretation of neutrality— that neutral ships could carry any goods they pleased, or that "free ships make free goods." This led not only to severe protests from the Republicans, led by Jefferson and Madison, but to the Quasi-War, an undeclared naval conflict with France, occasioned by French seizures of U.S. vessels. France claimed that the United States had agreed to a broad definition of contraband devised by the British and had therefore broken the "free ships-free goods" rule of the 1778 Franco-American Treaty of Commerce.[16] It was not until

1800 that the Convention of Mortefontaine was signed, bringing the Quasi-War to an end.

American-French hostilities and negotiations aggravated the bitter conflicts at home between Federalists, who tended to be pro-British and anti-French, and Republicans, whose sympathies were reversed. The French revolutionary government sought to exploit these differences with the activities of Citizen Genet and in the XYZ Affair. Party strife in the United States was perhaps more severe in the Adams administration (1797–1801) than ever before, or since, in the United States, reinforced as it was by ideological differences and, on both sides, suspicions that the other was engaged in treason.[17]

The resumption of Anglo-French hostilities in 1803 led to new and eventually more serious political troubles for the United States, this time focusing on Britain. Eventually, a series of events led to the War of 1812 between Britain and the United States. Once again, domestic political quarrels were linked closely to foreign relations, although in this case regional differences and differences of economic interest were more important than ideological affiliation. Neither Britain nor Napoleonic France had a particularly appealing political system from the American point of view, although some Anglophilia remained among New England Federalists in particular. Pressures for war came principally from the South and West; representatives from New Jersey, New York, and New England voted heavily against the declaration of war. In general, agricultural interests favored war; mercantile sectors opposed it.[18]

The Anglo-American disputes of these years did not begin, however, with threats of war but with economic sanctions. In the years immediately before 1807, Britain and America were each other's best customers. Over 40 percent of American exports were to Britain; about one-third of British exports were shipped to the United States. Britain imported American foodstuffs and cotton; the United States imported British manufactured goods, particularly textiles. As the Anglo-French war continued, more and more of this trade was carried in American ships: the American merchant marine increased in tonnage by 80 percent between 1802 and 1810.[19]

Each side thought that the economic interdependence reflected in these figures was politically asymmetrical in its own favor—that a restriction of trade would damage the other country more than itself. British leaders believed that the United States, an upstart nation, could, and should, be subordinated to British policy. Americans, at the same time, thought that the British West Indies were at their mercy:

> The Americans believed that the West Indies need for food provided an obvious way of bringing pressure upon the entire empire. "If we shut up the export trade six months the Islands would be starved," a Republican commercial expert wrote in 1806; "the West India islands are dependent on it [the United States] for the necessaries of life, both for the white and black population."[20]

At the same time, Britain was suspected, with good reason, of using its war with France as an excuse to gain commercial advantages over the United

States. Henry Clay argued in 1811 that "the real cause of British aggression, was not to distress an enemy but to destroy a rival," and Perkins concludes that most British cabinets between 1805 and 1812 "sought not to foster trade but to monopolize it."[21]

The exigencies of war soon provided opportunities for the United States to test the belief of President Jefferson and his political allies that the United States could gain political advantage from economic sanctions. In 1805, in the *Essex* case, the British Admiralty ruled that Britain could legally seize American vessels carrying goods between the West Indies and France, or French allies, even if they stopped in the United States en route. This decision threatened the lucrative re-export trade. By January 1807, Napoleon had declared a blockade of the British Isles, and Britain had prohibited neutrals from engaging in coastwise trade in Napoleonic Europe. "For the first time the United States faced actual exclusion from carrying on any trade with the continent."[22]

Congress reacted to the *Essex* decision and high-handed British actions on the seas by passing the Nonimportation Act of 1806. This act, however, did not proscribe the importation of the most important American purchases from Britain—cottons, cheap woolens, iron, and steel—and was not enforced until the spring of 1808. In the meantime, Monroe and Pinckney negotiated a treaty with Britain in December 1806, which President Jefferson rejected on the grounds that it did not deal with the British practice of impressment— stopping American merchant vessels and forcing some members of their crews to join the British navy on the spot. When a British warship fired on the U.S.S. *Chesapeake* and forced it to turn over four of its crew members, some Americans urged a declaration of war. Jefferson sought to avoid this action. Responding to the British refusal to be conciliatory, he proclaimed a general embargo prohibiting American ships from leaving port, securing its adoption by Congress within a few days.[23]

Jefferson signed the Embargo Act on December 22, 1807. Although the Embargo was enforced unevenly, it did reduce American exports by almost 80 percent between 1807 and 1808; imports (including those for re-export) fell by 60 percent and imports for consumption by almost 50 percent. The share of British exports taken by the United States shrank from one-third to one-seventh.[24]

As a political instrument, however, this remarkable measure of dissociation was ineffective. Britain found new markets in the Spanish Empire for its exports after the Iberian revolt against Napoleon in the spring of 1808. Although the British West Indies were damaged by the American action, and prices rose, the British government made successful efforts, as the British minister in Washington urged, to show "the People of this Country that the Threat to starve His Majesty's Islands in the West Indies, is as vain as it is illiberal and disgusting."[25] Britain had overimported cotton in 1807, and therefore had a stockpile to cushion the effects of the embargo on its textile mills. The price of wheat in England did rise, but not enough to force the government to ban distilling: for Britain, the Embargo was, in the end, only an inconvenience.

For the United States, however, the Embargo's effects were more severe. Shipping interests suffered greatly, but so did cotton planters, since cotton prices dropped by half. Wholesale prices of western produce in New Orleans were 15 percent lower in 1808 than in 1807.[26] Political conflict and even threats of disunion followed. In New England, courts often failed to convict those charged with violations of the Embargo; and a mob at Gloucester even destroyed a revenue cutter. The Republican Joseph Story led opposition to the measures, which "had prostrated the whole commerce of America."[27] As opposition increased, Congress, at the end of February 1809, substituted a Nonintercourse Act for the hated Embargo. This act

> repealed the Embargo, closed trade, both export and import, with the British Empire and the areas controlled by Napoleon; prohibited armed British and French ships from entering American ports; and authorized the president to reopen trade with a power that ceased to violate American maritime rights. Nobody seriously believed that England and France, able to stand up against the Embargo, would be effectively coerced by this lesser pressure. "We have trusted our most precious interests in this leaky vessel," scoffed John Randolph in one of those colorful metaphors that studded his speeches, "and now, by way of amendment, we are going to bore additional holes in this machine, which, like a cask, derives all its value, if it have any, from being water-tight."[28]

Once American ships were allowed to leave port, their eventual destinations could not be controlled: "in the first four months of the new administration seventy-nine ships sailed from New York in nominal search of a market in the Azores."[29]

The justification for replacement of the Embargo with the Nonintercourse Act was not that the latter would be more effective internationally, but that it was less offensive at home. John Quincy Adams claimed that "I was the efficient cause of the substitution of the Nonintercourse for the embargo, which I verily believe saved the country from a civil war."[30]

In 1809 Congress adopted Macon's Bill No. 2, which repealed the Non-intercourse Act and freed commerce with Britain. This admission of political defeat allowed exports to increase to 60 percent of the 1807 level, triple that of 1808.[31] The bill also provided, however, that if one belligerent were to modify its edicts against American shipping, the United States would repeal measures against it and reapply the provisions of the Nonintercourse Act to the other. Napoleon took advantage of this provision, maneuvering the United States into a prohibition of all British imports in February 1811. In conjunction with numerous other grievances between the United States and Great Britain, as well as the desire of some Southerners and Westerners for war and British unwillingness to yield, this sequence of events led to the War of 1812 (1812–15) between Britain and the United States.[32]

The United States was neither economically strong enough, nor sufficiently coherent politically, to impose an embargo successfully on Great Britain, even when Britain was involved in an arduous war against France. The strategy of dissociation could not insulate the United States from the ramifications of a European conflict amounting to an Atlantic, if not a world, war. Indeed, dissociation aggravated internal fissures in the American polity to the point that responsible political leaders worried about civil war. It led to a series of half-measures that not only failed to secure U.S. maritime objectives but that helped to drag the country into a military conflict that it could not win.

During the period between 1793 and 1815, as a whole, the United States was in a position quite unlike the situation faced by less-developed countries today. Economically, international developments at first favored the United States by stimulating demands for American shipping and American exports. Policies of close association with the European powers were therefore economically advantageous, at least in the short run. Politically, however, the United States was severely threatened by the side effects of the Napoleonic Wars, and when the Embargo eventually took effect, it had a strong adverse impact on national income. Although numerous manufacturing industries developed between 1808 and 1815, they did not compensate for the loss of export and shipping revenue. It was not until about 1820 that U.S. per capita income once again reached the levels of 1807. The value of United States exports did not reach the 1807 level again until 1835, although apart from re-exports, the 1807 level was surpassed by 1816.[33] Politically, as we have seen, the Embargo and subsequent War of 1812 aroused severe resistance, especially in New England.

Yet at this time the United States was less dependent on the world economy than many LDCs are now, and this enabled it to weather the storm. In 1810 83 percent of the labor force was engaged in agriculture, much of it in the form of almost self-sufficient family farms. Domestic supplies of essential food and energy were abundant. Ratios of exports to GNP, although higher than subsequently, did not exceed the range of 14–20 percent.[34] Unlike many contemporary less-developed countries, the United States did not have to face choices between production of crops for export and provision of sufficient food to meet basic human needs at home, nor could it be cut off from supplies that were essential for the functioning of its agricultural economy.[35] Without the support of significant allies, the United States was treated harshly by the great powers of the period; the American government had little success in maneuvering between the superpowers. Yet its high degree of national economic self-sufficiency helped it to withstand foreign pressure and to overcome the effects of its own political fragmentation.

American Economic Growth: 1815–1860

The period between the end of the War of 1812 and the beginning of the Civil War was one of considerable economic growth: indeed, a recent economic history textbook characterizes it as the crucial period in which United States economic growth accelerated and began to be self-sustaining.[36] Real per capita income growth seems to have been around 1.3 percent per year for the period as a whole, while the total population and labor force grew at per annum rates of over 3 percent—higher than in any subsequent period of twenty years or more.[37]

Part of this strong performance can be accounted for by the expansion of cotton production during this period. The invention of the cotton gin made it commercially worthwhile to grow cotton throughout wide areas of the South, just as innovations in the textile industry, particularly in Britain, increased the demand. Cotton production rose from less than 200,000 bales in 1815 and 400,000 bales in 1820 to an average of over 4 million bales in the three years preceding 1860.[38] Although cotton prices fell by about 25 percent between 1820 and 1860, the value of cotton exports increased more than eight times over the same forty years. By 1860 cotton accounted for almost 60 percent of total U.S. exports, up from about 30 percent in 1820. Since import prices fell more than export prices, U.S. terms of trade sharply improved between 1820 and 1860, being especially strong in 1834–39 and 1847–60.[39]

During this period, international conditions were remarkably favorable for the cotton sector. The demand for cotton grew annually by 5 percent between 1830 and 1860.[40] Since the American South was the dominant supplier of the material to the world market, it possessed some degree of monopoly power.[41] Cotton supply was elastic to demand over a range of output that could be produced using available land suitable for cotton; but when demand outpaced available land (as in the 1830s and 1850s), prices rose rapidly, since there was a lag of about four years between increased land sales (stimulated by higher cotton prices) and increased cotton supply.[42]

Cotton was important for the North as well as the South: ports such as New York flourished, the American shipping industry grew, and Northern financiers provided credit for Southern planters. Cotton became the chief raw material for Northern industry. Nevertheless, it did not provide the major engine of growth for the economy of the North and West.[43] On the contrary, the most important stimulus for Northern and Western growth during this period was the construction of canals and railroads linking the Eastern Seaboard with areas across the Appalachian Mountains. This internal "transportation revolution" led to dramatic declines in costs: inland freight rates fell during the nineteenth century to one-fiftieth of their late eighteenth century values.[44] Interregional exports (among the Northeast, South, and West) increased from $109 million in 1839 to $480 million in 1860, compared to an increase in exports to other countries from $102 million to $316 million.[45] West-South trade was relatively small and did not grow rapidly; Northeast-West trade was both more dynamic and more important.[46] Intraregional trade seems to have risen even faster, as improved transportation facilitated the widening and deepening of markets within sectors of the country—as New Yorkers, for example, traded with each other via the Erie Canal. Only the South, with its export orientation, failed to develop this pattern of intraregional trade.[47] Thus, as a result of internal transportation improvements, the ratio of exports to gross domestic product fell: Paul David estimates that between 1800–10 and the 1830s it dropped from about 14–20 percent to 8–9 percent.[48]

Growth led to changes in the structure of the economy, both in the Northeast and in the West. Cotton textiles were the initial leading sector: between 1815 and 1833, this sector expanded at a rate of 16 percent annually.[49] During the period between 1808 and 1815, numerous American manufacturing firms had been formed, especially in the cotton textile sector, but also to produce woolens, iron goods, and other products formerly imported from Britain or the European continent. These industries faced a postwar crisis when British products again could appear in American markets. A number of American manufacturers were driven into bankruptcy, but after the crisis had passed, American cotton-textile and woolen manufacturers were competitive in the home market, even without the tariff protection extended in 1816, 1824, and 1828.[50]

The growth of textile manufacturing was followed, especially during the 1840s, by a surge in the output of the Pennsylvania-based iron and steel industry, and by the development of a more diversified domestic manufacturing sector. Extraordinarily high rates of capital accumulation contributed to rapid rates of output growth in manufacturing: almost 10 percent annually in the 1840s and almost 6 percent annually during the 1850s.[51] Between 1820 and 1860, the proportion of the gainfully employed labor force occupied outside of agriculture increased from 21 to 47 percent.[52] Although total factor productivity growth in agriculture during the 1815–1860 period increased only by about .6 percent per year, in cotton textiles it rose by over 3½ percent annually, and in transportation by over 4½ percent.[53] Even before the Civil War, the Northeast was becoming industrialized.

As this was taking place, the West was expanding; the frontier moved beyond the Mississippi to the Great Plains. What is now the Middle West developed a diversified and market-oriented agricultural economy, replacing pioneer self-sufficiency. By 1860 the Northeast and West together had more railroad mileage per capita than any other region of the world, with the South not far behind.[54] The Northeast and West were becoming increasingly closely linked to one another, as intrasectoral ties were also being deepened.

The capital accumulation that propelled this growth came principally from Americans rather than from abroad. Domestic savings rates increased throughout the period, but particularly after 1835.[55] Net foreign capital invested in the United States did rise from $70 million to $380 million between 1790 and 1860, but this was a "trivial" amount compared with indigenous capital formation.[56] Nevertheless, at particular times external sources of capital were important: 1815–18, 1832–39, and 1850–57 were periods of especially large foreign borrowing. In particular, the boom of the 1830s was fueled by foreign investment and the consequent inflow of specie into the United States. As a result, in periods such as this one, the United States was in a classically dependent situation. Milton Esbitt argues, for instance, that "American economic growth in the 1830s depended on a healthy British economy, just as Europe's in the late 1940s and early 1950s did on that of the American economy."[57] When the Bank of England reacted to the effects of a poor domestic grain harvest by tightening its monetary policy in 1837, credit for cotton purchases was reduced, cotton prices collapsed, and specie was exported to Britain from the United States. The result in the United States was monetary contraction, financial distress for borrowers and their banks, and depression—the panic of 1837.[58]

Instability was fostered by loose lending practices and poor performance by borrowers. Land speculation in the West left many investors vulnerable to the price collapses in cotton that took place in 1837 and 1839. During this period, Nicholas Biddle of the United States Bank of Pennsylvania (formerly the Second Bank of the United States) attempted to maintain the price of cotton, in an early form of commodity price stabilization that predates Brazilian efforts in coffee as well as recent commodity agreements and demands for a Common Fund. The 1839 crash brought down Biddle's bank and led to widespread defaults on obligations to British creditors.

Public investors added to the difficulties. Much of American borrowing in the 1830s was carried on by public enterprises—creations of state and local governments—for transportation projects, particularly canals: 70 percent of the canals built in the United States during this period were constructed with public funds borrowed from private investors.[59] Many of these projects had been stimulated by the success of the Erie Canal and rivalry among cities for access to the interior of the country; often they were ill-conceived and failed to generate sufficient revenue to repay the loans that had been contracted. This led in the 1840s to widespread defaults on state debts.[60]

As a result of the crash of the late 1830s, during the 1840s "there was no market in London for any American security." The contemporary counterpart to the International Monetary Fund, the House of Rothschild, apparently blacklisted the United States for a time. As Jenks reports it, "'You may tell your government,' said the Paris Rothschild to Duff Green, 'that you have seen the man who is at the head of the finances of Europe, and that he has told you that they cannot borrow a dollar, not a dollar.'"[61] The U.S. Congress was asked by the creditors to assume the debts of the states, but failed to act after considering the issue in 1842.

Like contemporary developing countries, the United States was subject to temporary disciplinary actions by creditors, but these were not sustained over long periods of time. Unlike many contemporary developing countries, American debts were relatively small. Aggregate U.S. foreign indebtedness, which stayed below $100 million until 1833, with the brief exception of 1817, rose to $297 million by 1839, fell sharply during the 1840s, then rose to about $380 million in 1860. Interest and dividends on foreign indebtedness amounted to about 7 percent of export earnings in 1820, about 6½ percent in 1830, over 9½ percent in 1850, and about 7½ percent in 1860.[62]

In contrast to the Northeast and the West, the South did not diversify its economy. Nor did it industrialize. Instead, it exploited its comparative advantage in cotton production by extending that production westward, using slave labor. Whether the economic success of plantation agriculture could have been maintained beyond 1860 is controversial. Fogel and Engerman claim that slavery could have continued to prosper as cotton production expanded.[63] Wright, on the contrary, has argued that even without the Civil War, the Southern economy would have declined after 1860.[64] Both sides agree that demand for cotton continued to increase after 1866, but only by 1.5 percent per year rather than 5 percent. The issue is whether to place more importance on the continued increase in demand or on the decline in the rate of increase.

In either case, the South before 1860 experienced what would now be called "growth without development":

> The general prosperity of the late antebellum era of southern history, and its basis in the prosperity of plantation slavery, are facts beyond serious dispute. Their historical significance, however, is another matter. Consideration of the sources and of the nature of this movement suggests that the prosperity of the period was not only unprecedented but evanescent. The southern economy, at this time, was absorbing the benefits of strong and rapidly growing demands for raw cotton in international markets—demands connected with the process of industrialization elsewhere. Yet full advantage was not being taken of these fortuitous circumstances to lay more permanent foundations for prosperity— foundations that at a future date might have sustained a cumulative process of economic transformation and growth in the South itself.[65]

I will argue below that this pattern of southern growth had serious implications for the Union. Indeed, it could be argued that external economic conditions were too benign for the United States during the decades before 1860, since strong demand for cotton, with a Europe at peace, created incentives for plantation agriculture to maintain itself and to spread. Yet it would have been difficult for contemporary economists (even armed with twentieth-century ideas) to object. American produce was in strong demand; funds could be borrowed for internal development without serious sanctions for default; and hard-working immigrants arrived in substantial numbers from Europe. From a strictly economic point of view, before 1860, association "worked."

The American South in the World Economy: Slavery and Civil War

Much of the historiography of the Civil War has revolved around the question of the importance of slavery in precipitating the conflict. The conventional view emphasizing the central role of slavery was challenged in the 1920s by Charles and Mary Beard, who emphasized that the war "had not been a contest over principles but a struggle for power—a clash of economic sections in which freedom did not necessarily combat slavery but industrialism most assuredly combated the planter interests."[66] The South was an agrarian economy, closely associated with Britain; its interests lay in low tariffs and competitive conditions in shipping and banking. Northeastern manufacturers, by contrast, sought a protective tariff, wishing to take advantage of Southern cotton for their textile mills.

Yet as Barrington Moore has pointed out, there is no inherent reason why capitalists and aristocratic planters cannot collaborate: the Bismarckian alliance between the capitalists of the Rhineland and the East Elbian Junkers illustrates this possibility. Moore asks the right *political* question raised by the economic determinist thesis: "Why did Northern capitalists have no need of Southern 'Junkers' in order to establish and strengthen industrial capitalism in the United States?"[67] His answer, essentially, is that slavery made the southern planters an unattractive coalition partner. Western farmers feared the extension of slavery and were therefore unwilling to collaborate with the Southern agrarians, although both factions would have had similar interests in low tariffs and internal improvements. The collapse of the Democratic party in the 1850s indicates how slavery—particularly the issue of slavery in the territories—tore apart the Jacksonian coalition.[68] Northern industrialists were not only reluctant to become closely associated with the planters on ideological grounds (many of them were linked to abolitionists and free-soilers); they also had an attractive alternative partner, since the Western fear of slavery in the territories made free-state farmers more willing to align with industrialists against the South. Thus the Whig party—formerly the party of propertied men, North and South—collapsed even before the Jacksonians did; and a new Republican majority of North and West was formed. As Moore characterizes the realignment:

> The essence of the bargain was simple and direct: business was to support the farmers' demand for land, popular also in industrial working-class circles, in return for support for a higher tariff. "Vote yourself a farm—vote yourself a tariff" became Republican rallying cries in 1860. In this fashion there came to be constituted a "marriage of iron and rye"—to glance once more at the German combination of industry and Junkers—but with western family farmers, not landed aristocrats, and hence with diametrically opposite political consequences.[69]

Only after slavery had been abolished, and a period of time had elapsed after the war, did the Southern planters once again become a candidate for a winning political coalition. This realignment took place in 1876, when the disputed Hayes-Tilden election was settled by bringing an end to Reconstruction and permitting Southern whites eventually to disenfranchise and dominate Southern blacks. As Moore argues:

> When Southern "Junkers" were no longer slaveholders and had acquired a larger tincture of urban business and when northern capitalists faced radical rumblings, the classic conservative coalition was possible. So came Thermidor to liquidate the "Second American Revolution."[70]

Moore's argument suggests that it is futile to seek to disentangle slavery from "economic" or "political" causes of the Civil War. Moore explicitly recognizes this, although he views the economic causes as fundamental:

It is impossible to speak of purely economic factors as the main causes behind the war, just as it is impossible to speak of the war as mainly a consequence of moral differences over slavery. The moral issues arose from economic differences.[71]

David M. Potter makes a similar point, without Moore's emphasis on the primacy of economic forces. He acknowledges that even antislavery Northerners were generally racists by modern standards and did not have the interests of black people at heart. "The North did not hate slavery enough to go to war about it; slavery was too close to capitalism to justify the old antithesis of industrialism versus agrarianism; the conflict of economic interests was negotiable." Yet he goes on:

> Nevertheless, in every aspect, slavery was important. Economically, it was
> an immensely powerful property interest, somewhat inimical to the interests
> of free farming, because the independent farmer could not compete with the
> slave. Socially, it was the keystone of a static society of social hierarchy which
> challenged the dynamic, mobile, and equalitarian modes of life and labor that
> prevailed in the free states. Ideologically, it was a negative of the basic American
> principles of freedom and equality. It is futile to draw analytical distinctions
> between the slavery issue and (a) economic conflict of interest, (b) cultural
> incompatibilities, and (c) ideals as a social force. For the slavery issue was
> not, for explanatory purposes, an alternative to any of the others. It was part
> of the essence of all of them.[72]

If slavery is crucial to understanding the Civil War, an adequate analysis of the conflict must take into account changes in the world economy, since slavery was so intimately tied to the South's role in the international division of labor. Strong demand for cotton, particularly from Britain, led to exponential growth in production between 1820 and 1860. This led to the extension of cotton production to what was then the Southwest from the Old South; and to the movement of the center of gravity of slavery from Virginia and the Carolinas in 1790 to Georgia by 1860.[73] There seems to be general agreement now that slavery was profitable, both for plantations in the Old South (net "exporters" of slaves) and plantations in the better cotton-growing areas of the Southwest.[74] This profitability of slavery resulted from the suitability of the area for cotton cultivation, combined with the lack of other available cotton-producing areas to supply the mills of Lancashire: "The American South was the dominant supplier of cotton to the world market at the time, and this conveyed some degree of monopoly power."[75]

As slavery became increasingly profitable, southern commitment to it increased. At the time of the Declaration of Independence, "both North and South had moved in unison to condemn slavery as an evil":

> Southern and northern congressmen alike had joined in voting to abolish
> the importation of slaves after the year 1808. Slavery was barred from the
> Old Northwest by the Ordinance of 1787; it was confined, even within the
> South, mostly to the limited areas of tobacco culture and rice culture, both

of which were static. At this point, it seemed to many men in both sections only a question of time until the institution would wither and die.[76]

By the 1830s, however, the Southern mood had changed, and the South "had begun to formulate a doctrine that slavery was permanent, morally right, and socially desirable." By the 1850s, a Southern majority on the Supreme Court had ruled that Congress could not exclude slavery from the territories, and in his "House Divided" speech, Abraham Lincoln warned that the Court might, in the future, even go so far as to hold that "the Constitution of the United States does not permit a *state* to exclude slavery from its limits."[77] The profitability of slavery increased both Southern commitment to it and Northern fear of its extension.

British demand for cotton thus had fateful effects on the Union, by committing Southerners more strongly to slavery and giving Northerners more reason to fear it. From the Northern standpoint, extension of slavery would have created a country, not just a region, inhospitable to freedom and to individual economic opportunity. Moore even argues that a Southern victory would have put the United States "in the position of some modernizing countries today, with a latifundia economy, a dominant antidemocratic aristocracy, and a weak and dependent commercial and industrial class unable and unwilling to push forward toward political democracy."[78] This puts in modern terms what many Northerners feared. From the standpoint of Southern elites, acceptance of restriction of slavery to states in which it already existed could have maintained the institution temporarily although any profits to be gained from exploiting new areas for plantation agriculture would have been sacrificed. But Southern planters would have had to remain citizens of a country in which they would have been increasingly despised. They would have had to worry more about slave revolts. Their position of political and military power in the United States would have steadily deteriorated, so a later contest would have been more one-sided. And they would have lived with the realization that their way of life was ultimately doomed to extinction.

In the preceding section of this paper, we saw that from a strictly economic point of view, the ante-bellum association of the United States with the world economy "worked." Understanding the effects of association on slavery and the sectional conflict, however, leads to a severe qualification of this conclusion. In the long run, growth without development might have proven to be an inadequate economic strategy for the South. This hypothetical economic danger is dwarfed, however, by the political reality. The effects of close association with the world economy—the entrenchment of slavery and (to a considerable degree) the Civil War—were almost disastrous for the Union and tragic for a large proportion of Americans. Although fewer than five million men voted in the election of 1860, 600,000 men died in the subsequent war.[79] Relative to population, the American Civil War was the bloodiest war in American history. In the absence of dissociative policies, the United States became the victim of forces in the world economy that—

in conjunction with intersectional cultural differences and the impact of ideals—tore the Union apart.

UNITED STATES POLICIES

As we have seen, American economic development was strongly influenced by political and economic events abroad. Yet United States policies also played a role. Alexander Hamilton laid the basis for close transatlantic economic ties with his funding of foreign, domestic and state debts, and the establishment of the first Bank of the United States.[80] These measures were designed to enable the United States to borrow abroad and to begin the construction of an indigenous capital market.

Economic association between the United States and the Old World was promoted more, however, by lack of policy than by positive governmental action. For the most part, the government let forces of comparative advantage operate: it is difficult to find a consistent or self-conscious U.S. strategy of foreign economic policy in the antebellum years. Between 1793 and 1807 the United States allowed shipping and the export of agricultural produce to expand rapidly despite the vulnerability of these activities to wartime disruption and loss. No sustained program to promote manufacturing was undertaken, despite Hamilton's advice in the *Report on Manufactures*. After the War of 1812, the United States was content to let cotton exports rise, even though this pattern of development intensified conflict over slavery. Thus, despite serious negative externalities attached to associative development, public measures were not taken to alter these patterns of growth. On the whole, American policy was passive and could be characterized as one of "unmanaged association."

The most dramatic exception to this generalization is, of course, the period between 1808 and 1815 when Jefferson's Embargo, subsequent legislation, and then the War of 1812 cut the United States off from most of its foreign trade. Here a policy of virtually complete dissociation was tried, although not for economic reasons but in reaction to dire political circumstances. A more limited instance of dissociative policy is provided by U.S. protective tariff legislation, particularly between 1816 and 1833 and again between 1842 and 1846. High tariffs on textiles and iron, as well as other manufactured products, distorted patterns of comparative advantage. Henry Clay's "American System" expressed a widespread desire, at least in the 1820s, for a more self-sufficient national economy.

This section considers the brief but remarkably complete dissociation of the embargo period and the selective dissociation of the protective tariff. For each episode the reasons for deviating from the usual laissez-faire approach and the consequences of policies actually followed will be noted. Some observations on the implications of economic policies for political cohesion conclude the section.

Dissociation: The Embargo and the War of 1812

As indicated earlier, the period between 1808 and 1815 saw real income in the United States decline as established patterns of economic development were ruptured. This fact could be used to indicate that associative policies had been beneficial. However, all sudden changes in the structure of an economy involve adjustment costs, and temporary losses in national income could have been subsequently overshadowed by long-run gains. High immediate costs of dissociation therefore do not necessarily imply policy failure.

In the period between 1808 and 1815, American manufacturing industries did grow strongly, aided by the strong protection provided by the Embargo, its successors, and the War of 1812. Taussig comments:

> The embargo, the non-intercourse acts, and the war of 1812 rudely shook the country out of the grooves in which it was running, and brought about a state of confusion from which a new industrial system could emerge more easily than from a well-settled organization of industry. The restrictive period may indeed be considered to have been one of extreme protection. The stimulus which it gave to manufactures perhaps shows that the first steps in these were not taken without some artificial help.[81]

Nevertheless, the subsequent collapse of many industries begun during this period suggests that many of them had not become competitive, even after an initial period of learning and innovation. Manufacturing output in the Northeast was apparently lower in 1820, after the crisis for manufacturing of the previous five years, than it had been in 1810.[82] The iron industry was not competitive, even in the home market, until the 1840s. Only for cotton textiles and woolens, and perhaps for some smaller industries, could it be argued that the embargo and wartime period had economic benefits by encouraging "learning by doing," helping entrepreneurs to overcome imperfections of capital markets and providing sufficiently high profits that investment was carried out despite externalities associated with innovation that could not be captured by the manufacturer himself.[83] At best, it seems that the embargo period may have speeded up the process of innovation and the growth of manufacturing, although in an abrupt and economically costly fashion. Certainly it would be difficult to hold it up as an example of the economic benefits of a dissociative policy.

Partial Dissociation: The Protective Tariff

Before 1816, the United States maintained relatively low tariffs. The Tariff of 1789 was, according to Taussig, "protective in intention and spirit," with specific duties imposed on certain items as a way of stimulating domestic production.[84] Yet the general duty was only 5 percent *ad valorem;* and even the specific duties were not high compared to what was to come later. Until 1808 tariffs continued to be moderate, although they were raised occasionally to provide additional revenue.

In 1816 Congress reacted to the flood of goods that entered the country after the War of 1812 by legislating a higher tariff, both in order to pay the war debt and to protect infant industries such as cotton and woolen textiles, and iron. Yet the highest rate of duty provided for in this tariff was only 25 percent. In 1824, however, a full-fledged protective tariff was adopted, increasing rates of duty on cotton and woolen goods to 33⅓ percent. In 1828 the "tariff of abominations" raised rates still further, although tariffs were moderated in 1833. In 1842 the Whigs passed another high-tariff measure, which was superseded in 1846 by a low-tariff bill adopted by a Democratic Congress. In 1857 duties were further reduced.[85]

It is a striking feature of this tariff history that the United States had no coherent international economic strategy of which tariffs were a part. The South was consistently against high tariffs; the Western and Mid-Atlantic states favored them; and New England was divided. Regional differences were compounded by party politics, with the Democrats generally favoring lower tariffs than the Whigs. Furthermore, at crucial junctures personalities, and presidential politics, entered into the equation. The 1820s were years of intense domestic political competition, in which tariffs became the central focus. The tariff of 1828 was enacted as a result of maneuvering by Jackson's supporters in the Congress, who planned to embarrass their political opponents, supporters of John Quincy Adams:

> A high-tariff bill was to be laid before the House. It was to satisfy the protective demands of the western and middle states, and at the same time to be obnoxious to the New England members. The Jackson men of all shades, the protectionists from the North and the free-traders from the South, were to unite in preventing any amendments; that bill, and no other, was to be voted on. When the final vote came, the southern men were to turn around and vote against their own measure. The New England men, and the Adams men in general, would be unable to swallow it, and would also vote against it. Combined, they would prevent its passage, even though the Jackson men from the North voted for it. The result expected was that no tariff bill at all would be passed during the session, which was the object of the southern wing of the opposition. On the other hand, the obloquy of defeating it would be cast on the Adams party, which was the object of the Jacksonians of the North. The tariff bill would be defeated, and yet the Jackson men would be able to parade as the true "friends of domestic industry."[86]

Unfortunately for the inventors of this complex maneuver, the Adams supporters favored the bill in the House, and crucial senators, particularly Daniel Webster, supported it in the Senate for fear for the political consequences of opposition. After the legislation was adopted, John Randolph said, "The bill referred to manufactures of no sort or kind, except the manufacture of a President of the United States."[87]

American tariffs may have contributed to American economic development through their fiscal effects: they taxed consumption and contributed to a reduction of the national debt, which reduced interest rates.[88] But they did not play a major role in stimulating the industries—textiles and iron—

toward which they were particularly directed. The iron tariffs of the 1820s were entirely unjustified, since as long as U.S. industry relied on charcoal, it could not be competitive with British iron (using coke) or Swedish and Russian iron (using cheaper labor). U.S. duties on iron placed a heavy burden on U.S. users, failed to stimulate or even retarded innovation in the domestic industry, and hindered U.S. economic growth. This was also true for the high iron tariffs of 1832 and 1842–46.[89] Cotton-textile and woolen tariffs had greater justification—since the industries they protected were viable in the medium-to-long-run—but economic historians generally regard them as redundant. United States tariff policy toward the cotton textile industry, says one observer, should be viewed as "a means of redistributing income in favor of the cotton textile producers."[90] Taussig claims that the United States developed "a new arrangement of its productive forces" after the crisis of 1818–19, with little assistance from protective legislation.[91]

In the American experience before 1860, therefore, little could be said for policies of dissociation on purely economic grounds. The dissociation of the embargo period was economically costly, and was imposed for non-economic reasons. Tariff policies were also expensive. In the long run, the passivity of the government, which accepted associative development, seemed economically wise.

Economic Policies and Political Cohesion

Between 1776 and 1815, the United States government established control over its own policy and asserted its independence vis-à-vis Britain and France. It did not do so, however, as a unified government leading a united people. Indeed, the internal divisions associated with the policy of dependence reduction involved severe political conflicts and even threats of secession. In the 1790s, the Alien and Sedition Acts were passed, and severe differences erupted over the degree to which the United States should assert its independence of Britain. Likewise the years preceding the War of 1812 were stormy ones, and in 1814 the Hartford Convention raised the threat of possible New England secession. As is often the case today, external relations for a dependent country led to internal political stress.

Associative economic development contributed, as we have seen, to the political fragmentation that led to the American Civil War. The direction that rapid economic growth took was destabilizing for the Union. In the case of the United States, as with contemporary developing countries, it would be myopic to evaluate economic policies on the basis of their economic consequences alone.

The pattern of antebellum development had important social consequences as well, although their political implications were overshadowed by the Civil War. Most striking is the fact that income and wealth inequalities increased sharply between 1820 and 1860. America during this period is often seen as a Jacksonian democracy, in which every white man (not yet, every person) was substantially equal. Alexis de Tocqueville, writing in 1835, observed that "America exhibits in her social state an extraordinary phenomenon":

> Men are seen there on a greater equality in point of fortune and intellect,
> or in other words, more equal in their strength, than in any other country of
> the world, or in any age of which history has preserved the remembrance.[92]

As a comparison with Europe, this may well have been correct, although it should also be recalled that Tocqueville warned about the dangers of a "manufacturing aristocracy."[93] But when changes over time are considered, it appears that "inequality in income and wealth rose sharply in America between 1820 and 1860." In 1860 the richest 1 percent of free-wealth-holders held 29 percent of total assets, up from an estimated 12.6 percent in 1774; the richest decile held 73 percent of assets compared to less than 50 percent in the earlier year. Williamson and Lindert argue that in "four short decades" between 1816 and 1856, "the American Northeast was transformed from the 'Jeffersonian ideal' to a society more typical of developing economies with very wide pay differentials and, presumably, marked inequality in the distribution of wage income." Capital accumulation led to mechanization and to a rise in the demand for skilled as opposed to unskilled labor.[94] It is not clear that increasing inequality can be attributed to associative policies; nevertheless, the conjunction between capital accumulation and inequality observed in the nineteenth century United States parallels similar patterns in the contemporary Third World, which have been criticized by advocates of more egalitarian policies entailing dissociation.

Despite the widening inequalities, Northeastern and Western development was successful from an aggregate standpoint: efficient economic patterns were established and real incomes rose. By 1840 United States per capita income "approached that of Great Britain and was somewhat greater than that of France."[95] The open frontier provided opportunities for many, under less comfortable but more egalitarian conditions than those available in metropolitan centers. Yet growth in the South was economically problematic and politically disastrous. As indicated earlier, the South experienced "growth without development." Its maintenance of slavery was reinforced by the openness of the United States to the world economy and the strong British demand for cotton. The economic success of associative policies cannot be celebrated without the sober realization that the export economy of the American South upheld slavery and that the ruling elites of the South eventually sought to secede from the Union at the cost of a long and bloody civil war.

WERE SUPERIOR STRATEGIES AVAILABLE?

In terms of economic growth alone, it is hard to object to associative American policies in the period between 1789 and 1860. The costs lay elsewhere: in the social and political patterns that this type of economic growth fostered. The major issues here are two:

1. Policies followed between 1793 and 1807 permitted, and even encouraged, the development of the U.S. shipping industry, despite the

fact that an extensive shipping industry could be preyed upon by belligerents, which might lead to war, and despite the losses that would be incurred when shipping was cut off.

2. Policies followed after 1815 permitted the rapid expansion of the cotton economy, which increased the dependence of the United States on Europe, entrenched slavery by making it more profitable in a wider area of the South, and led to a sharp conflict of interest between the Northeast and West, on the one hand, and the South, on the other.

In both cases, associative policies led to the imposition of burdens on others that were not borne by the merchants and landowners who benefited from trade. Shipowners and shipbuilders did not, alone, pay the costs of increased defense expenditures or of the disruptions and losses of war; slaveholding planters were not morally outraged by slavery, nor did they bear the physical and moral costs of slavery inflicted on the slaves themselves. Eventually, their descendants (and the descendants of other Southerners, black and white), bore the costs of the Civil War and its aftermath, as well as the long-term costs of growth without diversification that the South had experienced; but these consequences were not anticipated by the planters of the 1830s, 1840s, and 1850s.

As shown earlier, the Embargo, the War of 1812, and later tariffs seem to have had negative economic effects on the United States. Nevertheless, a mildly dissociative international economic policy during the 1793–1807 period could have had some strategic benefits, even if it had been economically costly. The shock of the embargo would not have been so great; in particular, American shipping would not have grown so rapidly and would therefore not have been so vulnerable to restrictions on trade. New England's political reaction to federal government policies after 1807 might also, therefore, have been less extreme.

Such dissociative policies have become commonplace for countries preparing for, or trying to avoid, war. Nazi Germany is a prime example of the former.[96] More generally, many national policies in this century—including U.S. policies ranging from minerals stockpiling to oil import quotas—have been sincerely or hypocritically put forward as being justified by national security. Yet, given the weakness of the manufacturing sector before 1808, and the ferocity of party quarrels, it hardly seems likely that a conscious policy of protection for the sake of national defense could have been implemented. Nevertheless, something could have been said for it.

The associative policy of the post-1820 period was a great tragedy, insofar as it helped to entrench slavery and contributed to the Civil War. In retrospect, it would seem that the United States should have been willing to pay a considerable price to avoid that result. A path of economic development that would have made slavery uneconomic would certainly have had major benefits.

Once again, however, it is difficult to regard such a policy as politically feasible. Not only the South, but the Northeast and the West, gained from the cotton export trade. The cotton economy, resting on slavery, was not merely one sector among others but one of the most important and dynamic sectors, and a principal generator of foreign exchange. Even if Northern and Western interests had been willing to sacrifice their indirect gains from the slave-labor plantation system, legislation sufficient to stop the spread of slavery, even if it could have been enacted, might well have led to secession and civil war in the 1820s or 1830s. Discrimination against the cotton sector, for example, by imposing an export tax, was prohibited by the Constitution (Article I, section 9, paragraph 5), in a clause insisted upon by the Southerners at the constitutional convention in 1787.[97]

The constitutional prohibition against an export tax suggests, as David M. Kennedy has put it, that "in some serious sense it is not proper to speak about 'The United States' as an integrated economic or political entity in the early nineteenth century," or as Walter Dean Burnham wrote, "the chief distinguishing characteristic of the American political system before 1861 is that *there was no state*."[98] In the absence of a coherent state, North and South followed different economic strategies:

> The South *did* have a consistent and coherent associationist strategy, just as the North had a consistent and coherent dissociationist strategy in this period. The problem was that neither of them fully dominated the national political apparatus until after the Civil War decided things.[99]

In the absence of a strong state, the momentum of southern association, given the incentives working for it, was so great that it was impossible to stop. Even had the state been stronger and more coherent, extraordinary vision and political leadership would have been necessary to achieve such a result: people would have had to be more farsighted than they could reasonably be expected to be.

The U.S. experience therefore suggests that dissociative strategies should not be seen as simply a matter of choice. In the American experience, dissociation only occurred when it was forced onto the country by external events. For much of the period, associative strategies were so advantageous economically to dominant interests that they seem to have been virtually inevitable. The experience of Venezuela provides a relevant comparison. Despite their awareness of the dangers of external dependency, the Venezuelans have pursued an economic policy based on the export of petroleum: the ease with which oil produces large revenues makes this course of action virtually irresistible. Very poor or isolated countries have to be self-reliant, since they have little to sell and can only borrow with difficulty. Countries that can export on the world market under favorable terms of trade find that the lure of wealth prevents decisive moves toward dissociation: the United States between 1820 and 1860, Argentina around the turn of the century, and Mexico and Venezuela today, seem "doomed to association." The United States and Argentina might have managed associative strategies better than they did; it is to be hoped that Mexico and Venezuela will be more successful in this respect during the rest of the century. But for countries this fortunate in their resource bases, relative to prevailing patterns of demand in the world economy, it is difficult to envision dissociation as a viable long-term option. The efficiency benefits of tying themselves closely to the world economy—exporting, borrowing for infrastructural development, and using the funds (if leadership is farsighted) to diversify their industrial structure—will be too attractive for dominant elites to resist, even if they are unusually willing to forego the huge rents that can accrue to those who mediate between a wealthy export economy and the outside world.[100]

If dissociation becomes a viable option, it is unlikely to do so as a result of purely economic calculations. The major instance of dissociative American policy—the Embargo of 1807—constituted a desperate effort to preserve autonomy, honor, and peace simultaneously. This policy seemed to American leaders to be forced on them by foreign powers. It was hardly the result of a long-term strategy designed to reduce ties between the United States and the rest of the world.

CONCLUSIONS

It is impossible to draw simple parallels between the situation of the United States in the early nineteenth century and the less-developed countries in the world economy today. After 1820 the United States found itself in a peculiarly advantageous situation. Demand was strong for cotton, and capital was often available in Britain. Technological gaps between British and American industry were relatively small; trade barriers were low and declining; and the United States did not have to contend with highly organized multinational corporations, although it did have to deal with a small set of European bankers who communicated effectively with one another. Perhaps most important, the United States had a growing and prosperous agricultural sector outside of the Southern plantation economy. These farmers were not closely tied to the world economy, but they did generate demands for manufactured goods (many of which could be produced in the United States); and expectations of further agricultural expansion stimulated efforts to extend railroad and canal networks westward.[101] Westward expansion, facilitated by the transportation revolution of the antebellum era, stimulated growth.

It should not be inferred from this that the international economy of the nineteenth century was, in general, more favorable to growth by peripheral countries than the period since the end of World War II. By historical standards, LDC growth rates since the end of World War II have been much higher. For most countries on the periphery of the world economic system there was little *per capita* income growth before 1860.[102] As we have seen, U.S. gross domestic product per capita grew at about 1.3 percent annually in this period. Between 1960 and 1975 median per capita growth rates for non-oil less-developed countries were about 2 percent per year.[103] Northeastern and Western success in economic growth was not a matter of extraordinarily rapid development but rather of managing to cultivate virgin lands, assimilate millions of immigrants, and maintain substantial social mobility, while sustaining steady rates of growth in *per capita* income. This performance was the result less of government policy than of the open frontier. Apart from the South, the United States was not only "born free," in Louis Hartz's phrase; it was "born lucky."

The United States experience suggests that the strengths and weaknesses of associationist development strategies are not unique to the contemporary world. The United States had, in effect, two economies: the export-oriented plantation economy of the South and the relatively self-sufficient, increasingly balanced economy of the Northeast and West. In the South, associative strategies led to growth without development and a reinforcement of inegalitarian social patterns that failed to meet the basic human needs of much of the population. Slavery denied the most basic rights to millions of individuals. In the Northeast and West, by contrast, maintenance of openness to the world economy had beneficial effects: after 1815 there was little danger of excessive dependence on external trade; and European funds helped pay for the transportation networks that bound West and North together.

The American experience helps to reinforce a generalization sometimes made about the contemporary world. Countries with relatively well-integrated political economies, which have prospects for indigenous balanced development, may be wise to follow relatively open policies toward the world economy, while countries with large plantation sectors producing for export need to be more cautious, lest they perpetuate patterns of dualism and great social inequalities. Countries such as the nineteenth-century United States, containing both types of regions, may find that close association with the world economy tends to accentuate interregional divisions.

Ironically, however, political and economic patterns appear to be somewhat at odds with one another. Dominant landed elites in export enclaves will have strong interests in associative policies, since they benefit so much from their comparative advantage on a world scale. Their class interests, especially in the short term, reinforce long-term dependence and dualism. Yet in more balanced economies, which may benefit from openness, sentiments for protectionism are likely to be fostered by the very strength of import-competing sectors. Thus, in the United States, the South stood for free trade, while much of the Northeast and West favored protection.

Early United States development suggests strongly what other essays in this volume argue or imply for the contemporary world: strategies of association or dissociation cannot be assessed in a vacuum, but only in the context of particular, historically given circumstances. It was the resources of the West, and the availability of capital and free labor to develop them, that made close association with the world economy tolerable for the United States. Without these resources, interregional and intraregional trade would not have grown so fast, and foreign trade ratios would have remained higher. A policy of openness toward Europe could have made a less well-endowed United States much more dependent than it in fact became.

American experience also suggests that dissociation may sometimes be chosen as a political means to establish control over one's own policy—to assert one's autonomy as in the Embargo—rather than as a strategy designed to achieve economic development. In the contemporary world, development rhetoric may be used to legitimize a strategy of autonomy, but this should not blind analysts to the real motivations of the policy.

A review of American foreign economic policy also makes it easier to understand why certain governments in the Third World—China being the most obvious example—have returned to more associative policies after a period of dissociation. The United States itself behaved in this way, cutting ties with Europe between 1808 and 1815, then reopening its economy to foreign trade and capital. Dissociation may be unattractive as a long-run policy for countries with large internal resources and the potential for economic development at relatively modest levels of dependence; but it may nevertheless be an appropriate short-term policy, as a way of establishing one's autonomy and thus creating the conditions under which a self-directed policy of association can be successfully undertaken.

Growth took place in the antebellum United States as a result of a conjunction of favorable internal and external conditions. The United States prospered without developing a coherent economic growth strategy, either of dissociation or managed association. Yet its economic successes were accompanied by the political failure of secession and civil war. Despite this mixed record, and the difficulties of generalizing from the American experience (or from myths about it) to contemporary less-developed countries, Americans characteristically view their own history as demonstrating the virtues of laissez-faire and economic openness. In this respect, American ideology reinforces the interest of the twentieth century United States in maintaining a liberal world economy. It is therefore difficult to persuade United States policymakers of the virtues of state-run strategies of "self-reliance" in the Third World. To a country that was born free and born lucky, the protective actions of the less free and the unlucky do not strike a responsive chord.

ACKNOWLEDGMENTS

Sylvia Maxfield volunteered her energy and her talents as a research assistant in the summer of 1980, when she helped me prepare the first draft of this essay. For comments on later drafts I am indebted to Walter Dean Burnham, Barry Buzan, William Domke, Alexander Field, Jeffrey Hart, Peter Hall, Terry Karl, Peter J. Katzenstein, David M. Kennedy, David D. Laitin, Patrick McGowan, John Gerard Ruggie, and Aristide R. Zolberg. Paul A. David, Morton Keller, Daniel Smith, and Ann Tickner provided me with valuable references. The Center for Advanced Study in the Behavioral Sciences made available its marvelous facilities during July 1982, when I completed the final major revision, on which Nannerl O. Keohane made helpful suggestions.

NOTES

1. This quotation is from a set of comments on an earlier draft of this paper, kindly sent to me by Professor Walter Dean Burnham of MIT.

2. Sidney Ratner, James H. Soltow, and Richard Scylla, *The Evolution of the American Economy* (New York: Basic Books, 1979), p. 240, provides the estimate on per capita income; data on population for the United States (slightly over 5 million in 1800 and over 31 million in 1860) are from Paul A. David, "The Growth of Real Product in the United States Before 1840: New Evidence, Controlled Conjectures," *Journal of Economic History* (June 1967), 27(2):165; data on population for Great Britain, including Ireland (over 15 million in 1801 and almost 29 million in 1861) come from *European Historical Statistics, 1981*, pp. 31, 34.

3. David M. Potter, *The Impending Crisis, 1848–1861*, Don E. Fehrenbacher, ed. (New York: Harper & Row, 1976), p. 241. Potter points out that the wave of immigration during this decade was greater, as a percentage of population, than the great immigration of 1905–1914. In private correspondence, Aristide R. Zolberg has pointed out to me that U.S. capitalists encouraged immigration, especially after 1830, in a conscious effort to increase their labor supply; and that this was seen by British investors in the United States as beneficial to them as well.

4. Twenty years ago Seymour Martin Lipset examined the early United States experience from the perspective of the literature on "political development" in the postcolonial areas of the world, in *The First New Nation: The United States in Historical and Comparative Perspective* (New York: Basic Books, 1963). In a general sense, the impetus behind my paper is similar, although my focus is specifically on the relationship of the United States to the world economy and on the effects of foreign economic policies on the failure to develop such policies. My analysis is also indebted, in its emphasis on policies and institutions, to the work of Douglass C. North. See particularly his *Structure and Change in Economic History* (New York: Norton, 1981).

5. Curtis P. Nettels, "British Mercantilism and the Economic Development of the Thirteen Colonies," *Journal of Economic History* (1952), 12:105–14.

6. Curtis P. Nettels, *The Emergence of a National Economy, 1775–1815* (New York: Holt, Rinehart & Winston, 1962), pp. 50–60; Douglass C. North, *The Economic Growth of the United States, 1790–1860* (Englewood Cliffs, N.J.: Prentice-Hall, 1961), p. 21.

7. North, p. 19.

8. Quoted in *ibid.*, pp. 21–22. See also Paul Varg, *Foreign Policies of the Founding Fathers* (Lansing: Michigan State University Press, 1963), p. 98.

9. North, *Economic Growth*, p. 20.

10. Nettels, *Emergence*, p. 64.

11. This experience recalls two later situations. Under the pre-1914 gold standard, Britain could draw gold from peripheral countries by raising interest rates. Cyclical fluctuations were therefore more severe on the periphery than in the center. See Alec G. Ford, *The Gold Standard, 1880–1914: Britain and Argentina* (Oxford: Clarendon Press, 1962); and Peter H. Lindert, *Key Currencies and Gold, 1900–1913*, Princeton Studies in International Finance, No. 24 (International Finance Section, Princeton University, 1969). The second case refers to American economic policy toward Europe after 1920. Like Britain in the 1780s, the United States imposed direct restrictions on trade but allowed financial flows to take place without corresponding restraints. As in the 1780s, the eventual consequence at the end of the 1920s was financial panic, when it became impossible to pay interest or repay principal on the loans that had been contracted to finance an unbalanced trade account. See Charles P.

Kindleberger, *The World in Depression, 1929–1939* (Berkeley: University of California Press, 1974).

12. Varg, *Foreign Policies*, p. 175.

13. North, *Economic Growth*, pp. 25, 221, 229.

14. F. W. Taussig, *The Tariff History of the United States* (New York: Putnam, first published, 1892; 8th ed., 1931), p. 16.

15. Claudia G. Goldin and Frank D. Lewis, "The Role of Exports in American Economic Growth during the Napoleonic Wars, 1793 to 1807," *Explorations in Economic History* (January 1980), 17:21–22.

16. Varg, *Foreign Policies*, pp. 95–116; Alexander DeConde, *The Quasi-War* (New York: Scribners, 1966), p. 10.

17. For a discussion see DeConde, *The Quasi-War*. Not all strife in this period followed party lines: mutual suspicions and conflict also divided the Federalist cabinet of John Adams.

18. Bradford Perkins, *Prologue to War: England and the United States, 1805–1812* (Berkeley: University of California Press, 1961), pp. 32–66, 409.

19. *Ibid.*, pp. 22–31.

20. *Ibid.*, p. 23.

21. *Ibid.*, pp. 21–22.

22. Varg, *Foreign Policies*, p. 193.

23. Perkins, *Prologue to War*, pp. 153–56.

24. The figures on American exports and imports can be found in North, *Economic Growth*, pp. 221, 228. The information on the share of British exports taken by the United States appears in Perkins, *Prologue to War*, p. 168.

25. Perkins, p. 169.

26. *Ibid.*, p. 171.

27. North, *Economic Growth*, p. 55.

28. Perkins, *Prologue to War*, pp. 231–32.

29. *Ibid.*, p. 232.

30. *Ibid.*, p. 179.

31. North, *Economic Growth*, p. 221; Perkins, *Prologue to War*, p. 244.

32. Varg, *Foreign Policies*, pp. 244, 282. Madison, who had been the chief architect of the restrictions, sought to enforce them effectively during the War of 1812, but with indifferent success. See Donald R. Hickey, "American Trade Restrictions during the War of 1812," *Journal of American History* (December 1981), 68(3):517–38.

33. David, "Growth of Real Product," pp. 186–93; North, *Economic Growth*, pp. 58, 221, 233.

34. David, "Growth of Real Product," p. 191.

35. I am indebted for the elaboration of this point to comments by Professor Barry Buzan of Warwick University.

36. Ratner et al., *Evolution of the American Economy*, p. 240.

37. David, "Growth of Real Product," pp. 165, 183–88; Jeffrey G. Williamson and Peter H. Lindert, *American Inequaltiy: A Macroeconomic History* (New York: Academic Press, 1980), p. 206.

38. Robert William Fogel and Stanley L. Engerman, *Time on the Cross: The Economics of American Negro Slavery* (Boston: Little, Brown, 1974), p. 90.

39. *Ibid.*, p. 91; North, *Economic Growth*, p. 233.

40. Gavin Wright, "Prosperity, Progress, and American Slavery," in Paul A. David, Herbert G. Gutman, Richard Sutch, Peter Temin, and Gavin Wright, *Reckoning with Slavery* (New York: Oxford University Press, 1976), p. 309.

41. David et al., "Time on the Cross and the Burden of Quantitative History," in David et al., *Reckoning with Slavery*, p. 352.

42. North, *Economic Growth*, pp. 72–73.

43. This is the thesis of North, *Economic Growth*.

44. Ratner et al., *Evolution of the American Economy*, pp. 121–22.

45. Albert Fishlow, "Antebellum Interregional Trade Reconsidered," *American Economic Review* (May 1964), 54(3):363.

46. *Ibid.*; Albert Fishlow, *American Railroads and the Transformation of the Ante-Bellum Economy* (Cambridge: Harvard University Press, 1965); William N. Parker, ed., *The Structure of the Cotton Economy of the Antebellum South* (Washington: Agricultural History Society, 1970), originally the January 1970 issue of *Agricultural History*.

47. Ratner et al., *Evolution of the American Economy*, p. 224.

48. David, "Growth of Real Product," pp. 190–92.

49. Ratner et al., *Evolution of the American Economy*, p. 198.

50. Taussig, *Tariff History*, pp. 25–45; Paul A. David, "Learning by Doing and Tariff Protection: A Reconsideration of the Case of the Ante-Bellum United States Cotton Textile Industry," *Journal of Economic History* (1970), 30:521–601.

51. Williamson and Lindert, *American Inequality*, pp. 162, 232.

52. David, "Growth of Real Product," p. 166.

53. Williamson and Lindert, *American Inequality*, pp. 170–71.

54. Fogel and Engerman, *Time on the Cross*, p. 256.

55. Williamson and Lindert, *American Inequality*, p. 256.

56. Ratner et al., *Evolution of the American Economy*, p. 218.

57. Milton Esbitt, *International Capital Flows and Domestic Economic Fluctuations* (New York: Arno Press, 1978), p. 361.

58. Leland H. Jenks, *The Migration of British Capital to 1875* (New York: Knopf, 1927), discusses both the crisis of 1837 and the crisis of 1857, precipitated by actions of the Bank of France. On the crisis of 1857, see also North, *Economic Growth*, pp. 212–14.

59. Ratner et al., *Evolution of the American Economy*, p. 115.

60. Jenks, *Migration of British Capital*, pp. 78–106.

61. Both quotations are from Jenks, *Migration of British Capital*; they appear on pp. 99 and 106, respectively.

62. These debt service ratios are lower than recent ratios for "middle income" developing countries. World Bank figures indicate that in 1978 the debt service ratio of these countries averaged about 13.8 percent. *World Development Report, 1980*, pp. 134–35.

63. Fogel and Engerman, *Time on the Cross*, pp. 96–97.

64. Wright, "Prosperity, Progress, and American Slavery," in David, *Reckoning with Slavery*, p. 309.

65. David et al., "Time on the Cross and the Burden of Quantitative History," in David et al., *Reckoning with Slavery*, p. 349.

66. David M. Potter, *The South and the Sectional Conflict* (Baton Rouge: Louisiana State University Press, 1968), p. 91.

67. Barrington Moore, Jr., *Social Origins of Dictatorship and Democracy: Lord and Peasant in the Making of the Modern World* (Boston: Beacon Press, 1966), p. 115. Professor Peter Katzenstein of Cornell and Professor Pat McGowan of Arizona State reminded me of Moore's brilliant chapter on the American Civil War.

68. Potter, *The Impending Crisis*, discusses this collapse, which took place despite the almost heroic efforts of Stephen A. Douglas to prevent it. In a sense, the failure

of Douglas's efforts at compromise revealed that the Democratic party by 1860 no longer existed.

69. Moore, *Social Origins*, p. 130. The ideological opposition to slavery of Northern industrialists is crucial to this argument. Such opposition can be seen, following a recent discussion by David Laitin of British suppression of the slave trade, as an attempt to institutionalize a particular "moral order" in a manner that was consistent with Britain's own efforts to exert "ideological hegemony." Laitin comments: "If [Britain's acceptance of a hegemonic role] meant for the other states in the core the internationalization of free trade, it meant for the periphery the internationalization of a new moral order." Since the American North was in the core and the South in the periphery, it is not surprising that British hegemony had different meanings in these two sections of the United States. See David D. Laitin, "Capitalism and Hegemony: Yorubaland and the International Economy," *International Organization* (Autumn 1982), 36(4):711.

70. *Ibid.*, p. 149.

71. *Ibid.*, p. 123.

72. Potter, *The South and the Sectional Conflict*, p. 118.

73. Fogel and Engerman, *Time on the Cross*, p. 45.

74. Fogel and Engerman make this a major part of their thesis; see also Moore, p. 118; David et al., p. 349; Ratner et al., *Evolution of the American Economy*, pp. 147–48.

75. David et al., "Time on the Cross," in David et al., *Reckoning with Slavery*, p. 352.

76. Potter, *The Impending Crisis*, p. 38.

77. The quotations in this paragraph are from Potter, *The Impending Crisis*, pp. 39 and 349, respectively.

78. Moore, *Social Origins*, p. 153.

79. Potter, *The Impending Crisis*, pp. 443, 583.

80. Varg, *Foreign Policies*, pp. 77–82; North, *Economic Growth*, p. 46.

81. Taussig, *Tariff History*, pp. 62–63.

82. North, *Economic Growth*, p. 165.

83. Taussig, *Tariff History*, pp. 25–67; David, "Learning by Doing and Tariff Protection." David's article provides an excellent discussion of the conditions that must apply for the "learning by doing" or "infant industry" argument to be correct.

84. Taussig, *Tariff History*, p. 14.

85. *Ibid.*, pp. 68–115.

86. *Ibid.*, pp. 88–89.

87. *Ibid.*, pp. 101–2.

88. Ratner et al., *Evolution of the American Economy*, pp. 177–78.

89. Taussig, *Tariff History*, pp. 55 ff., 134; Williamson and Lindert, *American Inequality*, p. 138.

90. David, "Learning by Doing and Tariff Protection," p. 600.

91. Taussig, *Tariff History*, pp. 62–63. Christopher Chase-Dunn has recently published an article based on the hunch that the United States movement from a semiperipheral or peripheral status in the world economy, to a core position, might have been based on U.S. high-tariff policies in the antebellum period. The problem with such an analysis is that tariffs did not seem to make much difference in the development of U.S. manufactures in this period. Professor Chase-Dunn acknowledges this, but curiously persists in an enterprise premised on the opposite assumption. See Christopher Chase-Dunn, "The Development of Core Capitalism in the Ante-Bellum United States: Tariff Politics and Class Struggle in an Upwardly Mobile Semi-

periphery," in Albert Bergesen, ed., *Studies of the Modern World System* (New York: Academic Press, 1980).

92. Alexis de Tocqueville, *Democracy in America* (New York: Knopf, Vintage Edition, 1957), 1:55. (Originally published in 1835.)

93. Williamson and Lindert, *American Inequality*, p. 37.

94. For the source of these data, see Williamson and Lindert, *American Inequality*. The quotations appear on pp. 95 and 68, respectively. Asset data is to be found on p. 36 and the conclusion about capital accumulation on pp. 165 and 232. Williamson and Lindert criticize the thesis that there was a causal connection between accumulation and inequality (see ch. 12).

95. Ratner et al., *Evolution of the American Economy*, p. 239.

96. Albert O. Hirschmann, *National Power and the Structure of Foreign Trade* (Berkeley: University of California Press, 1945).

97. I was reminded of this constitutional provision by both Professor Walter Dean Burnham of MIT and Professor David M. Kennedy of Stanford. In the short run, a cotton export tax (even in constitutional) might not have hurt the cotton industry sufficiently to discourage slavery, since the American South held a predominant export position in cotton before 1860. Furthermore, if Fogel and Engerman are correct, and slavery was profitable in urban areas as well as on cotton plantations, merely to have limited the cotton economy would not necessarily have been sufficient to halt the growth of slavery.

98. These quotations are from the communications of Professors Kennedy and Burnham to me with respect to an earlier draft of this paper.

99. David M. Kennedy's comments to the author.

100. For this point I am indebted to the work of Terry Karl. See "The Political Economy of Petrodollars: Oil and Democracy in Venezuela" (Ph.D. diss., Stanford University, 1981).

101. Fishlow, *American Railroads and the Transformation of the Ante-Bellum Economy*.

102. W. Arthur Lewis, *Growth and Fluctuations, 1870–1913* (London: Allen & Unwin, 1978), p. 29.

103. Stephen D. Krasner, "North-South Economic Relations," in Kenneth Oye et al., *Eagle Entangled: U.S. Foreign Policy in a Complex World* (New York: Longman, 1979), p. 131.

CHAPTER 9

State Power and Industry Influence: American Foreign Oil Policy in the 1940s

Irvine H. Anderson. *Aramco, the United States and Saudi Arabia: A Study of the Dynamics of Foreign Oil Policy, 1933–1950.* Princeton: Princeton University Press, 1981.

Aaron David Miller. *Search for Security: Saudi Arabian Oil and American Foreign Policy, 1939–1949.* Chapel Hill: University of North Carolina Press, 1980.

Michael B. Stoff. *Oil, War and American Security: The Search for a National Policy on Foreign Oil, 1941–1947.* New Haven: Yale University Press, 1980.

During the quarter-century between 1948 and 1973, the production, transportation, and marketing of oil from the Middle East and other oil-exporting areas were controlled by arrangements established by the United States, Great Britain, and the major integrated oil companies. State power played an important role in assuring that control, which rested both on America's special relationship with Saudi Arabia and on the ability and willingness of the United States and Britain to intervene in defense of their petroleum interests—as they did with the Mossadegh government in Iran between 1951 and 1953. Yet it was the major integrated oil companies—the "seven sisters"—that owned and handled the oil, and negotiated with governments over royalties, taxes, and posted prices. Complementary roles were played by the public and private sectors. A remarkably stable system of relationships evolved, which provided the companies with ample profits and enabled consumers in industrialized countries to import petroleum at declining real prices. As contemporary critics argued, those prices were still above pure competitive levels, since the oil industry was controlled by a rather smoothly-meshed oligopoly; but by post-1973 standards, oil was provided at prices that were reasonable indeed.

After 1973, these arrangements collapsed. American state power became much less effective: [between] the 1973–74 OAPEC embargo and [1980], the United States government [was] unable to "break OPEC," to reduce oil prices, or even to guarantee adequate supplies in emergencies. The position of the "seven sisters"

[was] also eroded. In 1973, the seven most important international oil firms produced most all of OPEC's oil and distributed 90 percent of it. In 1980, however, about 45 percent of internationally traded oil was being sold directly by producing countries, to governments, to independents, on the spot market, or through other arrangements. Only about 55 percent was handled by the major integrated petroleum companies.[1]

It is trite to observe that these radical changes in the world oil market reflect[ed] the decline of American dominance in the international political economy. Such an observation begs not only the question of how and why American hegemony has eroded, but of how it was created in the first place. After all, the United States did not become the world's leading power in a fit of absent-mindedness or through an excess of altruism: in oil, as in other areas, deliberate planning and strategic action played major roles. Understanding how the American petroleum empire was constructed may provide some clues, at least, to its eventual demise.

The 1940s were critical years for United States foreign oil policy. American officials during World War II had clear objectives, which they sought to attain through policies that required the cooperation of both the integrated international oil firms and the domestic industry. Yet after series of unsuccessful attempts to implement governmental initiatives, responsibility for maintaining the flow of oil from the Middle East was placed in the hands of the major international firms, with periodic military and political support from Washington. State officials had their own purposes, and were not merely the tools of private interests, but they were constrained, step by step, by the political power of the oil companies.

This is not to say that the companies themselves were united. Indeed, one of the clearest themes to emerge in the history of this period is the difference between the interests and policies of the integrated international firms, on the one hand, and the U.S. domestic petroleum industry, on the other. Officials in the government found it much easier to work out joint strategies with the five American firms counted among the "seven sisters" than with the myriad small producers from Louisiana, Oklahoma, Texas, and Wyoming. In the end, domestic producers achieved their objectives by limiting imports of oil into the United States—that is, by restricting the scope of American public policy. International firms were faced with the more delicate task of encouraging governmental activism in defense of their foreign oil interests, while simultaneously ensuring that the companies would retain both their autonomy and their ability to capture oligopolistic rents. It is, in a way, a remarkable achievement that they also succeeded in securing their objectives.

Thus the history of American foreign oil policy in the 1940s contributes to our understanding of business-government relations in the formulation of foreign economic policy. United States oil policy is shaped both by state initiatives and by industry influence, with the industry in a consistently strong position. The 1940s provide something of a test of the limits of state initiatives, since government officials' actions toward the industry then were more vigorous than they have ever been since. The inability of a Harold Ickes to get his way during the Roosevelt administration cannot be attributed to lack of energy, intelligence, bureaucratic skill, or ties to top political leaders. Thus Ickes's failure suggests inferences about the importance of domestic political structures, since more fleeting personal and conjunctional factors seem to have favored forceful state action.

The major theme of this essay is therefore a familiar one: in the United States, the influence of powerful societal interests often prevents the formulation and execution of strong and consistent state policies. Since this is a review article, our minor theme has to do with questions of historiography. The three books under review are all based on original research in American and British archives, as well as in personal papers, contemporary publications, and secondary works. Anderson has also drawn extensively on interviews with former corporate and government officials. How has archival work, supplemented by other research, altered our understanding of American oil policy during the 1940s?

In our discussions of historiography, we are particularly concerned with the role of social scientific analysis in the writing of history. Anderson is familiar with some major works of political science and sociology, and he self-consciously discusses his method in an extensive appendix. Since *Aramco, the United States, and Saudi Arabia* turns out to be a better work of history than the books by Miller and Stoff, it will be worthwhile to return to this point briefly toward the end of our review.

Anderson, Miller, and Stoff deal by and large with the same issues and must attempt to solve the same puzzles. We begin by defining their common task and introducing three issues—the Petroleum Reserves Corporation, the Anglo-American Petroleum Agreement, and the termination of the Red Line Agreement—that are crucial both to an understanding of American oil policy in the 1940s and to a fair assessment of their books.

THE HISTORIANS' TASKS

Anderson, Miller, and Stoff agree on the main lines of wartime and postwar American oil policy. Before the war, the United States had sought to secure access by American companies to concessions in areas dominated politically by Britain and France; in particular, under the Red Line Agreement of 31 July 1928, American firms (linked together in the Near East Development Corporation) received a 23.75 percent share in the Turkish Petroleum Company, with concessions in what is now Turkey, Syria, and Iraq. Within the "Red Line Area," which included the Arabian peninsula, members of the Turkish Petroleum Company (later the Iraq Petroleum Company) were required by the agreement "to refrain from obtaining concessions or purchasing oil independently in any part of what was construed to have been the old Ottoman Empire" (Anderson, p. 18). This was part of a network of agreements made in the 1920s to restrict supply of petroleum and ensure that the major companies, working together, could control oil prices on world markets.

During the 1930s, a number of significant oil discoveries were made. The greatest impact at the time, at least for the United States, was probably exerted by the discoveries of rich fields in east Texas in 1930. But from a long-term international standpoint, the most important find took place in March 1938, when oil in commercial quantities was discovered in Saudi Arabia by the California Arabian Standard Oil Company, or Casoc (later the Arabian American Oil Company, or Aramco), a jointly owned subsidiary of Socal and Texaco. In 1940 these field produced five million barrels of oil, and by 1941 both the companies involved and the Saudi monarchy recognized that the area's petroleum reserves might be enormous.

During the war, American policymakers were warned that the United States would soon become a net importer of oil. Secretary of the Interior Ickes responded, first, by attempting to establish a Petroleum Reserves Corporation (PRC) to buy a controlling interest in Casoc. When this failed, the Department of State, along with Ickes, sought to achieve secure control over Middle Eastern oil through the negotiation of a petroleum agreement with Great Britain. This agreement was negotiated and then renegotiated, but failed to be ratified by the U.S. Senate. Having been thwarted in attempts at national and international control, the United States government turned to the major oil companies. It supported the entry of Exxon and Mobil into Aramco, which required breaking the Red Line Agreement over French objections.[2] By 1950, American policy toward foreign oil rested on controlling Saudi reserves through the instrument of Aramco.

Any account of U.S. oil policy during the 1940s must concentrate on American-Saudi relations: thus the books under review explore a common subject. Yet there are some differences in emphasis. *Search for Security* emphasizes the bilateral relationship rather than U.S. foreign oil policy. Miller includes extensive discussions of American concern about British influence in Saudi Arabia between 1940 and 1943, and of the Palestine issues at the time of the recognition of the state of Israel by the United States in 1948. The major theme of *Search for Security* is the attempt by the United States to develop influence in, and access to, Saudi Arabia through the use of economic resources, which ranged from Lend-Lease to subsidies, the building of the Dharan air base, Export-Import Bank loans, and the famous 50-50 tax arrangement of 1950 by which the United States allowed oil companies to take U.S. tax credits for royalties paid on crude oil production. Nevertheless, behind the development of U.S. policy toward Saudi Arabia lay overall U.S. oil policy; to understand American-Saudi relations, one has to understand that policy.

To be successful, therefore, each of the three books under review must provide a coherent account of American foreign oil policy during the 1940s. Such an account requires an analysis of the three main policy efforts of United States governments during these years: the attempt by the Petroleum Reserves Corporation to purchase much of Aramco; the Anglo-American Petroleum Agreement; and the entry of Exxon and Mobil into Aramco. Other issues, such as the construction of a pipeline to the Mediterranean, are also important; but for purposes of this review, it is sufficient to concentrate on these three. Some aspects of each issue seem particularly puzzling:

1. *The Petroleum Reserves Corporation.* Why did the leading oil policy official of the United States government—Interior Secretary and Petroleum Administrator for War Ickes—propose the nationalization of all or part of Aramco? For the leading capitalist government to suggest such a policy seems anomalous. Why

did the initiative fail? Which actors were decisive in blocking the purchase of all or part of Aramco by the Petroleum Reserves Corporation, and how did this take place?

2. *The Anglo-American Petroleum Agreement.* What purposes was the agreement meant to serve by the State Department officials who first developed this scheme in late 1943 and early 1944? How and why were major modifications made in the agreement before it was submitted to the U.S. Senate in revised form in November 1945? Why did it fail of ratification?

3. *The reconstruction of Aramco and the termination of the Red Line Agreement.* Why were Socal and Texaco interested in selling substantial shares in Aramco to Exxon and Mobil? They held such a huge pool of oil under their control that one might expect greater reluctance to share it. Why did the United States government support the termination of the Red Line Agreement rather than insisting on a different arrangement that could have maintained the old structure of the Iraq Petroleum Company and avoided difficulties with France?

We will explore these issues in turn, and in so doing will assess the contributions of the three works under review to the historiography of the period. It should first be noted that the works by Miller and Stoff preceded Anderson's book. Miller and Stoff do not appear to have read each other's works before publication, but Anderson had the benefit of reading both *Search for Security* and *Oil, War, and American Security*, even though most of his research was clearly carried out before those works became available to him. All three books are substantial works of scholarship and make important contributions to our knowledge of the period. If Anderson's work appears to be the most thorough and perceptive treatment of these issues, this may reflect not only his great skill as an historian, but also the advantages gained by being about to read the works by Miller and Stoff before the publication of his own.

The Petroleum Reserves Corporation

The works under consideration greatly amplify previous accounts of the formation of the Petroleum Reserves Corporation, and correct those accounts in several important respects. Interest in Saudi reserves had been stimulated by fears of wartime and postwar oil shortages, and in particular by the lobbying that went on in Washington in February 1943 to extend Lend-Lease aid to Saudi Arabia. The main corporate figures in this lobbying effort were Harry D. Collier, president of Socal, and William Rodgers, president of Texaco. They proposed, in return for Lend-Lease, that their joint venture, Casoc, would create an oil reserve in Saudi Arabia whose contents would be made available to the United States government at prices below those on the world market. Following approval of Lend-Lease, the State Department's Committee on International Petroleum Policy, chaired by Economic Advisor Herbert Feis, proposed the formation of a Petroleum Reserves Corporation in March 1943. The PRC was to acquire option contracts on Arabian oil. After the State Department made this suggestion, however, Harold Ickes and representatives of the military services (particularly the Navy) proposed that the PRC directly acquire reserves by purchasing all of Casoc's stock. This plan was approved by Roosevelt in late June 1943.

What is striking about these events is the extent of support for government ownership of oil reserves, and particularly the enthusiasm with which American military officials proposed actions that were sure to be opposed by major business interests. The Board of Directors of the PRC was to consist of the secretaries of state, interior, war and the navy, without private-sector participation; the right to manage the reserves was to be allocated not necessarily to Socal and Texaco (although they were to be given preference) but to those companies submitting the best bids. As Anderson comments, "the audacity of the overall plan was possibly reflective of the mood of wartime Washington" (p. 55).

These accounts add detail to earlier discussions of the PRC. The archival work done by all three authors also reveals clearly that the State Department, rather than Ickes or the Navy, first developed the idea for the PRC.[3] Furthermore, all three authors argue that the State Department, not the oil companies, was the prime mover behind the Lend-Lease decision of 18 February. As Miller notes, "the papers for the Lend-Lease decision had been sitting on the president's desk since early January, almost a month before Casoc-Socal representatives descended on Washington" (Miller, p. 71). The implication in works by such authors as Kolko and Turner that in this case oil companies "manipulated parent governments for their own purposes" seems clearly refuted by the archival data.[4] The recent findings therefore support the general argument offered by Stephen D. Krasner that state policy makers sought to "implement a consistent set of preferences," the second most important of which was increasing security of supply.[5] The Lend-Lease and PRC initiatives are better explained in terms of those preferences than in terms of lobbying by oil companies, even though the Lend-Lease decision was probably facilitated by the actions of Collier and Rodgers.

The Secretary of the Interior and representatives of the military, with the reluctant acquiescence of the State Department, had persuaded the President to create a Petroleum Reserves Corporation that would own huge quantitites of Saudi oil. In the face of this powerful coalition, and during a war in which executive authority was increased and military prestige was immense, how was the initiative defeated?

The prevailing view of this episode has been that Socal and Texaco refused to sell even a minority interest in Casoc, after negotiations in which the government scaled down its requests to that point. Krasner, for instance, notes that Rodgers recalled that Ickes had broken off discussions, but comments that "this interpretation seems disingenuous," since the official minutes of the PRC indicated that the company representatives "had been unable or unwilling to appreciate the urgency of and need for the assistance of the Government."[6] Miller and Stoff, also relying on government records, tell the same story. Miller argues that Casoc was interested in government sponsorship in Lend-Lease, but not in ownership, quoting Feis to the effect that the companies had "gone fishing for a cod and had caught a whale" (p. 82). Stoff, like Krasner, mentions Rodgers's statement, but discounts it: he believes that "the companies entered into negotiations to fortify their position in Saudi Arabia, not to surrender their concesssion or any part of it" (p. 85).

Anderson, however, has discovered that these versions of the story are incorrect; in particular, that they rely on Ickes's misleading congressional testimony and on PRC minutes that he had altered to conceal the truth of the matter. As Anderson states,

> A careful examination of newly accessible material in Ickes' confidential diary, the original records of the Petroleum Reserves Corporation, and unpublished State Department documents, reveals quite another story. There is strong evidence that Casoc and The Texas Company had almost completed an agreement to sell a one-third interest in return for government financing of the Ras Tanura refinery when Ickes himself terminated the negotiations because of pressure brought to bear by Socony-Vacuum and Jersey. Ickes simply omitted mention of the role of the other two companies in his congressional testimony. Feis was not privy to this part of the story, and the published minutes of the PRC board differ significantly from the version in the original PRC records. (p. 56)

As Anderson reconstructs events, rumors of negotiations between the government and the two companies (Socal and Texaco) led to intense opposition by members of the Foreign Operations Committee of the Petroleum Administration for War (PAW). This committee included senior representatives of all major international oil companies based in the United States. Exxon and Mobil were particularly outspoken in their attacks on the proposed government oil purchase. Ickes was alarmed by the industry attacks:

> Ickes' rather formidable power within the bureaucracy rested heavily on his close relationship with Roosevelt, which in turn was based on his proven ability to get results. If this corporate revolt were to undermine cooperation with the PAW itself, the consequences would be serious. Ickes had great courage and skill as a bureaucratic infighter, but part of his success lay in knowing when to fight and when to deftly change direction.[7]

The denouement came on 15 October 1943, in the midst of critical negotiations between Rodgers of Texaco and the PRC, of which Ickes was president. Ickes was visited that day by John Brown of Mobil, who indicated that his company "didn't like the idea of government competition." Ickes acknowledged in his diary that "there was a good deal to what he said"; and—more to the point—that afternoon, Ickes sent an assistant to adjourn negotiations with Rodgers. On 3 November, the matter was discussed in the PRC Board. Anderson comments:

> According to Ickes' confidential diary, and according to the original draft of the minutes of the meeting, Ickes discussed 'the reasons that had led to the discontinuance of our conversations' including the 'talk with Brown of Socony-Vacuum.' . . . The final minutes of that meeting were altered to omit all reference to Brown's intervention, and Ickes' subsequent testimony placed full responsibility for termination of the negotiations on Rodgers' unreasonableness. He obviously preferred not to discuss his yielding to quiet behind-the-scenes-pressure. (pp. 65–66)

Anderson's important discovery suggests the depth and thoroughness of his research, which consistently goes beyond the accounts of Miller and Stoff. It may also prompt reflection on why previous analysts have so readily accept Ickes's version of the story over that of Rodgers. Perhaps this represents a sort of "statist" bias in historiography: Ickes, as a representative of the public and a self-proclaimed spokesman for the "the public interest," could be trusted more than Rodgers, the shrewd oilman defending corporate interests. If we already think we know who is wearing the "black hat," we may therefore think we know whom to believe! But the credulity of historians toward Ickes's account also reflects the excessive faith often placed in "official documents." This episode reminds us that even apparently unimpeachable records, covered with archival legitimacy and dust, may be as misleading (even deliberately misleading) as obviously questionable sources such as oral interviews with participants. Richard M. Nixon was not the first official to try to revise the documentary history of his service to the nation.

The Anglo-American Petroleum Agreement

Failure of the PRC scheme brought to the fore another idea, which had been · discussed in the State Department during 1943 and which Ickes had embraced as well: the negotiation of a petroleum agreement with Great Britain. The saga of this agreement is a long story, complicated by bureaucratic infighting between Harold Ickes and the State Department. On the basis of previous work done before the opening of archival records on this subject, it was clear that the agreement had been negotiated in 1944, but had been withdrawn by Roosevelt from consideration in the Senate in early 1945 as a result of strong opposition by the industry and influential members of Congress. The treaty was then renegotiated with the intimate involvement of the U.S. oil industry, signed on 24 September 1945, and sent to the Senate on 1 November. But despite expectations at the time that it would be quickly ratified—Dean Acheson testified before the Eightieth Congress that "we have taken out every single solitary thing that anybody can even conjure up an objection about"—it never came to a vote on the floor of the Senate, although it was reported favorably by the Foreign Relations Committee on 1 July 1947. Finally, in 1952, it was returned to the State Department, unratified, by joint resolution of Congress.[8]

On the basis of the public record, the purposes of the agreement seemed obscure. Various officials, in testimony before Congress, argued that the agreement would do the following: first, it would help to resolve conflicts between the United States and Great Britain,[9] second, it would provide the basis for a wider international agreement on petroleum;[10] third, its would maintain the principle of equal opportunity in concessions—the open door;[11] fourth, it would protect British and American concessions in the Middle East against Soviet or other threats;[12] and fifth, it would prevent British discrimination against dollar-denominated oil.[13]

Krasner contends that state officials proposing the agreement "basically saw it as a device for giving American companies protection against British pressure and easier access to areas within Britain's sphere of influence. There was also some concern with integrating new supplies into the world market once the war ended." Even on the basis of the public record, it seemed that the latter reason was perhaps very important: as Krasner notes, independent domestic oilmen feared that "the pact might open the American market to cheap foreign petroleum." In the hearings, governmental officials were consistently on the defensive, attempting to allay fears that the chief purpose of the agreement was to facilitiate conservation of indigenous supplies by promoting the development of Middle Eastern fields.[14]

All three of the volumes under review—particularly those by Stoff and Anderson—make it clear that the anxieties of domestic oilmen were justified. The essential purpose of the agreement was to reduce the drain on western hemisphere oil reserves by developing Middle Eastern resources for marketing in Europe, and perhaps even in the United States. As Acting Petroleum Advisor James Sappington wrote on 1 December 1943, for security reasons "it was advisable that Middle Eastern Oil be developed to the maximum and that supplies in this hemisphere be . . . conserved." He even remarked that "if Middle Eastern oil should enter the United States to meet the postwar need for oil imports, the result should be a further conservation of the reserves" of the western hemisphere.[15]

Beyond this point, the accounts by Miller, Stoff, and Anderson diverge. Although he discusses the 1944 negotiations in some detail, Miller shows remarkably little interest in the fate of the agreement. He does not even note the reason for the critical fact that it was submitted as a treaty rather than an executive agreement, although this was previously known to have been the result of pressure from the Senate Foreign Relations Committee and Senator Connally in particular.[16] Miller discusses the nonratification of the agreement only in footnotes (nos. 56 and 57, p. 258), which do not go beyond what was previously known. He discusses neither the modifications in the treaty that took place during renegotiation, nor the reasons for its eventual demise. Yet the Anglo-American Petroleum Agreement, and its defeat, were of great importance. In intragovernmental discussions on it, officials agreed to make the development of Saudi reserves an American policy objective, and this has been fundamental to American oil policy ever since. The nonratification of the agreement, furthermore, by revealing once again the power of domestic oil interests, presaged the oil import quota policies of the 1950s and 1960s, which virtually foreordained the depletion of American reserves and our resulting dependence on the Persian Gulf. For a book on U.S.-Saudi relations, this lack of interest in the fate of the Anglo-American Petroleum Agreement is curious.

Stoff provides a much fuller account. In his book, we are told that the revised petroleum agreement—renegotiated with Britain in the wake of Senate opposition to the first version—"closely resembled its predecessor in form and substance" (p. 183), and that "in most essential respects the new draft retained the flavor of the original" (p. 184). Opposition from independent oilmen "found the agreement bereft of resolute defenders," since the international companies were lukewarm about it and Harold Ickes had left the government in February 1946, after a dispute with President Truman. State Department officials "had long since stopped . . . thinking of it as their property. Now that it was, they were no longer sure they wanted it. 'Now the orphan is on our doorstep,' one of them remarked upon Ickes's departure. 'Shall we smother it or adopt it?'" (p.

193). In Stoff's view, they made it a "foster child, neither abandoned nor embraced." Coupled with the intense oppositon, this doomed it to a quiet death.

Anderson's interpretation is quite different. In his judgment, the heart of the original agreement was the provision in Article III for the creation of an International Petroleum Commission, which would have recommended "production and exportation rates for the various concessions in the Middle East . . . [to prevent] . . . the disorganization of world markets which might result from uncontrolled competitive expansion."[17] In other words, it would have established what amounted to and Anglo-American oil cartel, fifteen years before OPEC. The major international firms supported this conception, provided that they would be furnished with immunity from antitrust prosecution: if so, the government would be achieving for them what they had long sought in world markets through informal collusion and more or less secret agreements.

Unfortunately for the planners of the agreement, it "ran aground in the domestic storm created by the Petroleum Reserves Corporation" (Anderson, p. 96). Industry opposition to an International Petroleum Commission (IPC) with powers to advise governments and recommend actions was intense and, as a comparison of the two agreements readily shows, the commission's role in the revised draft was limited to preparing reports and estimates. Anderson argues convincingly that the agreement was rendered virtually meaningless in the renegotiation. Ickes "moved to align himself with the new power center by supporting every one of the industry demands in the intragovernmental debates that followed" (p. 125). As a result, the State Department became lukewarm toward the agreement, since it would now exclude the U.S. industry and would rely entirely on voluntary compliance. State was strong enough, however, to delete the antitrust immunity clause, over Ickes's resistance; but this meant that "the majors now lost interest in the agreements. They gave Ickes credit for a good try, but from this point on [spring 1945] their support for the renegotiation process was also pro forma" (p. 129).

Thus Anderson argues that industry opposition in 1944 had been the turning point; after the death of Roosevelt, officials were only going through the motions. He also cites the State Department memo characterizing the agreement as an "orphan," but he goes further to argue that "although there is no documentary evidence that this course of action was ever formally adopted, there is strong circumstantial evidence that it was, in fact, the course taken."[18]

Anderson and Stoff agree on the original motivations for the Petroleum Agreement and on the lack of enthusiasm of the State Department for it after Roosevelt's death. Anderson, however, effectively refutes Stoff's characterization of the renegotiated agreement as closely resembling its predecessor "in form and substance"; and he shows more clearly that the crucial actions ensuring that the agreement would not be important—whether ratified or not—took place in late 1944, before the renegotiation with the British. The ambiguities in the public record, especially having to do with the weak and inconsistent case made for the agreement in the hearings, seem to be resolved. "In the process of negotiation, the real purpose had been masked with vague phrases," and later lack of enthusiasm or even covert opposition to ratification by State Department officials also seems to have contributed to the nature of testimony on its behalf (Anderson, p. 104). By late 1944 or early 1945, the precarious pro-agreement coalition of Ickes, the State Department, and the international oil majors had collapsed under pressure from the domestic industry. Only the shadow of a public international agreement remained.

The Reconstruction of Aramco and
the Termination of the Red Line Agreement

Public initiatives having failed, the major oil companies took direct action to secure control over Saudi oil. Between 1946 and 1948, Exxon and Mobil entered the Aramco consortium, and the old Red Line Agreement was dissolved. This took place over the objections of the French but with the diplomatic support of the State Department.

The story of how Exxon and Mobil maneuvered to dissolve the Red Line Agreement is told very well by Anderson, aided by interviews with participants. Fascinating though this tale of international legal intrigue is, however, the major puzzle in this episode is why Socal and Texaco would have been willing to sell shares in such a rich oil concession to two of their major competitors. It has long been known that high executives of Socal opposed the deal, on the grounds that Saudi oil would allow the company to expand rapidly at the expense of competitors if the latter were not allowed into Saudi Arabia. John Blair even went so far as to suggest that Socal sold its share because the Rockefeller family, who also controlled Exxon and Mobil, put their interests above those of the corporation itself.[19]

Miller dismisses this puzzle with scarcely a phrase, merely noting that "some in Aramco" opposed the deal, but that it offered "immediate advantages to the company" (p. 159). Stoff raises the issue more explicitly but provides no reason for Socal's decision. He simply asserts that Socal and Texaco responded positively to an initiative from Exxon and Mobil. Both Stoff and Miller rely heavily on published documents made available through congressional investigations.[20]

Anderson has once again gone farther than the other two historians. On the basis of interviews with former oil company officials, coupled with official documents, he argues that it was Socal, not Exxon, that took the first initiative to broaden Aramco's ownership. Collier of Socal and Rodgers of Texaco pursued a risk-averse strategy. They were about to invest $100 million in a pipeline, beyond the $80 million already sunk into Saudi Arabia; engaging in a full-scale marketing battle with the other majors would be fraught with uncertainty and danger; and unless they were very successful in this enterprise, they would not be able to sell enough oil to provide the Saudi monarchy with sufficient funds (at present royalty rates) to keep it happy.

Under the agreements made among the companies, Aramco received $76.5 million from Exxon and $25.5 million from Mobil, in return for 30 percent and 10 percent interests, respectively, in the business. In addition,

Anderson notes (p. 158) that a further agreement provided Socal and Texaco with "overriding payments out of Aramco's earnings over a number of years totalling $367.2 million," bringing the total amount received to almost $470 million.[21]

The other major issue with respect to this transaction (from the standpoint of American foreign policy) has to do with the United States government's position. Why did the U.S. support the companies so consistently, despite the costs this entailed for Franco-American relations? Paul Nitze, deputy director of the Office of International Trade Policy, did at one point suggest that the issue could be resolved without dissolving the Red Line Agreement and antagonizing the French, if Exxon sold its interest in IPC to Mobil and entered Aramco alone. Exxon and Mobil, however, rejected this suggestion, and (despite some misgivings) the State Department supported the companies' plan, since it would facilitiate the longstanding objectives of developing Middle Eastern oil and, by using that oil to supply Europe, of reducing the drain on western hemisphere reserves. Entry of Exxon and Mobil into the consortium would ensure that Aramco had the markets as well as the capital to develop Saudi oil sufficiently rapidly to satisfy leaders of the kingdom and would therefore help to keep relations smooth between the Saudis and the companies. With respect to these calculations of the State Department, Miller, Stoff, and Anderson tell essentially the same story.

HISTORICAL RESEARCH AND SOCIAL SCIENCE

On all three episodes—the PRC, the Petroleum Agreement, and the dissolution of the Red Line Agreement—*Aramco, the United States and Saudi Arabia* provides a richer, fuller, and more perceptive account than *Search for Security* or *Oil, War, and American Security*. As of the date of its publication in 1981, Anderson's book must be considered the definitive work on U.S. foreign oil policy in the 1940s.

The superiority of Anderson's work is presumably accounted for in part by his previous experience as an historian. The books by Miller and Stoff seem to be based on their Ph.D. dissertations, while Anderson is the author of an illuminating volume on the Standard-Vacuum Oil Company's activities in East Asia before World War II.[22] It is perhaps as a result of having written about this firm's foreign policies that Anderson is more interested in corporate behavior than Miller or Stoff. He appreciates intercorporate politics as well as bureaucratic or corporation-government politics, and inquires about strategies of Exxon or Mobil toward Socal and Texaco as readily as he asks about government policies and oil company lobbying. As we have seen, this insight into oligopolistic competition helped lead him to his discoveries about Mobil's intervention in the PRC affair, and Socal's initiative with respect to the partial sale of Aramco.

Anderson is much less dependent on official governmental files than are Miller and Stoff. Although he was not able to secure access to company files he conducted interviews with thirty-three former corporate and government officials. Most significantly he interview R. Gwin Follis of Socal, who had been involved in most of the events recounted. By contrast, Miller lists seven interviews (two by telephone) and Stoff none. Since none of the authors was able to use corporate records to any significant extent, Anderson's interviews with former oil company officials were particularly valuable.

As noted at the beginning of this essay, Anderson is the only one of these three authors to adopt a self-consciously social scientific methodology, influenced by the works of such authors as Allison, Mannheim, and Waltz. This orientation leads him to focus in comparable ways on each of the "entities"—such as the State Department, Foreign Office, or Texaco—involved in the events being discussed. Anderson thus adopts an approach that is in some ways similar to what Alexander L. George has called "the method of structured focused comparison."[23] As Anderson describes his method, he identified, "for each of the operative entities, its core belief system, its relative power *vis à vis* the others, its spatial context, its internal dynamics, and its specific objectives at each decision point" (Appendix A, p. 215). This method therefore drew his attention systematically to relations among corporations as well as between them and governments. His use of social scientific methodology does not lead, fortunately, either to the promulgation of pseudotheories on the basis of limited cases, or to a jargon-laden exposition: on the contrary, his use of social science is highly unobtrusive. But his superior insights into corporate behavior, and relations among organizations, may be accounted for, at least in part, by his understanding of the value of systematic analysis in the study of history. At a minimum, it liberates him somewhat from the tyranny of the official sources, which focus attention excessively on foreign offices and the State Department. The framework that Anderson imposes on his material seems to have encouraged him to reach out beyond those sources, and may thus have contributed to his healthy skepticism about the status of claims made in archival papers and to his effective use of interviews. The superiority of Anderson's work reflects the value of social science methodology for historical research when social science is used sensitively and combined with a careful reading of the documentary record.

CONCLUSION

American foreign oil policy during the 1940s illustrates the "paradox of external strength and internal weakness" that Stephen D. Krasner has discussed in the areas of commercial and monetary policy.[24] During this decade the United States dominated the international politics of oil as much as any country in the modern era has ever dominated any issue of critical importance to industrial society. Just before World War II, the United States accounted for 62 percent of world oil production,[25] and by 1945 it exercised major influence in most other major producing areas and in the principal importing countries. As a result, the United States was able to shape the oil production and marketing system to its aims during and after World

War II: Saudi Arabia, in particular, was brought within the American petroleum orbit. Nevertheless, this was not done as state policymakers would have preferred: resistance by oil interests led to reliance on the "private government of oil," in Robert Engler's phrase,[26] rather than on public authority.

All three authors under review appear to lament this situation. Miller's views are muted, but Anderson and Stoff are both explicit in their conclusions. Anderson comments that although the eventual American policy toward Saudi Arabia was "quite rational,"

> This policy was not one arrived at by strong executive leadership (as the Constitution suggests that it should be) or by political debate within a duly elected legislative body. Instead, it was the product of competing interest groups in and out of government finally reaching a compromise and resolving themselves into a coalition that appeared to serve each of their special interests. As should be abundantly clear from the events of late 1944 and early 1945, the government agencies involved were the weaker partners in the coalition, at least when it came to deciding on questions of method. (p. 204)

Stoff's view is more explicitly critical. He argues that the security achieved by U.S. oil policy in the 1940s, through "unregulated arrangements among private companies," was achieved at a high cost:

> The opportunity to shape a coherent national policy for foreign oil was lost. Through the Petroleum Reserves Corporation and more widely through the Anglo-American Oil Agreement, government planners had attempted to institutionalize public responsibility over oil in order to influence its development and distribution for the good of the nation, as those planners saw it. . . .
> The effort failed. . . . [American oil companies] became the agents of national policy because they could get the job done without the strains that attended public initiatives. The interests of those companies and of the United States government coincided in the first years after the war, as they had during it. But there was no guarantee that they would continue to do so. In the long run, private companies might find profit in commercial arrangements that worked against what public representatives determined as national interests. (pp. 207–8)

These laments for lost opportunities should not be interpreted as suggesting that plans for public control almost succeeded in the 1940s. The fate of these proposals does not reflect an aberration in American politics, but the reflection of normal patterns of behavior: that proposals for state control got as far as they did is more surprising than their eventual demise.

Nevertheless, the pattern of industry influence over oil policy, established in the 1940s, had serious long-run consequences. Tax arrangements were made in the 1950s to permit higher royalties for producing countries without reducing oil company profits; and oil import quotas were imposed, in the late 1950s, to protect the domestic industry in the name of national security. These government policies reflected industry influence. The former only transferred money from American taxpayers to sheiks and oil companies; the latter, in the long run much more serious, depleted indigenous U.S. reserves of petroleum and thus ran directly counter to the conservationist objectives of State Department officials such as Sappington and Loftus in the 1940s. Thanks to the power of domestic oil interests and the weakness of state institutions, we "drained America first."[27]

Recalling this sad story, it is tempting to conclude that public control of oil would have helped: that success of the Petroleum Reserves Corporation scheme or the oil agreement's cartel aspirations would have led to better outcomes for the United States or perhaps even for the world. It seems evident that if the initial State Department objectives for conserving American oil supplies had been attained, the United States would have been better prepared for the traumatic events of the 1970s. Yet it is important not to romanticize public power. In view of what we know about American politics, is it reasonable to suppose that governmental powers would have been employed autonomously, over a long period of time, free of manipulation by the industry most directly involved? And even had this been the case, what assurance would we have that government policies would have been wise, much less that they would have been beneficial to people outside the boundaries of the United States? Throughout the 1950s and 1960s, populist critics of "big oil" emphasized the high price of oil, relative to cost of production, and the high profits of the companies. They demanded cheaper oil for consumers in the United States and other industrialized countries. Such a policy would have led to even greater petroleum dependence and waste by the early 1970s than actually existed; and might also have contributed to more friction, earlier, with the governments of oil-producing countries. Public control may be a necessary condition for successful oil policies; but it is surely not sufficient.

Recent work on American oil policy in the 1940s makes the events of the 1970s appear more like the denouement to a classic tragedy than the climax of a melodrama. The predicaments created by dependence on Persian Gulf oil were not created by villainy or stupidity as much as by fundamental characteristics of American society. Fragmentation of public authority, pervasive business influence, and willingness of political leaders to follow the path of least resistance in the short run: these were the fatal flaws. In retrospect, it is difficult to imagine that—despite the farsighted wisdom of certain officials—the United States could have averted the oil crisis of the 1970s. Unfortunately, the prospect that these debilitating characteristics will persist makes it difficult to be optimistic about the future.

NOTES

1. Thomas L. Neff, "The Changing World Oil Market," in David A. Deese and Joseph S. Nye, eds., *Energy and Security* (Cambridge, Mass.: Ballinger, 1981), pp. 23–27.

2. I am using the current names for these firms. Exxon was known in the 1940s as Standard Oil of New Jersey, or simply "Jersey"; Mobil was referred to as "Socony-

Vacuum" or "Socony"; Texaco was known as the Texas Company. "Socal" is the customary abbreviation for the Standard Oil Company of California.

3. The concise account by Stephen D. Krasner, in *Defending the National Interest: Raw Materials Investments and U.S. Foreign Policy* (Princeton: Princeton University Press, 1978), p. 192, omits mention of the State Department initiative and is therefore incomplete. Krasner's book is a synthetic work of theory and interpretation, relying for information on secondary sources. It has been a rich source of ideas for this essay, as well as indicating what careful scholars knew about some of these episodes before the archives had been explored.

4. The quotation is from Louis Turner, *Oil Companies in the International System* (London: Allen & Unwin, 1978). Gabriel Kolko's pioneering book, *The Politics of War* (New York: Vintage, 1968), also ascribes a crucial role to the lobbying oilmen; see pp. 295–96. In a footnote (no. 31, p. 49), Anderson argues that the incorrect inference that Rodgers and Collier "were the prime movers behind Lend-Lease for Saudi Arabia" can be traced to a 1948 congressional study, *Petroleum Arrangements with Saudi Arabia* (U.S., Senate, Special Committee Investigating the National Defense Program, Part 41, 80th Cong., 1st sess.).

5. Krasner, *Defending the National Interest*, p. 214. For Krasner, "general foreign policy objectives" are most important, followed by increasing security of supply, then by maximizing the competitive structure of the market. Ibid., p. 331.

6. Ibid., pp. 193–94.

7. Anderson, p. 63. Krasner, *Defending the National Interest*, pp. 194–95, emphasizes congressional opposition to the purchase of stock in Casoc, and argues that the industry prevailed through its influence in Congress. It seems plausible to infer that Ickes may have been worried about both his standing with the industry and Roosevelt directly, and with the fate of any agreement in Congress. Anderson's account, however, somewhat undermines Krasner's argument (pp. 18–19) to the effect that Congress is the critical factor weakening central decision makers faced with opposition from private corporations. If Anderson is correct, industry opposition to the PRC purchase plan, even without Congress, would have given Ickes second thoughts.

8. This account of what was previously known, apart from records in the archives, is based on research that I did on this issue in 1977. The quotation from Acheson appears in *Executive Sessions of the Senate Foreign Relations Committee* (Historical Series), volume 1, 80th Congress, 1st and 2nd sessions, 1947–48 (Washington: Government Printing Office, 1976), p. 77. Important secondary sources available at that time included Herbert Feis, *Seen from E. A.: Three International Episodes* (New York: Knopf, 1947), and Benjamin Shwadran, *The Middle East, Oil, and the Great Powers* (New York: Praeger 1955). The hearings on the Agreement appear in U.S., Senate, *Petroleum Agreement with Great Britain and Northern Ireland*, Hearings before Committee on Foreign Relations, 80th Congress, 1st sess., June 1947. For information on Senate action (or inaction), see *New York Times*, 14 June 1947; *Congressional Record*, 80th Cong., 1st sess., p. 8289; and *Foreign Relations of the United States*, 1945, VI, p. 244.

9. Feis, *Seen from E. A.*, pp. 135–36; testimony by Ralph Davies and Charles Rayner at hearings, *Petroleum Agreement*, pp. 101, 135. By 1948 this theme was muted: Feis downplayed its importance under questioning before the Brewster committee, indicating that "I should not think that the British would be in any way eager to disturb our position out there at the present time." By 1948, American dominance was so firmly established that this justification could not be seriously offered as a major reason for the agreement. See U.S., Senate, *Petroleum Arrangements with Saudi Arabia*, Special Committee Investigating the National Defense Program, Pt. 41, 80th Congress, 1st and 2nd sess., p. 25309.

10. Feis, *Seen from E. A.*, p. 135; Rayner, in *Petroleum Agreement*, p. 35; Davies, in ibid., pp. 95, 101.

11. Rayner and Davies in *Petroleum Agreement*, pp. 36, 95, 104. Davies refers to the Red Line Agreement as an example of the kind of restrictive agreement that the treaty is aimed against.

12. This was a muted theme in early testimony (Rayner, *Petroleum Agreement*, pp. 35–36) but became more prominent in later discussions. See Acheson's testimony in 1947 (*Executive Sessions*), and Feis's testimony before the Brewster Committee (*Petroleum Arrangements with Saudi Arabia*).

13. Davies' testimony, *Petroleum Agreement*, pp. 112, 242–43. Such discrimination did later take place, as Anderson recounts.

14. Krasner's account is accurate within the limits of the published information available at the time he wrote. See *Defending the National Interest*, pp. 199–205. The quotations in this paragraph appear on pp. 200 and 204 of his work.

15. "Memorandum on the Department's position," folder, "Petroleum Reserves Corporation Activities, 7/3/43–1/1/44," box 1, records of the Petroleum Division, RG 59, National Archives (cited by Anderson, fn. 27, p. 78). All three authors agree that the major impetus for the agreement came from the desire of governmental officials to conserve American petroleum reserves, although for political reasons attempts were often made to conceal this motivation. The head of the Petroleum Division in 1945, John A. Loftus, expressed similar views to those of Sappington. See Loftus memo, 31 May 1945, National Archives, decimal file 1945–49, Box no. 5849, file no 841.6363/5-3145.

16. Krasner, *Defending the National Interest*, p. 201.

17. Anderson, p. 95, quoting a memorandum by John A. Loftus of the Petroleum Division, Department of State, 9 November 1944. Anderson conveniently reprints both versions of the Agreement in Appendix B, pp. 216–28.

18. Anderson, p. 131. The memo in question is one from Clair Wilcox to Will Clayton, 19 February 1946. National Archives, Record Group 59, decimal file 800.6363/2-1946.

19. John M. Blair, *The Control of Oil* (New York: Vintage Books, 1976), p. 39.

20. In addition to Blair's account, previous discussions of the breaking of the Red Line Agreement can be found in the following: U.S., Senate, *The International Petroleum Cartel*, staff report to the Federal Trade Commission, submitted to the subcommittee on monopoly of the Select Committee on Small Business, 22 August 1952 (reprinted, 22 April 1975); U.S., Senate, *Multinational Oil Corporations and U.S. Foreign Policy*, Committee on Foreign Relations, subcommittee on multinational corporations (1975), chap. 2, "The 1947 Aramco Merger," pp. 45–55.

21. Of the three books under review, only Anderson's mentions these overriding payments. Miller shows no interest in the sale price at all, and Stoff put it simply at $102 million (p. 198).

22. Irvine H. Anderson, *The Standard-Vacuum Oil Company and the United States East Asian Policy, 1933–1941* (Princeton: Princeton University Press, 1975).

23. Alexander L. George, "Case Studies and Theory Development: The Method of Structured, Focused Comparison," in Paul Gorden Lauren, ed., *Diplomacy: New Approaches in History, Theory, and Policy* (New York: Free Press, 1979), pp. 43–68.

24. Stephen D. Krasner, "United States Commercial and Monetary Policy: Unraveling the Paradox of External Strength and Internal Weakness," in Peter J. Katzenstein, ed., *Between Power and Plenty: Foreign Economic Policies of Advanced Industrial States* (Madison: University of Wisconsin Press, 1978), pp. 51–88.

25. Joel Darmstadter and Hans H. Landsberg, "The Economic Background," in Raymond Vernon, ed., *The Oil Crisis: In Perspective*, special issue of *Daedalus* (Fall 1975), pp. 31–33.

26. Robert Engler, *The Politics of Oil: A Study of Private Power and Democratic Directions* (Chicago: University of Chicago Press, 1961).

27. An excellent recent account of decisions by the Eisenhower administration to institute an oil import quota program can be found in William J. Barber, "The Eisenhower Energy Policy: Reluctant Intervention," in Craufurd D. Goodwin, ed., *Energy Policy in Perspective: Today's Problems, Yesterday's Solutions* (Washington, D.C.: Brookings, 1981), especially pp. 229–61. During these years, as earlier, it was domestic oil and coal interests, and their supporters in the administration and Congress—not the military or civilian leaders of the Defense Department—who pressed for import controls during the Truman presidency, see Craufurd D. Goodwin, "Truman Administration Policies toward Particular Energy Sources," in *Energy Policy in Perspective*, especially pp. 84–90 and 104–7.

CHAPTER 10

Hegemonic Leadership and U.S. Foreign Economic Policy in the "Long Decade" of the 1950s

In the 1950s Henry Luce's short-lived "American century" was at its height. The United States was by far the world's most powerful country, economically as well as militarily; and it was willing to exercise leadership to realize its vision of the future. The "long decade" of the 1950s can be dated from 1947, the year of the Truman Doctrine and Marshall Plan, to 1963, the year of the test-ban treaty and the Interest Equalization Tax. During those sixteen years, the cold war coexisted with active and successful efforts by the United States to reconstruct an open, dynamic, world capitalist system.

It is hardly any wonder that American students of international political economy often seem to view the 1950s with nostalgia. In those years, it is argued, foreign economic policy was harnessed to responsible world leadership rather than to the search for petty and often ephemeral gains at the expense of one's allies and trading partners. During the "long decade," the United States used its own vast political and economic resources to construct the basis for a strategy of "hegemonic leadership"—in which the United States provided benefits for its allies but also imposed constraints upon them.

This paper explores what American leadership in the world political economy actually meant in the period between 1947 and 1963. How did the United States exercise leadership, what were the preconditions for such activity, and what were the results? America's successes and failures in the 1950s may shed some light on the problems facing the architects of U.S. foreign economic policies during the [late 1980s and 1990s].

To assess the meaning of American leadership in the 1950s, it is necessary to have a clear understanding about the material base from which that leadership was exercised, that is, to explicate a conception of "hegemony." Hegemony in the world political economy is twofold, resting both on economic advantages and on political dominance.

Immanuel Wallerstein has defined hegemony in economic terms as "a situation wherein the products of a given core state are produced so efficiently that they are by and large competitive even in other core states, and therefore the given core state will be the primary beneficiary of a maximally free world market."[1] This is an interesting but poorly worked out definition, since under conditions of overall balance of payments equilibrium, each unit—even the poorest and least developed—will have some comparative advantage. The fact that the United States in 1960 had a trade deficit in textiles and in basic manufactured goods (established products not, on the whole, involving the use of complex or new technology) did not indicate that it had lost hegemonic status.[2] Indeed, one should expect the economically hegemonic power to import products that are labor-intensive or that are produced with well-known production techniques. An economically hegemonic power can better be defined as one with a comparative advantage in goods with high value added, yielding relatively high wages and profits. These may well be goods on which there is some sort of monopoly, deriving, for instance, from political power or from technological advantages. In this case, the hegemonic power will be a price maker, and its partners, by and large, will be price takers.

Politically, a hegemonic power can be defined as one that "is powerful enough to maintain the essential rules governing interstate relations, and willing to do so."[3] Not every country that would be considered hegemonic on an economic definition could be considered politically hegemonic, as the examples of Holland in the 1640s and (perhaps) Japan in the 1980s or '90s will indicate.[4] The United States in the 1950s met both these conditions, at least for the world capitalist system, as fully as any state has done in the modern era. Even at the end of the decade, U.S. gross domestic product was double the sum of the GDPs of Britain, France, Germany, and Japan combined; and the United States had trade deficits only in the categories of food, crude materials, minerals, petroleum, basic manufactured goods, textiles, and footwear.[5]

Fred Hirsch and Michael Doyle define hegemonic leadership as follows: "This label implies a mix of cooperation and control; economic relations, created by political and economic means, have been mainly cooperative; and political relations, solidified by economic means, have been cooperative-hegemonic."[6]

The dominant power provides positive incentives for cooperation, as well as persuading its allies that they should join in a common cause. To a considerable extent, the hegemonic power focuses on "milieu goals" rather than "possession goals"; it seeks a favorable order even at the expense of foregoing attempts to maximize its short-term advantage.[7]

At the same time, hegemonic leadership does not prevent the dominant state from pursuing its own interests, within limits. It may even use coercion and pressure to set the boundaries of legitimate action by its allies; within these limits, it may place reliance on persuasion and positive inducements. Under hegemonic leadership, the leader invests tangible resources in building stable and favorable international arrangements, but at the same time, it may extract resources from particular areas of its domain, and it can be expected, within limits, to look after the interests of its own nationals and its own firms.

Hirsch and Doyle argue, on the basis of evidence about trade and monetary policies, that after 1947 the United States followed a hegemonic leadership strategy. I concur with this argument. Yet the "long decade" rested not only on stable money and nondiscriminatory trade but on cheap oil from the Middle East provided largely through American companies for America's allies in Europe and Japan. Between 1943 and 1954, the United States, through state action by using its international oil companies, assured itself of control of Saudi oil resources and a large share of control of oil in Iran and Kuwait.[8] These policies led not only to actions in the Middle East—with which this paper will not deal extensively—but to repercussions in relations between the United States and its European partners. The nature of American "hegemonic leadership" will become clearer if we refer not only to familiar work on money and trade but also discuss oil issues in some detail. Since oil [was] the source of crucial American weaknesses in the [early] 1980s, this emphasis may also help us understand the sources of our [recent] dilemmas.

The main body of this paper attempts to show what American hegemonic leadership meant by exploring how it worked in the areas of money, trade, and oil. For the reasons given above, we will focus on oil. Three petroleum cases will be discussed in detail: American efforts to ensure control of Saudi Arabian oil between 1943 and 1948; the sterling-dollar oil problem of 1949–50; and the Emergency Oil Lift Program in the wake of the abortive Anglo-French invasion of Egypt in 1956. The concluding sections of the paper address the question of how hegemonic leadership can be established and how it can be maintained in the long run by discussing the preconditions for American exercise of such leadership and the failure of American policies to recreate the conditions that made hegemonic leadership viable.

THE OPERATION OF HEGEMONIC LEADERSHIP

The story has often been told of how, in 1947–48, the United States readjusted its monetary and trade policies in response to the Soviet threat (as perceived by decision makers) as well as the failure of Britain's attempt to restore sterling convertibility in the summer of 1947. As Hirsch and Doyle point out, this did not represent an abandonment of earlier policy objectives:

> The United States—by providing massive additional *financing* and accepting trade and payments liberalization by *stages*—saved rather than abandoned its earlier objective of ultimate multilateralism in 1947–48. Such a policy was then possible because of the fundamental characteristic of the international political economy of the time: United States leadership on the basis of only qualified hegemony. The strategy, as is well known, was a major success: the moves toward progressive regional liberalization, undertaken by European economies that were strengthened by the aid injections, paved the way for a painless adoption of multilateralism at the end of the 1950s, with the moves to currency convertibility and the ending of trade discrimination against dollar imports.[9]

With respect to Europe, the United States during the 1950s made short-term sacrifices—in financial aid, or in permitting discrimination against American exports—in order to accomplish the longer-term objective of creating a stable and prosperous international economic order. Except where domestic politics interfered—as, most markedly, on trade policy, particularly in agriculture—the United States was quite successful in using its tremendous economic resources to provide incentives to European countries to subscribe to the American vision of a restructured world economy.[10]

The most striking and far-reaching example of United States leadership is perhaps provided by American efforts, dating from 1949, to assure most-favored-nation treatment for Japan. From the autumn of 1951 onward, Japan sought, with American support, to be allowed to join the General Agreement on Tariffs and Trade (GATT). The struggle was long and difficult: Britain in 1951 even opposed allowing Japan to send an official observer to GATT; in 1953 it was finally agreed that Japan could participate in GATT without a vote; and in 1955 Japan became a Contracting Party. Even then, other members that accounted for 40 percent of Japan's exports immediately invoked Article 35, making GATT's nondiscrimination provisions inapplicable to their relations with Japan. For a decade the United States helped Japan persuade other GATT members to disinvoke Article 35, thus ending discrimination against Japan; this was accomplished for all major trading partners by the mid-1960s. American policy was based on a combination of political and economic calculations. If Japan were to prosper, it would need to trade with other industrialized countries; hence American markets must be open to Japanese exports. Given this politically determined necessity, discriminatory restrictions imposed on Japan by other nations would result in a heavier burden placed on the United States: Goods not imported by others would have to be absorbed by the American market. Since the United States, as leader, was resolved to keep Japan in the American-led system, it had strong incentives to persuade or pressure its allies into helping out. "Free world interest" combined with U.S. interests to mandate a leadership strategy.[11]

American success in exercising hegemonic leadership was greatly facilitated by the existence of a perceived threat from the Soviet Union, and by the economic conditions fostered by the Korean war and rearmament policies in the early 1950s. Historians of various schools have emphasized the importance of the cold war for the British loan and the Marshall Plan. Harry Truman is reported to have said that the Marshall Plan and the Truman Doctrine were "two halves of the same walnut."[12]

As noted above, we shall consider three cases of American hegemonic leadership in oil. The first of these—American efforts to establish control of Saudi Arabian oil between 1943 and 1948—illustrates the lengths to which the U.S. government was willing to go to assure that it, or at least U.S. companies, retained exclusive possession of these petroleum resources. The ability later of the United States to dispense oil to its allies, or to assure them of supplies despite their own lack of military power, depended on the success of this initial effort at self-aggrandizement. The sterling-dollar oil incident provides a revealing glimpse into the cross-pressures under which American policy makers were operating in the period before the Korean war as they sought to protect American interests in the Middle East, to defend U.S. companies against discrimination, and also to build a cooperative alliance system under Washington's leadership. The Emergency Oil Lift Program illustrates the tremendous capabilities that the United States commanded at the height of its dominance in the mid-to-late 1950s, and the ability of the U.S. government, in a crisis, to mobilize those capabilities even against formidable domestic resistance.

The major theme of these cases is the efficacy of American action. The United States had so many resources—economic, political, and military— that it was able to attain its essential objectives in each of these situations. Hegemonic leadership rested on the deployment of tangible as well as intangible assets. The minor theme of these cases, most evident in the events surrounding the Anglo-American Petroleum Agreement in 1944–45 and those having to do with the emergency oil lift in 1956–57, concerns the impact of domestic politics in thwarting certain governmental initiatives and shaping others. As we shall observe at the end of this chapter, the fragility of American hegemonic leadership—reflected in the fact that it lasted, in full force, for a "long decade" rather than a century—can be accounted for in good measure by the refusal of domestic interests to adjust, or to sacrifice, for the sake of the long-term power position of the United States.

SECURING SAUDI OIL: 1943–48

Concern about future domestic oil shortages, and information about the vastness of Saudi Arabian reserves, led planners in the U.S. government in 1943 to pay attention to the problem of how to assure continued American control of the Saudi concession, held jointly at the time by Standard of California (Socal) and the Texas Company (Texaco). At first, worry centered on British designs, although "nowhere in the accessible British archives is there any evidence of a British plan in the 1940s to actually displace the American concessionaire."[13]

Having recognized the importance of Saudi oil in the postwar world, American planners moved vigorously to secure it for the United States. The first attempt, led by Interior Secretary Harold Ickes, centered on the development of a government-owned Petroleum Reserves Corporation (PRC). This extraordinary enterprise was to purchase all the stock in the California-Arabian Standard Oil Company (Casoc), then owned by Socal and Texaco; its board of directors was to consist of the secretaries of state, interior, war and navy. Although Ickes pushed hard for this plan, the State Department was always lukewarm at best. Eventually, negotiations for the purchase of Casoc were terminated as the result of pressure brought to bear on Ickes by Standard Oil of New Jersey (Jersey) and Socony-Vacuum (Socony).[14] The PRC later attempted to make arrangements for a government-owned pipeline from the Persian Gulf to the Mediterranean, a scheme that was also blocked by competitors of Socal and Texaco.[15]

Meanwhile, the State Department was urging a different route to secure control of Saudi oil: a petroleum agreement with Great Britain. The Anglo-American Petroleum Agreement was negotiated and signed first in 1944, and after severe criticism from the oil industry, renegotiated with industry participation during 1945; but it was never ratified as a treaty by the U.S. Senate. The complex story of the fate of the agreement has been well told elsewhere,[16] so a brief review will suffice.

The original agreement, signed in 1944, would have in effect established a government cartel for the management of world oil supplies. The joint Anglo-American Petroleum commission would "recommend production and exportation rates for the various concession areas in the Middle East [to prevent] . . . the disorganization of world markets which might result from uncontrolled competitive exploitation."[17] Middle Eastern production would be managed and markets guaranteed. Yet this proposal came up against a formidable coalition of interests. Members of the Senate Foreign Relations Committee had insisted successfully from the outset that the agreement be submitted to the Senate as a treaty. In a sense this sealed its fate, since the governmental cartelization approach "ran counter to the vested interests of the American independents, the antitrust philosophy of the Department of Justice, the laissez-faire ideology of a remnant of New Deal opponents, and State's long-standing practice of not supporting one domestic interest group over another.[18] Even had this not been sufficient to kill it, the proposal ran afoul of a fierce bureaucratic battle for the control of oil policy between Harold Ickes and the dominant forces in the State Department.

Having failed to secure Saudi oil either by direct government ownership or through international regulation, the U.S. government then turned to a policy of support for the efforts of major American oil companies—Socal, Texaco, Socony, and Jersey in particular—to guarantee their control of Middle Eastern oil. In 1946, Socal and Texaco found themselves with prolific reserves of oil in Saudi Arabia and a joint venture, now named ARAMCO, operating there with a skilled production team; but they also faced large demands for capital and uncertain markets for the huge quantities of oil that would be produced. Standard Oil of New Jersey, by contrast, was chronically crude-short, and concerned about being excluded from the richest, lowest-cost concession in the world. Moved by the business conservatism of their leaders, and over the strenuous objections of other company officials (at least in Socal), Socal and Texaco decided, in early 1946, to invite Jersey to purchase a share in ARAMCO. Eventually, Socony was also asked to participate, and arrangements were made for a 30 percent purchase in ARAMCO by Jersey and 10 percent participation for Socony.[19]

Yet to consummate this deal it was necessary somehow to nullify the restrictions of the Red Line Agreement of 1928. This agreement had required the partners in the Iraq Petroleum Company (IPC) to produce or purchase oil within the Red Line Area (including Arabia as well as Iraq, but not Iran) *only* through the IPC. In other words, IPC member companies were not to compete with the IPC itself within the Red Line Area. By 1946 the

IPC companies were Anglo-Iranian (23.75 percent), Shell (23.75 percent), Compagnie Française des Petroles (CFP, 23.75 percent), Socony (11.875 percent), Jersey (11.875 percent), and the Gulbenkian interests (5 percent). Socal and Texaco, not being members of the IPC, were not restrained from producing in Saudi Arabia; but Socony and Jersey were. For these companies to join ARAMCO would constitute a violation of the Red Line Agreement.

In early negotiations, Shell assured the American companies that it would participate in drafting new arrangements for IPC, and Jersey placated Anglo-Iranian with an agreement to purchase large amounts of Iranian and Kuwaiti oil from it, over a twenty-year period, and to construct a new pipeline (never built) from Abadan to the Mediterranean. CFP and Gulbenkian posed more serious problems. Fortunately for the American companies, however, during World War II CFP and Gulbenkian had operated within Nazi-controlled territory and had in 1940 been construed by a distinguished British barrister as having become "enemy aliens," thus rendering the Red Line Agreement null and void. This served as a sufficient pretext in 1946 for Jersey Standard and Socony to argue that the agreement was legally dissolved and to open negotiations for a new agreement free of the restrictive clauses of the earlier one.[20]

Not surprisingly, CFP objected strenuously. Not only were its leaders presumably insulted by being labeled "enemy aliens" as a result of the defeat of France; they feared that the effect of the ARAMCO deal would be to reduce production from Iraq, where CFP shared an interest. CFP therefore sought participation in ARAMCO itself, along with Jersey and Socony. In addition, the French government protested strongly, holding the U.S. government responsible, and threatening to take direct action in France against Jersey in retaliation for its actions.[21]

The companies and the State Department recognized the seriousness of French protests. Negotiations ensued, with the State Department providing "firm diplomatic support" for the companies.[22] The negotiations actually took place among the companies concerned, and with Gulbenkian personally, but were followed closely by the interested governments.

CFP's proposal for participation in ARAMCO was blocked by King 'Abd-al-'Aziz of Saudi Arabia, who declared that he would not agree to the sale of any part of ARAMCO to a non-American firm.[23] In February 1947 officials in the State Department proposed that Socony purchase the 11.875 percent holding of Jersey in the IPC and withdraw from the ARAMCO deal.[24] Had this been done, the Red Line Agreement would not have been violated. This scheme was not accepted by the companies, however.

The terms worked out dissolved the Red Line Agreement but did give the French the right to draw larger shares of oil from IPC production than their proportionate holdings in IPC would have allowed, and involved a commitment by Jersey and Socony to support increased IPC production. Protracted negotiations took place with Gulbenkian, who reportedly told John C. Case of Socony that he simply would not respect himself unless he "drove as good a bargain as possible." Gulbenkian's ace in the hole was the fact that he had filed suit in London, threatening to open the complex affairs of IPC to the public; the day before arguments were to begin, the suit was settled.[25]

Although the U.S. government stayed in the background on the Red Line issue, it clearly supported its companies in their efforts to solidify their control of Saudi Arabian oil while they, and the United States, were strong relative to European firms and governments. As in financial and commercial policy, establishment of dominance preceded exercise of hegemonic leadership.[26] With respect to the objective of securing U.S. control over Saudi oil, American policy was consistent, vigorous, and successful: Resistance outside the United States could be dealt with from a position of strength. The vehicle for American policy, however, had to be adapted to the realities of American society: Plans for government ownership or control were abandoned in favor of support for the expansion of private corporations. U.S. policy was shaped both by the opportunties abroad for extension of national power and the constraints, as well as opportunities, engendered by the institution of capitalism at home.

THE STERLING-DOLLAR OIL PROBLEM

Even during the war the British government anticipated a shortage of foreign exchange during the postwar years and insisted, in negotiations on a petroleum agreement, on "the right of each country to draw its consumption requirements, to the extent that may be considered necessary, from the production in its territories or in which rights are held by its nationals."[27] In 1949 Great Britain decided to take such measures to save on dollar costs by discriminating against American-owned oil companies, contrary to agreements reached between the British government and U.S. companies in the 1920s and '30s. British measures not only affected imports into the United Kingdom but also reduced sales of American firms in countries such as Argentina and Egypt, with which Britain made barter agreements, providing oil in return for other goods. The British government also, in the spring of 1949, ordered British bankers

> to refuse to transfer funds in payment for American-supplied oil from sterling balances in London of countries outside the sterling area. Consequently, such countries as Finland, Sweden, Norway, and Denmark, which were so short of dollars as to require that all or part of their oil needs be purchased with sterling, were unable to draw on their sterling balances in the United Kingdom to pay for imports supplied by American companies. Consequently, they had to buy sterling oil.[28]

Since real money was at stake, the U.S. companies protested, claiming that Britain's actions were meant less to save dollars than to strengthen the position of British companies in the world oil industry at the expense of their American competitors.[29] The glut of oil that had emerged, at current prices, made it impossible for the companies to sell all the petroleum that they could produce; so the Americans' loss was the British firm's gain. Furthermore, a cutback in markets for U.S.-owned Eastern Hemisphere oil was seen in the State Department as having ominous implications for America's security interests:

> This situation raises serious security, political and economic problems in view of the fact that the foreign oil concessions, refining and marketing facilities and organizations of American oil companies depend upon the maintenance of foreign market outlets. If the American oil companies producing abroad are faced with the shrinkage in the market for their output they must necessarily curtail production. If the American companies are forced to cut back production at the same time the British companies are expanding their output, the former are placed in a difficult political and financial position which may in turn prejudice U.S. national security interests.[30]

An internal State Department memo in December focused directly on the implications of British policy for the U.S. position in Saudi Arabia:

> Loss of one-quarter annual revenue might stalemate Saudi Arabia progress while neighboring states advance, jeopardizing the unique cooperation and friendship now existing between U.S. and Saudi Arabia. Western orientation of Saudi Arabia, which counters Arab reaction to Western support of Israel, would suffer.[31]

Not everyone in the U.S. government saw the national interest and the interests of the ARAMCO partners as so closely linked. Oil was selling at several times its cost of production, yet neither the American nor British companies were seriously considering reducing prices as a response to stagnation in demand. The British financial situation was much more serious than the plight of already-wealthy American oil companies:

> The important interests of the United States would not be served if the dollar and other economic drain on the British is maintained at anywhere near the present or projected levels. $710 million in fiscal 1950 and well over $600 million in 1953 seems an impossible drain for anyone to contemplate. The absolute maximum savings of dollars and economic resources on the sterling area's oil accounts are desperately needed in view of Britain's present balance of payments and budgetary positions and the uncertain outlook for future ECA [Economic Cooperation Administration] appropriations. . . . It would sound very badly to have it publicized that the Government imposed serious burdens on the British economy, thereby nullifying part of the U.S. foreign aid program, in order to win for the five big American oil companies in the Persian Gulf the unique privilege denied to all American farmers and other American businesses of selling for sterling in third countries, on the ground of threat to the U.S. national interest, when the companies are selling Persian Gulf oil at a price between three and five times the cost of its production.[32]

The problem was essentially one of adjustment costs: Who should have to pay the costs of adjusting to a slacker oil market? Different possible outcomes were associated with different patterns of cost:

1. Intense price competition could have taken place, sharply reducing the cost of imported oil in Europe and elsewhere. Consumers would have benefited from this outcome, which would have facilitated European industrial recovery. Indeed, the ECA exerted some downward pressure on prices, leading to a fall in the per barrel "company take" in the Middle East from $1.52 in 1948 to $1.14 in 1949, but no general price war ensued.[33]

For obvious reasons, neither the British nor American companies wished to "solve" the problem of an oil glut by reducing prices precipitously. Nor did the governments display enthusiasm for this solution. Britain did not use sterling devaluation, in 1949, to encourage British companies to undersell U.S. firms, or to prevent British companies from increasing their profits from oil for which costs were incurred in sterling. Britain was presumably worried about the effects on its current account of reduced oil company profits, and repatriation of profits, as well as on those profits per se (which were shared by the government through its partial ownership of British Petroleum). Those American officials concerned with Saudi Arabia and other producing countries would not have been happy with the adverse effects of lower oil prices on relations with these states. Taken together, the vested interests arrayed against a market solution to the problem were powerful and well organized.

2. The United States could have accepted greater oil imports, thus reducing excess supply on world markets, at the expense of U.S. *domestic* production. American independent firms would have borne much of the cost of adjustment. Despite the fact that this arrangement would have been efficient, and would have permitted a continued (but slower) growth of U.S. domestic production, "a solution on this basis would be strongly opposed by U.S. independent producers, however, and it would probably not permit nearly as large an expansion of U.S. output in the Middle East as U.S. companies have been planning."[34]

3. Great Britain could have withdrawn its restrictions on American companies' operations. In this case the burden of adjustment would have fallen chiefly on the British economy, since the dollar drain would have not been reduced.

4. The United States and Britain could have *jointly* forced adjustment costs on to others by requiring purchasers of oil outside the United States and Britain "to pay at least the dollar cost in dollars of the oil supplied." This was the essence of a plan presented in November 1949 by W. L. Faust of the Socony-Vacuum Oil Company. This was a proposal for duopolistic action; as the U.S. Counselor for Economic Affairs in London noted, "Of course, many consumers would object, but if all American and British oil were marketed in this pattern they would have no alternative but to accept it." Nitze argued similarly that "it may be desirable for the Governments of U.S. and U.K. to attempt to regulate, on a formal or informal basis, the

production and flow of oil products. Competition in the usual sense is unlikely and probably undesirable."[35]

5. Great Britain could have permitted U.S. companies to sell oil for sterling outside the sterling area, only converting into dollars the dollar cost of that oil; "unconverted pounds would be used by United States oil companies to purchase goods and services from the sterling area." This would have removed the discrimination against American firms (*vis-à-vis* British firms) while—according to Caltex (a Socal-Texaco company) and American officials who supported the scheme—not increasing the dollar drain on Britain beyond what would be incurred by *British* companies increasing their production abroad.[36]

Solutions 1, 2, and 3 were vetoed by powerful actors: The companies resisted price-cutting, U.S. domestic interests prevented large increases in oil imports, and the British government's concern for its financial position stood in the way of unilateral British concessions. The Faust Plan was unattractive to many elements of the U.S. government since it would not alleviate the general dollar shortage but merely transfer part of the dollar crisis from Britain to oil-consuming countries, many of which were also subsisting on U.S. aid. Furthermore,

> [t]he "third" countries, faced with paying a portion of the cost of petroleum in dollars, might demand similar treatment for their own exports of other commodities. . . . If this pricing policy became common we would be introducing an additional complicating element in international trade that seems clearly undesirable. Our general policy is in the opposite direction; for example, in our work on European integration our objective is to avoid the need for dollar settlements.[37]

The Faust Plan was essentially a proposal for a duopolistic imperial regime, which would extract resources from countries other than the United States and Britain for the benefit of U.S. and British oil companies. The U.S. Government could not accept it precisely for this reason: It conflicted too strongly with American policies in money and trade that emphasized hegemonic leadership and restabilization of the capitalist world economy. The great sympathy within the U.S. government, and in the Congress, for the oil companies seems to have inhibited the government from rejecting the Faust Plan out of hand, but the Caltex proposal (solution 5) was more congenial because it did not involve third-party complications and resulting threats to American milieu goals. Thus by December 1949 the Caltex proposal had essentially become the basis of the U.S. position:

> After extended interagency discussion, the U.S. government has proposed to the British that American companies be allowed to sell part of their production to third countries against sterling payment. U.S. companies would be allowed to convert into dollars an amount equal to dollar outlays British companies would have to make to replace equivalent existing U.S. production capacity.[38]

Acceptance of this proposal by the British would have ended the discriminatory advantages that British companies were then, according to the United States, gaining as a result of British governmental policy, and would have protected ARAMCO from unfair British competition:

> British companies are expanding at rates double normal estimates of increased demand and using surplus oil to displace United States oil through currency and trade restriction rather than through competition action such as price reductions, superior products, efficiency, etc.[39]

Yet the British government not only failed to accept this proposal but in December 1949 imposed new restrictions requiring affiliates of American companies to buy oil for import into the sterling area from British and British-Dutch companies rather than from American-owned firms (even members of their own group). "An American owned affiliate thereafter could import oil from sources owned by American companies only insofar as the volume of oil required to meet its needs was beyond what the companies having sterling status could supply. Jersey oil thus became marginal in its most important Eastern Hemisphere markets."[40] Jersey calculated that it would lose $85 million worth of sales during 1950 as a result of this regulation.

The American companies responded to this attack on their interests in two ways. First, they pressed the U.S. government to intervene more actively on their behalf. In January 1950 Tom Connally, then chairman of the Senate Foreign Relations Committee and a leading spokesman for petroleum interests (although especially for the Texas independents), advocated a cutoff of all Economic Cooperation Administration assistance to Britain. This was not done, but the ECA did suspend assistance to projects for expanding the British oil industry.[41] In April the State Department "presented a note to the British Government insisting on the right of United States companies to trade anywhere in the sterling area."[42]

At least some of the companies, of which Jersey is an example, also entered into direct negotiations with the British government. Having secured the support of the U.S. government,

> Jersey's Howard Page finally negotiated a complicated but satisfactory settlement directly with the British treasury in May 1950. The British agreed to end gasoline rationing, and Jersey undertook to supply all of the additional gasoline required by its British affiliates with payment in sterling. Instead of remitting profits to the United States in dollars, Jersey would use the sterling proceeds to purchase needed goods and equipment manufactured in Britian. Along with a series of similar agreements worked out by Page in 1950 and 1951, this arrangement essentially solved the dollar oil problem.[43]

This solution was facilitated by the economic boom that took place after the Korean war broke out in June of 1950. Increased economic activity quickly eliminated the oil surplus and improved Britain's balance of payments position.

The sterling-dollar oil problem illustrates the combination of pursuit of narrowly defined self-interest and concern for alliance management that characterized U.S. hegemonic leadership. American companies were being discriminated against, and the State Department therefore came to their aid; but even before the Korean war broke out, the American desire to rebuild a strong Western Europe—reinforced and rationalized by the Soviet threat— inhibited the government from pushing the oil companies' case too hard. The United States was not willing to permit discrimination against powerful American interests under the guise of financial necessity; but its reaction was restrained. The outbreak of the Korean war, by stimulating rearmament and preventing a recurrence of serious recession, removed the initial economic difficulty of oversupply that had led to the issue in the first place. The intensity of the cold war after 1950 removed the major oil problem between the United States and Britain while reinforcing the inclination of both governments to settle their differences amicably.

THE EMERGENCY OIL LIFT PROGRAM, 1956–57

In July 1956 a series of disputes erupted between Egypt and the major Western powers, in particular the United States, Britain, and France. On July 19, the United States withdrew its offer to contribute $56 million toward financing the Aswan Dam; one week later, Egypt nationalized the Suez Canal. This led to an international crisis, the climax of which involved the invasion of Egypt by Israeli, British, and French forces in late October and the collapse of that invasion under pressure from the United States as well as resistance from Egypt and threats from the Soviet Union. As a result of the military actions, the Suez Canal, which at that time was the main route for oil shipments between the Persian Gulf and Europe, was suddenly blocked, leading to a potentially severe oil shortage in Europe.[44]

The reaction of the U.S. Government to this crisis provides a clearer illustration of hegemonic leadership in action. The United States used its great economic and political resources, and its links with major international oil companies, to cope successfully with the oil shortfall and achieve its own political purposes in the process.

Immediately following nationalization of the Suez Canal, the United States set up a Middle East Emergency Committee (MEEC), [composed] of fifteen major U.S.-based oil companies, under the provisions of the Defense Production Act of 1950. The companies declared that they could not devise alternative tanker schedules for a crisis in any detail until it was known what the situation would be; but they established the organizational structure of the MEEC and acquired the requisite antitrust waivers from the government to allow them to coordinate among themselves. Planning was left to the companies: The role of the government, according to the director of the Office of Defense Mobilization, was to encourage voluntary agreements among the companies and to exempt them from antitrust laws.[45] In September the British, Dutch, and French governments sponsored the establishment of a parallel committee composed of the major European-based oil companies (Royal Dutch Shell, British Petroleum, and Compagnie Française des Petroles).[46]

In response to the British-French-Israeli invasion of Egypt, the United States suspended the operations of the MEEC, and it did not meet thereafter until December 3, 1956.[47] The U.S. government was clearly using the threat of an oil shortage to put pressure on Britain and France, during November, to withdraw their troops from Suez. By the end of November, however, it had become clear to American leaders that further pressure on the Europeans was unnecessary and would weaken the Atlantic alliance. President Eisenhower ordered reactivation of the MEEC to permit it not only to arrange tanker schedules but to enter into arrangements on a collective basis with the Organization for European Economic Cooperation (OEEC), in order properly to plan for oil allocations. The Oil Committee of the OEEC established a Petroleum Industry Emergency Group from the industry (involving the United States as well as European companies), which advised the Oil Committee on procedures for allocation of scarce oil supplies among the European countries.[48] The United States insisted that the OEEC rather than the United States or the companies take the responsibility for allocating oil by country. One reason for this was to deflect Arab criticism of the United States, which would have been intense if America had aided Britain and France directly.[49]

Yet the United States played far from a passive role. It urged the OEEC to take immediate action to allocate supplies on a pro rata basis; and the MEEC reinforced the pressure to do so by deciding on December 28 not to cooperate on allocation arrangements in Europe without an OEEC decision, which was eventually forthcoming on January 7. Meanwhile, the MEEC approved tanker schedules allowing more efficient shipments of crude oil and refined products from Venezuela and the United States to Europe, replacing in good measure the long haul around the Cape of Good Hope for oil from the Persian Gulf.[50]

During the early phase of the crisis—between the closure of the canal and early January—the problem was essentially one of transportation: "not one of a shortage of oil but a shortage of the means of bringing it to Europe."[51] If normal tanker patterns had been maintained. Europe would have received little more than 60 percent of its estimated needs. Yet reallocation of tanker patterns was remarkably easy; indeed, even before the MEEC was reactivated, international oil companies had increased their shipments from the United States to Western Europe from an average of 50,000 barrels a day to 370,000 barrels a day, and had increased shipments to Europe by a further 224,000 barrels a day by increasing shipments from the Caribbean and diverting Middle Eastern crude from the United States to Europe.[52]

The more serious problem after the beginning of January was not tanker availability but the supply of crude oil. Increases in shipments from the

United States were accomplished largely by drawing down stocks, which could not continue indefinitely. But the Texas Railroad Commission, which controlled production in Texas, refused to increase allowable production in January, and only increased it slightly in February, despite the European crises. The commission sought higher oil prices—an increase of 12 percent did take place in early January—and feared a later oil glut if supply were increased too rapidly. Independent Texas producers far from the coast opposed the supply increase since their output was effectively limited by transport problems, and they would benefit from higher prices. Furthermore, Europe needed heavy crude oil, but U.S. producers feared that as a consequence of increasing crude oil shipments to Europe, they would be stuck with large supplies of gasoline, which would depress the U.S. market. Thus there was what the *Oil and Gas Journal* called a "transatlantic feud" between the United Kingdom and the Texas Railroad Commission. The commission wanted the UK to end gas rationing and purchase gasoline from the United States in return for increased Texas production. European diplomats were pressuring the State Department for increased production, the assistant secretary of the Interior was calling for increased U.S. production, but the state regulatory agencies dragged their feet.[53]

Finally, President Eisenhower took a direct hand in the matter. In his presidential news conference of February 6, 1957, the following colloquy took place:[54]

William McGaffin, Chicago Daily News: The United States has been lagging on oil deliveries to Western Europe, one reason being that the Texas Control Board has not okayed a step-up in production in Texas. According to latest reports, Great Britain is down to about two weeks' oil supply. What do you intend to do?

President Eisenhower: Well, of course, there are certain powers given to the President where he could move into the whole field of state proration. I think the federal government should not disturb the economy of our country except when it has to. On the other hand, I believe that the business concerns of our country, the people that operate the tanker lines, the people that produce the oil, and all the other agencies, including those of the proration boards, should consider where do our long-term interests lie. Certainly they demand a Europe that is not flat on its back economically. . . .

Now all of this oil must flow in such a quantity as to fill up every tanker we have operating at maximum capacity. And if that doesn't occur, then we must do something in the way, first, I should say, of conference and argument and, if necessary, we would have to move in some other region or some other direction, either with our facilities or with others. But it must be done.

Faced with this barely veiled threat of federal action, the Texas Railroad Commission shortly thereafter increased the allowable production for March by 237,000 barrels per day over the February figure, to a point that was 380,000 barrels per day over pre-Suez levels. The big international firms favored the increase, and independents were now willing to go along because stocks had been reduced and prices had been raised during the first two months of the year.[55]

Once this had been done, the crisis evaporated quickly. With a mild winter, and more Gulf oil available, drains on stocks were arrested from February onward; tanker schedules were canceled on April 18, 1957, and the activities of the MEEC and its European partner organizations were effectively ended by May.[56]

The Emergency Oil Lift Program illustrates, in striking form, the paradox of external strength and domestic weakness that Stephen Krasner points to in his account of U.S. foreign economic policy.[57] The United States had overwhelming power internationally: It was able not only to stop the Anglo-French-Israeli invasion of Suez but, in the wake of that episode, to persuade European countries to decide on oil allocations and to use its own oil companies, with their tanker fleets, and its unused petroleum capacity at home, to supply Europe adequately with oil during the winter. Policy coordination between the U.S. government and the multinational companies, between U.S. and European companies, and between the U.S. and European governments was arranged harmoniously. The United States controlled immense resources that it could reallocate at little cost to itself; it was therefore able to exercise leadership *vis-à-vis* the Europeans, who had little choice but to follow. The key difficulties faced by the Eisenhower administration were internal—with the Texas Railroad Commission in particular. Federal-state policy coordination was so difficult that it required a threat of drastic action to achieve the desired results; U.S.-European coordination was easy by comparison. In this case, at least, the management of interdependence indeed depended on what happened at home.[58]

PRECONDITIONS FOR
HEGEMONIC LEADERSHIP

Characteristic patterns of international economic behavior during the long decade of the 1950s seem to merit the labels of economic interdependence, or liberalism. Discrimination in international trade was gradually reduced, tariff barriers fell somewhat, and the international monetary system was reconstituted on the basis of pegged exchange rates with the dollar as international money. The volume of international trade, payments, and investment increased enormously. Concomitantly, economic growth was rapid, fueled by ample supplies of petroleum, the price of which was falling.

Politically, the decade could be described in terms of the growth of "complex interdependence," involving growing transnational, intergovernmental, and transgovernmental relationships among the advanced capitalist countries.[59] Force was banished as a direct, explicit means of influence among their governments; at the same time, the connections between domestic political economy and international political economy seemed to become more important—as illustrated by the Emergency Oil Lift Program of 1956–57. U.S. foreign economic policy fit the pattern of hegemonic leadership that Hirsch and Doyle describe: The United States both played a crucial role in bringing complex interdependence about, and adapted effectively to it.

Yet it would be mistaken to infer from these patterns of interdependence that power had been eliminated from international political economy. As Robert Gilpin has emphasized: "An economic system does not arise spontaneously owing to the operation of an invisible hand and in the absence of the exercise of power. Rather, every economic system rests on a particular political order; its nature cannot be understood aside from politics."[60]

Complex interdependence, and the relatively benign attention that the United States gave to the political economy of Western capitalism, rested on American industrial and financial dominance, as well as on American politico-military power. This is revealed especially well by examining U.S. policy, issue by issue, *before* American dominance had been achieved. In each case, the United States was less accommodating when it was seeking to establish its position of dominance than it later became after that position was secure.

In its first term the Roosevelt administration had been careful not to exercise international financial leadership; indeed, President Roosevelt virtually forced the adjournment of the London Economic Conference of 1933 with his famous message declaring that "the old fetishes of so-called international bankers are being replaced by efforts to plan national currencies with the objective of giving those currencies a continuing purchasing power."[61] As the 1930s depression continued and war grew closer, the United States became somewhat accommodating, particularly in the Tripartite Agreement of 1936, but this was only a very cautious step toward international cooperation. The Bretton Woods Conference of 1944 and the British Loan of 1945–46 marked a sharp change in American policy toward exercise of international leadership; but it is important to note that the terms offered by the United States for its cooperation were still very tough. At Bretton Woods, the United States stood for its interests as a creditor country, seeking to avoid becoming involuntary lender to the world.[62] According to revisionist historians, the U.S. government deliberately attempted to keep Britain just strong enough financially to be able to adopt liberal trade and payments policy but weak enough that it could not forego postwar U.S. credits.[63]

In part, this financial policy was a result of American commercial policy, which sought to ensure that Britain, and other capitalist countries, would dismantle preferential trade arrangements and cooperate in the establishment of nondiscriminatory international trade. The stringent terms imposed by the United States, in particular the Treasury Department, on the loan granted to Britain in 1945–46 reflected this aim.[64] As we have seen, only when British weakness had been revealed in 1947 was there a pronounced change in this policy. Although the long-run objective of assuring multilateralism remained, the conditions perceived by the United States had changed: Now it was clear that the United States was the dominant Western power and that it no longer had to fear the strength of its partners. Indeed, since their weakness had become the chief problem, it was appropriate to shift from a vigorous policy of breaking down trade barriers to one of combining support for rebuilding European economies, temporary acceptance of discrimination against American exports, and long-run moves toward liberalized trade.

In petroleum policy, as we have seen, vigorous actions to attain American objectives—whether through government ownership of oil reserves, a bilateral cartel, or support for enterprising American petroleum firms—also preceded the more benign phase of hegemonic leadership, as represented by the Emergency Oil-Lift Program. The United States sought control over crucial resources before it was willing to be generous in their disposition.

MAINTAINING THE VIABILITY OF HEGEMONIC LEADERSHIP

Any strategy that is viable in the long term has to re-create the conditions for its own existence. If the strategy requires maintenance of national strength, following the strategy must generate strength, or the strategy will eventually collapse. Any hegemonic leadership strategy, therefore, must seek to maintain the national base of resources upon which governmental influence, and leadership, rest.

Over the whole postwar period, U.S. policy has failed to assure this condition for long-term success. The United States has remained a major, although not dominant, factor in international trade, but during the 1960s and '70s its sectoral trade balances deteriorated severely in a number of major areas involving relatively advanced technology, such as motor vehicles; and concern was expressed about American advantages in such leading sectors as semiconductors and aircraft. American influence over international monetary regimes had rested during the 1950s on the stability of the dollar, and the confidence people had in it; stability and confidence both declined precipitously in the wake of persistent American current deficits during the late 1960s and early '70s, and the refusal of the U.S. government, after 1973, to support the value of the dollar in international markets. In oil, the decline in American resources was even more dramatic: in 1956, the United States imported 11 percent of its oil consumption and had excess capacity of 25 percent for an overall surplus of 14 percent; by 1973, imports amounted to 35 percent of consumption (on their way to 45 percent +) and excess production capacity was a mere 10 percent of consumption by comparison.[65]

The failures to maintain American dominance seem to have had somewhat diverse sources. In trade, comparative advantage shifted as Europe and Japan recovered from the war and as formerly unindustrialized countries began to industrialize. In the monetary area, the United States attempted to fight the Vietnam war without making the requisite financial adjustments, and then continued, through much of the 1970s, to maintain an inflationary economy that continued to undermine the value of the dollar. Since the United States was the world's dominant financial power, it could refuse to adjust and at least temporarily shift the burden of adjustment onto others; but the eventual consequences for its currency and for its financial leadership were severe.

In petroleum, the sources of American weakness lay in the political power of domestic interests. As we saw earlier, the Anglo-American Petroleum Agreement was defeated by a coalition of interests led by independent domestic oilmen. In addition to securing U.S. control of Saudi oil reserves, planners in the State Department had sought to use the agreement to conserve domestic petroleum reserves by drawing down those of the Eastern Hemisphere. Acting Petroleum Adviser James Sappington argued in a memo of December 1943 that Middle Eastern oil should be "developed to the maximum and that supplies in this hemisphere be . . . conserved." Sappington even contemplated the possibility of Middle Eastern oil displacing domestic oil in the U.S. market, thus achieving "a further conservation of the reserves of [the Western] . . . hemisphere."[66]

In May 1945 the same objective obtained, although the State Department, in its public statements, was at pains to deny this. At that time, the head of the Petroleum Division, John A. Loftus, described the essential objectives of the Anglo-American Petroleum Agreement in a confidential memorandum as follows:

> We want the operating policies of British private petroleum companies to be in reasonable conformity with our general policy objective of effecting a relative increase in the rate of exploitation in the Eastern Hemisphere (particularly Middle Eastern) petroleum reserves, and a relative decrease in the rate of exploitation in the Western Hemisphere. This is an objective which probably cannot be stated in precise or quantitative terms without provoking acute internal political controversy here; and even if precision were possible a quantitative agreement on petroleum production would sufficiently approximate a cartelization of the petroleum industry as to be subject to serious criticism in terms of our general economic foreign policy. Therefore . . . the best, if not the only, approach appears to be to obtain from the British an agreement upon certain broad principles governing petroleum development. In this case the principles would be of such a character as to permit and facilitate the expansion of Eastern Hemisphere (Middle Eastern) oil production.[67]

By this time State Department planners probably realized that the aspiration to increase imports of petroleum into the United States, at the expense of domestic production, was unrealizable, but they continued to seek to limit the necessity for the export of Western Hemisphere petroleum to the Old World. Independent oilmen and senators from oil-producing states discerned the true purpose of the agreement, despite misleading statements from its proponents; they suspected correctly that "the object of the treaty is to permit the movement of petroleum from the Near East throughout the world and, if necessary, into the United States, rather than developing, or further developing, the oil resources of the United States."[68]

The defeat of the petroleum agreement, which was reported by the Foreign Relations Committee to the Senate in July 1947 but never voted upon,[69] illustrates once again the domestic Achilles heel of American foreign economic policy. State Department officials correctly foresaw the folly of "draining America first" while foreign oil could still be obtained easily and cheaply; but they could not prevail against domestic interests in a protected energy market. Defeat of the treaty was followed, in the 1950s, by the development of import quotas on oil, which further accelerated the exhaustion of American petroleum resources and therefore U.S. power resources in the world economy. The seeds of destruction of the hegemonic leadership policy had been planted before the policy itself had ever been implemented.

CONCLUSION AND IMPLICATIONS

The United States did indeed follow a hegemonic leadership strategy during the long decade of the 1950s. In the short to intermediate term, this strategy was a success: It assisted in the economic and political recovery of Europe and Japan, and maintained the milieu goals that the American government sought during the cold war. American leadership rested heavily on the dominance achieved by the United States, by 1947–48, in the major areas of foreign economic policy including finance, trade in manufactured goods, and petroleum. Stable money, nondiscriminatory trade, and cheap energy were the foundations for the American decade. The cold war legitimated U.S. leadership, but the resources used by the United States were derived from its own sources of political-economic strength.

In the longer run the hegemonic leadership strategy was self-liquidating; rather than perpetuate the conditions for its success, it permitted their demise. It is arguable that a decline in U.S. dominance was inevitable in trade; but the difficulties in finance and oil were more clearly of America's own making. The United States refused to adjust to a weakened financial position, in the late 1960s and '70s, instead resorting to financing its deficits and maintaining consumption through a process of disinvestment. In petroleum, special interests prevented the implementation of a farsighted strategic policy of conservation, which officials of the State Department were perceptive and public-spirited enough to envisage and support. In the crucial areas of finance and oil, American policy was crucially—indeed, fatally—weakened by the inconsistency of domestic policies with long-run international imperatives.

Thus the United States contracted a disease of the strong: refusal to adjust to change. Small states do not have the luxury of deciding whether or how fast to adjust to external change. They do not seek adjustment. It is thrust upon them, because they are not powerful enough to control the terms through which they relate to the international economic system. Powerful countries can postpone adjustment; and the stronger they are, the longer it can be postponed. Where adversity is temporary, this helps the powerful country to ride out the storm. But where adverse secular shifts are taking place, it merely postpones the inevitable, making it more difficult to deal with in the future. In this case, the ability to avoid costs in the short term simply gives myopic leaders, or institutions that yield myopic policy results despite leaders' preferences, the chance to dissipate their advantages. For Spain in the sixteenth century, discoveries of bullion in America had ultimately disastrous rather than beneficial effects: They contributed to the ruin of the economy and the crashing defeat of overextended Spanish armies.[70] For Britain in the nineteenth century, the existence of the Empire, into which it could retreat, fatally delayed a national reaction to industrial decline.[71] For the United States during the 1950s and '60s, its overwhelming economic superiority after World War II, buttressed by the deference that it received as the head of a cold-war alliance, also seems to have made it oblivious to the need for policy change.

It would be hard to argue that the United States has gone as far down the road toward economic oblivion as Spain had by the seventeenth century or Britain by 1914. Yet it seems clear that an enduring revival of American influence will not be produced by the return of cold war (if such should happen) alone. Internal measures—to adjust to change, to build up industrial strength through investment and technological development to bring energy consumption and production more closely into balance—are necessary conditions for successful reassertion of U.S. leadership. As in the 1950s, interdependence can be managed only if the resources are available, if investments in national power, as well as in wealth, have been made. If capabilities are lacking, slogans about leadership will be to no avail.

NOTES

1. Immanuel Wallerstein, *The Modern World System II: Mercantilism and the Consolidation of the European World-Economy, 1600–1750* (New York: Academic Press, 1980), p. 38.

2. For the data, see Stephen D. Krasner, "United States Commercial and Monetary Policy: Unraveling the Paradox of External Strength and Internal Weakness," in *Between Power and Plenty: Foreign Economic Policies of Advanced Industrial States*, ed. Peter J. Katzenstein (Madison: University of Wisconsin Press, 1978), pp. 68–69.

3. Robert O. Keohane and Joseph S. Nye, Jr., *Power and Independence: World Politics in Transition* (Boston: Little Brown, 1977), p. 44.

4. For a discussion of Holland's "hegemony," see Wallerstein, *Modern World System*.

5. GDP data from Robert O. Keohane, "The Theory of Hegemonic Stability and Changes in International Economic Regimes, 1967–1977," in *Change in the International System*, ed. Ole Holsti, Randolph Siverson, and Alexander L. George (Boulder, Col.: Westview, 1980), p. 144. Trade data from Krasner, "U.S. Commercial and Monetary Policy."

6. Fred Hirsch and Michael Doyle, "Politicization in the World Economy: Necessary Conditions for an International Economic Order," in Hirsch, Doyle, Morse, *Alternatives to Monetary Disorder* (New York: McGraw-Hill for Council on Foreign Relations, 1977), pp. 27–28.

7. Arnold Wolfers, "The Goals of Foreign Policy," in Wolfers, *Discord and Collaboration: Essays on International Politics* (Baltimore: Johns Hopkins University Press, 1962), chap. 5.

8. For a lucid and concise general account, see Stephen D. Krasner, *Defending the National Interest: Raw Materials Investments and U.S. Foreign Policy* (Princeton: Princeton

University Press, 1978), pp. 119–128, 188–215. New information on the period up to 1950 can be found in the thoroughly researched study by Irvine H. Anderson, *Aramco, the United States, and Saudi Arabia: A Study in the Dynamics of Foreign Oil Policy, 1933–1950* (Princeton: Princeton University Press, 1981). Anderson goes well beyond two other recent books on the subject: Aaron David Miller, *Search for Security: Saudi Arabian Oil and American Foreign Policy, 1939–1949* (Chapel Hill: University of North Carolina Press, 1980); and Michael B. Stoff, *Oil, War, and American Security: The Search for a National Policy on Foreign Oil, 1941–1947* (New Haven: Yale University Press, 1980).

9. Hirsch and Doyle, "Politicization in World Economy," pp. 31–32.

10. The literature on American financial and trade policies after World War II is voluminous. For a good overview, see Krasner, "U.S. Commercial and Monetary Policy." On monetary affairs, see Richard Gardner, *Sterling-Dollar Diplomacy* (New York: Oxford University Press, 1956); Fred Block, *The Origins of International Economic Disorder* (Berkeley: University of California Press, 1976); Alfred Eckes, *A Search for Solvency: Bretton Woods and the International Monetary System, 1941–1971* (Austin: University of Texas Press, 1975). On trade, see E. F. Penrose, *Economic Planning for the Peace* (Princeton: Princeton University Press, 1953); Clair Wilcox, *A Charter for World Trade* (1949); Robert E. Hudec, *The GATT Legal System and World Trade Diplomacy* (1975), pp. 3–58; and Gardner, *Sterling-Dollar Diplomacy.*

11. For a discussion, see Gardner Patterson, *Discrimination in International Trade: The Policy Issues* (Princeton: Princeton University Press, 1966), pp. 271–305.

12. Walter LaFeber, *America, Russia and the Cold War, 1945–71* (New York: John Wiley, 1972), p. 53.

13. Anderson, *Aramco,* chap. 2.

14. Ibid.

15. Ibid., chap. 3.

16. Anderson, *Aramco,* has the most complete and detailed account. Stoff also discusses the agreement at some length, although he does not sufficiently appreciate the differences between the first draft and the second, or the loss of enthusiasm in the State Department for the redrafted version. See Stoff, *Oil, War, Security,* pp. 178–95; compare with Anderson, chap. 5.

17. Memorandum, "The Petroleum Division," October 1944, pp. 38–39 (Box 48, Harley Notter files, Record Group 59, National Archives); cited by Anderson, *Aramco,* chap. 3, note 76. It should be noted that for this paper, I have worked from the uncorrected galley proofs of Anderson's book, kindly lent to me by Sanford Thatcher of Princeton University Press. Page numbers for the text are therefore unavailable, and it is possible that final footnote numbers will be different from those given here.

18. Anderson, *Aramco,* chap. 3.

19. Ibid., chap. 5. Anderson has made a significant historiographical contribution by showing that Socal and Texaco took the initiative in offering part of ARAMCO to Jersey; it was formerly believed that Jersey pressed first for participation.

20. The essentials of the story in the last two paragraphs can be found in the materials listed below, on which the first draft of this paper relied. The most comprehensive and solidly researched account, however, is in Anderson, *Aramco,* chap. 5. For the other materials, see *The International Petroleum Cartel* (staff report to the Federal Trade Commission, submitted to the subcommittee on monopoly of the Select Committee on Small Business, U.S. Senate, 22 August 1952; reprinted 22 April 1975); *Multinational Oil Corporations and U.S. Foreign Policy, Hearings of the Subcommittee on Multinational Corporations,* U.S. Senate, Committee on Foreign Relations (93-2), 1974, p. 8, Appendix 2; *Multinational Oil Corporations and U.S. Foreign*

Policy (U.S. Senate, Committee on Foreign Relations, subcommittee on multinational corporations, 1975), chap. 2, "The 1947 Aramco Merger," pp. 45–55; John M. Blair, *The Control of Oil* (New York: Random House, 1976). For the draft contract between Jersey and the Anglo-Iranian Oil Company, see National Archives (Record Group 59, Box 4231, file no. 800.6363/1-2847), material dated 20 December 1946, with a covering letter from a Jersey Standard official to the head of the Petroleum Division of the Department of State, indicating that this contract was the basic document in the transaction. See also Anderson, *Aramco*, chap. 5.

21. Dispatches of 14 and 20 January 1947 from the Embassy in London to the State Department (Record Group 59, Box 4231, file no. 800.6363/1-1447 and 800.6363/1-2047).

22. Anderson, *Armaco,* chap. 5.

23. Ibid.

24. Memo from Paul Nitze to Will Clayton, 21 February 1947 (National Archives, Record Group 59, Box 4231, file no. 800.6363/2-2147).

25. Anderson, *Aramco,* chap. 5. The Church subcommittee on multinational corporations alleged in 1975 that "although Exxon and Mobil eventually reached an IPC settlement the French never forgave the Americans for keeping them out of Saudi Arabia." *Multinational Oil Corporations and U.S. Foreign Policy,* p. 55. No evidence, however, is adduced for this assertion, of which no trace appears in Anderson's account. Indeed, certain pieces of evidence suggest the contrary. The U.S. Embassy in London reported on 14 March 1947 that the French seemed to like the idea that they could purchase more than their regular quota of oil from IPC (Record Group 59, Box 4231, file no. 841.6363/3-1447). On 29 May 1947, the Embassy reported satisfaction in London with "the only cloud on the I.P.C. horizon at the moment is the difficulty the major partners are having with Gulbenkian" (Record Group 59, Box 4231, file no. 800.6363/5-2947).

26. Linda Cahn argues that leadership strategies on commodity policy (wheat, sugar, tin) have been consistently followed by the United States only in situations where US hegemony was assured. See "National Power and International Regimes: United States Commodity Policies, 1930–1980" (Ph.D. dissertation, Stanford University, 1980).

27. Memorandum, "The Petroleum Division," October 1944, p. 35 (Box 48, Harley Notter files, National Archives, Record Group 59). Cited in Anderson *Aramco*, chap. 3, note 73.

28. Henrietta M. Larson, Evelyn H. Knowlton, and Charles S. Popple, *New Horizons, 1927–1950,* vol. 3 of *History of Standard Oil Company (New Jersey)* (New York: Harper & Row, 1971), p. 706.

29. William Adams Brown Jr., and Redvers Opie, *American Foreign Assistance* (Washington, D.C.: Brookings Institution, 1953), p. 226. See also Larson et al., p. 707; *New Horizons,* and Anderson, *Aramco,* chap. 6.

30. Memorandum of Conversation of a meeting called by Paul Nitze of the Bureau of Economic Affairs, Department of State, on 9 April 1949, "to discuss the major aspects of the dollar-sterling oil problem and the views thereon of the interested offices of the Department" (Record Group 59, Box 4232, file number; 800.6363/4-949).

31. "Working Paper, Near East Conference," 20 December 1949, p. 4 (Box 2, Records of the Petroleum Division, Record Group 59). Anderson also refers to this working paper, considering it as expressing "the basic State Department position for the duration of the 'dollar oil' crisis." See Anderson, *Aramco,* chap. 6, note 94.

32. Personal memo of George Eddy of the Office of International Finance, Treasury Department, referred to in a memo from Eddy to Henry Labouisse in the State

Department, on 16 December 1949. (Record Group 59, Box 4232, 800.6363/12-1649). Eddy's personal memo had somehow fallen into the hands of the British, who were using it in their arguments with the American government. Raymond Mikesell, in the Department of State, also criticized high oil price policies: "I hope that some consideration will be given to the consumer, who thus far has been the forgotten man in this picture!" (Record Group 59, Box 4232, file no. 841.6363/7-649 CS/RA).

33. Brown and Opie, *American Foreign Assistance*, pp. 227–30. For the figures, see Hanns Maull, *Europe and World Energy* (London: Butterworth, 1980), p. 211.

34. Memo from Paul Nitze of the Bureau of Economic Affairs to the Secretary of State, 27 April 1949. (Record Group 59, Box 4232, file no. 800.6363/4-2749).

35. The quotes all come from documents in the National Archives of the United States (Record Group 59, Box 4232): (1) Memo of Conversation of meeting between B. Brewster Jennings, President, Socony-Vacuum Oil Company, Inc. and various members of the Department of State staff, 21 December 1949 (file no. 841.6363/12-2149; (2) letter of 2 December 1949, from Don C. Bliss, counselor for Economic Affairs of the United States Embassy in London to Henry R. Labouisse, Jr., Office of British and Northern European Affairs, Department of State (file no. 800.6363/12-249; and (3) Memorandum of Conversation of a meeting called by Paul Nitze of the Bureau of Economic Affairs, Department of State, April 9, 1949, "to discuss the major aspects of the dollar-sterling oil problem and the views thereon of the interested offices of the Department." Record Group 59, Box 4232, file number 800.6363/4-949.

36. For the quotation and the argument, see a memorandum to Ambassador Childs from R. Funkhouser, "Background on Current US-UK Oil Talks" (National Archives, Record Group 59, Box 4232, no file number, no date). It appears to have been written in September 1949.

37. Memorandum from Mr. Rosenson of the State Department Monetary Affairs Staff to Henry R. Labouisse, Jr., Office of British and Northern European Affairs (Record Group 59, Box 4232, file no. 800.6363/12-1349), 13 December 1949.

38. Working Paper, Near East Conference, 20 December 1949. (Record Group, Box 4232, no file number), p. 1.

39. Ibid., p. 3.

40. Larson et al., *New Horizons*, pp. 706–07.

41. Brown and Opie, *American Foreign Assistance*, p. 226. Within ECA, Walter Levy, ranking petroleum officer, had pointed out as early as February 1949 the difficulties posed for American companies by ECA plans to finance refinery construction in European countries by European firms (See National Archives, Record Group 59, Box 4232, file number 800.6363/2-1048, for E. L. McGinnes, Jr., memo on meeting of International Petroleum Policy Committee, 10 February 1949).

42. The quotation is from Joyce and Gabriel Kolko, *The Limits of Power* (New York: Harper & Row, 1972), p. 461. In a meeting held on 9 December 1949 a representative of the Socony-Vacuum Oil Company, had "emphasized that the oil companies were convinced that they would be unable to get anywhere with the British unless and until the State Department took a firm position with the British and insisted that a settlement of the matter be reached" (Memorandum of Conversation, Department of State, Record Group 59, Box 4232, file no. 841.6363/12-949, 9 December 1949), p. 2.

43. Anderson, *Aramco*, chap. 6.

44. For general accounts, see Robert Engler, *The Politics of Oil* (University of Chicago Press, 1961), pp. 260–63; Shoshana Klebanoff, *Middle East Oil and US Foreign Policy* (New York: Praeger, 1974), esp. p. 119; Paul Johnson, *The Suez War* (New

York: Greenberg Press, 1957). The *Economist* (London) offered thorough coverage of the crisis throughout.

45. Testimony of Arthur Flemming, Director, Office of Defense Mobilization, U.S. Government, in *Emergency Oil Lift Program and Related Oil Problems, Joint Hearings before Subcommittees of the Committee on the Judiciary and Committee on Interior and Insular Affairs, U.S. Senate* (85th Congress, 1st sess.), 5–21 February 1957, p. 12.

46. Organization for European Economic Cooperation (OEEC), *Europe's Need for Oil: Implications and Lessons of the Suez Crisis* (Paris, 1958), p. 21.

47. Engler, *Politics of Oil*, pp. 261, 307. *Emergency Oil Lift Program* hearings (henceforth *EOLP*), pp. 2543–48.

48. *Europe's Need for Oil*, pp. 28–29; *Petroleum Survey*, "1957 Outlook," *Hearings before the Committee on Interstate and Foreign Commerce, House of Representatives* (85th Congress, 1st sess.), February–March 1957, pp. 111–13; *EOLP*, p. 595. Eisenhower declared on 30 November 1956 that "the contemplated coordination of industry efforts will insure the most efficient use of tankers and the maximum availability of petroleum product." *Public Papers of the President, 1956*, p. 902.

49. For discussions of relations between the MEEC and the OEEC, see *EOLP*, pp. 1884–1931, 2451–52, 2538–49, 2583–89.

50. *EOLP*, p. 1983.

51. *Europe's Need for Oil*, p. 33.

52. Ibid., pp. 34, 29.

53. *Economist* (London), 12 January 1957, pp. 113, 133; *Oil and Gas Journal*, 21 January 1957, p. 74; 4 February 1957, p. 80.

54. *Public Papers of the President, 1957*, p. 124.

55. *Oil and Gas Journal*, 25 February 1957, p. 78.

56. *Europe's Need for Oil*, p. 38.

57. Krasner, "U.S. Commercial and Monetary Policy."

58. For a discussion of similar problems, see Peter J. Katzenstein, "Introduction: Domestic and International Forces and Strategies of Foreign Economic Policy," in Katzenstein, *Between Power and Plenty*.

59. Keohane and Nye, *Power and Interdependence*, chap. 1.

60. Robert Gilpin, *U.S. Power and the Multinational Corporation: The Political Economy of Foreign Direct Investment* (New York: Basic Books, 1975), p. 41.

61. Kindleberger, *The World in Depression*, p. 219.

62. Gardner, *Sterling-Dollar Diplomacy*, esp. p. 117.

63. Gabriel Kolko, *The Politics of War: The World and United States Foreign Policy, 1943–45* (New York: Vintage Books, 1968), p. 283. In his account of Bretton Woods and the British loan, Fred L. Block follows Kolko's version. See *The Origins of International Economic Disorder*, p. 59.

64. See the accounts of Hirsch and Doyle, (note 6), Block and Gardner (note 10), and Kolko (note 63).

65. Joel Darmstadter and Hans H. Landsberg, "The Economic Background," in *The Oil Crisis*, ed. Raymond Vernon, special issue of *Daedalus* (Fall 1975): 30–31.

66. Both quotes are from Anderson, *Aramco*, quoting "Memorandum on the Department's Position," Sappington, 1 December 1943, folder: "Petroleum Reserves Corporation Activities, 7/3/43-1/144" (Box 1, Records on the Petroleum Division, Record Group 59). Other memos on the subject, according to Anderson, supported Sappington's reasoning.

67. Memo by John A. Loftus, 31 May 1945 (National Archives, decimal file 1945–49, Box no. 5849, file no. 841.6363/5-3145).

68. Question by Senator Robertson of Wyoming, *Petroleum Agreement with Great Britain and Northern Ireland, Hearings before the Committee on Foreign Relations, U.S. Senate* (80th Congress, 1st sess.), June 1947, p. 51. A principal opponent of the treaty by the time it came to the Senate, in its rather truncated form, was Harry F. Sinclair. See Davies testimony, *Petroleum Agreement* hearings, p. 117, and W. L. Connelly, *The Oil Business as I Saw It; Half a Century with Sinclair* (Norman: University of Oklahoma Prss, 1954), p. 154.

69. *Congressional Record*, 80th Congress, 1st sess., records that the treaty was reported favorably by the Committee to the full Senate on 3 July 1947 (p. 8289). It was never debated; the only statement on the subject in the 80th Congress was a statement opposing it strongly by W. Lee O'Daniel of Texas. The State Department still supported it officially, if perfunctorily, as of 5 February 1948, when Willard L. Thorp included a paragraph about it in testimony before a House committee. *Petroleum for National Defense, Hearings Before the Special Subcommittee on Petroleum, Committee on Armed Services, House of Representatives* (80th Congress, 2nd sess.), 1948, p. 315. During 1948 the treaty simply dropped from view; during that year, it was not mentioned to any significant degree in the *New York Times* or the *Oil and Gas Journal*.

70. Perry Anderson comments, "If the American Empire was the undoing of the Spanish economy, it was its *European* Empire which was the ruin of the Hapsburg State, and the one rendered the extended struggle for the other financially possible." *Lineages of the Absolutist State* (London: New Left Books/Humanities Press, 1974), p. 74.

71. Marcello de Cecco comments: "Britain's retreat into Imperial markets, and her staunch defence of the privileges she enjoyed there, is one of the principal keys to an understanding of world economic history in [1890–1914]." *Money and Empire: The International Gold Standard, 1890–1914* (Totowa, N.J.: Rowman and Littlefield, 1975), pp. 28–29.

Index